Data Protect   8
A Practical Gui

by

Heather Rowe, Partner
Lovells, London

Co-chairman of the International Bar Association,
Committee R (Technology and E-commerce)

and

Chairman of the International Chamber of Commerce (ICC)
International Working Party on Data
Protection and Privacy and of ICC UK's Committee
on Technology, Telecommunications and Information Policy

and of

The Centre for the Study of Financial Innovation's
Regulatory Working Party on the Internet

A member of the Reed Elsevier plc group

Published by
Tolley
2 Addiscombe Road
Croydon, Surrey CR9 5AF England
020 8686 9141

Printed in Great Britain by
Bookcraft Ltd, Bath

Preface

This text analyses the main tenets of the UK Data Protection Act 1984 (DPA 1984) (to set the scene for the new Data Protection Act 1998 (DPA 1998)), looks at some key issues arising from the EU general Data Protection Directive passed in 1995, and looks at how DPA 1998 (published in January 1998 and given Royal Assent on 16 July 1998) has replaced DPA 1984 and implemented the Directive. So far as possible, this paper will highlight changes from DPA 1984 and areas where the DPA 1998 contains new provisions for English law.

It will also look at the related data protection legislation designed for the telecommunications sector which is particularly important because, despite its name which suggests it should only attract the interest of telecommunications companies, it will have wide-reaching effect for anyone who, for example, records or monitors telephone calls or uses the telephone or fax for direct marketing.

This book is also prepared with the benefit is having seen the DPR's own publication The Data Protection Act 1998, An Introduction produced in October 1998 (the 'Introduction') and available, free of charge, from the Office of the Data Protection Registrar, Wycliffe House, Water Lane, Wilmslow, Cheshire SK9 5AF (tel: 01625 545745 or fax: 01625 524510). Its ISBN Number is 1 870 466 21 7. The Introduction does not extend to the entire DPA 1998, but it is helpful in looking at some of the key areas -- including consent to processing and the interpretation of the complex transitional provisions, etc.

This book expressly acknowledges the use of the Introduction and quotes relevant passages from that publication as it represents the most up-to-date statement by the DPR's office in this area as at the date of publication. It seems sensible to quote the text of the Introduction, rather than seeking to paraphrase it, since following the express wording of the advice could be important for data controllers to show they are seeking to comply fully with DPA 1998, as interpreted by their national regulatory authority.

This book also acknowledges the paper produced by the DPR's office The Data Protection Registrar's legal analysis and suggested 'good practice approach' to assessing adequacy, including consideration of the issue of contractual solutions, a preliminary view document produced on 29 July 1999. This document addresses the issues that arise when transferring data outside the EEA to countries which may not provide an adequate level of protection for personal data and gives some very helpful comments. This is available from the DPR's office and from its website on www.open.gov.uk/dpr/dprhome.htm or their new website: www.dataprotection.gov.uk. There is also a more recent paper of February 2000 which amplifies the original paper.

Contents

Contents

10

Contents

Contents

15

Contents

1 – Data Protection Act 1984

Application [1.1]

The *Data Protection Act 1984* (*DPA 1984*) received Royal Assent in July 1984. It was an Act to:

> 'regulate the use of automatically processed information relating to individuals and the provision of services in respect of such information'.

DPA 1984 applied throughout the UK and there is also data protection legislation in Jersey, Guernsey and the Isle of Man.

Definitions [1.2]

To understand *DPA 1984* fully it is necessary to understand certain core definitions upon which it was built.

Broadly, *DPA 1984* affected users of personal data (data users) and individuals who were the subject of personal data (data subjects).

Data User [1.3]

For a data user, *DPA 1984* was relevant if:

○ it kept (or had kept on its behalf) data in a form that could be automatically processed (defined as, in relation to data, as amending, augmenting, deleting or rearranging the data or extracting the information constituting the data and, with personal data, means performing any such operations by reference to the data subject);
○ some or all of that data related to living individuals and were data that formed part of data which was processed or intended to be processed (note that company data and that of 'legal persons' were not covered but data on individuals in partnerships were);

O the individual concerned was either identifiable from the data or from the data combined with other information the data user had in non-computerised form (e.g. a card index or code book); and

O the data was more than an indication of the data user's intentions regarding the individual and included facts or expressions of opinion about that individual (this included statements as to the creditworthiness of individuals).

Data Users and Computer Bureaux   [1.4]

DPA 1984 distinguished between:

O a **data user** – who controlled what information was kept and processed and what it was used for; and

O a **computer bureau** – which processed personal data for data users or allowed them to use its equipment to process data.

For the purposes of *DPA 1984*, a computer bureau did not control the contents and use of personal data.

Personal Data   [1.5]

Personal Data could include audio and video data. The Data Protection Registrar (DPR) said that:

'...audio and video recording equipment generally has the ability to operate automatically in response to instructions and is therefore potentially within the scope of the Act. If the information recorded on the audio or video tape or other storage medium relates to a living individual, then provided that individual could be identified from the information on the tape or from that information and other information in the possession of the data user, the recorded information will be personal data.

However these personal data will only be "processed" if, in a particular case, the audio or video equipment has the facility to automatically perform its processing operations "by reference to a data subject" and the data user makes use of this facility.'

DPA 1984 did not regulate personal information that was not kept in a form that could and was intended to be processed automatically, notably information held in paper form.

Data Subjects' Rights [1.6]

A data subject had a right (subject to certain exceptions):

○ of access to any personal data maintained;
○ to have such data corrected by various means; and
○ to compensation for inaccuracies in certain circumstances.

Registration [1.7]

Under *section 5* of *DPA 1984*, all data users were required to register with the DPR.

A registration had to show full details of the data user, including:

○ a description of personal data;
○ the purposes for which it was to be held;
○ the sources of the data;
○ likely people to whom the data would be disclosed; and
○ the countries the data might be sent to outside the UK.

Offences [1.8]

Under *DPA 1984*, it was an offence:

○ for data users not to register when they should have done;
○ not to keep the registered particulars up-to-date or to give particulars that were deliberately or recklessly false or misleading;
○ under *section 5* of *DPA 1984*, knowingly or recklessly to:
  ● hold/use personal data save as described on the Register,
  ● use personal data for a purpose not on the Register,
  ● obtain information from sources not on the Register,
  ● transfer personal data to countries/territories other than those to which it has stated on the Register it intends to transfer such data,

O   for a computer bureau to disclose personal data, knowingly or recklessly, without authority of the data user for whom they were held (*section 15, DPA 1984*).

If *DPA 1984* applied to personal data held there was a further twist, in that there was the possibility of personal liability on directors, managers, the company secretary or similar officers of that company (*section 20, DPA 1984*).

Compensation [1.9]

DPA 1984 contained limited rights of compensation for data subjects who suffered loss from inaccurate or lost data.

If a data subject suffered damage from inaccurate personal information held about them, *section 22* of *DPA 1984* entitled them to compensation from the data user for damage resulting from such inaccuracy.

If personal data were lost or destroyed without the data user's or the computer bureau's authority (as the case may be), or disclosed without authority, resulting in the data subject suffering damage, they were entitled to compensation under *section 23* of *DPA 1984*.

Note that a data subject entitled to compensation for damage was also entitled to compensation for any distress suffered.

Data Protection Principles [1.10]

There were eight Data Protection Principles listed in *Schedule 1* to *DPA 1984* which had to be, in the interests of data subjects, observed by data users in respect of personal data.

A breach of one of the Data Protection Principles was not, of itself, a criminal offence. However, the DPR could take certain actions against a data user if it breached a Principle and, if the data user failed to comply with the DPR's requirements, they would then be committing a criminal offence.

If the DPR found out about a breach, action would be taken. Proceedings for an offence could only be instigated by the DPR and by/with the consent of the Director of Public Prosecutions.

The eight Data Protection Principles under *DPA 1984* were as follows.

'1.   The information to be contained in personal data shall be obtained, and personal data shall be processed, fairly and lawfully.

2.   Personal data shall be held only for one or more specified and lawful purposes.

3.   Personal data held for any purpose or purposes shall not be used or disclosed in any manner incompatible with that purpose or those purposes.

4.   Personal data held for any purpose or purposes shall be adequate, relevant and not excessive in relation to that purpose or those purposes.

5.   Personal data shall be accurate and, where necessary, kept up to date.

6.   Personal data held for any purpose or purposes shall not be kept for longer than is necessary for that purpose or those purposes.

7.   An individual shall be entitled –

(a)   at reasonable intervals and without undue delay or expense –

(i)   to be informed by any data user whether he holds personal data of which that individual is the subject; and

(ii)   to access any such data held by a data user; and

(b)   where appropriate, to have such data corrected or erased.

8.   Appropriate security measures shall be taken against unauthorised access to, or alteration, disclosure or destruction of, personal data and against accidental loss or destruction of personal data.'

The *DPA 1984* and the DPR gave additional guidance on some of the Principles, the most important of which is addressed below.

First Data Protection Principle [1.11]

The First Data Protection Principle was one which the DPR has issued considerable guidance about.

'(1)   Subject to subparagraph (2) below, in determining whether information was obtained fairly, regard shall be

had to the method by which it was obtained, including
in particular whether any person from whom it was
obtained was deceived or misled as to the purpose or
purposes for which it was to be held, used or disclosed.'

There was no specific guidance as to the matters to be taken into account
in deciding whether or not processing was 'fair' for the purposes of
DPA 1984. Fairness needed to be judged by reference to the purpose
of the processing, the nature of the processing itself and to its
consequences for the individual affected by it.

To assess the proper standards, the DPR would use the standpoint of
'the common man'. Thus, the DPR could have decided that a data
user had contravened the First Principle even though the data user
did not intend to be unfair and did not consider himself to be acting
unfairly.

Questions to Ask [1.12]

The DPR recommended in written guidelines, questions that should
be asked in order to determine fairness.

○ Did the data user explain why the information was required and
why it might be used or disclosed?
○ Was the person under the impression that the information would
be kept confidential by the data user? If so, was that impression
justified by the circumstances?
○ Was any unfair pressure used to obtain the information?
○ Did the data user have any particular knowledge about the person
from whom he obtained the information? If he had no such
knowledge, would the explanation he gave concerning the
collection and intended use be understood by the ordinary man
in the street?

Uses and Disclosures [1.13]

The data user should try to make sure that no-one was misled as to
why the information was required or why it would be used or disclosed.
Where there may be additional uses and disclosures which the person
supplying the information could not reasonably be expected to know,
the duty to obtain information fairly required taking steps to make

him aware of the true position and it did not matter if the data user intended to deceive/mislead the data subject. A general description of the intended purposes, disclosures and data users would usually be sufficient. So where personal data has been obtained from a data subject which would be used, for example, for direct marketing in a way not obviously apparent from the circumstances of collection of that data, the First Principle would have been breached.

The DPR has said that it would have rarely been sufficient simply to tell an individual who was a data subject that the information he or she was being asked to supply may be held, used or disclosed as described in the data user's register entry. That was not clear enough or easy enough for the data subject to check.

Codes of Practice [1.14]

The DPR has also encouraged codes of practice to be developed by groups of data users to encourage the provision of helpful explanations to individuals about their position under the data protection legislation. For example, the Banking Code of Practice contains various references to the data protection legislation and requires banks to remind their customers of various provisions of that Code insofar as it affects them.

General Observations [1.15]

It is also worth making one or two general observations about the First Data Protection Principle. The first is that the DPR considered that the data user must be fair and act lawfully in relation to personal data in relation to each individual. Even though a data user could show that the information was obtained and processed fairly and lawfully in relation to most persons and on most occasions, even if there was only one person in relation to whom the processing might have been held to be unfair, this would still have been a contravention of the First Principle.

The Data Protection Tribunal has also stated that it was quite clear from *DPA 1984* as a whole, and in particular, from the Data Protection Principles, that the purpose of *DPA 1984* was to protect the rights of the individual about whom data were obtained, stored, processed or supplied, rather than those of the data user.

The Data Protection Tribunal has also taken the view that, in deciding whether processing was fair, the most important single consideration is the interest of the data subject. The Tribunal considered that it should weigh the various considerations, as it had done in the case in question, and that it was entitled to give more weight to the interests of the individual.

Finally, the DPR has always been particularly concerned about direct marketing and ensuring that this was done in accordance with the First Principle. (See further **Chapter 18**.)

Second Data Protection Principle [1.16]

DPA 1984 set out guidance on interpreting the Second Data Protection Principle, providing that:

> '...personal data should not be treated as held for a specified purpose unless that purpose is described in particulars registered under this Act in relation to the data.'

A 'specified purpose' is one which was described in the relevant register entry. Data users could comply with this Principle by ensuring that they registered all their purposes and by establishing procedures to ensure that new purposes were added to the register entry as and when they arose.

Eighth Data Protection Principle [1.17]

DPA 1984 gave additional interpretation of the Eighth Data Protection Principle and an explanation of the factors to consider when assessing if appropriate security existed.

> 'Regard shall be had:
>
> (1) to the nature of the personal data and the harm that would result from such access, alteration, disclosure, loss or destruction as were mentioned in this Principle; and
> (2) to the place where the personal data were stored, to security measures programmed into the relevant equipment and to measures taken for ensuring the reliability of staff having access to the data.'

This Principle had to be observed by data users and by computer bureaux for personal data which they processed for others, or which were processed on equipment in the bureau's possession.

This Principle was of particular importance for the maintenance of databases of personal data of customers for example. This Principle, and a simplified registration procedure, were the only parts of *DPA 1984* that applied to computer bureaux. The position is easier for computer bureaux under *DPA 1998*.

Matters to Consider [1.18]

Matters which should be taken into account when deciding whether security measures were 'appropriate' included the:

O   nature of the data and the harm that would result from a breach of security;
O   place where personal data were stored (i.e. access to the building, precautions against burglary, fire, etc.); and
O   security measures programmed into the relevant equipment (e.g. knowledge of passwords).

Security Policy [1.19]

The prime responsibility for creating and putting into practice a security policy rested with the data user. The policy should have sought to ensure that:

O   personal data could only be accessed, altered, disclosed or destroyed by authorised people;
O   those people act only within the scope of their authority; and
O   should the data be accidentally lost or destroyed, they could be recovered so as to prevent any damage or distress from being caused to the data subjects.

The DPR recognised that no security policy could be foolproof. A breach of security would not of itself cause him/her to take formal action. The absence of appropriate security measures, as well as a breach of this Principle, may also lead to a data subject being entitled to compensation if they suffered loss from, say, unauthorised disclosure.

The DPR's Powers [1.20]

The DPR was under a duty to promote compliance with the Data Protection Principles and was given powers to ensure this happened. The DPR had four main powers in relation to breaches. These were:

O refusal of registration application;
O enforcement notices;
O de-registration notices; and
O transfer prohibition notices.

Refusal of Registration Application [1.21]

When a data user applied for registration under *DPA 1984*, the DPR could refuse an application if she was satisfied that the applicant was likely to contravene any of the Data Protection Principles. However, it is unclear how the DPR would know this at this point.

Enforcement Notices [1.22]

The DPR also had the power to serve an enforcement notice if she considered that there was a contravention of a Data Protection Principle. In deciding whether to serve such a notice, the DPR could consider whether the contravention had or was likely to cause damage or distress.

By such a notice, the DPR could:

O cause rectification or erasure of data; or
O order that certain steps be taken or activities ceased.

De-registration Notice [1.23]

The DPR could also serve a de-registration notice which meant that the registration was cancelled (and clearly, thereafter, no further processing could take place or it would be a criminal offence).

The DPR would not normally serve a de-registration notice unless she considered that the contravention not only was causing or could cause damage or distress but that the breach in question could also not be adequately secured by service of an enforcement notice.

Transfer Prohibition Notice [1.24]

The DPR could also serve a transfer prohibition notice which could prevent the transfer of the data to a place outside the UK if this could lead to a contravention of the Data Protection Principles. No particular conditions were to be satisfied by a data user before such a transfer would be permitted.

A transfer prohibition notice was the only way the DPR could really police cross-border transfers of data and was used only once or twice. Note that under *DPA 1998* the situation is very different.

2 – Data Protection Directive

Background [2.1]

Directive 95/46/EC on the protection of individuals with regard to the processing of personal data and on the free movement of such data (the *Directive*) was adopted in October 1995, after much criticism and many changes along the way. It represents privacy legislation, something not really hitherto known in the UK. Most of the *Directive* was to have been implemented by Member States by October 1998.

The expressed intention of the *Directive*, in its Preamble, is to ensure that the differences in levels of protection of the rights and freedoms of individuals, notably the right to privacy, which currently exist between Member States, are adjusted so that these differences would not prevent the movement of such data between Member States. The level of protection is to be equivalent in all Member States to remove any obstacles to flows of personal data.

Specific Concerns [2.2]

Much of the *Directive* is known to EU Member States because it is based on the 1981 Council of Europe Convention for the Protection of Individuals with Regard to Automatic Processing of Data and slightly earlier OECD Guidelines from 1980. However, in many areas the *Directive* goes further.

The *Directive*, as did *DPA 1984* and as does *DPA 1998*, only applies to personal data. However, the Commission instigated a study in 1998 to consider whether the protection of the *Directive* whether in whole or in part, should be extended to data about 'legal persons'. The study compared the law and practice in Member States which already applied their data protection laws to legal persons (Austria, Denmark, Italy and Luxembourg) to the laws in five other Member States which do not (France, Germany, Ireland, The Netherlands and the UK). It also compared the data protection laws in those countries that do extend protection to legal persons to the laws in three other countries outside the European Union, where such protection is also provided (Iceland, Norway and Switzerland).

The study concluded:

> '...it is recommended that consideration be given to extending specific elements of the protection of the Directive to legal persons in specific areas'.

One area mentioned was the protection of interests of legal persons in relation to direct marketing and another was protection of the interests of legal persons in relation to the processing of business information by credit reference agencies, warning agencies and the like. Therefore, it is not out of the question that at some future date the European Commission might follow these recommendations and seek to extend the protection of the *Directive*, in a limited number of areas, to legal persons rather than just natural persons.

Manual Data [2.3]

Most importantly, the *Directive* applies not only to automated data but also to personal data contained in certain manual files. The preamble to the *Directive* states that it covers situations where:

> '...the data processed are contained or are intended to be contained in a filing system structured according to specific criteria relating to individuals, so as to permit easy access to the personal data in question'.

Personal data is any form of data, computerised or manual. The principles of the *Directive* apply to sound and image data, although this was already the case under *DPA 1984* if that data was personal data and could be processed automatically by reference to a data subject.

In relation to manual data, the *Directive* is expressed, in its preamble, '...as regards manual processing...to cover only filing systems, not unstructured files' (although many have a problem with the *Directive's* definition of a 'personal data filing system' because they see it applying to bulky correspondence files). It goes on to say:

> '...in particular, the content of a filing system has to be structured according to specific criteria relating to individuals allowing easy access to personal data...'.

The *Directive* contains a definition of personal data similar to that in *DPA 1984* but the scope of the *Directive* applies to the processing of personal data *whether or not* by automatic means. This includes manual data if it is in a personal data filing system. In the *Directive*, 'personal data filing system' means:

> '...any structured set of personal data which are accessible according to specific criteria, whether centralised, de-centralised or dispersed on a functional or geographical basis'.

The cautious English lawyer who would like to give a meaningful interpretation of such wording could say that a structured set of personal data accessible according to specific criteria could include each of their correspondence files if set up in date order, on a treasury tag, in a file and/or with the name of the data subject as the heading on each page. Hopefully, read with the above extracts from the Preamble, this analysis is over-cautious. This is relevant to matters such as the data subject's right to have copies of such files in permanent form − an administrative nightmare (and a costly one if the correspondence file is three inches thick!). This general concept of a personal data filing system may have come from the legal systems of other countries within the EU (for example, Germany) and in that country the concept is given a *narrow* interpretation limited to structured files such as card indexes. This looks like it will prove to be the case under *DPA 1998* as well (see **4.5** below for the DPR's preliminary views on *DPA 1998* and its applicability to manual files).

Processing [2.4]

Under the *Directive*, 'processing of personal data' means:

> '...any operation or set of operations which is performed upon personal data, whether or not by automatic means, such as collection, recording, organization, storage, adaption or alteration, retrieval, consultation, use, disclosure by transmission, dissemination or otherwise making available, alignment or combination, blocking, erasure or destruction;'

As can be seen from the definition of processing, there is now very little that is not processing of data. In addition, data can be 'processed' under the *Directive* by automated and non-automated means − underlying the fact that the *Directive* can extend to certain structured manual filing systems.

The definition of processing is much wider than the definition under *DPA 1984* which was relatively restrictive. It catches sending E-mail. It even, arguably, could catch the shredding of the paper contents of confidential bins in a solicitor's office.

Consent [2.5]

The preamble to the *Directive* makes its clear that:

> '...in order to be lawful, the processing of personal data has to in addition be carried out with the consent of the data subject or be necessary with a view to the conclusion or performance of a contract binding on the data subject, or as a legal requirement, or for the performance of a task carried out in the public interest or in the exercise of official authority, or in the legitimate interests of a natural or legal person provided that the interests or the rights and freedoms of the data subject are not overriding.'

Concepts such as the 'legitimate interest' or 'overriding interest' of a data subject, and certain other concepts that are in the *Directive*, are not really familiar to English lawyers although they would be understood in France, for example.

The 'data subject's consent' is defined in the *Directive* as any:

> '...freely given specific and informed indication of his wishes by which the data subject signifies his agreement to personal data relating to him being processed'.

In obtaining consent, the data user (called, in the *Directive*, the data controller) has to get a 'specific' consent to the proposed processing and the consent has to be 'informed' – so the data subject has to be clearly told in advance all about the proposed processing. Again the consent cannot be coerced, which is consistent with the DPR's approach under *DPA 1984*. This could require changes for example, to application forms, to the scripts currently being used by call centre operatives or to a company's standard terms and conditions with customers.

There is nothing in the *Directive* that says that consent has to be in writing so a fully informed oral consent would probably be acceptable in many areas.

Permissible Circumstances for Processing [2.6]

Article 7 provides that Member States have to ensure that personal data may only be processed in certain circumstances. The definition of 'processing' is very wide and includes:

> '...any operation or set of operations which is performed upon personal data, whether or not by automatic means, such as collection, recording, organisation, storage, adaption or alteration, retrieval, consultation, use, disclosure by transmission, dissemination or otherwise making available, alignment or combination, blocking, erasure or destruction'.

These circumstances are if:

○ the data subject has given his consent unambiguously;
○ processing is necessary for the performance of a contract to which the data subject is party or in order to take steps at the request of the data subject prior to entering into a contract;
○ processing is necessary for compliance with a legal obligation to which the controller is subject;
○ processing is necessary in order to protect the vital interests of the data subject;
○ processing is necessary for the performance of a task carried out in the public interest or in the exercise of official authority vested in the controller or in a third party to whom the data are disclosed;
○ processing is necessary for the purposes of the legitimate interests pursued by the controller or by the third party or parties to whom the data are disclosed, except where such interests are overridden by the interests for fundamental rights and freedoms of the data subject which require protection under the *Directive*.

Only one of the conditions listed needs to be satisfied to enable processing to continue.

The first two exceptions and probably the last one are those that would most likely be relevant to companies which will want to ensure they can process or continue to process data. The first two exceptions are really to get an 'unambiguous' consent to processing (which presumably has to be before the processing starts) or to be satisfied that there is a contract in place for which the relevant processing is *necessary*. The latter would be the case where, for example, a data subject asks his bank to transfer funds electronically to another person's account. It would be necessary to process personal data about the customer to do this and it should be possible to argue that it would be necessary to do this processing to fulfil the banker customer/relationship.

The last exception would involve a data controller being absolutely satisfied that it needs to process the relevant data as part of its proper conduct of its business and that there is no right of the data subject that would be adversely affected as a result of such processing so, for example, if a data subject has been fully informed of the uses to which their data may be put and nothing about the manner of that processing could cause any detriment to the data subject (and consent is not required under the *Directive* for any other reason) then this provision could apply and consent would not be necessary.

Scope [2.7]

Article 3 details the scope of the *Directive*. It makes it clear that the *Directive* applies to the processing of personal data wholly or partly by automatic means and to the processing otherwise than by automatic means (i.e. of manual files) of personal data which form part of a filing system or are intended to form part of a filing system. This of course begs the question of what constitutes a filing system. Could a *single* structured correspondence file be such a system?

The *Directive* does not apply to the processing of personal data which falls outside the scope of Community law (which potentially makes it narrower in scope than *DPA 1984*).

Applicability of National Law [2.8]

Article 4 provides for the national law applicable to processing. How it has been implemented in the UK is addressed in **Chapter 4**.

Article 4 states:

'1.　Each Member State shall apply the national provisions it adopts pursuant to this Directive to the processing of personal data where:
(a)　the processing is carried out in the context of the activities of an establishment of the controller on the territory of the Member State; when the same controller

is established on the territory of several Member States, he has to take the necessary measures to ensure that each of these establishments complies with the obligations laid down by the national law applicable;

(b)   the controller is not established on the Member State's territory, but in a place where its national law applies by virtue of international public law;

(c)   the controller is not established on Community territory and, for purposes of processing personal data makes use of equipment, automated or otherwise, situated on the territory of the said Member State, unless such equipment is used only for purposes of transit through the territory of the Community.

2.   In the circumstances referred to in paragraph 1(c), the controller has to designate a representative established in the territory of that Member State, without prejudice to legal actions which could be initiated against the controller himself.'

The provisions of *Article 4* have caused a degree of uncertainty amongst international jurists since the provisions are unclear. Some have been concerned that the way *Article 4* is worded would mean that one country would be expected to try and apply its laws to its citizens in another country, which is really rather a complex concept.

From the *Directive* and its preamble, it can be concluded that the form of the 'establishment' is not the essence in determining the application of the national provisions of the *Directive* but 'effective and real exercise of activity through stable arrangements' is. The intention behind this Article appears to be the prevention of circumvention of national rules by the subsidiaries through the application of one national rule by the parent company.

According to the preamble clause (19), an:

'...establishment...implies the effective and real exercise of activity through stable arrangements; whereas the legal form of such an establishment, whether simply branch or a subsidiary with a legal personality, is not the determining factor in this respect...'.

Furthermore, it adds that:

'...when a single controller is established on the territory of several Member States, particularly by means of subsidiaries, he must ensure, in order to avoid any circumvention of national rules, that each of the establishments fulfils the obligations imposed by the national law applicable to its activities.'

In one specific area, where a controller of data in the EU uses a data processor outside the EU, the European Commission appears to be interpreting this to mean that where there is a data processor in a country outside the EU which provides data processing services to a company inside the EU, where that service is provided for the benefit of the establishment of the data controller in the EU, it would appear that the transfers of data would be controlled under the law of the country where the data controller is established in the EU. This seems to be being interpreted as requiring the EU data controller to impose restrictions of the kind set out in *Article 17* on its data processor outside the EU.

As will be seen at **Chapter 15** below, this analysis is consistent with the provisions of *Article 17* which require a company in the EU to impose certain provisions (particularly in relation to security) on any data processor that it uses.

The Equivalent of the Data Protection Principles   [2.9]

Article 6 contains the *Directive's* equivalent of the Data Protection Principles under *DPA 1998* and provides, for example, that Member States shall ensure that personal data are:

> '...collected for specified, explicit and legitimate purposes and are not further processed in a way incompatible with these purposes'.

Clearly, the terms and conditions of use adopted by data controllers will probably, to the extent that they do not already do so for a number of other reasons, need to include provisions specifying why personal data is being collected and the purposes for which those data will be used.

Criteria for Making Processing Legitimate   [2.10]

The *Directive* requires Member States to provide that personal data may be processed (which, as we have seen at **2.4** above, is very widely defined) only if one of the following conditions can be satisfied.

○ The data subject has unambiguously given his consent.
○ processing is necessary for the performance of a contract to which the data subject is party or in order to take steps at the request of the data subject prior to entering into a contract.
○ Processing is necessary for compliance with a legal obligation to which the controller is subject.
○ Processing is necessary in order to protect the vital interests of the data subject.
○ Processing is necessary for the performance of a task carried out in the public interest or in the exercise of official authority vested in the controller or in a third party to whom the data are disclosed.
○ Processing is necessary for the purposes of legitimate interests pursued by the controller or by the third party or parties who whom the data are disclosed, except where such interests are overridden by the interests for fundamental rights and freedoms of the data subject which require protection in accordance with the *Directive*.

These conditions to processing are new to English law and have required changes to be made to UK legislation.

Special Categories of Processing [2.11]

Article 8 provides for Member States to be able to impose higher levels of protection for individuals where the data being processed reveal:

○ racial or ethnic origin;
○ political opinions;
○ religious or philosophical beliefs;
○ trade union membership; or
○ concerns health or sex life.

Indeed, Member States are to ensure that legislation which protects such information is put in place adequately.

In fact, *DPA 1984* contained a provision whereby a higher level of protection could be applied to such data by subsequent regulation, but no such regulation was ever passed.

Article 9 provides for what has been loosely (and inaccurately) called the 'press exemption'. It provides for the relaxation of certain provisions of the *Directive* in relation to processing of personal data:

'...carried out solely for journalistic purposes or the purposes of artistic or literary expression only if they are necessary to reconcile the right to privacy with the rules governing freedom of expression'.

The position of the press generally is considered further in **Chapters 7** and **8**.

Information in Cases of Collection of Data from the

Data Subject   [2.12]

Article 10 requires the data controller or his representative to supply certain information to data subjects from whom data are being collected. Data controllers will be required, when collecting data from data subjects, to notify the data subject of:

○   the identity of the data controller;
○   the purposes of the processing for which the data are intended; and
○   any further information (such as the recipients of the data or whether replies to the questions are obligatory or voluntary) in so far as such further information is necessary, having regard to the specific circumstances in which the data are collected, to guarantee fair processing in respect of the data subject.

Preamble clause (38) states:

'Whereas, if the processing of data is to be fair, the data subjects must be in a position to learn of the existence of a processing operation and, when data are collected from him, must be given accurate and full information, bearing in mind the circumstances of the collection'.

This goes beyond the UK position under *DPA 1984* which did not contain any express notification requirement. However, the DPR has said, in her *Introduction* to *DPA 1998* in October 1998, that many of the new requirements to notify data subjects were part of the requirements of *DPA 1984*, in any event, although perhaps not set out in the wording of that Act, but that this is how the interpretation of *DPA 1984* had evolved in practice.

This notification requirement is going to be of practical importance for data controllers. They will need to include an appropriate statement to this effect in:

○ communications with data subjects (including on web sites);
○ standard terms and conditions;
○ mail shots; and
○ their agreements and dealings with employees.

Otherwise, the subsequent processing of the data collected could well be unfair and have ramifications for the data controller. (See **Chapter 11**.)

Information Where the Data Have not been Obtained from the Data Subject [2.13]

Article 11 provides that where data have not been obtained from the data subject, Member States shall provide that the data controller will have to at the time of undertaking the recording of personal data or, if its disclosure to a third party is envisaged, no later than the time when the data are first disclosed to a third party, provide the data subject with various further items of information.

This includes the:

○ identity of the controller (and of his representative if applicable);
○ purposes of the processing;
○ categories of data concerned;
○ recipients or categories of recipients;
○ existence of the rights of access and rectification of data; and
○ details of his representative;

insofar as such further information is necessary, having regard to the specific circumstances in which the data are processed, to guarantee the fair processing of that data in respect of that specific data subject.

This goes beyond the UK position under *DPA 1984* as to what information is to be given to data subjects and when. For example, *DPA 1984* did not expressly require data users to notify any purposes direct to data subjects (although the purposes did have to be stated in a data user's registration). However, the general fairness concept is interpreted by *DPA 1984* to mean that whilst it was not necessary to tell data subjects about uses of their data which were obvious, they did need to be told about non-obvious uses.

Preamble clause (39), which addresses the situation where information are not obtained from the data subject, states:

> 'Whereas certain processing operations involved data which the controller has not collected directly from the data subject: whereas, furthermore, data can be legitimately disclosed to a third party, even if the disclosure was not anticipated at the time the data were collected from the data subjects: whereas, in all these cases, the data subject should be informed when the data are recorded or at the latest when the data are first disclosed to a third party.'

Preamble clause (40) is also quite helpful in explaining how *Article 11* is to work. It says:

> 'Whereas, however, it is not necessary to impose this obligation if the data subject already has the information: whereas, moreover, there will be no such obligation if the recording or disclosure are expressly provided for by law or if the provision of information to the data subject proves impossible or would involve disproportionate effort, which could be the case where processing is for historical, statistical or scientific purposes: whereas, in this regard, the number of data subjects, the age of the data, and any compensatory measures adopted may be taken into consideration.'

Again, this has practical procedural consequences for data controllers as to how they provide this information to data subjects.

Data Subjects' Rights [2.14]

Data Subjects are given a number of rights under the *Directive*.

Right of Access [2.15]

Article 12 provides that Member States shall guarantee every data subject:

○ the right to obtain details of information held about them;
○ communication of a copy of what is held; and
○ knowledge of the logic involved in any automatic processing of data concerning them.

The first two provisions are very similar to those that existed under *DPA 1984* (particularly as interpreted by the DPR) and, therefore, should not be unfamiliar in the UK.

Right to Object [2.16]

Article 14 could prove problematical because it provides that Member States shall grant data subjects the right in certain circumstances to object on 'compelling legitimate grounds relating to his particular situation' to the processing of data relating to him. More importantly for the direct marketing industry and those companies which use direct marketing techniques, the data subject has to be given a right:

> '…to object, on request and free of charge, to the processing of personal data relating to him which the controller of the data anticipates processing for the purposes of direct marketing'.

Automated Individual Decisions [2.17]

Article 15 provides that every person who may be subject to a decision which produces legal effects about them or significantly affects them and which is based solely on automated processing intended to evaluate certain of his personal aspects such as credit worthiness, shall have the right not to be subject to such a decision.

There are exceptions, for example, where the decision is taken in the course of entering into a contract, provided the request for entering into the contract is made by the data subject and that request has been granted as a result of the automated decision. Alternatively, if the effect of the decision is not to grant the data subject's request, the data subject must be otherwise safeguarded by, for example, 'arrangements allowing him to put his point of view' (*Article 15(2)(a)*).

The effect of this, in relation to *DPA 1998*, is considered in **Chapter 5**.

Exemptions and Restrictions [2.18]

Article 13 permits exemptions from certain rights, such as the right of subject access. For example, exemptions can be put in place in situations where it is necessary to safeguard:

O   national security;
O   defence;
O   public security; or
O   the prevention, investigation, detection and prosecution of criminal offences or breaches of ethics for regulated professions.

Confidentiality of Processing   [2.19]

Article 16 addresses confidentiality and security of processing. It provides that any person acting under the authority of the controller or of the processor of data, including the processor himself, who has access to personal data shall not process them except on instructions from the controller, unless he is required to do so by law. This links very closely with *Article 17* described at **2.20** below.

Security of Processing   [2.20]

Article 17 could ultimately prove to be a problem for data users because it provides that Member States should ensure that data controllers have to implement appropriate technical security and organisational measures to protect personal data against accidental or unlawful destruction or accidental loss or unauthorised alteration, disclosure or access.

In deciding whether or not the protective measures are adequate, it would appear that Member States must have 'regard to the state of the art and the cost of their implementation' and, therefore, this seems to impose obligations on data subjects to keep an eye on what is 'state of the art' on the basis that they may set in train a series of procedures in the year 2000 which are, at that time, deemed to be adequate security only to find themselves a year later no longer complying with the state of the art.

Whilst they can (thankfully) take the cost of implementation into account, if the state of the art on technical security for data advances, it is not just the cost that is the concern – there is also the disruption factor for business of regular changes to security procedures and technologies. Indeed, technological improvements may not necessarily be substantially more expensive, so does a company *have to* make those improvements if cost is not really an issue? Relaxation of US Government restrictions on the use of strong encryption is one obvious example. If they do relax export restrictions on strong cryptography, so that stronger products become available in Europe, should data controllers be upgrading their systems to those products?

The obligation of security is on the data controller. The question arises as to who is the data controller in the context of networks? Preamble clause (47), gives some guidance as to who is the data controller in the context of transmission systems. It says:

> 'Whereas where a message containing personal data is transmitted by means of a telecommunications or electronic mail service, the sole purpose of which is the transmission of such messages, the controller in respect of the personal data contained in the message will normally be considered to be the person from whom the message originates, rather than the person offering the transmission services: whereas, nevertheless, those offering such services will normally be considered controllers in respect of the processing of the additional personal data necessary for the operation of the service:'

Notifying the Supervisory Authorities [2.21]

Under *Article 18*, Member States shall provide that the controllers of data or their representatives (if any) have to notify the national supervisory authority set up under the auspices of the *Directive* before carrying out processing operations. This will be a particularly important provision for any countries in Europe which do not already have a notification procedure to some sort of central body.

Article 28 requires the establishment of a supervisory authority in every Member State, with complete independence, to administer data protection matters. The supervisory authority is to be given quite extensive powers. This is not onerous for the UK which already has central registration with the DPR.

Contents of Notification [2.22]

Under *Article 19*, the notification to the supervisory authority has to cover at least the:

○ name and address of the data controller and any representative;
○ purpose(s) of the processing; and
○ category(ies) of data subject.

Prior Checking [2.23]

Article 20 requires Member States which determine that processing operations are 'likely' to present specific risks to the rights and freedoms of data subjects to provide that these processing operations are examined *prior* to the start of processing.

This prior checking concept is new to the UK. Those in the UK have been brought up on the simple concept that, if you are registered, then acting within your registration and the Data Protection Principles is the key consideration. The DPR has not in the past interested herself so much in the detail of processing procedures (other than mainly in relation to security).

Publicising of Processing Operations [2.24]

Article 21 requires Member States to take measures to ensure that processing operations are publicised and a register of such activities kept in accordance with various other Articles of the *Directive* such as *Articles 18* and *19*.

Judicial Remedies, Liability and Sanctions [2.25]

Articles 22–24 provide for remedies, liability and sanctions. Member States are required to provide for a judicial remedy for data subjects for breach of the rights guaranteed by the relevant national law established pursuant to the *Directive*. Again, given the remedies under *DPA 1984*, this not was an onerous requirement for the UK to implement in *DPA 1998*.

In addition, Member States shall provide that any person who has suffered damage as a result of an unlawful processing operation will be compensated.

Article 24 provides for sanctions to be imposed against data controllers which breach the *Directive*.

Transfer of Personal Data to Third Countries   [2.26]

The main causes for concern under the *Directive* for *international* businesses are *Articles 25* and *26* in relation to the transfer of personal data to third countries, which are almost certain to become more relevant as markets become truly 'global'. These Articles will clearly have ramifications for use of the Internet (or intranets/extranets) and for E-commerce generally. More basically than that, it could restrict the ability of groups of companies to centralise their data processing at their head office, if that head office is overseas and outside the EU.

Article 25 Principles   [2.27]

Article 25(1) states that cross border dataflows can only be permitted by Member States where the country to which the transfer takes place (other than another Member State in the EU) ensures 'an adequate level of protection' for that data.

In accordance with *Article 25(2)*, the 'adequacy' of the level of protection shall be assessed 'in the light of all the circumstances surrounding a data transfer operation'. Consideration is to be given to issues such as:

○   the nature of the data;
○   the purpose and duration of the processing operation;
○   the country of origin and of final destination;
○   the rules of law (both general and sectoral) in the third country in question; and
○   any professional rules and security measures which are complied with in the third country in question.

Member States and the Commission shall inform each other of any cases where they consider the appropriate level of protection is not available.

Obviously, this begs a question as to what is an adequate level of protection and the onus is on controllers to decide the adequacy issue. It is possible that there will be findings of the Commission, decisions which confirm whether the laws of a particular country do provide adequate protection for personal data. There could also be other methods of providing protection which could also be held to be adequate. Transborder dataflows could be adversely affected by the new procedures. This area is reviewed in more detail in **Chapter 15**.

Article 26 Derogations [2.28]

The prohibition in *Article 25* has some derogations from it in *Article 26*. Even if a third country does not ensure an adequate level of protection, *Article 26(1)* provides that a transfer may take place on condition that either the:

O   data subject has given his consent unambiguously to the proposed transfer;

O   transfer is necessary for the performance of a contract between the data subject and the controller or the implementation of pre-contractual measures taken in response to the data subject's request;

O   transfer is necessary for the conclusion or for the performance of a contract concluded in the interest of the data subject between the controller and a third party;

O   transfer is necessary on important public interest grounds, or for the establishment, exercise or defence of legal claims;

O   transfer is necessary in order to protect the vital interests of the data subject; or

O   transfer is made from a register which, according to laws or regulations, is intended to provide information to the public and which is open to consultation either by the public in general, or by any person who could demonstrate legitimate interest, to the extent that the conditions laid down in law for consultation are fulfilled in the particular case.

Where a country is perceived as not providing an adequate level of protection, a Member State could provide that the transfer may take place provided that the data subject has given his consent unambiguously to the proposed transfer – quite often, in practice, they would not necessarily have consented unambiguously (and it is very clear from the definition of a 'data subject's consent' in the *Directive* that consent has to be unambiguous, uncoerced and informed). If a transfer does not come within this provision, the other exceptions to the prohibition on transfer should be considered.

Article 26(2) provides that a Member State (i.e. without referring to the European Commission) may authorise a transfer of personal data to a third country which does not ensure an adequate level of protection for personal data where the data controller has adduced sufficient guarantees with respect to the protection of the privacy of the individuals. Such guarantees may, in particular result from 'appropriate contractual clauses'. So, a data controller could produce a contract to the local regulator which imposes tough obligations on its overseas contracting party outside the EU ensuring a high level of protection of any personal data transferred – which might pass this test. It could also be that the relevant national regulator might instead approve the method by which data are protected because that method provides adequate protection for the data. Contractual clauses are only one way that the lack of adequacy of protection could be rectified.

Under *Article 26(4)*, the European Commission can also submit contractual solutions of the type described above to a Committee set up under *Article 31* to vote upon such solutions and, if they vote in favour, those clauses will be approved for use in all Member States. For a detailed analysis in relation to crossborder transfers of date see **Chapter 15**.

Codes of Conduct [2.29]

Article 27 encourages codes of conduct to be set up, either nationally or internationally, for the proper implementation of the *Directive* and particularly to address the specific features of different industry sectors.

Supervisory Authority [2.30]

Article 28 requires the establishment of a supervisory authority in every Member State, with complete independence, to administer data protection matters. The supervisory authority is to be given quite extensive powers.

In the case of the UK, the DPR's office already existed so this particular provision is not a problem.

Working Party on the Protection of Individuals with Regard to the Processing of Personal Data [2.31]

Article 29 provides for the establishment of a Working Party on the protection of individuals with regard to the processing of personal data.

This Working Party is made up of the EU Data protection regulators or their alternates and has 'advisory status' only and shall 'act independently'.

Article 30 sets out the role and constitution of the Working Party. It states that the Working Party shall:

> '(1) look at questions about the application of national measures adopted under the Directive in order to contribute to the uniform application of such measures;
> (2) give opinions to the Commission about the level of protection in the Community and in third countries;
> (3) provide the Commission with advice on any proposed amendments to the Directive and on any additional measures or safeguards required to protect individuals with regard to the processing of personal data; and
> (4) give opinions on codes of conduct drawn up at Community level.'

The Working Party can also take the initiative and make recommendations on matters regarding protection of personal data in the Community. To the extent that action is taken by the Commission based on advice from the Working Party, the Commission will report back to them as to the steps that have been taken.

The Working Party has already produced numerous Working Documents and Recommendations on a number of matters including contractual solutions in the context of cross border dataflows (see **Chapter 15**) and the Internet (see **Chapters 16** and **17**). Their most relevant working documents (as far as the book is concerned) are set out in the bibliography in **Appendix B**.

The Committee   [2.32]

Article 31 sets up a Committee that has, perhaps, some greater power to make things happen (as compared to the advisory Article 29 Working Party) in approving data protection matters. This is a Committee set up of government representatives of Member States, as opposed to the Article 29 Working Party which is set up of representatives of the EU data protection authorities. The Committee is chaired by a representative of the Commission.

The role of the Committee is to assist the Commission. The Article 29 Working Party tends (some have said) to take a slightly conservative view of the law, given their express role (in many cases established by statute) to protect the individual's rights. It may be that the Article 31 Committee may take a slightly wider view on certain matters.

Article 31 provides that the Committee will look at measures submitted to them by the Commission and deliver an opinion. The opinion has to be delivered by a majority as set down in *Article 148* of the *EC Treaty*.

If an opinion from the Committee is delivered with the appropriate majority, then the Commission shall adopt measures which shall apply immediately. If, however, those measures are not in accordance with the opinion delivered by the Committee, the measures shall be communicated by the Commission to the Council of Ministers forthwith. Were that to happen, the Commission is not able to implement the measures proposed for a period of three months from the date of communication and the Council, acting by a qualified majority, may take a different decision within that time limit to that made by the Commission.

Other Provisions [2.33]

Article 32 contains complex transitional provisions which could allow a Member State to bring the entire *Directive* into force immediately or to allow this to happen a little later on or in stages.

The Commission is required (under *Article 34*) to report to the Council and the European Parliament at regular intervals on the implementation of the *Directive*. Their report could, if appropriate, contain proposals for amendments to the *Directive*. The Commission has to examine, in particular, the processing of sound and image data relating to natural persons and shall submit any appropriate proposals necessary, taking account of developments in information technology and in the light of progress in the information society.

There is no explanation given in the *Directive* as to why sound and image data is singled out for special note.

One can only assume that the Commission felt that such data had to be expressly covered in the *Directive* and otherwise would have fallen outside it. That would not be the DPR's view on such data – she has always said it is caught by *DPA 1984* if it could be processed automatically by reference to the data subject. Indeed, her extensive Guidelines to *DPA 1984*, Fourth Series, September 1997, mentioned 'automatic retrieval systems, telephone logging equipment and document image processing systems' as potentially within the ambit of *DPA 1984*.

3 – Background to DPA 1998

Introduction [3.1]

In the 1970s, the use of computers was already creating public concern in relation to the exploitation of data held within computers.

The earliest UK legislative proposals were, in fact, put forward in 1969 in shape of the *Data Surveillance Bill 1969*, introduced into the House of Commons by Mr Kenneth Baker. The *Bill* was introduced into the House of Lords as the *Personal Records (Computers) Bill*, but neither of these *Bills* reached the statute book. Again, the *Control of Personal Information Bill* was introduced in 1971, but did not become law.

In 1970, the then government established the Younger Committee to investigate the subject of privacy. The Younger Committee produced its report, the *Report on Privacy (Cmnd. 5012)*, in July 1972 that contained the results of the work of the Younger Committee which had worked on the report for nearly two years. Chapter 20 of the report is devoted to the subject of computers and much that is in the report found its way into *DPA 1984*.

In 1971, UNESCO had the International Commission of Jurists prepare a report on privacy and personal data. At that time, few countries had formalised legislation addressing computerised data and the first such national law was adopted in Sweden nearly three years later.

The Younger Report was followed by a UK government white paper *Computers And Privacy (Cmnd. 6353)* in 1975 and, as part of that process, the government decided that some form of data protection authority should come into existence. It set up a data protection committee chaired by Sir Norman Lindop to investigate privacy issues and a report was completed in 1978. Again, many recommendations in that report found their way into *DPA 1984*.

On 23 September 1980, the Council of the Organisation for Economic Co-operation and Development (OECD) adopted a Recommendation concerning Guidelines governing the protection of privacy and transborder flows of personal data. This Recommendation was the outcome of a number of years' work by an expert committee. The Guidelines contain provisions outlining the basic concepts to be adopted in order to give protection against the misuse of personal data although they do not themselves create a compulsory regime for data protection. However, Member States have certainly borne the Guidelines in mind when creating their own legislation domestically.

At the same time, in parallel, a European data protection convention was emerging, based on the available national legislation and legislative recommendations. The Council of Europe Treaty was the first international treaty to protect individual data from abuse. The relevant convention, number 108, 'for the protection of individuals with regard to automatic processing of personal data' ('the Convention') was opened for signature by Member States in 1981 and many of the principles we see in the *Directive* and in *DPA 1984* come from the Convention – e.g. the Data Protection Principles and the individual's rights to know what information is held about them on computer.

Following the Younger and Lindop reports and in the light of the OECD Guidelines and the Convention, the UK government determined to legislate, resulting in *DPA 1984*.

The passing of *DPA 1984* enabled the UK to endorse the OECD Guidelines and ratify the Convention.

The Advent of the Directive [3.2]

Attempts to establish a single market within the European Union showed that there were still considerable problems within the Convention and the first attempt at harmonising data protection legislation within the EU came with the draft *Data Protection Directive* in 1990, which was heavily revised in 1992.

An agreed common text was submitted to the Council of Ministers in 1995 and the *Directive* was finally adopted by the European Parliament on 24 October 1995.

Member States were allowed a three year period in which to implement the required legislation.

> 'The entry into effect of this Directive is good news for both individual citizens, who will enjoy safeguards concerning data held on them, and economic operators, who will benefit

from the free flow of information and the boost to consumer confidence'.

The European Commissioner for the Single Market, Mario Monti, has said.

'I am of course disappointed that some Member States are lagging behind on implementing the Directive in national law, and would not hesitate to open infringement procedures against them. However, I would like to stress that the Directive will be applicable from 25 October.'

This veiled threat proved to be true.

As of 11 January 2000, Germany, France, Luxembourg, the Netherlands and Ireland were the subject of a notification from the European Commission that they have decided to prosecute them for failure to notify all the measures necessary to implement the *Directive* on the protection of personal data. This step represents the third formal stage of formal infringement proceedings under *Article 226* of the *EC Treaty*. A previous notification also included the UK but one assumes that the European Commission dropped it because it was satisfied, by January, that the UK law would come into force on 1 March 2000.

In those Member States where the implementing legislation is not yet in place, under general European law principles individuals would be entitled to invoke the *Directive's* provisions before national courts, in accordance with the case law of the Court of Justice (*Marleasing* case, *C-106/89, 13 November 1990*). In addition, individuals suffering damage as a result of a Member State's failure to implement the Directive would be entitled to seek remedies before national courts, under the terms of the Court of Justice's case law in the *Francovich* case (*C-6/90 and C-9/90, 19 November 1991*). Additional information concerning the *Directive* is available on the Internet at http://europe/eu.int/comm/dg15/en/media/dataprot/index.htm.

In the UK, implementation has been effected by *DPA 1998*, which is substantially longer than its predecessor. *DPA 1998* has repealed and replaced *DPA 1984* in its entirety. *DPA 1998* has also enabled the implementation of the *Directive* by the UK. For this purpose, it should be noted that the UK does not include the Channel Islands and the Isle of Man, all of which are working towards new data protection legislation akin to the *Directive* so that there can be no suggestion that those jurisdictions (being heavily promoted as centres for E-commerce because of their favourable VAT Status — indeed, Jersey has passed an

E-commerce law) do not provide adequate protection for personal data and, therefore, *Article 25* (see **2.27** above) might apply.

New legislation will not solve all data protection problems completely. However, in some ways *DPA 1998* goes further than the *Directive*, because the *Directive* is only committed, on its terms, to amend aspects of UK data protection legislation which are inside the scope of European Community law. There is nothing to stop individual countries from addressing data protection in the context of activities that are outside the European Community law and, therefore, outside the competence of the *Directive*. This means that the laws in all Member States will not be completely uniform, notwithstanding implementation of the *Directive*.

What Happens if Implementation of the Directive by the UK is Challenged? [3.3]

EU Member States are required to implement EU Directives fully into their national laws. Occasionally, Member States are challenged by processes created by EU legislation for failing to implement. The new requirements to obtain consent to process data in *Article 7* of the *Directive* (see **2.6** above) require that 'the data subject has unambiguously' given his consent. In *Article 26(1)*, too, where transferring data outside the EU, the data subject had to have 'given his consent unambiguously to the proposed transfer'.

Where consent is addressed in *DPA 1998*, the word 'unambiguously' does not appear. Indeed, *DPA 1998* does not define 'consent' at all, whereas there is a definition of consent in the *Directive*. In theory, therefore, it could be said that there are differences between the way *DPA 1998* implements the *Directive* with regard to 'consent' and the wording of the *Directive* itself.

Another area where, perhaps, it could be said that *DPA 1998* may be slightly at odds with the *Directive* is in relation to the transitional provisions. This would not be surprising, since the transitional provisions in the *Directive* are awesomely complicated. There is at least an argument that the UK interpretation of the meaning of 'processing already under way' is more liberal that the wording of the *Directive* itself (on this point generally see **Chapter 14**).

If there were ever to be a suggestion that *DPA 1998* did not properly implement the *Directive*, the British Government runs the theoretical risk of:

O   being challenged under *Article 189* of the *EC Treaty* for failing to implement the terms of the *Directive* properly; and

O   the Data Protection Commissioner ('the Commissioner') could be subject to judicial review under English law for acting outside her powers.

Under that Article, a directive is binding as to the result to be achieved but the Member State may choose the form by which it is to be implemented. The directive must, however, be fully applied in a clear and precise manner. Once a directive has been enacted, the national courts are under a duty to interpret the legislation to achieve the result envisaged by the directive. If a Member State fails to properly implement the terms of the directive, an individual may still rely on its terms against the Member State.

An application for judicial review would be made under *section 31 of Supreme Court Act 1981*, to the High Court, on the grounds that the Commissioner had acted unreasonably, for example in failing to take into account the terms of *DPA 1998* when applying her interpretation of processing already under way.

An individual bringing a claim has to first obtain leave of the court and has to show that they have a sufficient interest in the matter, i.e. an individual right or claim. This would be established by reference to the consumer rights laid down in *DPA 1998*, which are curtailed by the interpretation of those rights by the Commissioner.

If the Commissioner's interpretation were to be challenged under either English or EU law, it is likely that the Commissioner would revert to a more literal interpretation of the provision in question.

Introduction of DPA 1998   [3.4]

The *Data Protection Bill* (as it then was) was published on 14 January 1998, some months after publication was originally intended. The first date for publication was interrupted by the UK General Election.

DPA 1998 received Royal Assent on 16 July 1998. Very little of the Act came into force with the Royal Assent – effectively, only the definitions section and power to generate the necessary subordinate legislation. It came into full force on 1 March 2000 once all the necessary subordinate legislation had been generated.

The *Directive* was adopted in October 1995 and had to be implemented in Member States by 24 October 1998 (and therefore there should have been implementing legislation in place in Member States by then). However, draft subordinate legislation needed to be in place in the UK before *DPA 1998* could be implemented, hence the delay.

DPA 1998 does not seek to address, expressly, the phenomenal changes in telecommunications and technology since 1984. It attempts to be technology neutral and set a general framework (as did the *Directive*) and focuses on what one can and cannot do with data – rather than seeking to be explicit about how the data is created and held or how it is processed, disclosed or transferred. Views differ as to whether the apparent lack of acknowledgement of technological advances is a good feature.

The Commissioner has said:

> 'In essence the Act is very close to the current law: at least 80% of compliance with the Act flows from compliance with the Data Protection Act 1984. Key elements which would continue under the new law include: the data protection principles of good practice; registration; an independent supervisory authority to oversee data protection legislation; and the data subjects' rights to access their personal data, to correct inaccurate data and to claim compensation for damage suffered in certain circumstances.'

Subordinate Legislation [3.5]

Eighteen sets of regulations were needed to give effect to *DPA 1998* or to create exemptions or exceptions to certain provisions in specific circumstances. Details of these are contained in **Chapter 23** and the **Legislation Annex**.

Interpretation of the Directive [3.6]

The Home Office have grappled manfully with the conceptual and linguistic problems arising from the implementation of an EU Directive and, rather than going for the simple option of 'copy out', (whereby the *Directive* simply becomes part of English law on its original wording), the Home Office have attempted to make practical sense of the *Directive* for the purposes of *DPA 1998*. This has obviously been no mean feat (and there will be those who say they have not gone far enough or have gone too far). They are, however, to be congratulated for the attempt.

Shortcomings of DPA 1998 [3.7]

The legislators have also sought to plug some perceived 'holes' or shortcomings in *DPA 1984*. For example, *DPA 1984* has itself been criticised as being unnecessarily 'regulatory' in certain respects. One example is the requirement for all data users to register with the DPR, subject to very limited exceptions. The exceptions to 'notification' under *DPA 1998* (a similar procedure) will not be so narrow.

The DPR's Office has also, in the past, commented on areas under *DPA 1984* which could usefully be changed. The DPR was concerned about her inability, in certain areas, to enforce her powers adequately. She was also concerned about the overly regulatory approach to registration under *DPA 1984*.

4 – Definitions and Interpretation

Introduction [4.1]

As with *DPA 1984*, the definitions are key to *DPA 1998*.

Data Subjects [4.2]

DPA 1998 only applies to 'data subjects' i.e. living individuals who are the subject of personal data. In fact, a literal interpretation of the *Directive* might arguably have applied the definition to individuals who had died, but the Home Office have interpreted this sensibly.

Data [4.3]

The definition of 'Data' under *section 1(1)* is information which:

(i)   is being processed by means of equipment operating automatically in response to instructions given for that purpose;

(ii)   is recorded with the intention that it should be processed by means of such equipment;

(iii) is recorded as part (or with the intention that it should form part) of a relevant filing system (i.e. any set of information relating to individuals to the extent that, although not processed as in (i) above, the set is structured, either by reference to individuals or by reference to criteria relating to individuals, in such a way that specific information relating to a particular individual is readily accessible); or

(iv)   does not fall within any of the above but forms part of an accessible record as defined in *section 68*).

Data can take many forms, including manual records, data held in a computer, video, compact disc or on tape.

Processing [4.4]

The *Introduction* states that from the definition of data it is clear that *DPA 1998* is now concerned not only with automatically processed or processable information but also data falling within the definition of a 'relevant filing system' (referred to in this book as 'manual data'). This is a significant development. Data controllers will have to consider whether information which is recorded manually comes within *DPA 1998*. Manual data may be subject to transitional relief until 2001 or 2007 (see further **Chapter 14**).

Data about companies are not caught by *DPA 1998* although the DPR did in the past give a view on ancillary personal data held on corporate files, e.g. computer-held customer mailing lists.

For example, suppose that where the customer is a company, the list contains both the company name and the name and/or the job title of the individual employee of the customer to whom the mailing is to be sent. The details about the individual are personal data. If the processing is aimed solely at communicating with the customer (in other words, the company) and the personal data is being used merely to send the mailing to the right part of the customer's organisation, then the data user did not 'hold' those personal data under *DPA 1984*.

If, on the other hand, the intention was to communicate with the named individual, then the personal data were 'held' because they were processed by reference to him/her. So, if the customer was a sole trader (an individual trading on his/her own account) the personal data relating to them would be held by the data user.

Under *DPA 1998*, holding data is in itself an act of 'processing'. There are now categories of data such as 'ancillary' data of the type described above which may fall within *DPA 1998* even though they would have been outside *DPA 1984*.

The new definition of 'processing' is much wider than under *DPA 1984*. *DPA 1984* extended to amending, augmenting, deleting or rearranging the data or extracting information from data, all of such operations being performed 'by reference to the data subject'. This latter phrase has led to a relatively restrictive interpretation of what is processing. The *Directive* has done away with this test.

Under *DPA 1998*:

'...processing...in relation to information or data, means obtaining, recording or holding the information or data or carrying out any operation or set of operations on the information or data, including:
- organisation, adaptation or alteration of the information or data,
- retrieval, consultation or use of the information or data,
- disclosure of the information or data by transmission, dissemination or otherwise making available, or
- alignment, combination, blocking, erasure or destruction of the data.'

It would appear that processing covers just about any activity involving data including, for example, sending E-mail, opening and reading a manual file or looking at data on a screen, arguably even if you did not personally call up that data onto the screen. *DPA 1998* would appear to catch *all* personal data held and processed. Therefore, persons holding such data will need to consider what word search facilities, for example, are available to locate all such data if they receive a request for subject access.

Under *DPA 1984*, there was a sort of exemption colloquially called the 'word processing' exemption. It excluded from the definition of processing any operation performed on data only for the purpose of preparing the text of documents. This express exemption has gone, although perhaps it is now slightly meaningless anyway, given that most word processing is done on PCs and the text could and is searched easily (an act of processing) and the fact that E-mails are often stored to locate names/ personal data and are used almost like a mini database, rather than held in relation to text preparation. Such complex computer equipment is rarely used for 'simple' word processing – solely so that letters could be typed, printed off for signature and then simply held on computer to print another copy, if required. On that basis, it is right that the 'exemption' should go.

Since the new definition of processing is so wide and might require system changes to deal with subject access, for example, the transitional provisions in *Schedule 8* of *DPA 1998* helpfully provide that for all purposes all automatic processing already under way before 24 October 1998, shall be treated until October 2001 as if the words 'by reference to the data subject' still appeared in the definition of processing. So, until October 2001, subject access has to be given only to automated personal data to which *DPA 1984* applied. It would not be necessary to find all data on a data subject wherever and however held, but only those which are processed 'by reference to the data subject'.

Relevant Filing System [4.5]

A 'relevant filing system' means:

> '...any set of information relating to individuals to the extent that, although the information is not processed by means of equipment operating automatically in response to instructions given for that purpose, the set is structured, either by reference to individuals or by reference to criteria relating to individuals, in such a way that specific information relating to a particular individual is readily accessible'.

This is a major new provision as far as English law is concerned.

It is still slightly unclear as to what files this catches, but what is clear is that the definition catches certain types of structured manual or paper filing systems. Even the Commissioner's office has been struggling to produce guidance as to what exactly is caught but has, however, addressed this area in the *Introduction*.

It is clearly helpful for 'data controllers' (see **4.14** below) to understand exactly what files *DPA 1998* applies to. The definition clearly covers, for example, systems like card index boxes and, perhaps, a filing cabinet containing *all* files on employees of a company, if it is fairly easy to locate and extract the file about one particular employee.

One of the authors of *DPA 1998*, Mr Graham Sutton of the Home Office, acknowledged in the early days of *DPA 1998* that there were still difficulties with what constitutes a relevant filing system. He even went so far as to give an example that a ringbinder containing an employee's data would not be a relevant filing system, even if organised in date order, but it could be if there were file divider cards in that ringbinder which divided the file up into different categories of data and made it more structured. Thinking on this continues to develop and be refined.

The Government believes that the wording in *DPA 1998* includes highly structured sets of data such as card index systems and excludes collections of paper which only incidentally contain information about individuals.

When introducing *DPA 1998* as a *Bill* at its second reading, Lord Williams of Mostyn acknowledged that how to address manual files is a difficult area. He indicated that the Government could have limited this to highly structured systems, but that would not have properly met the requirements of the *Directive*. He said:

'...we do not intend that it should catch files about named individuals where a variety of different kinds of documents are stored by date order. We want broadly to focus on much more highly structured files'.

In many ways, this interpretation seems to reflect the wording of the preamble to the *Directive* rather than the *Directive's* opaque definition of a 'personal data filing system'.

In a briefing paper produced in July 1998, the DPR's office said:

'It has...been put to us that "particular information" refers to information of a very specific nature. On this analysis information held in a file relating to an immigration application would arguably be covered as all the information in the file will, or should, be directly pertinent to that application. However, it has been argued that information held in a normal personnel file will not be "particular information" as there will be a range of information concerning such matters as sickness absence, performance, pay, next of kin. We find this distinction unconvincing. The range of information in a personnel file may be wide because there is a wide range of information relevant to an individual's employment. Nevertheless the information is "particular" in that it is all information held for, and relevant to, employment.'

The *Introduction* states that it is not wholly clear how this definition translates in practical terms in all situations. The Commissioner's Office can only give general guidance – the final decision in cases of dispute is a question for the courts. Whether or not manual information falls within this definition will be a matter of fact in each case.

Considerations [4.6]

In trying to assess whether a manual filing system is caught by *DPA 1998*, the Commissioner recommends that data controllers should consider the following.

Set of Information [4.7]

There has to be a set of information about individuals. The word 'set' suggests a grouping together of things by reference to a distinct identifier i.e. a set of information with a common theme or element. Examples might include a set of information on clients, suppliers or employees.

Sets of information about individuals need not necessarily be grouped together in a file or files. They may be grouped together in some other way, for example, by prefix codes, or by attaching an identifying sticker within a file or files. Similarly, the information does not necessarily have to be grouped together in the same drawer of a filing cabinet or even in the same filing cabinet. Nor does it necessarily have to be maintained centrally by an organisation. The set of information may be dispersed over different locations within the organisation, for example, different departments, branch offices, or via homeworkers but can still be a filing system.

Structure [4.8]

There has to be a structure to the set which works in one of two ways:

○ by reference to individuals themselves, for example, their name or identifying number/code; or
○ by reference to criteria relating to individuals, e.g:
  ● age;
  ● sickness record;
  ● type of job;
  ● credit history;
  ● shopping habits;
  ● entitlement to particular benefits; or
  ● membership of particular organisations.

Readily Accessible? [4.9]

The structuring has to work in such a way that specific information about a particular individual is readily accessible. This has two elements.

Firstly, the accessible information has to be specific information about a particular individual as opposed to the totality of information about that particular individual – what does or does not amount to such specific information will be a matter of fact in each individual case. It is suggested that in order to decide whether or not information is specific, data controllers should seek to identify what information they are reasonably likely to use in the course of their relationship with the individual concerned. If it is reasonably foreseeable that the information is likely to be so used, then it is specific information.

Secondly, such specific information has to be 'readily accessible'. *DPA 1998* does not define what is meant by this but the Commissioner suggests that the ordinary meaning of this phrase is that it is capable of being reached easily by virtue of the structure. Arranging papers in chronological order or lack of separation in the file by file dividers will not necessarily mean the information is not readily accessible — this would depend on the manner of structuring in the particular case (and this conflicts slightly with the comment of Mr Graham Sutton of the Home Office referred to at **4.5** above).

In deciding whether or not it is readily accessible, an approach suggested by the Commissioner is to assume that a set or sets of manual information which are referenced to individuals (or criteria relating to individuals), and which information is specific to an individual, is caught by *DPA 1998* if they are, as a matter of fact, generally accessible at any time to one or more people within the data controller's organisation in connection with the day-to-day operation of that organisation.

How This Affects Companies [4.10]

Organisations will have their own particular methods of arranging manual information. One organisation which has manual files containing, for example, customer information may fall within the definition whereas another organisation, which also has manual files containing customer information, may not. This is because the criteria in the definition of 'relevant filing system' are concerned with how this information is grouped, structured and accessed as opposed to its generic type.

Although it is recognised that there are certain areas of business where the question of whether manual information falls within the definition would be of particular significance, for example, personnel files, it is not possible for the Commissioner to state categorically whether or not certain types of information or files are caught by *DPA 1998* — it is necessary to look in each individual case at how the information is structured and whether, in the particular circumstances, the information forms (or is intended to form) part of a 'relevant filing system'.

In practice, data controllers may find that their manual files consist partly of information which forms, or is intended to form, part of a 'relevant filing system', and partly of information which does not. It is essential for data controllers to keep in mind that it is the information and the way in which it is structured which they should assess, rather than whether it is in itself a file or filing system. In other words the Commission is saying a file is not synonymous with 'relevant filing system'.

The *Introduction* says:

> 'In deciding whether manual information is part of a "relevant filing system", data controllers may find it helpful to undertake an audit of their manual information and filing systems and conduct a compliance evaluation, devoting resources to bringing manual data so identified into line with data protection standards in accordance with that evaluation. Manual information which forms part of clearly "highly structured" files, for example, card indexes or records, are likely to fall within the definition. The Commissioner recognises that data controllers may find that there are grey areas in determining whether or not certain manual information should be brought into line with the requirements of the Act. It is suggested that in those cases where data controllers are unsure whether or not manual information comes within the definition of data/"relevant filing system" they should make a further evaluation in the nature of a risk assessment. Data controllers should consider whether or not and, if so, the extent to which, a decision not to treat the information as being covered by the Act would prejudice the individual concerned. Where the risk of prejudice is reasonably likely then data controllers would be expected to err on the side of caution and take steps to ensure compliance. By way of an example of the suggested approach, a data controller should consider whether or not (or to what extent) the deprivation of the right of subject access or the right to rectify inaccuracy in relation to certain manual information is likely to prejudice the individual concerned.'

Transitional Relief [4.11]

Where manual information does comprise a relevant filing system, data controllers may not have to comply with *DPA 1998* in full, immediately – transitional relief may apply (see further **Chapter 14**).

Where it does, manual information falling within the definition (i.e. manual data) are exempt from the Data Protection Principles, *Part II* (Individuals' Rights, including subject access) and *Part III* (Notification) until 24 October 2001. Further (but less extensive) transitional relief may be available between 24 October 2001 and 23 October 2007. Where the data controller does not qualify for transitional relief, steps will have had to be taken to bring manual data into line with the new regime immediately *DPA 1998* came into force.

The Commissioner seems prepared to work closely with data controllers in the period after *DPA 1998* comes into force but one should expect that this relatively lenient attitude will not continue once data controllers (and the Commissioner) familiarise themselves with the new provisions and what is required for compliance – and certainly not once the initial three-year transitional period for certain manual data expires on 23 October 2001.

The Commissioner recognises that there will be cases where it is unclear whether manual information falls within the definition of 'relevant filing system', so becoming manual data subject to *DPA 1998*. In such cases, as has already been suggested, data controllers will have to make reasoned judgements.

Examples [4.12]

Broadly speaking, the concept of a 'relevant filing system' would catch:

- a rolodex in which names, addresses and other personal data are stored in alphabetical order;
- a card index box in alphabetical order;
- a filing system in which an employer keeps all its employee files in a filing cabinet in alphabetical order;
- a labelled looseleaf file in which a company keeps records of all its unpaid invoices in alphabetical (or, perhaps, date) order; or
- a looseleaf directory kept by a professional firm of experts instructed.

Other files would be more difficult. What about a file where all correspondence is stored in date order, wherever it has come from. Is such data readily accessible? On the current guidance, date order alone would not be enough.

If a senior officer in a company keeps a file of letters of complaint, not in any particular order or perhaps in date order. Is that enough to be a structured filing system? Probably not. Certainly not if a particular data subject cannot readily be identified on that file.

Action Companies Should Take [4.13]

Now the issue of relevant manual files is at least partly clarified, companies should set up internal guidelines on how to decide if manual files are caught by *DPA 1998* and, if so, at the same time remind employees of the data protection principles which require personal data to be kept accurate, up-to-date, adequate, relevant and not excessive for the purpose for which they are processed.

Old, out-of-date information, duplicates and drafts should perhaps all be disposed of. The decision to dispose of materials should be taken in the light of possible future claims or litigation. If, say, something might be useful to answer a future customer query, disposal might not be sensible.

Many companies already have guidelines as to how long computer records need to be kept and why they should be kept for specific periods and these should be borne in mind in deciding on how to restructure files. *DPA 1998* is no different to *DPA 1984* on this score and does not seek to interfere with company policies on data storage/destruction as long as the legislation is not breached. Indeed, for many companies a general corporate data policy (encompassing a data protection policy) would be prudent.

Data Controller [4.14]

A 'data controller', instead of being the person controlling the content and use of data as was the definition of 'data user' under *DPA 1984*, is the person who:

> '...(either alone or jointly or in common with others), determines the purposes for which, and the manner in which, personal data are, or are to be processed'.

Therefore, the test is, if anything, wider than under *DPA 1984* and may catch more persons.

It is important to note that there is a difference between the definitions of data user and data controller. The wider ambit of 'processing', together with the concept of determining 'the purposes for which and the manner in which' personal data are processed, go beyond the concepts of 'holding' and 'control of the contents and use' of data by which activities a data user was defined. Also, the term 'data controller' is defined by reference to personal data, as opposed to data generally.

Sharing Control [4.15]

The determination of the purposes for which and the manner in which any personal data are, or are to be, processed does not need to be exclusive to one data controller. Such determination may be shared with others. It may be shared jointly or in common. 'Jointly' covers the situation where the determination is exercised by persons acting together. Determination 'in common' is where data controllers share a pool of personal data, each processing it independently of the other. This could be the case where a number of companies in a group share a common database of all their employees, or customers, and all the companies can update the data as necessary.

The degree of control exercised by each data controller may vary, in that one data controller may have more control over the obtaining of the personal data and another data controller may have more control over the way that the personal data are used. A data controller has to be a 'person' – i.e. a legal person. This term comprises not only individuals but also companies and other corporate and unincorporated bodies. It is now possible to be a data controller even if you do not possess a computer, if you process manual records in a relevant filing system.

Data Processors [4.16]

A 'data processor' is:

> '…any person (other than an employee of the data controller) who processes the data on behalf of the data controller'.

The definition of data processor is simplified from the definition of a computer bureau under *DPA 1984*. A data processor is no longer required to notify details to the Commissioner's Office for registration as it did as a computer bureau under *DPA 1984*.

Processors were also required to comply with the Eighth Data Protection Principle of *DPA 1984* (providing security for data – see **1.17** above).

Instead, the Data Protection Principles contained in *DPA 1998* require data controllers to impose controls on the activities of their data processors by contract (see *Schedule I, Part II, paras 11* and *12* – analysed in **Chapter 11**) but the data processors are not themselves directly required to comply with *DPA 1998* (unless they are also data controllers).

Personal Data [4.17]

The definition of 'personal data' in *DPA 1984* talked about information which related to a living individual who could be identified from that information (or from that and other information in the possession of the data user). *DPA 1998* uses similar wording but goes further to talk about not only information which *is* in the possession of, but also information *likely to come into the possession of* the data controller.

It is questionable how fair it is to apply a test like this unless all the relevant data is physically in someone's possession. Perhaps future guidance from the Commissioner will clarify this, since the *Introduction* does not analyse the distinction.

Another departure from *DPA 1984* is that under *DPA 1998* personal data includes not only expressions of opinion about the individual but also:

> '…any indication of the intentions of the data controller or any other person in respect of the individual'.

This may be important, for example, for those in human resources departments who previously would not have had to disclose their intentions in relation to employees. Note that the definition now also extends to any expressions of opinion by *any other person*.

There is also an exemption from subject access in *Schedule 7* for confidential references given by the data controller (which could, of course, contain indications of intentions about employees and which would otherwise be subject to subject access). It is also possible that promotion planning and expressions of intention in regard to this are exempt from subject access under *Schedule 7, para 5* which covers data processed for the purposes of 'management forecasting' or 'management planning' to assist the data controller in the conduct of any business or other activity.

Section 7(4) provides that subject access need not be given where to do so would disclose confidential information without the consent of a third party identifiable from that information. This may, therefore, exempt from subject access references given in confidence by third parties but the Commissioner's Office has indicated that a request for subject access overrides confidentiality and, whilst the name of the referee could be deleted, the reference should be disclosed.

Third Party   [4.18]

Under *DPA 1998*, 'third party', in relation to personal data, means any person other than:

○ the data subject;
○ the data controller; or
○ any data processor or other person authorised to process data for the data controller or processor.

The expression third party does not include employees or agents of the data controller or data processor, which persons are for the purpose of this expression to be interpreted as being part of the data controller or processor. As such, this expression is distinguishable from 'recipient', which effectively separates employees/agents of the data controller/ processor from the data controller/processor itself.

General Interpretation   [4.19]

The definitions also include certain provisions of general interpretation which are new. For example, *section 1(2)* says that 'obtaining' or 'recording' in relation to personal data, includes obtaining or recording the information to be contained in the data and that 'using' or 'disclosing', in relation to personal data, includes using or disclosing the information contained in the data.

The interpretation provisions contained in *section 1(3)* provide that, in determining for the purposes of *DPA 1998* whether any information is recorded with the intention either:

'(a) that it should be processed by means of equipment operating automatically in response to instructions given for that purpose, or
(b) that it should form part of a relevant filing system,
it is immaterial that it is intended to be so processed or to

form part of such system only after being transferred to a
country outside the European Economic Area (EEA).'

In other words, this is included to ensure that it is not a way of flouting
the restrictions under *DPA 1998* in relation to cross-border data flows
by sending diverse data items overseas (perhaps in manual form) with
the intent that they be subsequently assembled into a relevant file there.

The references to the EEA in *DPA 1998* include Norway, Liechtenstein
and Iceland, as well as the EU Member States.

Sensitive Personal Data [4.20]

Under *DPA 1984*, there was no special treatment for sensitive data.
DPA 1984 gave the Secretary of State power to modify the Data
Protection Principles by order, so as to provide additional safeguards
in relation to:

O   personal data on racial origin;
O   political/religious/other opinions and beliefs;
O   physical/mental health/sexual life; or
O   criminal convictions.

However, this power was never exercised.

A special provision is made in *DPA 1998* for sensitive data (*section 2*)
which covers all of the data categories mentioned in *DPA 1984*,
although it excludes the 'other opinions and beliefs' category and
extends the 'religious' category to 'his religious beliefs or other beliefs
of a similar nature'. *DPA 1998* slightly widens the sensitive data
categories to include:

O   trade union membership;
O   alleged commission of offences;
O   proceedings for any offence alleged to have been committed by
    the data subject;
O   the disposal of such proceedings; or
O   the sentence of any court in such proceedings.

The primary relevance of the concept of sensitive personal data is that,
under *DPA 1998*, certain additional steps have to be taken by data
controllers before they can process such data to ensure such processing
is fair (see further **Chapter 12**).

Interesting questions arise such as can video or a photograph be sensitive data? Can the colour of somebody's skin or the fact they wear a turban or other distinctive style of dress be an indication of racial or ethnic original or religious beliefs? Indeed, can a name itself be sensitive personal data?

Special Purposes [4.21]

Section 3 is new and is very important as far as the Press are concerned. It defines 'the special purposes' which means one or more of:

- O   the purposes of journalism;
- O   artistic purposes; and/or
- O   literary purposes.

This is relevant for the 'media exemption' and various provisions specific to the media (see **Chapter 7**).

The Data Protection Principles [4.22]

Section 4 requires all data controllers to comply with the Data Protection Principles, which are a similar but expanded version of the eight Principles in *DPA 1984*.

However, there are now a number of conditions attaching to the processing of any personal data in certain circumstances (*Schedule 2*) and there are additional conditions attaching to the processing of personal data which is also sensitive personal data (*Schedule 3*). The data controller has to comply with *DPA 1998* in respect of all personal data, even if it is not obliged to notify its details or details of that data to the Commissioner (see **Chapter 6**).

Schedule 1, Part II sets out in some detail how the Principles would be interpreted. No doubt, we will in due course receive extensive guidelines on interpretation from the Commissioner, once her office has familiarised itself more fully with *DPA 1998* and its practical ramifications. The first such detailed guidelines are published in the *Introduction*, and do look at some aspects of the expanded Data Protection Principles, such as the meaning of 'consent'.

Persons to Whom DPA 1998 is Applicable [4.23]

Section 5(1) analyses those persons to whom or to which *DPA 1998* applies. These are a data controller in respect of any data only if:

'(a) the data controller is established in the United Kingdom and the data are processed in the context of that establishment, or

(b) the data controller is established neither in the United Kingdom nor in any other EEA State but uses equipment in the United Kingdom for processing the data otherwise than for the purposes of transit through the United Kingdom.'

For the purposes of *section 5(1)(b)*, a data controller falling within that subsection has to nominate a representative established in the UK. Data subjects have to be told of the existence of such a representative (*Schedule 1, Part II, paras 2* and *3*).

For the purpose of *section 5(1)(a)*, a person is 'established' (under *section 5(3)*) in the UK if he is:

'(a) an individual who is ordinarily resident in the United Kingdom,

(b) a body incorporated under the law of, or of any part of, the United Kingdom,

(c) a partnership or other unincorporated association formed under the law of any part of the United Kingdom, and

(d) any person who does not fall within paragraph (a), (b) or (c) but maintains, in the United Kingdom –
(i) an office, branch or agency through which he carries on any activity, or
(ii) a regular practice,'

Thus, the existence of a UK branch of a company incorporated overseas and trading here would mean that company is 'established' in the UK.

The concept of a 'regular practice' is somewhat vague. How often does that practice have to take place before it is regular? Indeed, what is a 'practice'? This should perhaps be clarified.

The reference to being established in any other EEA State has a corresponding meaning to that for a person being established in the UK.

Where a data controller is not established in the UK but uses equipment here, it is assumed that this could also include equipment owned either by the data controller or equipment owned or controlled by a third party data processor (processing on behalf of the data controller). This is consistent with the approach in *DPA 1984* which applied to overseas companies with an agent in the UK processing data here for that overseas company. The provision in the same sub-section which excludes equipment used 'for the purposes of transit' through the UK is helpful. For example, when using the Internet it is quite possible that your E-mail message could pass through the UK, without you even knowing of it and this data would not fall within *DPA 1998*. Again, this definition should not catch those who might have telecoms switching or routing equipment of some kind in the UK which transfers telephone calls or data through the UK telecommunications network where the UK is not the destination of the message.

The Home Office has acknowledged that the relevant provisions on jurisdiction in the *Directive* could lead, for example, to overlapping jurisdictions applying in different Member States. In its consultation paper on the *Directive* in 1996 it was said:

> 'While some of the provisions relating to geographical extent are clear enough, others are obscure and possibly ambiguous. There is, therefore, the potential for inconsistent approaches being adopted in different Member States. The danger is that this could make it possible for the national law of more than any Member State to apply to a single processing operation, or for no Member State's law so to apply.'

We do not yet have any guidance from the DPR on the interpretation of *section 5(1)* as such.

A big unanswered question is, assuming a UK company is a data controller, what is meant by the phrase 'in the context of' a UK establishment? If the processing is not such processing, *DPA 1998* does not apply. It could be argued that it means 'relating to' or 'having a connection with' or 'for the benefit of'. Otherwise it should be construed that it is processing which is necessary for the proper functioning of the relevant UK business.

The Commissioner and the Tribunal [4.24]

Section 6 redesignates the DPR as the 'Commissioner'. *Article 28(1)* of the *Directive* requires there to be a 'supervisory' authority in each Member State for monitoring the application in its territory of the provisions adopted by that Member State pursuant to the *Directive*. This is the Commissioner for the UK.

Article 28(3) of the *Directive* requires the UK government to give the Commissioner various powers, including investigative powers and powers of access to data to perform their functions, together with other powers such as a power to bring legal proceedings.

The provisions of *Article 28* were already largely covered in *DPA 1984*, although in some cases, the provisions had to be widened slightly. For example, *DPA 1984* already enabled international co-operation between countries party to the European Convention. *Section 54* reflects this, but also provides for the Commissioner to be the supervising authority in the UK for the purposes of the *Directive*.

Section 6 provides for the continuance of the Data Protection Tribunal originally established under *DPA 1984*. Broadly speaking, the existing Data Protection Tribunal structure continues. It will have a chairman appointed by the Lord Chancellor, after consultation with the Lord Advocate, together with such number of deputy chairmen as the Lord Chancellor may determine, and with such number of other members appointed by the Secretary of State as he may determine.

Section 6 also sets out the minimum professional qualifications required for members of the Tribunal which is to be made up of a mix of:

O   senior lawyers;
O   persons to represent the interests of data subjects; and
O   persons to represent the interests of data controllers.

5 – Rights of Data Subjects

Introduction [5.1]

Part II creates new rights for data subjects and at least reiterates those that existed under *DPA 1984*. In many cases, those rights, such as the right of subject access, are enhanced under *DPA 1998*.

Access to Personal Data [5.2]

Section 7 sets out the individual's right of access to personal data. Such a right existed under *DPA 1984* but the information to be supplied to data subjects seeking access is now slightly expanded.

An individual is now entitled under *section 7(1)*, on making a written request:

'(a) to be informed by any data controller whether personal data of which that individual is the subject are being processed by or on behalf of that data controller,

(b) if that is the case, to be given by the data controller a description of –

  (i) the personal data of which that individual is the data subject,

  (ii) the purposes for which they are being or are to be processed, and

  (iii) the recipients or classes of recipients to whom they are or may be disclosed,

(c) to have communicated to him in an intelligible form –

  (i) the information constituting any personal data of which that individual is the subject; and

  (ii) any information available to the data controller as to the source of those data...'

This goes beyond *DPA 1984* which simply obliged the data controller to supply a copy of the information constituting personal data held by him. Certain particulars such as to whom data are to be disclosed had to be provided, under *DPA 1984*, but only to the public at large on the data user's register entry – they did not have to be provided individually to data subjects on request.

This change in *DPA 1998* is, however, understandable because the situation could arise in future that a data controller is legitimately not registered (as a result of a regulation to that effect passed as contemplated by *DPA 1998, Part III*), so this information is not publicly available because there is no public register entry, and this request for information is the only way this general information could be obtained by the data subject.

The obligation is also to provide a 'description', initially, rather than the personal data itself. What does that mean and how detailed has the description to be? Let us hope that some guidance is forthcoming on this in due course.

Disclosure of Sources [5.3]

Section 7(1)(c)(ii) is a particularly sensitive new area for those who are concerned about revealing their sources (e.g. the Press). *DPA 1984* only required sources to be registered on the data user's register entry in fairly general terms. Arguably the new provision is more onerous for the data controller, as they would have to supply any information as to the source of *particular* information. It is hoped that the Commissioner's approach to revealing sources will not require too much checking of these by the data controller, otherwise it would overly complicate compliance with subject access.

In addition, disclosure of sources is, presumably, protected to some extent by *section 7(4)* regarding restrictions on disclosure of data relating to third parties (see **5.9** below) so it should not be necessary to name names, merely categories of sources.

Data Used for Evaluation of an Individual [5.4]

Section 7(1)(d) provides that where the processing by automatic means of a data subject's personal data:

> '...for the purpose of evaluating matters relating to him such as, for example, his performance at work, his credit worthiness, his reliability or his conduct...'

78

has constituted or is likely to constitute the *sole* basis for any decision significantly affecting him, the data subject has the right to be informed by the data controller of the 'logic' involved in that decision-taking.

This provision could be particularly difficult for banks which now rely quite heavily on objective credit scoring of potential borrowers carried out automatically. Many companies with a large appetite for recruitment also use software programmes which automatically scan CV's and reject all those which have not got certain information in them or apply a points score to the qualities of a job applicant such as their academic record and years of experience. The Commissioner's Office has mentioned psychometric testing in this context.

In the various discussion papers put out by the Home Office and the Commissioner's Office prior to the publication of *DPA 1998*, it was made fairly clear that it would be sufficient for a company using such techniques to describe to its customers, in relatively generic terms, how their automatic scoring system works without going into too much detail.

Trade Secrets [5.5]

Section 8(5) states that the relevant section regarding automatic decision-making is not to be regarded as requiring the provision of information as to the logic involved in any decision-taking if that information constitutes a 'trade secret'. The generally accepted meaning of a trade secret is:

> 'information which is used in one's business, and which gives a person an opportunity to obtain an advantage over competitors who do not know or use it'.

Surely, in fairness, provided customers are aware of the fact that automatic credit scoring may take place and its general mechanics, there should be no need to go into any more detail, particularly if they have a right to make representations regarding the decision (see **5.22** below).

Payment of Fees [5.6]

Section 7(2) contains a distinct improvement, as far as organisations which receive a number of requests under this legislation are concerned. Data controllers are not obliged to give subject access (with some exceptions) until they have been paid the fee of the prescribed amount and have been given the necessary information that is reasonably required to identify the records of that individual. Whilst the prescribed sum is currently only £10 and will not change (save in 'prescribed cases', where the sum could be up to £50 (see further **Chapter 23**)), it seems fair that, given the fact that the cost of performing searches through major computer databases always outweighs the prescribed fee (sometimes considerably), companies are not obliged to provide information until the customer has at least paid them to carry out the search.

The relevant regulation regarding fees for subject access under *section 7* is *Data Protection (Subject Access)(Fees and Miscellaneous Provisions) Regulations 2000 (SI 2000/191)* which is summarised in **Chapter 23** and is set out in full in the **Legislation Annex**.

Under *DPA 1984*, the time limit for compliance started to run from the date of the request and, therefore, major institutions with a lot of databases had no choice but to start carrying out the searches even before they had been paid, simply to comply with the time frame. Hopefully this provision will deter the idly curious, although it does not really assist with the fact that the cost of such a search can often be considerable and the fee paid may go nowhere near the actual cost.

Refusal to Comply with the Request [5.7]

There are a number of circumstances in which a data controller can refuse to comply with the data subject's request.

Unsatisfactory Information [5.8]

A data controller is not obliged to comply with a request under *section 7* unless he is supplied with such information as he may reasonably require in order to satisfy himself as to the identity of the person making the request and to locate the information which that person seeks (*section 7(3)*). This is consistent with the approach under *DPA 1984*. This is also wholly reasonable, bearing in mind that now the concept of processing of data no longer applies only to data 'processed by reference to' a data subject.

There may well be wider categories of electronically held data to search through than there were previously in order to comply with a subject access request (as well as having to give subject access to manual information).

Information Relating to Another Individual [5.9]

Under *DPA 1984*, a data user was not obliged to comply with a subject access request if it could not comply with the request without disclosing information relating to another individual who could be identified from that information, unless that person had consented. This included a reference to information identifying that individual as the source of the information sought by the request. *Section 7(4)* is not to be construed as excusing a data controller from communicating so much of the information sought by the request as could be communicated *without* disclosing the identity of the other individual concerned, whether by the omission of names, other identifying particulars or otherwise.

However, under *section 7(4)*, where a data controller cannot comply with the request without disclosing information relating to another individual who could be identified from that information, they are also not obliged to comply with the request unless 'it is reasonable in all the circumstances to comply with the request without the consent of the other individual' *(section 7(4)(b))*.

This whole area is a slightly fraught one, particularly in relation to the area of subject access to employment references (see **19.9**).

Since parts of *section 7(4)* are new provisions to English law, *DPA 1998* gives assistance in deciding when it is reasonable to comply with a request to provide data without the consent of the other individual whose details might be revealed. Under *section 7(6)*, data controllers should look at:

O   any duty of confidentiality owed to the other individual (which is particularly important for e.g. banks, solicitors or medical professionals);

O   any steps taken by the data controller with a view to seeking the consent of the other individual;

O   whether the other individual is capable of giving consent; and

O   any express refusal of consent by the other individual.

Perhaps this wording has been included in *DPA 1998* by virtue of recent indirectly relevant case law, because it is certainly not wording required by the terms of the *Directive*.

For example, in *Gaskin v United Kingdom (1990) 12 EHRR 36*, Mr Gaskin claimed that he had been ill treated whilst a child in local authority care. During the proceedings, he sought discovery of all documents held by a relevant local authority which related to his case. Third parties such as doctors had prepared some of the documents and the local authority sought their consent to disclose the documents. In some cases consent was declined. The local authority therefore did not disclose those documents. The European Court of Human Rights disagreed with their conclusion and held that whilst Mr Gaskin did not have an entitlement to access all data, the failure to provide an independent review constituted a breach of his rights under *Article 8* (the right to privacy) of the *European Convention on Human Rights*. This represents quite a change to previous thinking on the extent of access.

In debate on the Bill in the House of Lords July 1998, Lord Williams of Mostyn said, of the right of access to records that it:

> '...is to consolidate in the Bill the access rights given in the other legislation to which I referred and thereby to give effetc in respect of the relevant records to the ECHR judgment in the case of Gaskin.'

Section 7(7) provides that:

> 'An individual making a request under this section may, in such cases as may be prescribed, specify that his request is limited to personal data of any prescribed description'.

Such cases could be prescribed by regulations, for example in *Data Protection (Subject Access) (Fees and Miscellaneous Provisions) Regulations 2000 (SI 2000/191)* (see the **Legislation Annex**).

The new provisions above regarding when a data controller should comply with subject access are perhaps more unfair to data controllers than they were to data users under *DPA 1984*. Before, they simply did not have to disclose data if that would also disclose personal data regarding other individuals without their consent. Now they are supposed to take a view on it. Suppose they get it wrong? If the third party suffers loss, might that person try and bring an action against the data controller? How, exactly, indeed, does this fit with duties of confidentiality? Does the duty of confidence prevail, or the data controller's statutory duty?

The prescribed period for responses to a request for subject access remains 40 days.

Provisions Supplementary to Section 7 [5.10]

Section 8 contains provisions supplementary to *section 7*. To comply with a subject access request, *section 8(2)* requires that a copy shall be provided in permanent form unless:

'(a) the supply of such a copy is not possible or would involve disproportionate effort, or

(b) the data subject agrees otherwise...'.

In addition, where any of the information referred to in *section 7(1)(c)* (see **5.2** above) is expressed in terms which are not intelligible without explanation, the copy has to be accompanied by an explanation of those terms. This would include such matters as a card index or code book which might explain codes used in relation to a data subject or a directory which explains abbreviations used.

Disproportionate Effort [5.11]

On the question of what might constitute a disproportionate effort, the Commissioner has said (in a paper produced in July 1998 and available from the DPR web site (see **Appendix B**) what she regards as the types of factors that might constitute a 'disproportionate effort' (admittedly in the context of giving notice of certain information to data subjects under the First Data Protection Principle – but no doubt the concept is not dissimilar here).

These include:

○ the cost to the data controller in providing the information, for example, postage and/or manpower/employee time expended weighed against the benefit to the data controller of processing the data;

○ the length of time it would take the data controller to provide the information, again weighed against the benefit to the data controller;

○ how easy or how difficult it is for the data controller to provide the information, also weighed against the benefit to the data controller.

These factors would always be balanced against the effect on the data subject, i.e. the extent to which the withholding of the information may be prejudicial to them. In this respect, a relevant consideration would be the likelihood that, or the extent to which, the data subject already knows about the processing of their personal data by the data controller.

Subsequent Requests [5.12]

Generally, when a data controller has previously complied with a request made under *section 7* to provide data, *section 8* provides that the data controller is not obliged to comply with a subsequent identical or similar request under that section by that individual unless a reasonable interval has elapsed since the previous request. Guidance is given as to what is a reasonable interval in the Commissioner's *Introduction*. Again, this should help stop spurious and vexatious applications.

Changing Data After Request is Made [5.13]

Information provided pursuant to a subject access request, (similar to the wording under *DPA 1984*), had to be supplied by reference to what existed at the date of the request and could be 'purged' during the interim period if (and only if) there was already a standard practice, say, to delete data after so many days and, therefore, this would usually be deleted as a matter of course during the period during which subject access has to be complied with, irrespective of receipt of a subject access request *(section 8(6))*.

The Commissioner reminds us in the *Introduction* that the information given in response to a subject access request should be all that which is contained in the personal data at the time the request is received. However, routine amendments and deletions of the data may continue between the date of the request and the date of the reply. To this extent, the information revealed to the data subject may differ from the data which are held at the time the request is received, even to the extent that data are no longer held. Importantly, having received a request, the data controller must not make any special amendment or deletion which would not otherwise have been made.

For example, if an E-mail system automatically clears 'Trash' and deletes it every 14 days, that may continue during this period, even if there might possibly have been a relevant E-mail which it thereby deleted. Clearly, there may be other reasons (especially related to data which may be relevant to litigation – actual or impending) which could cause individuals to take care as to what information they do and do not delete (irrespective of *DPA 1998*).

Practical Steps [5.14]

A practical implementation step companies should be considering is drafting *pro forma* response letters to subject access requests to help streamline the subject access process. These should include both a positive and negative letter. The 'negative' letter should state that no such data is held. The 'positive' letter should include a description of the types of data held and, at the very least, a general description of the sources of that data.

For some companies, it may be easy to draft a list of sources or categories of data being processed which applies to all data subjects, which could simply be despatched to any data subjects about whom data are held if they ask for subject access e.g. to members of a professional body, if that body *only* holds standardised information on all members. A different letter might be needed, say, for that body's employees.

In addition, those companies which use automated decision taking should prepare a standard paragraph to explain the logic of that process to data subjects to which it applies, in general terms (see **5.4** above).

It may even be possible to produce a standard letter seeking further information from a data subject, since a data controller is entitled to ask for information to satisfy itself as to the identity of the person making the request and, also, to locate where the information might be.

Presumably, these steps could also be carried out by telephone. For example, many telephone banking organisations or Internet service providers seek, as part of the registration process, an item of information such as the date of birth of a member of the applicant's family or their mother's maiden name. This could be the additional information which a company may wish to use to seek to verify the identity of the person requesting subject access to enable the organisation to satisfy itself as to that person's identity.

Credit Reference Agencies [5.15]

Section 9 provides that an individual making a request for personal data to a data controller, under *section 7* of *DPA 1998*, which is a credit reference agency, may limit the request to personal data relevant to their financial standing. Further, if there is no specific request to do this, the agency shall take him to have so requested. This takes the burden away from credit reference agencies to provide a vast quantity of information in response to what is likely to be a considerable amount of enquiries.

The agency is also obliged, when supplying information under *section 7*, to make a statement (in such form as may be prescribed by the Secretary of State by regulations) of the individual's rights:

O   under *section 159* of *Consumer Credit Act 1974 (CCA 1974)*; and
O   to the extent required by the prescribed form, under *DPA 1998*.

This is more specifically referred to in *Consumer Credit (Credit Reference Agency) Regulations 2000 (SI 2000/290)* and the *Data Protection (Subject Access)(Fees and Miscellaneous Provisions) Regulations 2000 (SI 2000/191)*.

Incorrect Data   [5.16]

Section 159 of *CCA 1974* gives a consumer the right to have incorrect entries in his file removed or corrected with procedures to ensure that this takes place, if correction is warranted – i.e. if it is proved the individual 'is likely to be prejudiced' if this is not done.

Various references appear in *DPA 1998* to *CCA 1974* and other statutes under which individuals are entitled to data about themselves. This is because the existing rights of subject access, correction of data and so on in relation to personal data under various statutes such as *CCA 1974* have been helpfully consolidated in *DPA 1998*.

Subject access was really first pioneered in *CCA 1974* which enabled individuals to obtain a copy of information held by a credit reference agency (*section 158*). *CCA 1974* procedures were not affected by the passing of *DPA 1984*. Many complaints about access received by the DPR under *DPA 1984* have related to the credit sector so it was considered the retention of two separate regimes might be rather unnecessary.

DPA 1998 now deals with the issue of access to data held by credit reference agencies which had previously been covered by *CCA 1974*. *DPA 1998* provides for different fee levels for subject access to be fixed by the Secretary of State. The intention is that access requests, which would formerly have been brought under *CCA 1974*, will remain subject to the lower fee (currently £1) payable under *section 9* of *CCA 1974*.

One issue concerning the change was the subject of discussion in Parliament. Under *CCA 1974*, a modified access procedure applies where the subject is a business person (*section 160*). Effectively, this limits the amount of information supplied so that, for example, the person asking for access would not receive information about adverse credit reports which had been provided by bankers or suppliers. Where the business constitutes a sole trader or partnership, the general access provisions of *DPA 1998* will replace the specialised provisions. Concern was expressed that the consequence might be that third parties would be reluctant to supply such information in the knowledge that it could be obtained, with the results being that small businesses might find it more difficult to obtain credit. The Government indicated at the time this was debated that it was not convinced that the concerns were justified and a proposal to amend the *Bill* to retain the current procedures was rejected. However, the Government has said it will keep this under review.

Processing Likely to Cause Damage or Distress [5.17]

Under *section 10*, an individual is entitled at any time by written notice to require a data controller to cease, within a reasonable time, or not to begin, processing, or processing for a specified purpose or in a specified manner, any personal data in respect of which he is the data subject, on the grounds that, for specified reasons:

'(a)   the processing of those data or their processing for that purpose or in that manner is causing or is likely to cause substantial damage or substantial distress to him or to another, and

(b)   that damage or distress is or would be unwarranted.'

Conceptually, this is much wider than *DPA 1984* because it enables, for example, a son to apply to have the processing of data stopped if he feels that it is causing substantial damage or substantial stress to another − his mother, for example. He must, of course, specify his reasons for this which might be quite difficult in practice. It is questionable whether this sort of provision is really appropriate and in what situations it could arise. One example might be if an individual is told that a data controller holds data about him which has been given to the data controller by a third party (as may be required by *Schedule 1, Part II, para 2* − see **Chapter 11**) the individual could then try and 'protect' himself by exercising this right.

Exceptions [5.18]

There are some exceptions to this (e.g. the processing is necessary for the performance of a contract with the data subject or the data subject's prior consent has been obtained, in which event, the *prior* consent appears to rule the day). However, it must not be assumed that a consent will necessarily last for all time. The Commissioner's general comments on consent should be considered, and also bear in mind the First Data Protection Principle to process data fairly (see **Chapters 11** and **12**).

Data Controller's Response [5.19]

The data controller has 21 days to respond confirming compliance with the request or disputing why the processing is warranted. It would then be for the courts to decide, on application by the aggrieved data subject, whether the processing may continue.

Pre-existing Consent [5.20]

It would appear that if the consent of the data subject to such processing is in place (or if certain other conditions in *Schedule 1* are satisfied), this right to call for such processing to cease will not apply – the pre-existing consent would prevail. Should data controllers therefore try to include in their consent clauses in contracts with customers a consent to all types of processing that might cause damage – perhaps processing data about someone's marital status or other information about their financial status (e.g. that they were formerly a bankrupt)?

Whether such data should be held in the first place is, of course, subject to the Data Protection Principles and the data subject's separate right under *section 14* to have data rectified, blocked, erased or destroyed in certain circumstances (see **5.26** below). In principle, there is no legal reason why such a clause could not be included. In practice, the key determining factor must be the adverse PR effect that would be generated if such provisions appearing expressly in a contract. Again, it is worth a further reminder that the holding of the 'distressing' data, in the first place, is subject to compliance with the First Data Protection Principle (fair processing).

Processing for the Purposes of Direct Marketing [5.21]

Section 11 incorporates what appears to be an important new right, namely the right for the individual at any time, by written notice, to ask a data controller to cease (within a reasonable time) or not to begin, processing, for the purposes of direct marketing of personal data in respect of which he is the data subject.

For the purposes of this section 'direct marketing' means:

> '...the communication (by whatever means) of any advertising or marketing material which is directed to particular individuals'. (*Section 11(3)*.)

This goes considerably further than the express wording of *DPA 1984* and is required by virtue of the *Directive*.

It would appear that this right is exercisable at any time, even if there is a prior consent to direct marketing in place. This differs from *section 10* (right to prevent processing likely to cause damage or distress) where, if there is a prior consent in place, the prior consent appears to prevail (see **5.20** above). Direct marketing organisations and, indeed, all companies that adopt direct marketing techniques, must be aware of this and realise they cannot assume that once a consent to marketing is in place that it overrides a subsequent request under *section 11*, or that it lasts for ever.

Direct marketers also have to be aware of the possibility that individuals, (and in some cases companies), have rights to opt-out of unsolicited faxes or telephone calls for direct marketing purposes.

Clearly, in addition to compliance with *section 11* and the First Data Protection Principle, the direct marketer will need to comply with the notification requirements under *DPA 1998*.

The direct marketing implications of *DPA 1998* are discussed at length in **Chapter 18**.

Automated Decision Taking [5.22]

Section 12 is new to English law and is the specific section regarding automated decision-taking, and should be considered in conjunction with the comments made above regarding *section* 7 and the communication of the 'logic' contained in automated decision-taking (see **5.4** above).

Section 12 provides that, by giving notice in writing to a data controller, an individual could require that no decision made by or on behalf of a data controller which significantly affects the data subject may be based solely on the processing by automatic means of personal data in respect of which he is the data subject. This applies to a non-exhaustive list of areas, which includes information supplied for the purposes of evaluating matters relating to him such as performance at work, his creditworthiness, his reliability or conduct.

Even where no such notice has effect, the data controller has to tell the data subject if such a decision is made about him on such basis and the individual is entitled, within 21 days of that notification, to require the decision reconsidered or to require the data controller to take a new decision otherwise than on that basis. For companies which feel they might find themselves in such a situation, it might be worthwhile (as a practical point) to prepare a standard response to data subjects.

Importantly, the restriction on automatic processing does not apply provided that the conditions in *section 12(4)–(7)* are met.

Exempt Decision [5.23]

The first condition referred to is that the decision in question is an 'exempt decision', meaning it:

- ○ is taken in the course of steps taken:
  - ● for the purpose of considering whether to enter into a contract with the data subject;
  - ● with a view to entering into such a contract; or
  - ● in the course of performing such a contract; or
- ○ is authorised or required by an enactment.

The additional condition which has to be satisfied is either:

- ○ the effect of the decision is to grant a request of the data subject; or
- ○ steps have been taken to safeguard the legitimate interests of the data subject (for example, by allowing him to make representations).

The long and the short of this section appears to be that data subjects are entitled to know the generic details of any system taking automated decisions about them. However, the restriction that no decision can be made using such a device does not apply where:

O the decision is taken by, for example, a bank in the course of steps taken for the purpose of considering whether to enter into a specific contract with a data subject (e.g. a first time loan application); and

O the effect of the automated decision is to grant a request of the data subject (i.e. a request by him for the grant of a loan) or, if the loan is not granted, the application form includes some redress mechanism regarding the decision which is taken.

Section 12(7)(b) gives the specific example of giving an ability to make representations (similar to the provisions in *Article 15* of the *Directive*). From this, it would appear that provided data controllers structure their documentation so that it is expressed to be a request by the applicant to be considered for a loan (or whatever the product may be), there is a clear statement that the automated processing system is to enable it to help consider whether to enter into a contract with the data subject and provided the customer has clearly asked in the application for the data controller to take this decision and the application form includes a right to make representations, then the conditions in *section 12* which do away with the need to go through the notice procedures will have been satisfied.

What remains to be seen is whether it would be enough to give the right to make representations after the event in a rejection letter so that, rather than put it on application forms. In sending a notice of rejection of an application the wording could appear in that document. However, the former must surely be preferable.

The decision also has to 'significantly affect' the data subject. Rejection of a loan or a job might be within this concept.

Notice Handling Procedure [5.24]

Data controllers will have to establish a procedure for handling notices given under *section 12*. This could be extremely onerous for large institutions managed in separate divisions, in separate locations and with separate computer systems.

It will also be necessary to implement a procedure for registering and acting upon notices received from data subjects asking the data controller to reconsider the automated decision or take a new decision not on an automated basis. The data controller has 21 days to respond to a data subject's notice under *section 12* with details of the action he intends to take to comply with the notice.

More difficult would be if a bank, say, decided it wanted to be able to run these automatic procedures regularly during the life of a relationship with a customer without having to go back for consent or to keep notifying the customer each time.

Compensation for Failure to Comply with Certain Requirements [5.25]

Section 13 continues certain rights of the individual which existed under *DPA 1984*, including certain specific rights of damages and a right to damages for distress if in the latter case underlying damage could also be proven.

Where the contravention of the data subject's rights relates to the processing of personal data for the 'special purposes' (see **4.21** above) – e.g. journalism, it is not necessary to prove any damage at all before giving the individual data subject a right of damages for distress (a concept which is, in any event, rare under English law – see **5.17** above). Under *DPA 1984*, the right of compensation *only* arose from loss from for example, inaccuracy of or unauthorised disclosure of personal data. The new right of compensation is for damage caused by any breach of *DPA 1998*. Therefore, this does represent an extension of the data subject's rights.

There is a defence for a data controller which has taken such care as in all the circumstances is reasonably required to comply.

Rectification, Blocking, Erasure and Destruction [5.26]

Section 14 gives rights of rectification, blocking, erasure and destruction for the data subject in relation to personal data held about him. The right to ask for data to be blocked is new.

There has been some discussion as to what the distinction may be between erasure and destruction of data. It is suggested that the distinction may depend upon the nature of the storage medium involved. Manual files may well be 'destroyed' by physical destruction such as shredding or incineration. Computer records, on the other hand, are more accurately described as 'erased' because they can only really be completely eradicated by re-formatting the relevant storage medium.

A data subject may apply to the court for an order requiring the data controller to rectify, block, erase or destroy data and any other personal data in respect of which he is the data controller and which is inaccurate and any data which contains an expression of opinion which the court finds is based on inaccurate data.

Data are inaccurate if they are 'incorrect' or 'misleading' as to any matter of fact. The court can make an order, on application by a data subject, that the data subject has suffered damage by reason of a contravention by the data controller of any requirement of *DPA 1998* in respect of personal data, thereby entitling the data subject to compensation under *section 13* where there is a substantial risk of further contravention in respect of those data in such circumstances.

The court could order the data controller to notify third parties to whom the data in question have been disclosed of the fact that it has been rectified, blocked, erased or destroyed. The court decides whether it is reasonably practicable to give notice and the court would look at, in particular, the number of persons who have to be notified. This could potentially be quite onerous and it is hoped that it will be construed practically. It would mean, for example, that if a company sells a mailing list which is corrected by virtue of *section 13*, it may need to notify those to whom a copy of the list has been supplied. The same could apply to data supplied to credit reference agencies.

Another area might be where companies providing and participating in an Internet portal service and the telecoms company provides the Internet access might wish to share customers' data. The entity collecting the data will no doubt notify the customer that the data will be shared so the collection of the data will have been fair, but it could be required to notify changes to the other participants in the service by virtue of *section 13*.

Jurisdiction and Procedure [5.27]

Section 15 describes the jurisdiction and procedure under *sections 7–14*.

The jurisdiction conferred by these sections is exercisable by the High Court or a County Court in England and Wales or, in Scotland, by the Court of Session or the sheriff.

Section 7(9) of *DPA 1998* provides that if it is satisfied, on the application of any person who has made a request for subject access under *section 7*, that the data controller in question has failed to comply with the request in contravention of those provisions, the court may order him to comply with the request.

Section 15(2) provides that in determining whether an applicant is entitled to the information which he seeks, the courts may require the information sought (or information as to the logic involved in any decision-taking as mentioned in *section 7(1)(d)*) to be made available for its own inspection but shall not, until the question has been determined in favour of the data subject, permit the information to be disclosed to the data subject or his representatives.

6 – Notification

Introduction [6.1]

The notification procedure under *DPA 1998* is broadly similar to the registration procedure under *DPA 1984* but is slightly less formalistic. Sources of personal data no longer have to be registered.

Registrable Particulars [6.2]

Section 16 describes the 'registrable particulars' which have to be supplied. These are:

○ the data controller's name and address; and if he/she has nominated a representative for the purposes of *DPA 1998*, that person's name and address;
○ a description of the personal data being or to be processed by or on behalf of the data controller and of the category or categories of data subject to which they relate;
○ a description of the purpose(s) for which the data are being or are to be processed;
○ the description of any recipient(s) to whom the data controller intends or may wish to disclose the data;
○ the names, or a description, of any country or territories outside the EEA to which the data controller directly or indirectly transfers, or intends or may wish directly or indirectly to transfer, the data; and
○ in any case where personal data are being, or are intended to be, processed in circumstances where the restriction on processing without being notified (*section 17(1)*) does not apply (e.g. if by virtue of relevant notification regulations that particular description of processing is perceived as unlikely to prejudice the rights and freedoms of data subjects and therefore the restriction on processing without notification does not apply) and the notification does not extend to those data, then the registrable particulars must include a statement of that fact.

The relevant notification regulations are set out in full in the **Legislation Annex** with a summary in **Chapter 23**.

Security for Personal Data   [6.3]

Data controllers are obliged under *DPA 1998* to supply a general statement of the measures they take for the purposes of providing security for personal data under what is now the Seventh Data Protection Principle. Both the Commissioner's office and the Home Office went through a process of consulting interested parties as to how much should be required to be notified for this purpose.

One of the Home Office's suggestions was that data controllers indicate their adherence to BS 7799 – Information Security Standard and Certification Scheme (see further **16.7**). This allows companies to develop an Information Security Management System (ISMS) which involves three steps:

O   creation of a management framework for information;
O   an assessment of the organisation's security risks; and
O   selection and implementation of controls so that the identified security risks are reduced to an acceptable level.

Whilst the standard cannot make an organisation immune from security breaches, both the Department of Trade and Industry and the Commissioner's office are encouraging businesses to consider use of BS 7799 as their security procedure.

Now that the relevant regulations are in force, companies should be considering drafting a standard statement of their security policies. Someone should also be tasked within companies with keeping the statement up-to-date to reflect changes in procedures and check the text from time to time.

Prohibition on Processing Without Registration   [6.4]

Under *section 17*, it is still an offence (as it was under *section 5* of *DPA 1984*), if you *should* be registered, to process data *without* being included on the Register maintained by the Commissioner. This is effectively a strict liability offence as it does not have a defence built into it (see *section 21*).

However, *section 17(3)* provides that if it appears to the Secretary of State that processing of a particular description is unlikely to prejudice the rights and freedoms of data subjects, notification regulations may be brought in excluding that data from the need to notify, in which event such processing can take place *without* an entry being included in the Register in respect of that data controller (but the legislation generally still applies to that data controller).

In the Home Office Consultation Paper on Subordinate Legislation, published in August 1998, more 'processing' would be exempt from notification. Subject to detailed work, the Home Office said at that time that it hoped to exempt standard business processing such as:

○ processing for payrolls;
○ some personnel and work planning;
○ purchase and sales administration; and
○ general administration, including word processing.

The relevant notification regulations are set out in full in the **Legislation Annex** with a summary in **Chapter 23**.

Notification by Data Controllers [6.5]

Under *DPA 1998*, data controllers who have not notified their details or are not obliged to do so are nevertheless required to honour the Act *in all respects*.

In addition, broadly speaking, the obligation to file registrable particulars does not apply in respect of manual records recorded as part of a relevant filing system or with the intention that they should form part of a relevant filing system provided that the relevant filing system is already undergoing processing at 24 October 1998. This transitional exemption applies until October 2001 (see the transitional provisions in *Schedule 8* described in more detail in **Chapter 14**).

Under *section 18*, the data controller who wishes to be included in the register must supply the Commissioner with certain particulars (see *section 16*) and a general description of its security measures for the purpose of complying with the Seventh Data Protection Principle (see also **6.3** above).

Section 18 provides that notification regulations may also be passed giving more detail about how the information is to be supplied for notification and to make provision for matters such as the giving of notification by partnerships or in cases when two or more persons are the data controllers in respect of personal data.

Notification must be accompanied by a prescribed fee (for full details see the **Legislation Annex** and **Chapter 23**).

Exempt Categories of Data User [6.6]

A main benefit of the new notification procedures is that the Commissioner has powers to exempt categories of data user from the need to register.

Data processors (what were 'computer bureaux' under *DPA 1984*) do not need to register under *DPA 1998* unless they are also data controllers.

Under *DPA 1984*, data bureaux (now data processors) were regulated in that they had to register simple details with the DPR and were obliged to comply only with the Data Protection Principle regarding security. There were therefore few direct obligations on them.

DPA 1998 moves away completely from putting direct statutory liability on computer bureaux. Instead, data controllers have to impose contractual obligations on 'data processors' to act *only* on their instructions and to observe the Seventh Data Protection Principle as if they were a data controller. In that sense, therefore, the regime has been simplified because there is no need for a data processor (unless that data processor is also a data controller) to notify. Instead, the primary liability to ensure a data processor's compliance with the security requirements of *DPA 1998* is imposed on the person appointing a data processor. That person is legally obliged to include clauses in their contract with their data processor to protect the data being processed – otherwise data controllers would breach the First Data Protection Principle. It may be appropriate for data controllers to require their data processors to comply with BS 7799 or a similar widely accepted standard (see **6.3** above and **16.7** below).

Register of Notifications [6.7]

Section 19 provides for the Commissioner to keep the Register and that, by regulations, he can make provision as to:

O   the time as from which any entry is to be treated as having been made;

O   the fees payable; and

O   the period for which the relevant entry shall be retained in the register (although *DPA 1998* states the 'relevant time' is twelve months).

During the consultation process on notification, it was said:

> 'It will no longer be necessary to re-apply for registration every three years. Instead, a data controller will automatically remain on the register provided they pay their annual fee and keep their notified details up to date.'

Duty to Notify Changes   [6.8]

Under *section 20*, data subjects are obliged to notify changes to their entry. In tandem with this, the Commissioner is obliged to make necessary amendments to the Register to reflect any notification received.

So far as practical, notification requires that the entries in the Register contain the data controller's current name and address and describe the current practice or intentions of the data controller with respect to the processing of personal data and a general description of its security measures. These will need to be kept up-to-date.

This is not a strict liability offence. There is a defence under *section 21(3)* if the data controller can show that they have exercised all due diligence to comply with this obligation. Nevertheless, data controllers should put in place procedures for monitoring their registration.

Note that under *section 6* of *DPA 1984*, failure to keep the registered address up-to-date was a strict liability offence.

Offences   [6.9]

Under *DPA 1984*, *any* breach of the terms of a registration was a criminal offence. Under the new regime, such breaches could be the subject matter of an enforcement notice but are not automatically criminal offences. This is a much more sensible and practical way to approach this. Companies have an opportunity to explain what they are doing to the Commissioner and why, without the immediate prospect of having committed a criminal offence. Nevertheless, the Commissioner could take matters further if she finds the explanation unsatisfactory.

Preliminary Assessment by the Commissioner   [6.10]

Section 22 provides that where any processing is of a type which is subject to an order made by the Secretary of State because it appears to him particularly likely to cause substantial damage or substantial distress or otherwise significantly to prejudice the rights and freedoms of data subjects ('assessable processing') then, on receiving a notification under *section 18* or under notification regulations made under *section 20*, the Commissioner has 28 days in which to issue a notice to the data controller stating whether or not such proposed processing is likely to fall within these categories of processing.

It is an offence to proceed with processing where the Commissioner has not approved this under *section 22* unless the Commissioner has failed to respond within 28 days, in which event processing may proceed or, if during the 28-day period the data controller has received a notice from the Commissioner as to whether the proposed processing is likely to fall within the stated categories of processing. This is to implement the 'prior checking' provisions in the *Directive (Article 20)*.

In the consultation preceding *DPA 1998*, the Commissioner's office hinted that certain data matching techniques might come under this umbrella as such techniques could lead to unfair processing of data and a possible breach of the First Data Protection Principle. Data matching/mining was debated during *DPA 1998's* readings in the House of Lords. A section expressly addressing (and regulating) data matching was proposed by the opposition for inclusion but was not adopted by the Government.

In the House of Lords, during *DPA 1998's* second reading, Lord Williams of Mostyn said that the number of times that this prior checking procedure would be used would be 'very small'.

In the Consultation Paper on Subordinate Legislation, the Commissioner said:

> 'The July 1997 White Paper published by The Home Office identified three possible categories for this procedure:
> O   data matching;
> O   processing involving genetic data;
> O   processing by private investigators.
>
> The Government proposes to apply the preliminary assessment arrangements to these categories, either generally or in certain areas. It will develop the detail in the light of the comments

which are made in response to the White Paper, and any further comments made in response to this paper. Respondents might wish to consider in particular whether the preliminary assessment arrangements should be restricted to certain processing operations within the three main categories, and if so which ones.'

Regulations have not yet emerged which address this area.

Section 42 of *DPA 1998* provides that any person may ask the Commissioner to assess whether or not it is likely that any processing of personal data has been or is being carried out in compliance with *DPA 1998*. Dependent upon the Commissioner's assessment, which may involve the service of Information Notices by the Commissioner under *section 43*, this may lead to enforcement action being taken by the Commissioner pursuant to the complaint. (For further details, see Chapter 7 of the Commissioner's *Introduction* on Powers and Duties of the Commissioner which contains an excellent summary.)

This type of assessment should be distinguished from that described as a 'preliminary assessment' in *section 22*, which places a duty upon the Commissioner to make an assessment (upon receipt of an application for notification) as to whether or not the proposed processing, of a kind specified in an Order by the Secretary of State (termed 'assessable processing' in *DPA 1998*) is likely to comply with *DPA 1998*.

'Assessable processing' means processing which is of a description specified in an order made by the Secretary of State as appearing to him to be particularly likely:

O   to cause substantial damage or substantial distress to data subjects; or
O   otherwise significantly to prejudice the rights and freedoms of data subjects.

No Regulations have yet been produced.

Appointment of Data Protection Supervisors   [6.11]

The Secretary of State may under *section 23*, by way of an order, make provision under which a data controller may appoint a person to act as a 'data protection supervisor' responsible for monitoring the data controller's compliance with *DPA 1998* 'in an independent manner'. The order may also provide that, in relation to any data controller who has appointed such a person and where that person complies with such conditions as may be specified in the Order, the provisions of *Part III* of *DPA 1998* may have effect subject to such exemptions or other modifications as may be specified in the Order. In other words, companies which police their data protection procedures properly may be relieved from some of the general obligations on data controllers under *DPA 1998*.

Section 23 provides that an Order may impose duties on data protection supervisors in relation to the Commissioner and confer functions on the Commissioner in relation to data protection supervisors. In practice, one wonders why companies would wish to go this route, unless the Order makes the data protection regime considerably more relaxed for those companies that do appoint a supervisor. The role for the supervisor by regulations may prove to be more onerous than the role currently held by data protection officials within organisations. It is also perhaps questionable, if this role is burdensome, that a person would wish to take on this role unless recompensed/indemnified appropriately by his employer. Certainly, if it is a considerable new responsibility, an employee who has already been tasked with looking after compliance with *DPA 1984* might well be entitled to refuse to accept such a change of responsibilities.

This concept is new to English law. It has come from the *Directive*, but it is thought that the root of the particular provision has come from German law. If a company in Germany has appointed a data protection supervisor, in-house, who can be shown by the company to be suitably independent of the company's management, then it is possible that the Federal Data Protection Commissioner will exempt the data controller in question from the obligation to notify the Commissioner under the current German legislation. A new German law is not yet in place to implement the *Directive* (see **Appendix C, Part 2**), but one assumes that this provision will reappear in the new law, given that the *Directive* (*Article 18*) contemplates this. *Article 18* seems to suggest that where a Data Controller appoints a personal data protection officer, responsible for ensuring (in an independent manner) the internal application of the national law and the keeping of the register of processing operations required by the law, then Member States can provide for the simplification of or exemption from notification in those circumstances.

Section 23 is, therefore, broadly similar to the requirements of the *Directive* since it is the only part of *DPA 1998* that addresses notification from which data controllers can gain an exemption, *if* they appoint a data supervisor.

Duty of Certain Data Controllers to Make Certain Information Available [6.12]

Section 24 is somewhat complicated. Various categories of data need not be registered under *DPA 1998* or, by regulation. Nevertheless, on request by a data subject, the data controller has to make the relevant particulars available (free of charge) to the data subject within 21 days. This seems fair because those not required to notify as a result of any concessions or exemptions in that respect under *DPA 1998* have nevertheless to provide a copy of what they would have notified to the data subject (had they been obliged to register) on request, so that the data subject can still find this information out, albeit not from a public register.

Functions of Commissioner in Relation to the Making of Notification Regulations [6.13]

Section 25 expands on how detailed regulations on notification would be passed. The Commissioner was obliged, soon after *DPA 1998* was passed, to submit her recommendations on notification.

The relevant regulations are set out in the **Legislation Annex** and are described in **Chapter 23**.

Fee Regulations [6.14]

Section 26 gives the Secretary of State power to prescribe fees in relation to this part of *DPA 1998* and admits the possibility of different fees in different cases.

The relevant regulations mentioned above are set out in the **Legislation Annex** and are described in **Chapter 23**.

7 – Exemptions

Introduction [7.1]

As under *DPA 1984*, there are a number of exemptions under DPA 1998. These are detailed in *Part IV* and are either exemptions from the 'subject information provisions' or from the 'non-disclosure provisions'.

The subject information provisions are defined in *section 27(2)* as:

'(a) the first data protection principle to the extent to which it requires compliance with paragraph 2 of Part II of Schedule 1, and

(b) section 7.'

The non-disclosure provisions are defined in *section 27(4)* as:

'(a) the first data protection principle, except to the extent to which it requires compliance with the conditions in Schedules 2 and 3,

(b) the second, third, fourth and fifth data protection principles, and

(c) sections 10 and 14(1) to (3).'

Exemption from the non-disclosure provisions is available in circumstances where *DPA 1998* recognises that the public interest requires disclosure of personal data which would otherwise be in breach of *DPA 1998*.

The exemptions under *DPA 1998* are either full or partial exemptions and give an ability not to disclose certain data where they relate to:

○ national security;
○ crime and taxation;
○ health, education and social work;
○ regulatory activity, (a raft of organisations are listed to which the section applies – fairly large parts of this exemption are new, but the concept is not);
○ journalism, literature and the arts (all new);

○ research, history and statistics;
○ information available to the public by or under an enactment;
○ disclosures required by law or made in connection with legal proceedings etc;
○ use for domestic purposes; and
○ various miscellaneous exemptions in *Schedule 7* (see **Chapter 13**), some of them new.

A certificate of exemption, signed by a Minister of the Crown, is conclusive evidence of the requirements of the exemption having been met. Such a certificate may identify the personal data by describing it in general terms and may be expressed to have prospective effect.

National Security [7.2]

If required for the purpose of safeguarding national security, personal data are exempt from any of the provisions of:

○ the Data Protection Principles;
○ *Part II* (individual's rights);
○ *Part III* (notification);
○ *Part IV* (enforcement); and
○ *section 55* (prohibiting the unlawful obtaining of personal data).

Education [7.3]

The exemptions relating to education incorporate certain rights of access to personal data previously available under other statutes, the relevant provisions of which will be repealed.

Crime and Taxation [7.4]

Section 29 contains four categories of exemption which may be claimed if the personal data is being processed in relation to crime or taxation.

The three exemptions under *section 29(1)–(3)* only apply where there is likely prejudice to one of the crime and taxation purposes. *DPA 1998* does not explain the phrase 'likely to prejudice'. The Commissioner takes the view that, for any of these three exemptions to apply, there would have to be a substantial chance (rather than a mere risk) that in a particular case the purposes would be noticeably damaged. The data controller needs to make a judgement as to whether or not prejudice is likely in relation to the circumstances of each individual case.

Section 29(1)   [7.5]

Personal data processed for any of the crime and taxation purposes are exempt from:

O   the First Data Protection Principle *except* that part which requires compliance with the conditions for processing and the conditions for processing sensitive data; and
O   subject access,

to the extent to which the application of those provisions to the data would be likely to prejudice any of the crime and taxation purposes.

Section 29(2)   [7.6]

Personal data which:

O   are processed for the purpose of discharging statutory functions; and
O   consist of information obtained for such a purpose from a person who had it in their possession for any of the crime and taxation purposes,

are exempt from the subject information provisions to the extent to which the application of the subject information provisions to the data would be likely to prejudice any of the crime and taxation purposes.

Section 29(3)   [7.7]

Personal data are exempt from the non-disclosure provisions in any case where:

O   the disclosure is for any of the crime and taxation purposes; and

O   the application of those provisions in relation to the disclosure would be likely to prejudice any of the crime and taxation purposes.

This should not be construed as enabling disclosure of all personal data about a data subject to the Police, say. It must be data that, if disclosed, will assist with the crime and taxation purpose.

Section 29(4) [7.8]

This exemption can only be claimed where personal data are processed for any of the crime and taxation purposes, albeit limited to offences concerning fraudulent use of public funds, in addition to the assessment/ collection of any tax/duty. Further, it can only be claimed:

O   when the data controller is a relevant authority (i.e. a government department, a local authority, or any other authority administering housing benefit or council tax benefit); and

O   where the personal data consist of a classification applied to the data subject as part of a system of risk assessment which is operated for the crime and taxation purposes (as limited).

Where the exemption applies, personal data are exempt from subject access to the extent to which such exemption is required in the interests of the operation of the system.

Health, Education and Social Work [7.9]

Section 30 provides that, subject to an order by the Secretary of State bringing such provision into force and specifying the type of data to which the exemption applies:

O   personal data as to the physical or mental health or condition of the data subject;

O   personal data relating to present or past pupils of a school of which the data controller is the proprietor (as defined in *DPA 1998*) or teacher (similar provisions apply in Scotland); and

O   personal data processed by government departments or local authorities or by voluntary organisations or other bodies designated by the Secretary of State and which appear to them to be processed in the course of or for the purposes of carrying out social work in relation to the data subject or other individuals, may be exempt from the subject information provisions and any other provisions of *DPA 1998* that may be specified in an order made by the Secretary of State.

Regulatory Activity [7.10]

Section 31 provides an exemption from the subject information provisions for the processing of personal data by reference to numerous different categories of regulatory function exercised by public 'watch-dogs' which are all variously concerned with the protection of members of the public, of charities or of fair competition in business. This exemption is only available to the extent that the application of the subject information provisions would be likely to prejudice the proper discharge of those functions.

A number of bodies are specifically mentioned in *section 31(4)* such as the Northern Ireland Commissioner for Complaints and the Health Service Commissioner for England. There is also a specific provision in relation to the Director General of Fair Trading − *section 31(5)*.

The wording of *section 31* is much wider than that relating to this area under *DPA 1984*. In particular, the relevant function under *section 31* need not just be one imposed by a statute upon a relevant body. In addition to referring to any function conferred by an enactment as being a 'relevant function', it also applies to any function of the Crown, a Minister of the Crown or a government department and to 'any other function which is of a public nature and is exercised in the public interest'.

Journalism, Literature and Art [7.11]

This exemption is new to English law. Under *section 32*, personal data which is processed only for 'special purposes' i.e. journalistic, literary or artistic purposes (defined in *section 3*) is exempt from any provisions of *DPA 1998* relating to, *inter alia*:

O   the Data Protection Principles (save for requirements to keep data secure − the Seventh Data Protection Principle);
O   subject access;
O   the right to prevent processing likely to cause damage or distress;
O   prevention of automated decision-taking; and
O   rights to rectification, blocking, erasure and destruction.

The exemption only applies if the processing is undertaken *with a view to the publication* by any person of any journalistic, literary or artistic material (*section 32(4)*). It is unclear how firm the publication intention has to be for the exemption to apply. In addition, the exemption only applies if the data controller *reasonably believes* that:

O   having regard in particular to the special importance of the public interest in freedom of expression, publication would be in the public interest; and

O   in all the circumstances, compliance with that provision of *DPA 1998* is incompatible with the special purposes.

In considering whether the belief of the data controller that publication would be in the public interest is reasonable, regard may be had to his compliance with any relevant code of practice which is also designated by the Secretary of State for the purposes of this section (*section 32(3)*). This includes the Press Complaints Commission and Broadcasting Standard's Commission's codes of practice, which stipulate when breaches of privacy may be justified or warranted as in the 'public interest' (as defined in these codes). The data controller has other guidelines in the designated codes of practice mentioned in *Data Protection (Designated Codes of Practice) Order 2000*. If, therefore, the newspaper or broadcaster could show that it is complying with the relevant code of practice, then this should be sufficient to exempt it from the above and indeed other relevant requirements of *DPA 1998*.

Any proceedings against a data controller for access to or to prevent the processing of data (i.e. the equivalent of a restraining injunction) had to be stayed if the processing relates only to journalistic literary or artistic purposes and the material concerned had not been previously published by the data controller at the time 24 hours immediately prior to the application. The stay is until either the claim is withdrawn or the Commissioner makes a determination (*section 32(5)*).

This means that a 'gagging' order to prevent new revelations cannot be obtained under DPA 1998 since this would relate to material which had not been published by the data controller 24 hours immediately prior to the application. The definition of 'publish' (i.e. 'make available to the public or any section of the public' – *section 32(6)*) seems intended to prevent an argument that if, say, only a few copies of a newspaper had been published, the protection afforded by this subsection would still fail. However, the position in respect of weekly or monthly publications would appear to be less favourable.

If the media publish stories regarding living individuals this is likely to involve the 'processing' of personal data and this may involve a breach of the Data Protection Principles. This danger is particularly great if the personal data concerned is sensitive personal data (e.g. political opinions, religious beliefs or other beliefs of a similar nature or sex lives).

The media exemption would apply, however, if the publication is reasonably believed to be in the public interest (particularly the public interest in freedom of expression), which would probably be the case if a newspaper or broadcaster is complying with its approved code of practice.

In such cases, it would be possible for a complainant to obtain an order to prevent the processing (i.e. the publication) of the data about him if it had not been published by the data controller 24 hours immediately before the application is made.

Research, History and Statistics   [7.12]

Section 33 provides for various exemptions in respect of the processing (or further processing) of personal data for research purposes (including but not limited to statistical or historical purposes) provided that the processing (or further processing) is exclusively for those purposes and, also, that the following conditions are met, namely that the personal data are not processed to support measures or decisions relating to particular individuals and in such a way that substantial damage or substantial distress is, or is likely to be, caused to any data subject.

Where the exemption applies:

O   the further processing of personal data will not be considered incompatible with the purposes for which they are obtained (note that the exemption does not excuse the data controller from complying with that part of the Second Data Protection Principle which states that personal data shall be obtained only for one or more specified and lawful purposes);

O   personal data may be kept indefinitely despite the Fifth Data Protection Principle (which otherwise requires data only to be held as long as is necessary for the relevant purpose for which it is held); and

O   subject access does not have to be given if the results of the research or any resulting statistics are not made available in a form which identifies data subjects.

This means that subject access is not relevant where the data are never disclosed as a result of the research unless the data had been anonymised and can never be disclosed in a manner which would enable that individual to be identified.

Many industries, including the financial services industry and the pharmaceutical industry make extensive use of anonymised data. *Section 33(4)* confirms that, as long as the other provisions of the section are complied with, subject access need not be given to this information and, presumably, permits the sharing of anonymised data provided that the other requirements of *DPA 1998* in relation to the First Data Protection Principle are complied with.

Under *section 33(5)*, the exemption will not be lost just because the data are disclosed:

'(a)   to any person, for research purposes only,
(b)   to the data subject or a person acting on his behalf,
(c)   at the request, or with the consent, of the data subject or a person acting on his behalf, or
(d)   in circumstances in which the person making the disclosure has reasonable grounds for believing that the disclosure falls within paragraph (a), (b) or (c).'

This section is more detailed than its predecessor, *section 33(6)* of *DPA 1984*.

Information Made Available to the Public by or Under Enactment [7.13]

Section 34 of *DPA 1998* provides that when data consist of information which the data controller is obliged by or under any enactment, a rule of law or court order to make available to the public, personal data are exempt from:

- the subject information provisions;
- the Fourth Data Protection Principle (accuracy);
- *section 14(1)–(3)* (rectification, blocking, erasure and destruction); and
- the non-disclosure provisions.

There is no requirement to notify where the sole purpose of any processing is the maintenance of a public register.

There is currently quite a debate in the UK regarding uses that are made of the Electoral Roll, which is publicly available information. Many companies use the Electoral Roll for the purposes of direct marketing − to assist with mail shots, for example. The Commissioner is very keen to ensure that this information is not 'abused' and will be publishing guidance in connection with its use.

A company's share register may also fall within this exemption. Under *Companies Act 1985, section 709*, a company is obliged, on payment of a fee if it so provides, to supply any person with a copy of the share register.

This wording is very close to the wording that was contained in *section 34(1) of DPA 1984*.

Disclosures Required by Law [7.14]

Under *section 35*, where the disclosure of personal data is required by or under any enactment, by any rule of law or by the order of a court, personal data are exempt from the non-disclosure provisions. This presumably has to include orders of a foreign court, although the section does not expressly say so.

Legal Proceedings [7.15]

Disclosures that are made in connection with legal proceedings are dealt with in *section 35(2)*. Personal data are exempt from the non-disclosure provisions where the disclosure is necessary for the purpose of:

● or in connection with, any legal proceedings (including prospective legal proceedings);
● obtaining legal advice; or
● establishing, exercising or defending legal rights.

It is possible to claim the exemption even where legal proceedings have not yet started. However, it would be rash to claim such an exemption simply on a suspicion of proceedings. There would surely have to be some evidence that legal proceedings might ensue. However, the disclosure of information because it is necessary to establish a possible claim in legal proceedings, would appear to be permitted.

Domestic Purposes [7.16]

This is a wide-ranging exemption, whereby personal data are exempt from the Data Protection Principles and the provisions of *Part II* (individual rights) and *Part III* (notification) of *DPA 1998* where they are processed by an individual only for the purposes of that individual's personal, family or household affairs (including recreational purposes).

Whilst this is not clearly defined, it is clear that it covers the typical uses that individuals make of their computers at home for their personal correspondence, keeping a note of their personal household expenditure, playing computer games, corresponding with friends by E-mail, and so on.

A line would have to be drawn for those who work from home, perhaps, although this might properly be regarded as covered by their employers' registration, to the extent that there is nothing really different between the purposes for which they process the relevant data on their home computer and the purposes they use it for had that computer been on their desk at work. However, self-employed people who work from home may well have to register, notwithstanding that the computer is located in their domestic environment.

It should be noted that the exemption does not extend to *Part V* which deals with enforcement by the Commissioner. So, even if someone is not registered, they can still be subject to enforcement proceedings if they breach the provisions of *DPA 1998*.

Miscellaneous Exemptions [7.17]

Section 37 confers further miscellaneous exemptions which are listed in *Schedule 7* (see **Chapter 13**). Some of these exemptions, such as 'Management Forecasts', 'Confidential References given by the Data Controller' and 'Corporate Finance' are new (and potentially very important, particularly for human resources departments).

The provisions are also quite detailed and it is important to familiarise oneself with the new exemptions. For example, the exemption from subject access under *section 7* for confidential references does not apply to all references – only to references given *by* the data controller for an employee, *not* to any references given *to* the data controller *by a third party.* Clearly, the distinction is very important in practice when employers are giving subject access to employee files.

Power to Make Further Exemptions by Order   [7.18]

Section 38 contains a power for the Secretary of State by order to make further exemptions from the subject information provisions for certain types of data, the disclosure of which is prohibited or restricted under any enactment, if, and to the extent that, he considers it necessary to safeguard the interests of the data subject or the rights and freedoms of any other individual that the prohibition or restriction should prevail over those provisions.

He can also exempt personal data from the non–disclosure provisions in *DPA 1998* if he considers it necessary to safeguard the interests of the data subject 'or the rights and freedoms of any other individual'. It should be noted that the Commissioner, in making an order, can consider not only a specific data subject and his interests but any other individuals as well. It is hoped that this will not be construed too widely.

Transitional Relief   [7.19]

Section 39 provides that the transitional provisions in *Schedule 8* shall have effect. These are very complex provisions and are looked at in more detail in **Chapter 14**.

8 – Enforcement

Enforcement Notices [8.1]

If the Commissioner is satisfied that a data controller has contravened a Data Protection Principle, *section 40* permits the Commissioner to serve an enforcement notice requiring compliance with the principle in question, which either requires the data controller to take certain positive steps to rectify a problem or to stop pursuing a course of action (within a specified time).

In deciding whether to serve a notice, the Commissioner can consider the likelihood of distress or damage to any person.

Form [8.2]

To enable the data controller to plead their case, the enforcement notice has to state:

○   in reasonable detail which principle(s) have been or are being contravened;
○   the reason for that conclusion; and
○   particulars of the data controller's right of appeal.

There are detailed provisions for the form of a notice relating to the Fourth Data Protection Principle (where data has to be accurate and kept up-to-date or where the Commissioner is satisfied that personal data which are to be blocked, erased or destroyed, are inaccurate) which has to spell out clearly the steps a data controller has to take with respect to data to make it accurate or up-to-date.

Cancellation [8.3]

Section 41 allows for cancellation or variation of an enforcement notice if the Commissioner considers that all or any of its provisions need not be complied with to ensure compliance with the relevant Data Protection Principle.

Request for Assessment [8.4]

Section 42 provides that if any person is (or believes themselves to be) directly affected by any processing of data, that person can apply for an assessment of the likelihood that the processing has been, or is being, carried out in compliance with the provisions of *DPA 1998*.

This concept of a preliminary assessment by the Commissioner is new. On receiving notification from any data subject, the Commissioner shall make an assessment in such manner as appears to be appropriate, unless the Commissioner has not been supplied with such information as she may reasonably require in order to satisfy herself as to the identity of the person making the request and to enable her to identify the processing in question.

In determining in what manner to make an assessment, the Commissioner will look at:

○   the extent to which the request appears to raise a matter of substance;
○   any undue delay in making the request; and
○   whether or not the person making the request is entitled to make an application under *section 7* (subject access) in respect of the personal data in question.

Where the Commissioner receives such a request she will notify the person who has made the request whether she has made an assessment and, to the extent that she considers appropriate (having regard to any exemption from *section 7*), of any view formed or action taken as a result of the request.

From the way that *section 42* is drafted, it would appear that data subjects will not be able to use this assessment procedure as a 'fishing' exercise to get hold of information that would not otherwise be available to them directly through their subject access rights under *section 7*.

Information Notices [8.5]

Section 43 gives the Commissioner a new power. If she receives a request under *section 42* in respect of any processing of personal data or reasonably requires any information for the purposes of determining whether the data controller has complied or is complying with any of the Data Protection Principles, he can serve an 'Information Notice' on the data controller requiring that within such time as is specified in the notice, the Commissioner be furnished with such information relating to the request or to compliance with the principles as is specified in the notice and in such form as is specified.

An Information Notice has to state, as appropriate, either that the Commissioner:

O   has received a request for assessment under *section 42* in relation to the specified processing; or
O   regards the specified information as relevant for the purpose of determining compliance with the Data Protection Principles and his reasons for regarding its as relevant for that purpose.

It sounds quite a wide new right for the Commissioner, but its exercise could be challenged on the basis that the Commissioner is not acting 'reasonably' in requiring certain information.

The Commissioner has powers to seek information as a matter of urgency but has to give reasons for this, although the period of notice cannot be shortened below seven days.

Right of Appeal [8.6]

The Information Notice has to contain details of the right to appeal and shall not expire before the end of the period within which it can be appealed. If an appeal is brought against the notice (see **8.12** below), the information need not be furnished and the Commissioner cannot apply for a warrant pending the determination or withdrawal of the appeal.

The Commissioner has already said that she is not entirely happy with the data controller's ability to appeal against an Information Notice to the Data Protection Tribunal.

The practical effect of the current provisions is that ascertaining whether a data user has properly responded to a subject access request could take a number of weeks involving the issue of a formal Information Notice, an appeal against such a Notice and a tribunal hearing. Perhaps there is an argument that, if a warrant cannot be obtained during that period, an unscrupulous data controller might be able to 'sanitise' its activities prior to a warrant being obtained.

Exempt Information [8.7]

Nothing in *section 43* requires anyone to supply the Commissioner with information in respect of any communication between a professional legal adviser and his client in connection with the giving of legal advice to the client with respect to his obligations, liabilities or rights under *DPA 1998* or any communication between a professional legal adviser and his client, or between such an adviser or his client and any other person made in connection with or in contemplation of proceedings under *DPA 1998* (and for the purposes of such proceedings).

This is consistent with *Schedule 7* which provides an exemption from the subject information provisions in respect of information to which a claim of legal professional privilege can be maintained. Clearly, data protection laws should not be used as a way of sidestepping the established procedures for access to papers to be disclosed by parties to legal proceedings as a way of accessing data earlier than the procedures of the courts would allow.

A person shall not be required to furnish information under this section if to do so would reveal evidence of the commission of any offence, other than an offence under *DPA 1998*, and might expose him to proceedings for that offence. This is, again, consistent with a 'self-incrimination' exemption in *Schedule 7* (see **Chapter 13**).

Special Information Notices [8.8]

If the Commissioner has received a request for assessment or has reasonable grounds to suspect that, in a case in which proceedings have been stayed under *section 32*, the data are not being processed for the special purposes or otherwise are not in compliance with *section 32*, he may serve the data controller with a 'Special Information Notice' which, again, could specify what information is required, in what form and by when.

As with an Enforcement Notice, the Special Information Notice has to explain how it has come to be served (e.g. a request under *section 42*) and contain details of the rights of appeal.

It will be interesting to see how the Commissioner exercises this power and what types of information are asked for. Again, the Commissioner has to show 'reasonable grounds' for suspecting a breach of the relevant provisions of *section 32*.

Determination by the Commissioner as to the
Special Purposes [8.9]

Section 45 provides that if at any time the Commissioner considers (whether having been through the Special Information Notice procedure or otherwise) that personal data are not being processed for the special purposes or are not being processed with a view to publication as contemplated by *section 32*, she can make a written determination to that effect and serve it on the data controller, accompanied by details of the data controller's right of appeal.

Restriction on Enforcement in the Case of Processing
for the Special Purposes [8.10]

Section 46 provides that the Commissioner cannot serve an Enforcement Notice on the data controller with respect to the processing of personal data for the special purposes unless a determination under *section 45* has taken effect and the court has granted leave for the notice to be served. It will only do so if it is satisfied that the Commissioner has reason to suspect a contravention of the Data Protection Principles which is of 'substantial public importance' and (except in cases of emergency) the data controller has been given notice, in accordance with the rules of the courts, of the application for leave.

The procedure should give the data controller a sufficient opportunity to argue why, in the interests of free speech, it is exempt from the requirements of *DPA 1998*.

Failure to Comply with a Notice [8.11]

Under *section 47*, failure to comply with an Enforcement Notice, an Information Notice or a Special Information Notice is an offence. It would also be an offence for a person who, in purported compliance with an Information Notice or Special Information Notice makes a statement which he knows to be false in a material respect or he is reckless as to whether it is false in a material respect.

It will be a defence for a person charged under this section to prove that he exercised 'all due diligence' to comply with the notice in question.

Rights of Appeal [8.12]

Section 48 provides for rights of appeal to the Data Protection Tribunal in respect of Enforcement Notices, Information Notices and Special Information Notices and further detail of the procedures are set out in *Schedule 6*.

Determination of Appeals [8.13]

If, on an appeal under *section 48*, the Data Protection Tribunal considers that a notice against which the appeal is brought is not in accordance with the law or, to the extent that the notice involved an exercise of discretion by the Commissioner, that the Commissioner ought to have exercised her discretion differently, the Tribunal shall allow the appeal or substitute such other notice or decision as should have been served or made by the Commissioner. In any other case the Tribunal shall dismiss the appeal.

In considering an appeal, the Tribunal can review any determination of fact on which the notice is based and, if there has been a change of circumstances, the Tribunal may vary or cancel a notice in question.

9 – Other Functions of the Commissioner

General Duties of the Commissioner [9.1]

Section 51 sets out the general duties of the Commissioner including a duty to promote the following of good practice by data controllers and, in particular, the observance of the requirements of *DPA 1998* by data controllers. The Commissioner shall arrange for dissemination to the public of information about 'good practice' under *DPA 1998*.

'Good practice' is defined as such practice in the processing of personal data as appears to the Commissioner to be desirable having regard to the interests of data subjects and others and includes (without limitation) compliance with *DPA 1998*.

Codes of Practice [9.2]

Where the Secretary of State so directs by order, or the Commissioner considers it appropriate to do so, he can (after consulting relevant trade associations, data subjects or persons representing data subjects as he thinks appropriate) prepare and disseminate appropriate Codes of Practice for guidance as to good practice or he can encourage trade associations to do so.

He may notify trade associations whether in his opinion Codes submitted by them promote the following of good practice. An order of the Secretary of State as described above shall describe the personal data or processing which the Code would relate to and the persons/ classes of persons to whom it is to relate.

Any Code of Practice which is drawn up in compliance with the direction of the Secretary of State has also to be laid before each House of Parliament by the Commissioner unless he has included such Code in his general or other reports referred to at **9.5** below.

Dissemination of Information [9.3]

The Commissioner shall also arrange for the dissemination in such form and manner as he considers appropriate of any 'Community finding' (as defined by *Schedule 1, Part II, para 15(2)* – see **Chapter 11**) established pursuant to the *Directive* or any decision of the European Commission, under the procedure provided for in *Article 31(2)* of the *Directive*, (relating to transfers of data outside the EEA to countries which may not provide adequate protection for personal data). She may also disseminate such other information as it may appear to her to be expedient to give to data controllers in relation to any personal data about the protection of the rights and freedoms of data subjects in relation to processing of personal data in countries outside the EEA.

This latter obligation is important, because Community findings are the decisions which, for example, may designate a country outside the EU as one which does provide an adequate level of protection for personal data and, therefore, exports of data to that country would be permitted under the Eighth Data Protection Principle because the country to which the export is to take place satisfies the 'adequacy' test (see **Chapter 15** below).

Recommendations have been made by the Article 29 Working Party (see **2.31** above) that the laws in Switzerland and Hungary are perceived as providing an adequate level of protection for personal data – Although no formal Community finding has yet been made confirming this. The laws in six other countries have also been the subject of an external study commissioned by the European Commission but, again, no community finding has emerged in the light of that study.

Assessment [9.4]

Under *section 51(7)* the Commissioner has power, with the consent of the data controller, to assess any processing of personal data for the following of good practice and shall inform the data controller of the result of the assessment. If the Commissioner agrees to provide this service to a data controller, he can charge such sums for it as he may, with the consent of the Secretary of State, determine.

Report [9.5]

Section 52 provides that the Commissioner has to present a general report on the exercise of his functions to each House of Parliament on an annual basis and, from time to time, such other reports with respect to his functions as he thinks fit. This reflects the current practice.

Cases Involving Processing for Special Purposes   [9.6]

Under *section 53*, as soon as reasonably practicable after receiving an application by a data subject who is an actual or prospective party to proceedings under various provisions of *DPA 1998* in relation to the 'special purposes', the Commissioner shall consider the application and decide whether or not to grant it. She shall only grant it if the case involves a matter of substantial public importance.

If the Commissioner does decide to provide assistance, he has to let the applicant know as soon as practicable and state the extent of the assistance that would be provided. If he decides not to give assistance, he has to notify this as soon as practicable and, if he thinks fit, explain the reasons for it.

International Co-operation   [9.7]

Section 54(1) provides for the Commissioner to take over the role of the DPR and the Commissioner is formally appointed the 'supervisory authority' for the UK for the purposes of the *Directive* – e.g. being involved in ongoing data protection co-operation matters in the EU (and EEA) (as well as remaining the designated authority under the *1981 Council of Europe Convention on Data Protection*).

The Secretary of State may, by order, make provision as to co-operation by the Commissioner with the European Commission and supervisory authorities in other EEA States. Particular regard will be had to exchanges of information and the exercise, within the UK, at the request of a supervisory authority in another EEA State (in cases excluded by *section 5* from the application of the other provisions of *DPA 1998*), of functions of the Commissioner specified in the order. *Data Protection (International Co-operation) Order 2000 (SI 2000/190)* relates to international co-operation. It is summarised in **Chapter 23** and set out in full in the **Legislation Annex**.

In certain circumstances, the *Directive* provides for the European Commission to authorise certain contractual or other solutions to permit transfers of data outside the EU because the contract or other procedure provides an adequate level of protection for the data. *Section 54* provides that the Commissioner shall comply with any such authorisation and implement it in the UK and will notify the European Commission and supervisory authorities in other EEA States of circumstances in which the Commissioner is satisfied that personal data is transferred outside the EEA from the UK on terms which ensure adequate safeguards for the rights and freedoms of data subjects, which could include use of appropriate contractual solutions (see *section 54(7)*). For a further explanation see **Chapter 15**.

Disclosure of Information [9.8]

Section 58 provides that no enactment or rule of law prohibiting or restricting the disclosure of information shall preclude a person from furnishing the Commissioner or the Data Protection Tribunal with any information necessary for the discharge of their functions under *DPA 1998*.

Confidentiality of Information [9.9]

Section 59 imposes duties of confidentiality on the Commissioner, members of the Commissioner's staff or an agent of the Commissioner in relation to information on identified or identifiable individuals or businesses furnished to him for the purposes of *DPA 1998*. There are exceptions to this (e.g. where it is made for the purposes of discharging the Commissioner's functions under *DPA 1998* or where the consent of the relevant individual, or of the person for the time being carrying on the relevant business, is obtained).

Service of Notices by the Commissioner [9.10]

Section 65 sets out the procedures generally for service of notices under *DPA 1998*.

Notices to be given by the Commissioner may be served on a person who is an individual by:

○   delivering it to him;
○   sending it to him by post addressed to him at his usual or last known place of residence or business; or

○ leaving it for him at that place.

The notice can be served on a body corporate or unincorporate:

○ by sending it by post to the proper officer of the body at its principal office;
○ by addressing it to the proper officer of the body and leaving it at that office; or
○ if the person is a partnership in Scotland, by sending it by post to the principal office of the partnership or by addressing it to that partnership then leaving it at that office.

A 'principal office' in relation to a registered company, means its registered office and the 'proper officer' in relation to any body means the secretary or other executive officer charged with the conduct of its general affairs.

Section 64 is new and applies to:

○ notices or requests made under *Part II* (rights of data subjects and others);
○ notices requiring data controllers to make available certain information under *section 24(1)*; or
○ applications to cancel or vary an enforcement notice due to a change in circumstances under *section 41(2)*.

However, it does not apply to anything required to be served in accordance with rules of court.

The requirement that any notice, request, particulars or application to which this section applies has to be in writing will be satisfied where it is transmitted by electronic means, is received in legible form and is capable of being used for subsequent reference. The Secretary of State has the power to make regulations providing that the electronic transmission of notices, etc. does not apply in such circumstances as may be prescribed by the regulations. It seems strange that no other notices under *DPA 1998* can be given electronically.

10 – Offences and Liability

Unlawful Obtaining etc. of Personal Data [10.1]

It has been recognised in the past that there has been a problem with enforced subject access, where data subjects are forced to obtain access to their data in order to supply it to third parties, such as prospective employers.

With effect from February 1995, *section 161 of Criminal Justice and Public Order Act 1994 (CJPOA 1994)* introduced into *DPA 1984* the offence of procuring the disclosure of personal data in contravention of that Act where the person procuring the disclosure knew or had reason to believe that such disclosure constituted a contravention of *DPA 1984*.

Section 55 of DPA 1998 reflects (but does not quite mirror) the provisions that were introduced by this section. In fact the provisions of *DPA 1998* differ in several material respects.

Section 55(1) provides:

> 'A person must not knowingly or recklessly, without the consent of the data controller –
> (a) obtain or disclose personal data or the information contained in personal data, or
> (b) procure the disclosure to another person of the information contained in personal data'.

The first important change is that the procurer has to be acting 'knowingly or recklessly' whereas, under *CJPOA 1994*, the test was whether the procurer knew 'or had reason to believe' that the disclosure constituted a contravention. This change makes it clear that mere negligence by the 'procurer' is not enough to make him criminally liable. In order to be liable under *DPA 1998*, they would have to have actual knowledge or be turning a blind eye to the obvious.

In addition, a procurer only becomes liable if the information is obtained without the consent of the data controller. On the face of *section 55*, if the data controller consents to the release of the information, even if that disclosure is in breach of *DPA 1998*, the procurer will not be criminally liable even though a data controller would. This is a surprising result but is consistent with the strict wording in *section 55*.

It is also an offence under *section 55* for a person to sell personal data obtained in this manner.

Defences [10.2]

In addition to the defence which was available under *section 28* of *DPA 1984* (prevention or detection of crime/prosecution of an offender), *DPA 1998* introduces three new defences for the alleged procurer, that:

O   he acted in the reasonable belief that he had in law the right to procure the disclosure of the information;

O   he acted in the reasonable belief that he would have had the consent of the data controller if the data controller had known of the obtaining, disclosing or procuring and the circumstances of it; or

O   in the particular circumstances the procuring is justified as being in the public interest.

The first of these defences is unusual in the context of English law where it is not normally a defence to argue that you are mistaken as to your legal rights. In practical terms, one would not envisage many circumstances in which this defence could apply although it clearly gives scope for argument.

The second of these defences arguably creates further uncertainty. It is very difficult to predict when such a defence might be successful. For example, how do you establish what the data controller might have done if he had known that the information was being procured? Secondly, how does the court assess the reasonableness of the procurer's belief that the data controller would have given his consent?

The third defence is potentially the most important for the alleged procurer. As noted above, that section provides a defence where the information has been procured for the purposes of preventing or detecting crime or the apprehension or prosecution of offenders. The new 'public interest' defence is potentially broader than *section 28* of

DPA 1984. For example, a reasonable argument could be made that the detection of fraud and the chasing of the proceeds of fraud, even where it takes place purely on behalf of a private party, is in the public interest.

Prohibition of Requirement to Produce Certain Records [10.3]

It is an offence under *section 56* for a person to require, in connection with the recruitment of another person as an employee, the continued employment of another person, or any contract for the provision of services to him by another person, that that other person or a third party should supply him with a relevant record or produce a relevant record to him. Likewise, a person who provides goods, facilities or services to the public (whether or not remunerated for the same) has not to require that other person or a third party, as a condition of providing the goods, facilities or services, to supply him with a relevant record or to produce a relevant record to him.

A person who can show that the requirement is in accordance with any enactment, rule of law, order of court, or in particular circumstances justified as being in the public interest, is exempted from this prohibition.

'Relevant record' means any record which has been or is to be obtained by a data subject from any data controller listed in the table set out in *section 56*, which includes (amongst others) a chief officer of police in England, the Secretary of State, the Department of Health and Social Services for Northern Ireland.

This is considered in more detail in **Chapter 19**, in an employment context.

Avoidance of Certain Contractual Terms Relating to Health Records [10.4]

Section 57 renders void any condition or term of a contract insofar as it purports to require an individual to supply any other person with a record (or copy, or part thereof) to which *section 57* applies or to produce to any other person such a record, copy or part. This section applies to any record which has been or is to be obtained by a data subject in the exercise of the right to subject access under *section* 7, (right of access to personal data) and which consists of information contained in any health record (defined in *section 68(2)*).

Prosecutions and Penalties [10.5]

Section 60 provides that no proceedings for an offence under *DPA 1998* can be instituted without the consent of the Director of Public Prosecutions, or unless such proceedings are commenced by the Commissioner herself.

Criminal offences under *DPA 1998* carry, on summary conviction, a fine not exceeding the statutory maximum (currently £5,000) or on conviction on indictment, a fine that can be unlimited.

Any person guilty of an offence under *Schedule 9, para 12* (intentionally obstructing a person executing a warrant under *DPA 1998*) shall be liable to a fine.

Liability of Directors etc. [10.6]

Section 61 mirrors *section 20* of *DPA 1984* and provides that where an offence under *DPA 1998* has been committed by a body corporate and has been committed with the consent or connivance of, or would be attributable to neglect on the part of, a director, manager, secretary or similar officer who is purporting to act in any such capacity, they (as well as the body corporate) shall be guilty of the offence and shall be liable to be proceeded against and punished accordingly.

Where the affairs of a body corporate are managed by its members, this section applies to the acts and defaults of a member in connection with his functions of management as if he were a director.

The term 'officer' could include senior staff with management functions and also potentially the person within an organisation (who need not be a director or the secretary) in charge of data protection issues.

Company secretaries and directors should not assume someone is dealing with necessary public filings, for example, under *DPA 1998* – they should ensure it!

Application to the Crown [10.7]

Section 63 provides that *DPA 1998* binds the Crown and provides that, for the purposes of *DPA 1998*, each government department shall be treated as a person separate from any other government department.

Neither a government department or a person who is a data controller by virtue of the detailed provisions of *section 63* shall be liable for prosecution under *DPA 1998*, but *section 55* (unlawful obtaining of personal data) and the provisions in relation to obstructing the execution of a warrant (*Schedule 9, para 12*) shall apply to a person in the service of the Crown as they apply to any other person. Thus, as under *DPA 1984*, there is a limited ability to enforce *DPA 1998* as against the Crown/government departments.

11 – The Data Protection Principles

Introduction [11.1]

The Data Protection Principles were probably the single most important part of *DPA 1984* and surely remain so under *DPA 1998*.

The text of the new Data Protection Principles is set out below. Note that the underscore of key phrases is added for emphasis – this does not appear in *DPA 1998*.

1. Personal data shall be processed fairly and lawfully and, in particular, shall not be processed <u>unless</u> –
    (a)   <u>at least one</u> of the conditions in Schedule 2 is met, <u>and</u>
    (b)   in the case of <u>sensitive</u> personal data, <u>at least one</u> of the conditions in <u>Schedule 3</u> is <u>also</u> met.

2. Personal data shall be obtained only for one or more specified and lawful purposes, and shall not be further processed in any manner incompatible with that purpose or those purposes.

3. Personal data shall be adequate, relevant and not excessive in relation to the purpose or purposes for which they are processed.

4. Personal data shall be accurate and, where necessary, kept up to date.

5. Personal data processed for any purpose or purposes shall not be kept for longer than is necessary for that purpose or those purposes.

6. Personal data shall be processed in accordance with the rights of data subjects under this Act.

7. <u>Appropriate technical and organisational measures</u> shall be taken against unauthorised or unlawful processing of personal data and against accidental loss or destruction of, or damage to, personal data.

8. Personal data <u>shall not be transferred</u> to a country or territory <u>outside the European Economic Area unless</u> that country or territory ensures an <u>adequate</u> level of protection for the rights and freedoms of data subjects in relation to the processing of personal data.

Key Changes [11.2]

There are a number of key changes between the Data Protection Principles under *DPA 1984* and those under *DPA 1998*.

First Principle [11.3]

The First Data Protection Principle is one of the core provisions of *DPA 1998* and contains a lot of new provisions which have to be mastered as they will affect many companies and their procedures for collecting, holding and using personal data.

The reference to fairly and lawfully obtaining and processing personal data that existed under *DPA 1984* has been removed because 'obtaining' is now encompassed in the definition of 'processing'.

The First Principle is also subject to at least one of the conditions in *Schedule 2* being satisfied and, where the data is *sensitive* data, at least one of the conditions in *Schedule 3* also being satisfied. Data subjects must also be notified about the purposes for which their data are disclosed.

These are very important requirements which businesses need to be aware of.

Second Principle [11.4]

The Second Data Protection Principle has changed. It now encompasses both the Second and Third Principles from *DPA 1984*.

Sixth Principle [11.5]

The Sixth Data Protection Principle simply states that data shall be processed in accordance with the 'rights of data subjects under this Act'. This is a notable change from the more detailed provisions of the Seventh Principle of *DPA 1984* which it replaces.

Seventh Principle [11.6]

The Seventh Data Protection Principle (formerly the Eighth Principle under *DPA 1984*) now refers to 'technical and organisational measures' thereby replacing 'security measures'.

The *DPA 1984* reference to 'unauthorised access to, or alteration, disclosure or destruction of' data has been replaced with the term 'unauthorised or unlawful processing' (understandably, as the new definition of processing in *DPA 1998* covers all of these activities). *DPA 1984* reference to 'accidental loss or destruction of' data has been re-drafted to read 'accidental loss or destruction of, or damage to' data.

Eighth Principle [11.7]

The Eighth Data Protection Principle regarding export of data outside the EEA, is completely new. It is required by virtue of *Articles 25* and *26* of the *Directive* (see **2.26** above).

Schedule 4 sets out certain conditions which, notwithstanding the fact that the transferee country provides inadequate protection for personal data, the transfer can still take place where one of them is satisfied as this will permit the export of personal data where the Eighth Principle applies.

Interpretation Guidance [11.8]

The new Principles are accompanied by text to aid interpretation. It is very important to read this as it is necessary to help understand the reasons for, and more detailed thinking regarding, *DPA 1998*.

First Principle [11.9]

The new explanatory notes for the First Principle contain important requirements which are based upon *Articles 10* and *11* of the *Directive*. These state that certain information must be given to the data subject. The timing of the provision of this information and whether data controllers have to provide it differs, depending upon whether the data are collected direct from the data subjects or provided by third parties.

The requirements of *Schedules 2* and *3* (certain conditions need to be satisfied to ensure fair processing of personal data) *also* have to be satisfied, even where the personal data comes from a third party.

These say:

The First Principle

1. (1) Subject to paragraph 3, for the purposes of the first principle personal data are not to be treated as processed fairly unless:
   (a) in the case of data obtained from the data subject, the data controller ensures so far as practicable that the data subject has, is provided with, or has made readily available to him, the information specified in sub-paragraph (3); and
   (b) in any other case, the data controller ensures so far as practicable that, before 'the relevant time' or as soon as practicable after that time, the data subject has, is provided with, or has made readily available to him, the information specified in sub-paragraph (3).
   (c) it should be noted under (a) above that it is not essential to inform the data controller (or his colleagues) or sister companies, of visits but it certainly helps create group awareness of data.

One could speculate what would constitute notification 'as soon as practicable' under (b) above. Does this mean specific contact has to be made for this purpose or, alternatively, would it be enough to notify the data subject the next time the data controller has to make contact with the data subject e.g. when their next regular statement is sent out by their bank or the next newsletter is sent by their association? The whole point of the legislation is that data subjects are fairly treated. But, in addition, if a data controller does not provide the information under the first principle, the processing may still be fair if the data subject has, 'is provided with, or has made readily available to him, the information...' Being available could mean placing it in a clearly accessible location on a website. It could perhaps mean some form of public notice. Whether or not this test is complied with will clearly vary from situation to situation.

(2) In sub-paragraph 2(1)(b) above 'the relevant time' means:
  (a) the time when the data controller first processes the data, or
  (b) in a case where at that time disclosure to a third party within a reasonable period is envisaged:
    (i) if the data are in fact disclosed to such a person within that period, the time when the data are first disclosed,
    (ii) if within that period the data controller becomes, or ought to become, aware that the data are unlikely to be disclosed to such a person within that period, the time when the data controller did become, or ought to become, so aware, or
    (iii) in any other case, the end of that period.

In the case of data acquired from a third party this means, (given that simply holding data falls within the definition of processing,) that the prescribed information has to be provided as soon as practicable after it is received from the third party, for example, as soon as a leased or purchased customer list is received from a direct marketing company.

(3) The information referred to in sub-paragraph 2(1) above is as follows, namely:
  (a) the identity of the data controller,
  (b) if he has nominated a representative for the purposes of this Act, the identity of that representative,
  (c) the purpose or purposes for which the data are intended to be processed; and
  (d) any further information which is necessary, having regard to the specific circumstances in which the data are or are to be processed, to enable processing in respect of the data subject to be fair.

Schedule 2, para 2(3)(d) is very important. It states that in order to make processing fair in respect of any particular data subject, any particular circumstances that might affect whether particular processing of their data are fair need to be drawn to their attention. One example might be if the data on an individual are being sent outside the EEA to a country perceived as providing inadequate protection for the rights and freedoms of data subjects. The data subject should be told this.

Fourth Principle   [11.10]

It is important to note that under *DPA 1998* it is no longer necessarily enough for a data controller to say that, because the information is obtained from either the data subject or a third party, they have done all that they could reasonably do to ensure the accuracy of the data at the time.

Data controllers may now have to go further and take reasonable steps to ensure the accuracy of the data themselves. Whether or not a data controller would be expected to take such steps would be a matter of fact in each individual case.

Seventh Principle [11.11]

Data controllers have to honour certain obligations in their relationship with data processors. Informal arrangements between data controllers and data processors are insufficient – contracts are necessary.

There are positive practical steps data controllers should be taking.

O   Users should check their standard forms for appointment of third parties to process their data and ensure that appropriate references to the Seventh Principle are incorporated as well as including references to the appropriate level of control of the data by the data controller.

O   Users should ask themselves who is a data processor. Is it the person who processes a company's payroll (almost certainly yes) but what about the person who shreds confidential paperwork. Could that be personal data?

O   Users should also consider, when appointing a new processor, incorporating detailed questionnaires in tender documents, say, requiring the prospective processor to describe its security measures so that they can be carefully assessed.

O   The Commissioner has suggested that data controllers should review that their existing security measures are appropriate for the types of data they are processing. She has suggested that reference to the British Standards Institute standard BS 7799 may help data controllers assess the adequacy of their current data protection regime (see **16.7** below).

O   New contracts must contain an ongoing right of audit/inspection of the processor's security procedures.

Specimen wording that could go into a contract with a processor is set out in **Appendix E**.

Eighth Principle [11.12]

An adequate level of protection is one which is adequate in all the circumstances of the case, having regard in particular to:

(1)   the nature of the personal data;
(2)   the country or territory of origin of the information contained in the data;
(3)   the country or territory of final destination of that information;
(4)   the purposes for which and period during which the data are intended to be processed;
(5)   the law in force in the country or territory in question;
(6)   the international obligations of that country or territory;
(7)   any relevant codes of conduct or other rules which are enforceable in that country or territory; and
(8)   any security measures taken in respect of the data in that country or territory. (Emphasis added.)

The Eighth Principle does not apply to a transfer falling within any paragraph of *Schedule 4*, except in such circumstances and to such extent as the Secretary of State may by order provide.

Where:

(a)   in any proceedings under *DPA 1998* any question arises as to whether the requirement of the eighth principle as to an adequate level of protection is met in relation to the transfer of any personal data to a country or territory outside the European Economic Area; and
(b)   a Community finding has been made in relation to transfers of the kind in question;

that question is to be determined in accordance with that finding.

The fact that the data subject has to 'signify' his agreement means that there has to be some active communication between the parties. Data controllers cannot infer consent from non-response to a communication, for example from a customer's failure to return or respond to a leaflet.

The adequacy of any consent or purported consent has to be evaluated. For example, a consent which is later found to have been obtained under duress or on the basis of misleading information will not be a valid basis for processing.

Even when consent has been given it will not necessarily endure forever.

Whilst in most cases consent will endure for as long as the processing to which it relates continues, data controllers should recognise that the individual may be able to withdraw their consent.

Consent has to be appropriate to the particular circumstances. For example, if the processing to which it relates is intended to continue indefinitely or after the end of a trading relationship, then the consent should clearly cover those circumstances.

There is a distinction in *DPA 1998* between the nature of the consent required to satisfy the condition for processing data generally and that which is required in the case of the condition for processing sensitive data where the consent has to be 'explicit'. The use of the word 'explicit' suggests that the consent of the data subject should be absolutely clear. In appropriate cases where explicit consent is required, (and that will cover many instances), the consent should cover the specific detail of the processing, the particular type of data to be processed (or even the specific information), the purposes of the processing and any special aspects of the processing which may affect the individual, for example disclosures which may be made of the data.

As can be seen from the above, the level of detail appropriate to a consent will vary. In some cases implied consent may be sufficient. In others nothing less than clear written consent will suffice. A blanket consent to the processing of personal data is unlikely to be sufficient as a basis on which to process personal data, particularly sensitive personal data. The more ambiguous the consent being relied upon by data controllers in any particular case the more likely there are to be questions about its existence or validity.

Compliance with the 'Fair Processing Code' should in most cases ensure that consent is both 'specific' and 'informed'. This is provided that, in appropriate cases, data controllers supply data subjects with:

> 'any further information which is necessary, having regard to the specific circumstances in which the data are or are to be processed, to enable processing in respect of the data subject to be fair'. (*Schedule 1, Part II, para 3(d)*.)

Compliance with the Fair Processing Code should also ensure that the data subject is informed of the purpose or purposes for which the data are intended to be processed.

Controllers should recognise that compliance with the relevant conditions in *Schedules 2* and *3* in any case may not, in itself, ensure that processing is fair and lawful. There may be circumstances where, notwithstanding compliance with one or more of the relevant conditions, the processing is unfair or unlawful for other reasons. Factors which would need to be considered over and above satisfying at least one of the relevant conditions would include the question of compliance with the Fair Processing Code. There are circumstances in which processing may be in breach of the first principle, notwithstanding the fact that the data controller complies with at least one of the conditions for processing, for example, processing in breach of an obligation of confidence.

In deciding whether and, if so, what further information is 'necessary' to satisfy the above requirement, data controllers should consider what processing of personal data they shall be carrying out once the data are obtained and consider whether or not their relevant data subjects are likely to understand the following:

○ the purposes for which their personal data are going to be processed;
○ the likely consequences of such processing; and
○ more particularly, whether particular disclosures could reasonably be envisaged.

It will surely be the case that, the more unforeseen the consequences of processing, the more likely it is that the data controller will be expected to provide further information.

12 – Conditions Relevant to the First Principle

Schedule 2 [12.1]

Schedule 2 reflects the requirements of *Article 7* of the *Directive*, (criteria for making data processing legitimate) and mirrors the conditions necessary for the processing of *any* personal data to take place. The wording is very similar to *Article 7*.

The conditions are:

1. The data subject has given his <u>consent</u> to the processing.
2. The processing is necessary:
    (1) for the <u>performance of a contract</u> to which the data subject is a party, or
    (2) for the <u>taking of steps at the request of the data subject with a view to entering into a contract</u>.
3. The processing is necessary for compliance with any legal obligation to which the data controller is subject, other than an obligation imposed by contract.
4. The processing is necessary in order to protect the vital interests of the data subject.
5. The processing is necessary:
    (1) for the administration of justice,
    (2) for the exercise of any functions conferred on any person by or under any enactment,
    (3) for the exercise of any functions of the Crown, a Minister of the Crown or a government department, or
    (4) for the exercise of any other functions of a public nature exercised in the public interest by any person.

Consent [12.2]

One of the conditions to be satisfied is that 'consent' is obtained.

The *Directive* requires consent to be 'unambiguously' given, but that word does not appear in *Schedule 2*. Indeed, *DPA 1998* does not define consent.

Perhaps that means that the details of the processing need only be made known to the data subject in general terms in obtaining consent, or that consent could be oral (or even implied). This is another area where more guidance is probably necessary from the Government and/or the Commissioner. To be unambiguous, the consent probably needs to be obtained with the data subject having knowledge of all the relevant facts.

Various definitions of consent suggest that it is a positive act rather than, for example, someone sending a letter saying that unless an objection is received consent will be assumed. That is surely not enough for *DPA 1998*. The definition of consent in the *Directive*, which is presumably the one that the European Court of Justice would look at, if ever anyone challenged the UK's implementation of the *Directive*, provides that consent:

> '...shall mean any freely given specific and informed indication of his wishes by which the data subject signifies his agreement to personal data relating to him being processed.'

A very clear and easy opt-out, whereby a data subject is given the opportunity to refuse to have their data used for a particular purpose (such as direct marketing – see **Chapter 18**) should be enough because, if they do not opt-out in circumstances where it is very easy to do so, they implicitly consent. However, this will really work best for matters such as application forms when the data subject will be sending the form back anyway. There it is made very clear what the purposes are and the ability to opt out is easy. In such cases, an opt out should still be a valid compliance with *DPA 1998*. On the wording of the *Directive*, arguably opting in is the appropriate way to show consent – a positive agreement to the use of data.

Discussions with the Commissioner's Office on this topic suggest that, particularly in the area of direct marketing, provided that the marketer makes available to the potential marketing target a very clear explanation of the fact that their data may be used for marketing purposes, accompanied by a very simple and easy way to opt out, this would still be regarded as complying with the consent requirement of *DPA 1998*.

It is assumed that an oral consent could suffice. This would obviously be important in the context of a call centre collecting data on new customers or an on-line application for car insurance. However, even in these cases it would be prudent to put in place a system for keeping records that consent is obtained, such as recording the call itself (subject to complying with the legal requirements for recording telephone calls) or including tick boxes in the scripting software to prompt the call centre operative to remember to ask for consent and to record that it was given. Clearly, an employee could falsify this but if it is a term of their employment contract to follow such procedures properly, employees would be more unlikely to flout the system.

Schedule 3 [12.3]

Schedule 3 mirrors fairly closely the provisions of *Article 8* of the *Directive*. The conditions which have to be satisfied before sensitive data can be fairly processed (including obtaining) are:

1. The data subject has given his explicit consent to the processing of the personal data.

2. – (1) The processing is necessary for the purposes of exercising or performing any right or obligation which is conferred or imposed by law on the data controller in connection with employment.
(2)   The Secretary of State may by order –
-   (a)   exclude the application of sub-paragraph (1) in such cases as may be specified, or
-   (b)   provide that, in such cases as may be specified, the condition in sub-paragraph (1) is not to be regarded as satisfied unless such further conditions as may be specified in the order are also satisfied.

3. The processing is necessary –
-   (a)   in order to protect the vital interests of the data subject or another person, in a case where –
    -   (i)   consent cannot be given by or on behalf of the data subject, or
    -   (ii)   the data controller cannot reasonably be expected to obtain the consent of the data subject, or
-   (b)   in order to protect the vital interests of another person, in a case where consent by or on behalf of the data subject has been unreasonably withheld.

4. The processing –
-   (a)   is carried out in the course of its legitimate activities by any body or association which –
    -   (i)   is not established or conducted for profit, and
    -   (ii)   exists for political, philosophical, religious or trade-union purposes,
-   (b)   is carried out with appropriate safeguards for the rights and freedoms of data subjects,
-   (c)   relates only to individuals who either are members of the

body or association or have regular contact with it in connection with its purposes, and

(d)   does not involve disclosure of the personal data to a third party without the consent of the data subject.

5. The information contained in the personal data has been made public as a result of steps deliberately taken by the data subject.

6. The processing –

(a)   is necessary for the purpose of, or in connection with, any legal proceedings (including prospective legal proceedings),

(b)   is necessary for the purpose of obtaining legal advice, or

(c)   is otherwise necessary for the purposes of establishing, exercising or defending legal rights.

7. – (1) The processing is necessary –

(a)   for the administration of justice,

(b)   for the exercise of any functions conferred on any person by or under an enactment, or

(c)   for the exercise of any functions of the Crown, a Minister of the Crown or a government department.

(2)   The Secretary of State may by order –

(a)   exclude the application of sub-paragraph (1) in such cases as may be specified, or

(b)   provide that, in such cases as may be specified, the condition in sub-paragraph (1) is not to be regarded as satisfied unless such further conditions as may be specified in the order are also satisfied.

8. – (1) The processing is necessary for medical purposes and is undertaken by –

(a)   a health professional, or

(b)   a person who in the circumstances owes a duty of confidentiality which is equivalent to that which would arise if that person are a health professional.

(2)   In this paragraph "medical purposes" includes the purposes of preventative medicine, medical diagnosis, medical research, the provision of care and treatment and the management of health care services.

9. – (1) The processing –

(a)   is of sensitive personal data consisting of information as to racial or ethnic origin,

(b)   is necessary for the purpose of identifying or keeping under review the existence or absence of equality of opportunity or treatment between persons of different racial or ethnic origins, with a view to enabling such equality to be promoted or maintained, and

(c)   is carried out with appropriate safeguards for the rights and freedoms of data subjects.

(2)   The Secretary of State may by order specify circumstances in which processing falling within sub-paragraph (1)(a) and (b) is, or it not, to be taken for the purposes of sub-paragraph (1)(c) to be carried out with appropriate safeguards for the rights and freedoms of data subjects.

10. The personal data are processed in circumstances specified in an order made by the Secretary of State for the purposes of this paragraph.

Here 'explicit' consent is required. The word 'explicit' appears in *Article 8* of the *Directive*. However, explicit consent is not defined in *DPA 1998* (or the *Directive*) but obtaining such consent clearly has to be more onerous than the 'consent' required for *Schedule 2*. But what is the difference? It would be helpful to know what the Home Office or the Commissioner expects when obtaining 'explicit' consent. Does it need to be in writing? How much information has to be given? How is this different in practice to obtaining 'consent' under *Schedules 2* or *4*?

Guidance [12.4]

The Commissioner's *Introduction* flags that there is a distinction in *DPA 1998* between the nature of the consent required to satisfy *Schedule 2* and that which is required in the case of the condition for processing sensitive data under *Schedule 3*. It states:

'The use of the word "explicit" suggests that the consent of the data subject should be absolutely clear. In appropriate cases it should cover the specific detail of the processing, the particular type of data to be processed (or even the specific information), the purposes of the processing and any special aspects of the processing which may affect the individual, for example disclosures which may be made of the data.

As can be seen from the above, the level of detail appropriate to a consent will vary. In some cases implied consent may be sufficient. In others nothing less than clear written consent will suffice. A blanket consent to the processing of personal data is unlikely to be sufficient as a basis on which to process personal data, particularly sensitive personal data'.

13 – Miscellaneous Exemptions

Categories of Exemption [13.1]

Schedule 7 sets out various miscellaneous provisions exempting personal data from the subject information provisions and/or the non-disclosure provisions of *DPA 1998*. These are detailed below.

The Data Controller's Confidential References [13.2]

Schedule 7, para 1 provides a new exemption that excludes from subject access a reference 'given or to be given in confidence' by the data controller for the purposes of:

'(a) the education, training or employment, or prospective education, training or employment, of the data subject;

(b) the appointment, or prospective appointment, of the data subject to any office; or

(c) the provision, or prospective provision, by the data subject of any service.'

Schedule 7, para 1(c) is particularly interesting because it gives exemption from subject access for a reference not merely in relation to employment but in relation to the provision of *any* service. Presumably this could also include consultancy services, maintenance services, software development; or any other type of service.

However, it has to be borne in mind that it only relates to a reference given *by* the data controller. If there is a reference on file from a previous employer, this would appear to be caught by the subject access provisions in *DPA 1998*.

If there is a legal obligation to disclose a reference from a third party, then it is interesting how this could interact with the fact that references are often given in confidence. Arguably, the legal obligation to give subject access overrides the fact that a reference is given 'in con~~fidence~~' but there is uncertainty in this area.

It is perhaps possible to argue that *section 7(4)* could apply if, for example, it could be argued that this is in some way disclosure of information about a third party i.e. the giver of the reference. *Section 7(4)* states that in deciding whether to disclose information relating to another individual, data controllers are entitled to take into account whether there is any duty of confidentiality to that individual. Also you are entitled to withold data where disclosing it would disclose data about a third party. Arguably the name of a person who gives a reference falls within this, but *section 7(5)* points out that *section 7(4)* is not to be construed as excusing a data controller from communicating so much of the information sought by the request as can be communicated without disclosing the identity of the other individual. Arguably, one should blank out the name of the referee and then disclose the reference, but this is still unsatisfactory. In practice, most people ask a named person to give a reference, so the data subject will be able to guess who wrote the letter anyway.

Some guidance from the Commissioner's office on the relationship between duties of confidentiality and the obligation to give subject access would be most welcome and has been promised.

This exemption is considered in more depth in **Chapter 19**.

Management Forecasts, etc. [13.3]

Schedule 7, para 5 provides that:

> 'Personal data processed for the purposes of management forecasting or management planning to assist the data controller in the conduct of any business or other activity are exempt from the subject information provisions in any case to the extent to which the application of those provisions would be likely to prejudice the conduct of that business or other activity.'

This is a new exemption and potentially quite helpful in a business context. For example, it may exempt details of a company's plans to promote staff which would otherwise have to be provided pursuant to subject access.

It has to be fair that a person should not be able to use subject access as a means to find out about their future prospects before they would find out in the ordinary course of events. Presumably, this could potentially exempt plans to ask employees to move to different offices, so that one employee cannot find out prior to all employees being notified formally.

In the context of a professional practice, *Schedule 7, para 5* should exempt any interview notes or reports prepared as part of a partnership planning exercise. That is surely future planning for the organisation.

Presumably, even an expression of intention about somebody (which was excluded from the definition of personal data under *DPA 1984*) could still remain outside *DPA 1998* if that intention relates to a data controller's future planning – e.g. that they intend to outsource their operations or make staff redundant.

Corporate Finance [13.4]

Schedule 7, para 6 provides that where personal data are processed for the purposes of a corporate finance service (e.g. where advice is given on the placing of issues, or industrial strategy, or merger etc.) by a relevant person (defined, inter alia, as a person authorised under *Financial Services Act 1986*), the data are exempt from the subject information provisions to the extent to which it could affect the price of any existing instrument or instrument to be created, or to the extent the data controller reasonably believes it could affect the price of any such instrument.

If neither of the above applies, the data may be exempt from the subject information provisions in order to safeguard 'an important economic or financial interest in the United Kingdom'. The Secretary of State may by order specify matters to be taken into account in determining whether exemption from the subject access provisions is required to safeguard an important economic or financial interest, or circumstances where exemption is, or is not, to be taken to be required for that purpose.

The relevant regulations, *Data Protection (Corporate Finance Exemption) Order 2000 (SI 2000/184)*, are summarised in **Chapter 23** and set out in full in the **Legislation Annex**.

Negotiations [13.5]

Personal data which consist of records of the intentions of the data controller in relation to any negotiations with the data subject, are exempt from the subject information provisions in any case to the extent to which the application of those provisions would be likely to prejudice those negotiations.

This is new, and is different to the provision in *DPA 1984* which gave an exemption for indications of the intentions of the data user in respect of a data subject. This has now gone under *DPA 1998*. In many ways, it could be said to be narrower than the old provision which exempted expressions of intention in relation to a data subject because it is only an exemption in relation to negotiations with the data subject – e.g. perhaps in relation to negotiations with a business partner who is a sole trader or perhaps negotiations with an author about publishing his book. It would be helpful to know exactly what this exemption is aimed at.

In addition, when does the exemption cease? Does it cease when the negotiations cease, or does it apply for all time?

Examination Scripts etc.   [13.6]

Schedule 7, para 9 contains a new exemption. Personal data consisting of information recorded by candidates during their academic, or professional or other examination are exempt from subject access.

'Examination' is wider than answering an exam paper. It includes any process for determining the knowledge, intelligence, skill or ability of a candidate by reference to his performance in any test, work or other activity. That covers, for example, biometric testing and may even cover hand writing analysis.

Legal Professional Privilege   [13.7]

Under *Schedule 7, para 10*, if personal data consist of information in respect of which a claim to legal professional privilege can be maintained in legal proceedings, they are exempt from the subject information provisions. This closely reflects *section 31(2)* of DPA 1984.

Self-incrimination   [13.8]

A person need not comply with any request or order under *section 7* if compliance would, by revealing evidence of the commission of any offence other than an offence under *DPA 1998*, expose him to proceedings for that offence (*Schedule 7, para 11*). This is a new provision and goes on to say that information disclosed by any person in compliance with any request or order under *section* 7 shall not be admissible against him in proceedings for an offence under *DPA 1998*.

Other Categories [13.9]

Personal data are exempt from the subject information provisions:

❍ where the application of those provisions would be likely to prejudice the combat effectiveness of any of the armed forces (*Schedule 7, para 2*);

❍ where it is processed for the purposes of judicial appointment or honours (*Schedule 7, para 3*);

❍ where it is processed for the purposes of assessing any person's suitability for Crown employment and Crown or ministerial appointment (*Schedule 7, para 4*) (see also *Data Protection (Crown Appointments) Order 2000* (SI 2000/416) which are summarised in **Chapter 23** and set out in full in the **Legislation Annex**; or

❍ if they are examination marks (*Schedule 7, para 8*).

Transitional Provisions [13.10]

The Commissioner has said that it is important to stress that there is a three year transitional period (see further **Chapter 14**) for data controllers to bring processing already under way into compliance with the new law, and data already held in manual filing systems as at 24 October 1998 need not comply with many aspects of the new law until 2007.

Practical Pointers [13.11]

✓ Consider what practices to adopt as regards confidential references. Should they be reviewed, case by case, to see whether they could or should be disclosed pursuant to a subject access request? Do you wish to put something into your standard letters requesting a reference to the effect that, by giving the reference, the referee is consenting to its disclosure by you pursuant to a subject access request if you conclude the law so requires?

✓ Consider what need not be disclosed by virtue of the management forecasts exemption. This should exempt statements of intention in relation to employees as regards their dismissal, promotion or relocation.

This could extend, perhaps, to the closing of premises or proposals to move employees between sites. It seems primarily aimed at matters which will affect a company's staffing issues.

It could also extend to discussions regarding prospective new partners in professional firms and personal data regarding the renewal of consultancy contracts.

✓ Consider whether the corporate finance exemption applies, but this is quite narrow and really only relates to information which could affect share prices or the price of bonds, etc. There is an exemption order, *Data Protection (Corporate Finance Exemption) Order 2000 (SI 2000/184)* that applies a wider exemption where subject access, for example, might have a prejudicial effect on the orderly functioning of the financial markets or could adversely affect an important economical financial interest of the United Kingdom. One assumes that this test would also not apply in most cases involving corporate finance.

✓ Consider the effect of the exemption for 'negotiations' – this might cover negotiations with trade unions regarding salary or negotiating with individuals on commercial contracts – singers, authors, consultants, programmers and so on.

14 – Transitional Relief

Introduction [14.1]

There are a number of transitional provisions contained in *Schedule 8*. This Chapter focuses on the main ones relevant to the business community.

There is a three year transitional period for data controllers to bring processing already under way into compliance with the new law, and some data already held in a manual filing system need not comply with many aspects of the new law until 2007. The Government intends to ensure that data controllers can take full advantage of these provisions and the effect of this transitional relief should be borne in mind when considering the changes which are outlined below.

For the purposes of *Schedule 8*, personal data are 'eligible data' at any time if, and to the extent that, they are at that time subject to processing which is already under way immediately before 24 October 1998.

In *Schedule 8* 'eligible automated data' means eligible data which fall within paragraph (a) or (b) of the definition of 'data' in *Section 1(1)*, these refer to data being information which:

O   is being processed by means of equipment operating automatically in response to instructions given for that purpose;
O   is recorded with the intention that it should be processed by means of such equipment.

'Eligible manual data' means eligible data which are not eligible automated data.

'The first transitional period' means the period beginning with the commencement of *Schedule 8* and ending with 23 October 2001. 'The second transitional period' means the period beginning with 24 October 2001 and ending with 23 October 2007.

Exemptions Available Before 24 October 2001 [14.2]

Schedule 8 defines the period between the commencement of *DPA 1998* and 24 October 2001 as the first transitional period.

The Commissioner has said that:

> 'eligible data, which are data where processing was under way immediately prior to 24 October 1998, may benefit from a limited exemption from subject access during the transitional period. Subject access to eligible manual data held in a "relevant filing system" is not likely to begin until 2001 although access to "accessible" manual records, such as health records, will be available straight away. Eligible automated data will also be exempt from some of the new subject access requirements until 2001. However, data users should still give consideration as to what steps will be necessary to modify their existing subject access procedures to meet the new requirements.'

Eligible Manual Data [14.3]

Eligible manual data are exempt from the Data Protection Principles and *Parts II* (Rights of Data Subjects) and *III* (Notification by Data Controllers) of *DPA 1998* during the first transitional period.

The extent of the exemption of eligible manual data which form part of an accessible record and any data which fall within the definition of 'data' in *section 1(1)(d)* and are not subject to processing immediately before 24 October 1998 is set out in *Schedule 8, para 3(2)* and is not as wide as for eligible manual data.

There is an exemption for eligible manual data which consists of information relevant to the financial standing of the data subject and where the data controller is a credit reference agency (*Schedule 8, para 4*) similar to that for accessible records.

Eligible Automated Data [14.4]

Schedule 8, para 13(1) sets out the scope of the exemptions for eligible automated data during the first transitional period.

The Commissioner has said that, in effect, despite the fact that, strictly speaking, a data controller is not required to comply with the Fair Processing Code (the obligations to notify data subjects as set out in *Schedule 1*) if a *Schedule 8* exemption applies, nevertheless they should comply with the Code in so far as it equates to the existing criteria for assessing fair obtaining under *DPA 1984*. Data controllers should as a baseline take their existing systems set up under *DPA 1984* and work towards making them compliant by the relevant date.

Processing Otherwise than by Reference to the Data Subject [14.5]

During the first transitional period, eligible automated data are not to be regarded as being processed unless the processing is 'by reference to the data subject'.

The rationale behind this provision is that many businesses were very concerned that if the wording in *DPA 1984* that said it only applied to processing by reference to the data subject was to disappear, this would mean that data controllers would have to locate all information about the relevant data subject straight away, wherever it was located, even if that data is not really contained in a file which is obviously about the relevant individual. As long as the data subject could give a reasonable idea where to search, the search would have to be done.

The primary concern is that this sort of searching might require system changes, to provide full word search facilities which some systems might not have. Since most businesses have been prioritising grappling with the system changes necessary to cope with the advent of the year 2000 and, for many institutions, the need for their software to recognise and deal with the Euro, this could have been the additional system change to break the camel's back. For that reason, amongst others, these transitional provisions have been provided.

This will be helpful because, under *DPA 1984*, the DPR had said that the meaning of 'by reference to the data subject' was extremely important. This processing would occur under *DPA 1984* whenever the data user intended to locate and process information about an individual, whatever the technical means by which this object was achieved. However, if the fact that the information located or processed by the data user related to an individual was always purely incidental and irrelevant to the data user's purpose in processing it, then the personal data were never processed 'by reference to the data subject' and so were not regarded as 'held' by the data user and were outside *DPA 1984*.

One example which the Commissioner has given, in her earlier published Guidelines under *DPA 1984*, on interpreting this phrase is as follows:

> 'The names of senders and recipients of messages are stored in an electronic filing system with the text of the messages. Names and information relating to individuals may also occur in the body of the text. If the names are used simply to locate a particular communication, the individual's identity being irrelevant to the purpose for which the communication is being sought, then although the names are personal data they are not "held" by the data user. On the other hand, if the processing of the filed communications is directed to finding one or more of them because they have been sent or received by a particular individual or because they contain information relating to a particular individual, then the names and other information are "held" by the data user and fall within the Data Protection Act 1984.'

The above analysis would continue to apply where the relevant transitional provisions permit it.

Other Exemptions [14.6]

Schedule 8, Part I contains certain other specific provisions. For example, eligible automated data which are processed *only* for the purpose of replacing other data in the event of the latter being lost, destroyed or impaired (back-up data) are exempt from *section 7* (subject access) during the first transitional period. There are also specific provisions about certain exemptions for payrolls, accounts and unincorporated members' clubs and mailing lists.

However, the provision about back-up data may not be of much help to businesses which regularly back-up and store copies of their data. Many prudent businesses store back-up data for a number of years, and change and improve their storage systems. At the end of the first transitional period, access could in theory be sought to old back-up tapes or disks. This could be a very costly and time consuming exercise. Businesses should, therefore, consider whether, if such data falls within the subject access provisions, whether *section 8(2)* of *DPA 1998* would apply i.e. that finding that information would be a disproportionate effort. They should also consider why they have this information and whether it need to be stored or could be deleted. In fairness, many companies have well thought out policies as to how long they keep files – and why – but all companies should at least consider having such a policy and should think about why they might need one – data protection compliance being one reason. This is certainly not just a data protection issue. Does the business keep files for relevant limitation periods? Do they keep them merely to deal with customer queries?

As another example, some E-mail systems do not have word searching facilities, especially older systems. Surely it might not be reasonable of the Commissioner to expect such systems to be searched. To do so, to find a particular message, especially once stored as a back-up copy, would be a painstaking job as it may involve opening every message to check it. The Commissioner's Office has indicated that data controllers will have to look at the facts in such situations on a case by case basis. This is an area where the Commissioner's Office hopes to publish some guidelines in due course.

Exemptions Available After 23 October 2001 but

Before 24 October 2007 [14.7]

Schedule 8 defines the period after 23 October 2001 but before 24 October 2007 as the second transitional period.

Schedule 8, para 14 details the exemptions applicable to eligible manual data which are held immediately before 24 October 1998 during the second transitional period.

Note that these exemptions do not apply to any eligible manual data which are exempt as historical research under *Schedule 8, para 16* (see **14.8**).

Historical Research [14.8]

During the second transitional period, eligible automated data which are processed only for the purpose of historical research in compliance with the relevant conditions are exempt from the First Data Protection Principle, to the extent to which it requires compliance with the conditions in *Schedules 2* and *3* (*Schedule 8, para 17(1)*).

Eligible manual data which are processed only for the purpose of historical research in compliance with the relevant conditions (set out in *Schedule 8, para 16(1)* are exempt from certain provisions as detailed in *Schedule 8, para 16(2)*, during the second transitional period.

Eligible automated data which are processed:

○ only for the purpose of historical research;
○ in compliance with the relevant conditions; and
○ otherwise than by reference to the data subject

are exempt from the same provisions as eligible manual data.

It should be noted that this exemption applies only to research for historical purposes and not to all research data. Also, after 23 October 2001, there is still an exemption from having to satisfy the conditions in *Schedule 2* before processing the data (e.g. obtaining consent) but the Fair Processing Code will have to be complied with so, whilst data subjects need not be asked for their consent to processing, they will have to be fully informed about the purposes for which their data will be used.

Note also that there are separate exemptions from *DPA 1998* in the body of Act itself in relation to research. For example, *section 33* contains an exemption, for certain purposes, for information held for 'research purposes' which includes statistical or historical purposes (see **7.12**). If the conditions in *section 33* can also be complied with, then data held for research for historical purposes only may also be exempt from aspects of the Second and Fifth Data Protection Principles.

Exceptions   [14.9]

For the purposes of these provisions personal data are not to be treated as processed otherwise than for the purpose of historical research merely because the data are disclosed:
(a)   to any person, for the purpose of historical research only;
(b)   to the data subject or a person acting on his behalf;
(c)   at the request, or with the consent, of the data subject or a person acting on his behalf; or
(d)   in circumstances in which the person making the disclosure has reasonable grounds for believing that the disclosure falls within paragraph (a), (b) or (c). (*Schedule 8, para 18*.)

Exemption from Section 22 [14.10]

Processing which was already under way immediately before 24 October 1998 is not assessable processing for the purposes of *section 22* (preliminary assessment by the Commissioner), the 'prior checking' provisions.

The concept of prior checking (which is new to English law) was introduced by virtue of *Article 20* of the *Directive*.

Processing Already Under Way [14.11]

The clear concern with *Schedule 8* is what is meant by 'processing which is already under way' and 'immediately before' 24 October 1998. Does this mean data added to an old pre-24 October 1998 file is subject to DPA 1998 but older data on the same file is not? This would cause great confusion and subject access (if it is not negated by virtue of the transitional provisions) would be a nightmare.

This is a critical point. The Commissioner is saying that new data added to an existing system after 24 October 1998 would fall within the meaning of 'processing already under way' (and be exempt from various provisions of *DPA 1998* until October 2001) but it is slightly difficult to find a justification for her 'lenient' view. This more lenient interpretation is perhaps at odds with a literal interpretation of *DPA 1998* and the *Directive*. In addition, the Commissioner's Office have been unsure, when asked, when an existing system becomes a new system. For example, how much upgrading or change is required for this to effectively become a new system and subject to *DPA 1998*? This is clearly an area which it is hoped will be clarified with the passage of time and greater familiarity with *DPA 1998*.

Guidance [14.12]

According to the Commissioner's *Introduction*, if 'processing already under way' applies, this would permit:

O   amendments to existing personal data;
O   the addition of personal data on existing data subjects;
O   the addition of personal data on new data subjects; and

O   essential program and software changes to enable such processing
     to continue.

Thus, personal data added to and processed as part of an existing
database, in the same manner in which data was processed under that
system prior to 24 October 1998, would benefit from the exemptions.

The *Introduction* makes it clear that the purpose of the transitional
provisions is to facilitate a progressive move by data controllers to the
new regime created by *DPA 1998*. However, transitional relief would
only apply during the relevant transitional period for so long as, and
to the extent that, personal data are subject to processing already
under way. Therefore, if a data controller introduces new practices or
systems involving processing which is not already under way and
which are applied to such personal data, the transitional relief would
be lost even if this occurs before expiry of the relevant transitional
period.

Considerations   [14.13]

The definition of 'processing' in *DPA 1998* is much wider than that in
DPA 1984, so it is very likely that operations which did not fall within
the definition in *DPA 1984* will now involve 'processing'. Where
processing is different, but does not produce a new effect or result in
terms of the data controller's overall processing operation, it is likely to
be processing already under way. As such, in deciding whether
processing is already under way, the Commissioner suggests that data
controllers may find it helpful to review their overall processing
operations asking themselves a series of questions.

O   Is there something different about the processing?
O   If so, what is different about it? In deciding this, consider what
     processing is undertaken before and what processing is being or
     is to be undertaken from 24 October 1998, i.e:
     ●   Is the processing for a new purpose or new purposes?
     ●   Are the categories of data being processed the same?
     ●   Are the categories of data subject being processed the same?
     ●   Are the categories of recipient to whom the data are being
          disclosed the same?
     ●   Are the data to be stored for a different length of time?
     ●   Are the criteria for storage/destruction the same?
O   If the processing is different, what is the effect of this in relation
     to the data controller's overall processing operation? For example:

- Is the processing within a range of activities or business processes already undertaken by the data controller?
- Does the processing result in a new or different application of the data or part of the data?
- Is the processing carried out in order to achieve a new objective?
- Does the processing produce or result in a new or different effect upon the data subject?

This helpful list produced by the Commissioner's Office is not exhaustive. Other factors may need to be taken into account depending on the type of processing operation carried out by the data controller. However, this list of questions is probably the least that data controllers should ask themselves when trying to analyse their processing operations.

15 – Transborder Data Flows

Position under DPA 1984 [15.1]

Under *DPA 1984*, all data users had to register with the DPR. A registration had to include the names or a description of any countries or territories outside the UK to which they intended or may have wished directly or indirectly to transfer the data.

Holding and use of personal data was only permitted within the terms of the registration. Therefore, even if registered, it was a criminal offence under *section 5* for a data user (now a data controller) to knowingly or recklessly transfer personal data to countries/territories other than those to which it stated in its Register entry it intended to transfer such data.

Transfer Prohibition Notice [15.2]

The DPR's main sanction in relation to transfers of data outside the UK was to serve a transfer prohibition notice which could prevent the transfer of personal data to a place outside the UK if this could have led to a contravention of the Data Protection Principles. Even if the recipient country was named on a registration under *DPA 1984*, the DPR could still stop future transfers although this power was only ever exercised a handful of times.

Transfer prohibition notices either prohibited the transfer absolutely or until specified steps had been taken to protect the data subject's interests. The DPR's power to serve this type of notice varied, depending on whether or not the destination country was bound by the Council of Europe Convention on Data Protection No 108.

If the destination country was not bound by the Convention, the notice could be served if the DPR was satisfied that the transfer was likely to contravene, or lead to a contravention of, any of the Data Protection Principles.

If the destination country was bound by the Convention, the DPR's powers were more limited. Then, the DPR could only prohibit the transfer if satisfied either that the:

○   data user intended to give instructions for the further transfer of the personal data to another country not bound by the Convention and that further transfer was likely to contravene or lead to a contravention of any of the Data Protection Principles; or

○   data to be transferred were sensitive data about which the Secretary of State had altered or added to the Data Protection Principles and that that transfer was likely to contravene, or lead to a contravention of, any of the principles as so altered or added to.

Contravening a transfer prohibition notice could ultimately have meant that the DPR could commence proceedings for a criminal offence, but a data user would not be guilty if they could prove that they had used all due care to avoid contravening the notice.

The Directive [15.3]

The main causes for concern for international businesses under the *Directive* are *Articles 25* and *26* in relation to the transfer of personal data to third countries, which is almost certain to become more relevant as markets become truly 'global'. These Articles could clearly have ramifications for use of the Internet (or for intranets/extranets) and for E-commerce generally. They could equally cause concern for interactive satellite systems and advanced data communications systems.

Adequate Level of Protection [15.4]

Article 25(1) states that cross border dataflows can only be permitted by Member States where the country to which the transfer takes place (other than another Member State in the European Union) ensures 'an adequate level of protection' for that data.

The 'adequacy' of the level of protection shall be assessed 'in the light of all the circumstances surrounding a data transfer operation or set of data transfer operations'.

According to *Article 25(2)*, particular consideration is to be given to matters such as the:

O   nature of the data;

O   purpose and duration of the processing operation or operations;

O   country of origin and of final destination;

O   rules of law, both general and sectoral, in force in the country in question; and

O   professional rules and security measures which are complied with in the third country in question.

It is the person exporting the data who has to take a decision on adequacy. They may be helped by the EU Commission reaching a decision under *Article 25(6)* that a particular country does provide adequate protection. The Article 29 Working Party (see **2.31** above) has produced an opinion that the laws in Hungary and Switzerland would appear to pass the adequacy test and, if this is approved by the Commission, then the restrictions on export of personal data to them will not apply.

Obviously, this begs the question as to what is an adequate level of protection and there has to be an argument that, once you set in stone a Directive which clearly is regarded as adequate within all the Member States, this would tend to become the benchmark for adequacy. There are a number of very important jurisdictions such as the USA where there is little or no formal data protection legislation at all (there is certainly no federal statute similar to the *Directive*) and, therefore, the concern is that those jurisdictions would not be deemed to provide adequate security. The current active debate between the European Commission and the USA shows that the possibility of restrictions on transfers of data to the USA is of real concern. Transborder dataflows (and matters such as the development of E-commerce) could be adversely affected by the new procedures if they result in restricting data transfers.

A recent survey showed that less than 40 countries currently have meaningful data protection laws, and many of those are in the EU or are countries bound by the Council of Europe Convention, in any event.

Exceptions [15.5]

The prohibition in *Article 25* has some derogations from it in *Article 26(1)*. Even if a third country does not ensure an adequate level of protection a transfer may take place on condition that the:

O   data subject has given his consent unambiguously to the proposed transfer; or

○ transfer is necessary for the performance of a contract between the data subject and the controller or the implementation of pre-contractual measures taken in response to the data subject's request; or

○ transfer is necessary for the conclusion or for the performance of a contract concluded in the interest of the data subject between the controller and a third party; or

○ transfer is necessary on important public interest grounds, or for the establishment, exercise or defence of legal claims; or

○ transfer is necessary in order to protect the vital interests of the data subject; or

○ transfer is made from a register which, according to laws or regulations, is intended to provide information to the public and which is open to consultation either by the public in general, or by any person who could demonstrate legitimate interest, to the extent that the conditions laid down in law for consultation are fulfilled in the particular case.

How would the provisions of this Article effect, for example, a situation in which someone wished to transfer data to a country like the USA or Japan where there is no over-arching federal data protection legislation, although it provides quite a high level of data protection or privacy legislation in certain sectors or in certain states? There has to be an argument that, perhaps, since such a country does not have the levels of protection that are contained in the *Directive*, this could be regarded as a country where there is not an adequate level of protection. If so, a Member State can provide that the transfer may take place provided that the transfer to that data subject comes within one of the exceptions to the prohibition on transfer.

It may be, for example, that a transfer is necessary for the performance of a contract with the data subject – the data subject has a bank account overseas and the data controller is required by its UK customer, as part of the relationship it has with its UK customer, to send money there. Certain data may have to be exported to enable the transfer to happen. If another condition cannot be applied, the export can only take place if the data subject has given his consent unambiguously to the proposed transfer – quite often, in practice, he would not necessarily have consented unambiguously (and it is very clear – at least from the definition of consent in the *Directive* – that consent has to be unambiguous, uncoerced and informed)

Contractual Clauses [15.6]

There is another possible way to transfer data legitimately, if *Article*

26(1) cannot be complied with. *Article 26(2)* provides that a Member State may, without referring to the European Commission, authorise a transfer of personal data to a third country even if it does not ensure an adequate level of protection for personal data where the data controller has adduced sufficient guarantees with respect to the protection of the privacy of the individuals. Such guarantees may in particular result from appropriate contractual clauses.

Initial opinions generated by the Article 29 Working Party suggest that contractual solutions will need to be pretty tough on the importer of data overseas before being likely to be acceptable and there needs to be a way for the subjects of the data to access their data and some way that the subject's rights could be easily enforced against the entity abusing their data.

Whilst a local data protection authority within the EU can approve clauses for use, *Article 26(2)* states that a Member State may authorise a transfer or a set of transfers of personal data which receive adequate protection by use of contract clauses but, thereafter, the Member State is required (*Article 26(3)*) to inform the European Commission and the other Member States of the authorisations it grants under *Article 26(2)*.

Objection by the European Commission [15.7]

Under *Article 26(3)*, if a Member State or the European Commission objects on justified grounds to a proposed solution involving the protection of the privacy and fundamental rights and freedoms of individuals (whatever that means), the European Commission can take certain measures under the *Directive* to review the individual Member State's decision. So, a national regulator's decision to approve a contractual solution could, in theory, be subsequently overridden. This is clearly cumbersome and could serve, in a sense, to discourage local regulators granting that sort of approval if it could be 'disapproved of'.

The European Commission can also put forward contractual solutions of the type described above under *Article 26(4)*. This involves, first, the European Commission delivering a draft of the measures to be taken to a Committee set up under *Article 31* of the *Directive* (the Article 31 Committee) which shall deliver its opinion on the draft within any time limit stated. The opinion is delivered (by votes of Members of the Committee (who are the representatives of EU Member States) and, if the Committee votes, say, to adopt a particular set of model contract clauses, the European Commission shall adopt measures to implement the decision which shall apply immediately. Measures adopted by the European Commission which do not comply with the opinion of the Committee have to be communicated by the European Commission to the EC Council of Ministers forthwith, in which event there are further procedures which have to be gone through before any such measures are approved. If measures such as model contract clauses are approved, those clauses would then be approved for use in *all* Member States.

Self-regulation [15.8]

Is there a rôle for codes of conduct to satisfy the 'adequacy' test? It will remain to be seen whether such solutions or, indeed, something as non-binding as, say, a sectoral code of practice in the relevant third country will be regarded as adequate. One should anticipate that even to be considered as a possible candidate under *Article 26(2)*, a code of practice (as opposed to a law or model contract) would have to have sanctions built into it whereby the data controller could, say, be fined by a regulator if it breaches the restrictions on cross border data transfers. It remains to be seen how the 'safe harbor' debate between the EU and the US pans out, although the signs of a solution are encouraging (see **15.34** above).

The Working Document produced by the Article 29 Working Party in July 1998 does touch on the issue of self regulation as a permissible means to enable the export of personal data under *Articles 25* and *26*, particularly whether under *Article 25(2)* the adequacy test which has to be assessed 'in the light of all the circumstances surrounding a data transfer operation' could be satisfied not only by rules of law but also by 'professional rules and security measures which are complied with in that country'. For the purposes of their considerations, 'self-regulation' includes a self-regulatory code (or other instrument) and:

> '...should be taken to mean any set of data protection rules applying to a plurality of data controllers from the same profession or industry sector, the content of which has been determined primarily by the members of the industry or profession concerned.'

This broad definition would encompass, at one end of the scale, a voluntary data protection code developed by a small industry association with only a few members to the other end of the scale being detailed codes of professional ethics applicable to entire professions, such as doctors and bankers, which often have quasi-judicial force. In evaluating a self-regulatory code, the Working Party would regard one important criteria for judging the value of a code as being the degree to which its rules can be enforced. The cornerstones of any self-regulatory approach must be its effectiveness in achieving:

○ a good level of general compliance;
○ support and help to individual data subjects; and
○ crucially, appropriate redress (including compensation where appropriate).

Any code must have a high level of 'transparency' – in particular the code should be drafted in plain language and offer concrete examples, which illustrate its provisions. Furthermore,

> '...the code should prohibit the disclosure of data to non-member companies who are not governed by the code, unless other adequate safeguards are provided'.

Position under DPA 1998 [15.9]

Rather than make it an offence to make such a transfer, the Home Office has, rather neatly, made the restrictions in relation to cross border data flows the Eighth Data Protection Principle. This means that breach of the provisions is not immediately a criminal offence but is subject to the procedure for enforcing the Principles including enforcement notices and appeal, if appropriate.

Schedule 4 sets out those circumstances where, notwithstanding the fact that the transferee country provides inadequate protection for personal data, the transfer could still take place.

The conditions to satisfy to ensure that the Eighth Principle does not apply (only one of which needs to be met) are:

1. The data subject has given his consent to the transfer.
2. The transfer is necessary:
   (a) for the performance of a contract between the data subject and the data controller [Note: unlike Schedule 2, this refers to a contract between the data subject and the data controller], or
   (b) for the taking of steps at the request of the data subject with a view to his entering into a contract with the data controller.
3. The transfer is necessary:
   (a) for the conclusion of a contract between the data controller

and a person other than the data subject which–
  (i)   is entered into at the request of the data subject, or
  (ii) is in the interests of the data subject, or
 (b) for the performance of such a contract.
4.-(1) The transfer is necessary for reasons of substantial public interest.
  (2) The Secretary of State may by order specify–
   (a) circumstances in which a transfer is to be taken for the purposes of sub-paragraph (1) to be necessary for reasons of substantial public interest, and
   (b) circumstances in which a transfer which is not required by or under an enactment is not to be taken for the purpose of sub-paragraph (1) to be necessary for reasons of substantial public interest.
5.   The transfer–
 (a) is necessary for the purpose of, or in connection with, any legal proceedings (including prospective legal proceedings),
 (b) is necessary for the purpose of obtaining legal advice, or
 (c) is otherwise necessary for the purposes of establishing, exercising or defending legal rights.
6.   The transfer is necessary in order to protect the vital interests of the data subject.
7.   The transfer is of part of the personal data on a public register and any conditions subject to which the register is open to inspection are complied with by any person to whom the data are or may be disclosed after the transfer.
8.   The transfer is made on terms which are of a kind approved by the Commissioner as ensuring adequate safeguards for the rights and freedoms of data subjects.
9.   The transfer has been authorised by the Commissioner as being made in such a manner as to ensure adequate safeguards for the rights and freedoms of data subjects.

The Transitional Provisions   [15.10]

Data users who transfer data outside the EEA should consider whether or not they would be able to benefit from the transitional provisions which provide an exemption until 2001 from compliance with the Eighth Data Protection Principle for data which is subject to processing already under way. They should also consider whether they can satisfy any of the criteria set out in *Schedule 4* in which event the problem goes away. However, this is subject to the overriding general obligation to process personal data fairly and lawfully under the First Data Protection Principle.

What is a Transfer? [15.11]

To decide whether the Eighth Data Protection Principle even applies, it needs to be decided if, in fact, a 'transfer' of data overseas has taken place.

The Commissioner's Office produced the *Data Protection Registrar's legal analysis* (the 'Analysis') and suggested a 'good practice approach' for assessing adequacy including consideration of the issue of contractual solutions'. It must be stressed that the Analysis is a preliminary view. The paper attempts to analyse a number of issues in relation to the new Eighth Data Protection Principle.

DPA 1998 does not define transfer but the Analysis points out that the ordinary meaning of the word is transmission from one place, person, etc. to another. Transfer does not mean the same as mere transit. As such, the fact that the electronic transfer of personal data may be routed through a third country on its way from the UK to another EEA country does not bring such a transfer within the ambit of the Eighth Principle unless some substantive processing operation was being conducted upon the personal data in the third country in question.

Under *section 1(3)*, the transfer to third countries of information intended to be processed automatically or as part of a 'relevant filing system' only *after* it has been transferred, is specifically included in the ambit of *DPA 1998*. An example of this would be where information is provided by someone in the UK over the telephone to someone in a third country who then enters the information on a computer. Another common example would be mass data transfers from computer to computer using telecommunications systems.

Assessing Adequacy [15.12]

The Commissioner recommends a 'good practice approach' to identifying adequacy in her Analysis.

As a matter of good practice, data controllers proposing to transfer personal data to a third country (exporting controllers) are recommended to adopt a consistent approach to any assessment of adequacy. The Commissioner recommends that they should consider:

○ whether (or the extent to which) the third country in question is the subject of a Community finding or presumption of adequacy;

○ the type of transfer involved and whether this enables any presumption of adequacy (for example, in the case of controller to processor transfers), to be made;

○ and apply the Adequacy Test, including consideration of the application and use of contracts and/or codes of conduct to create adequacy;

○ where there is no adequacy, or where there is doubt in this respect, the derogations contained in *Schedule 4* of *DPA 1998*, pursuant to which the transfer may proceed if any are satisfied (such as consent).

Notwithstanding this good practice approach, the DPR recognises that, from a practical point of view, exporting controllers are likely to omit detailed consideration of the 'Adequacy Test'. Such an approach completely avoids any detailed consideration and analysis of adequacy and is based on the premise that transfers to third countries, in respect of which there is no Community finding and/or presumption of adequacy applicable, may proceed whether or not there is adequacy *provided that* one of the *Schedule 4* derogations is satisfied.

The Commissioner recognises this to be an alternative, pragmatic approach which will be widely adopted in practice, albeit that it is not considered by the Commissioner to equate to best practice in terms of data protection and notwithstanding the possibility that following this approach is more likely to be a breach of the Principles.

Overseas Processors   [15.13]

The good news is that one limited category or transfers is more likely to be held to be adequate – namely transfers to a 'processor' overseas. The Commissioner has made it clear that, in her view, a presumption of adequacy can be made in most, if not all, instances of transfers outside the EEA made by exporting controllers to overseas processors. This presumption is based on the fact that the exporting data controller in such circumstances necessarily remains, in law, the data controller in the UK for the purposes of *DPA 1998*, remaining subject to *DPA 1998* and the Commissioner's powers of enforcement and the enforcement of individuals' rights thereunder.

Subject to overall compliance with the requirements of *DPA 1998*, in particular the Seventh Data Protection Principle (relating to security matters) and the requirement of that Principle that there should be a written contract between the controller and processor, the Commissioner acknowledges that such transfers can ensure adequacy subject to there being no particular risks clearly apparent in the third country in question.

Model Contract Clauses [15.14]

As previously considered, there will be legitimate occasions where companies will not be able to satisfy one of the conditions in *Schedule 4*, but are prepared, by contract, to require an importer of data overseas to keep it secure and use it fairly. Model contracts therefore need to be available for use in such circumstances. The *Directive* contemplates it and so does *DPA 1998*, and some countries in the EU such as France and Germany have advocated use of such contracts in the past.

One hopes very much that the relevant authorities agree a model contract soon — especially because, whilst a 'safe harbor' may be agreed for the US (see **15.34** below), there are many other countries that may be caught by the restrictions in *Schedule 4*, where such a contract would be very useful.

The Commissioner's Attitude to such Clauses [15.15]

The Commissioner's Office has, in principle, indicated some degree of support for the concept of a model contract clause solution for the problems with the export of personal data from the EEA to countries which do not provide an adequate level of protection for personal data.

The Analysis touches on the issue of contractual solutions. It points out that: '...the Registrar has been consulted by a number of trade associations regarding the development of model contract clauses. She fully supports this initiative . . . '.

The Role of Contractual Solutions in the Context of Adequacy [15.16]

Probably the most interesting point from the Analysis is that it stresses the fact that the list of possible factors to be taken into account in *Article 25(2)* of the *Directive* in assessing adequacy is not exhaustive.

The Analysis states that, when exporting data where there is a question about adequacy, the data controller should:

> '...consider and apply the "adequacy test", including consideration of the application and use of contracts and/or codes of conduct to create adequacy'.

This is interesting since the *Directive* itself seems to contemplate the use of contractual solutions to rectify a situation where the level of protection is otherwise not adequate. Whereas the Commissioner's Office say you can take the contractual approval into account at an earlier stage to establish adequacy.

DPA 1998 provides a comparable basis for assessing what amounts to an adequate level of protection. *DPA 1998* provides that the level of protection must be 'adequate in all the circumstances of the case'. The interpretative provision of *DPA 1998* relating to the Eighth Principle states that, in assessing adequacy, consideration should be given:

> 'in particular to:
> O   the nature of the personal data,
> O   the country or territory of origin of the information contained in the data,
> O   the country or territory of final destination of that information,
> O   the purposes for which and period during which the data are intended to be processed,
> O   the law in force in the country or territory in question,
> O   the international obligations of that country or territory,
> O   any relevant codes of conduct or other rules which are enforceable in that country or territory (whether generally or by arrangement in particular cases), and
> O   any security measures taken in respect of the data in that country or territory.'

The Analysis seems to be saying that one can include a consideration of contract solutions as part of the overall adequacy test itself.

The Analysis states that one of the matters to address when assessing adequacy is that:

> '...where contracts are proposed to be used to try to secure adequacy – does the law of the third country in question recognise the fundamental importance of individuals/ businesses being able to contract freely with one another,

both domestically and internationally? If so, does the law of the third party enable enforcement of contractual obligations by parties to the contract/third parties?'

Until recently, English law did not permit a third party to a contract to enforce it. *UK Contracts (Rights of Third Parties) Act 1998* (the *UKC (RTP) Act*) received Royal Assent on 11 November 1999 and enables clauses granting rights to third parties not a party to a contract to grant enforceable rights to such third parties. It will now be possible to create an enforceable benefit for data subjects in a contract to which they are not a party (although equally the parties can expressly exclude this right). In relevant data protection contracts, the parties will need to include express wording granting this benefit or which could be so construed.

Section 1 of *UKC (RTP) Act 1998* (subject to other provisions of that Act) provides that a person who is not a party to a contract may in his own right enforce a term of the contract if:

◯   the contract expressly provides that he may, or
◯   the term purports to confer benefit on him.

This does not apply if, on a proper construction of the contract, it appears that the parties did not intend the term to be enforceable by him. *UKC (RTP) Act 1998* provides that the third party must be expressly identified in the contract by name, as a member of a class or in answering to a particular description but need not be in existence when the contract is entered into. It would be very easy to satisfy this requirement in the case of a class of data subjects and wording could be included in a contract for the export of data to this effect.

In order for *UKC (RTP) Act 1998* to apply, the third party must be expressly identified in the contract by name, as a member of a class or as answering a particular description but need not be in existence when the contract is entered into. In the case of a contract to export data, data subjects the subject of the export contract could be described as a class and, provided that this is done clearly, that ought to suffice. There should be no need to name particular data subjects.

One hopes that the Commissioner's office will be satisfied that there is a real ability for data subjects to enforce export contracts and, therefore, their objections to such a contract on the basis that the parties of the contract might not themselves enforce it will be alleviated. If *UKC (RTP) Act* applies, then, for the purposes of exercising his right to enforce a term of the contract, there shall be available to the third party (in the present case, the data subject) any remedy that would have been available

179

to him in an action for breach of contract if he had been a party to the contract (and the rules relating to damages, injunctions, specific performance and other relief apply accordingly).

The Commissioner recognises that it may be inappropriate, difficult, time-consuming and/or costly for exporting controllers to consider exhaustively the legal adequacy criteria in the case of every transfer and third country. This is an encouraging statement from the Commissioner because many small businesses would suffer very badly financially if they felt they had to have an intimate knowledge of worldwide data protection laws just because they want to establish a website.

The Commissioner further recognises that it would be unreasonable for her office to expect an exhaustive analysis of these criteria in every case. At the same time she also expects exporting controllers to be able to recognise those third countries which at any particular time represent a real and obvious danger to the rights and freedoms of individuals in relation to the processing of personal data. As such the Commissioner recognises that there will be circumstances when some or all of the criteria may not be considered by exporting controllers for different reasons. To the extent that this is the case, however, exporting controllers:

> 'should err on the side of caution in carrying out the adequacy/ risk assessment and deciding whether or not adequacy is ensured in the particular case'.

The Drawbacks [15.17]

The main drawbacks with any contractual solution is a lack of direct enforceability of the contract by the data subject and the data subject's potential inability to have access to the data held overseas. This was a particular problem under English law.

The Synthesis paper produced by the Article 29 Working Party in July 1998 appears to be saying it would be very difficult to create a contract which would fulfil the adequacy criteria the Working Party are suggesting. This is very disappointing as it is suspected that had this attitude been made widely known at the time the *Directive* was being drafted, there would have been even more resistance to *Articles 25* and *26*.

The core components that the Article 29 Working Party define as necessary for a solution to satisfy the adequacy test are detailed below.

The Core Components of an Adequate Contract   [15.18]

These include the:

- purpose limitation principle;
- data quality and proportionality principle;
- transparency principle;
- security principle;
- rights of access, rectification and opposition; and
- restrictions on onward transfers.

Purpose Limitation Principle   [15.19]

Data should be processed for a specific purpose and specifically used or further communicated only in so far as this is not incompatible with the purpose of the transfer. The only exemptions to this rule would be those necessary in a democratic society on one of the grounds listed in *Article 13* of the *Directive*.

The Data Quality and Proportionality Principle   [15.20]

Data should be accurate and, where necessary, kept up-to-date. The data should be adequate, relevant and not excessive in relation to the purposes for which they are transferred or further processed.

The Transparency Principle   [15.21]

Individuals should be provided with information as to the purpose of the processing and the identity of the data controller in the third country, and other information in so far as this is necessary to ensure fairness. The only exemptions permitted should be in line with *Articles 11(2)* and *13* of the *Directive*.

The Security Principle   [15.22]

Technical and organisational security measures should be taken by the data controller that are appropriate to the risks presented by the processing. Any person acting under the authority of the data controller, including a processor, must not process data except on instructions from that person.

The Rights of Access, Rectification and Opposition   [15.23]

The data subject should have a right to obtain a copy of all data relating to them that are processed, and a right to rectification of those data where they are shown to be inaccurate. In certain situations they should also be able to object to the processing of the data relating to them. The only exemptions to these rights should be in line with *Article 13* of the *Directive*.

Restrictions on Onward Transfers   [15.24]

Further transfers of the personal data by the recipient of the original data transfer should be permitted only where the second recipient (i.e. the recipient of the onward transfer) is also subject to rules affording an adequate level of protection. The only exceptions permitted should be in line with *Article 26(1)* of the *Directive* (see **2.28** above).

Additional Principles   [15.25]

Examples of additional principles to be applied to specific types of processing are detailed below.

Sensitive Data   [15.26]

Where 'sensitive' categories of data are involved (those listed in *Article 8* of the *Directive*), additional safeguards should be in place, such as a requirement that the data subject gives his explicit consent for the processing.

Direct Marketing   [15.27]

Where data are transferred for the purposes of direct marketing, the data subject should be able to 'opt-out' from having his data used for such purposes at any stage.

Automated Individual Decision   [15.28]

Where the purpose of the transfer is the taking of an automated decision in the sense of *Article 15* of the *Directive*, the individual should have the right to know the logic involved in this decision, and other measures should be taken to safeguard the individual's legitimate interest.

The Commissioner's Recommendations [15.29]

Exporting controllers should consider those aspects of the transfer which are relatively straightforward to assess, such as the:

O   nature of the personal data to be transferred;
O   purpose(s) of the proposed transfer;
O   period during which the data are intended to be processed; and
O   security measures taken in respect of the data.

For the purposes of the Analysis these matters, amongst others, are referred to as the 'general adequacy criteria'. The Commissioner stresses 'the general adequacy criteria can and should be assessed in every case because they are within the knowledge of the exporting controller'.

At the same time as considering the general adequacy criteria, the Commissioner recommends that exporting controllers should also consider other matters relevant to the transfer, being matters more particularly relating to the third country in question, such as the:

O   law in force in the third country (with particular consideration being given to the existence and content of any data protection law);
O   international obligations of that country and any relevant codes of conduct or other rules enforceable in that country.

The matters that exporting controllers are recommended to take into account for such analysis are referred to by the Commissioner as the 'legal adequacy criteria'.

Use of Contracts/Codes of Conduct [15.30]

Having established the general adequacy criteria and the legal adequacy criteria, the Commissioner indicates that determining adequacy then involves consideration of the extent to which contracts and/or codes of conduct may be used to secure adequacy, particularly in those cases where there may be elements of inadequacy highlighted by their consideration of the general and legal adequacy criteria or, indeed any failure in such consideration.

In the first instance, and in all cases, exporting controllers are advised to refer to any 'Community finding' (as defined in *DPA 1998*) which may have been published. *DPA 1998* provides that, where the European Commission makes a finding that a third country does, or does not, ensure an adequate level of protection within the meaning of *Article 25(2)* of the *Directive*, any question as to whether an adequate level of protection is met in relation to the transfer of any personal data to a third country shall be determined in accordance with that finding. At present there are no such findings in force although the Article 29 Working Party have provided papers indicating that Switzerland and Hungary may 'pass the test'.

In the absence of Community findings and/or presumptions of adequacy referred to above (or where the only presumption of adequacy/ inadequacy is based on the classification of transfer type considered above) exporting controllers are advised by the Commissioner to follow the Good Practice Approach and adopt a way of assessing adequacy which is consistent with that of both the *Directive* and *DPA 1998*. To do this, exporting controllers will need to consider various criteria applicable to the transfer by applying a test of adequacy. The test is designed to ensure that an assessment of adequacy, in the nature of a risk assessment, is made in relation to the majority of, if not all, transfers of personal data to third countries.

Type of Transfer [15.31]

The Commissioner recommends that, before considering the Adequacy Test, exporting controllers should attempt to put the proposed transfer in context by identifying the type of transfer involved – considering perhaps whether or not that type of transfer falls within any of the six types of international transfer which have been identified by the Confederation of British Industry (CBI) – a body which is doing a considerable amount of work in relation to model contracts.

In the case of certain transfers it may be possible for exporting controllers to approach the Adequacy Test with a strong presumption in favour of adequacy in terms of assessing the risk involved in the transfer. Not all transfers can be classified into one or other of the six types identified below.

O Transfers to a third party processor who remains under the control of the exporting data controller. Such a contract will need to satisfy *Article 17(3)* and *(4)* of the *Directive* (security of processing) there is the possibility of a presumption of adequacy in the case of such transfers – see above.

O Transfers within an international or multi-national company or group of companies where an internal agreement, policy or code may be more appropriate than a potentially large number of contracts.

O Transfers within a consortium of independent organisations set up to process international transactions in, for instance, the banking or travel sectors.

O Transfers between the providers of professional services such as lawyers or accountants whose clients' affairs are international in scope.

O Transfers which amount to a licence for use and probably a rental payment in respect of personal data used, for instance, in direct marketing.

O Transfers which amount to a sale of data to a third party with no continuing relationship either with the data subject or the purchaser.'

There is a presumption of inadequacy in relation to the last type of transfer described above. This quite clearly presents the greatest risk to the rights and freedoms of individuals in relation to the processing of personal data as there is no continuing relationship between the exporting controller and the importing controller. The International Chamber of Commerce (ICC), which is also working on a model contract, takes the same view in relation to this last category – that a special type of contractual solution would be needed in such a situation (if a contractual solution is even feasible) and so energies would be best expended on producing a contract or contracts to address the other situations first.

However, in the case of the other five types of transfer there is either a:

O continuing relationship (controller/processor);
O lack of permanency about the transfer and/or restriction(s) on use (list rental); or
O the added 'protection' of, for example, sectoral laws (banking), professional codes of conduct (legal); or
O requirement for a contractual relationship (controller/processor or travel industry consortia) or internal codes of conduct/company policies (multi-national).

The Commissioner suggests that the classification of the type of transfer may assist exporting controllers in placing the transfer in its correct context and in their assessment of the risks involved in such transfer.

However, not every transfer will be able to be classified in this way. This classification process is therefore not the only step to take in assessing adequacy. Nevertheless it is possible for strong presumptions in favour of, or against, adequacy to be made through such process.

The Genesis of the ICC Model Contract Clauses [15.32]

Over the years, various international organisations have promulgated the use of model contract clauses in contracts for transfers of data between countries. Probably the best known of such initiatives is the model contract clauses for use in contracts for the transfer of personal data to other countries produced by the International Chamber of Commerce (ICC) in 1992. Those clauses were produced in conjunction with the Council of Europe and endorsed by the European Commission and (subsequently) by the Organisation for Economic Co-operation and Development (OECD).

At that time, there was no overarching legislation such as the *Directive* or any other legislation which was insisting upon or encouraging such clauses, although at about the time when ICC model contract clauses were originally produced, there was an amendment to the draft Directive which added a reference in it to the possibility of the use of model contract clauses as a possible mechanism to enable transfers of personal data outside the EU under what is now *Article 26*.

Therefore, a model contract solution of the type advocated by the ICC was a possible solution to data expert problems, were the *Directive* to be adopted at a later date.

Many assumed, because the European Commission endorsed the ICC model clauses, that its attitude to contract clauses would be more positive than it now appears to be and that a model along the lines of the ICC version would be acceptable under the *Directive*. However, the European Commission has now said that contract clauses solutions will be rare. Had this been known when the *Directive* was adopted, one suspects *Article 25* would have caused even more debate. It is likely that a number of opponents to *Article 25* were less vociferous after the 1992 amendments because they saw model contracts appeared to be regarded as a real alternative to the other exceptions in *Article 26(1)*.

The original ICC Model Contract Clauses were designed to be consistent with the good data protection policies set out in certain guidelines produced by the OECD in 1980 and they are also consistent with the Council of Europe Convention No 108 of 1981. Neither of these has the force of law but both have been a very important influence in good data protection practices over the past 15 years or more. A number of European countries ratified the Convention and passed laws to do so, e.g. in England, *DPA 1984* (see **Chapter 1**).

The ICC clauses proved highly successful and a number of major organisations have, over the years, adopted them as part of their data protection and privacy policies. Although not then a legal requirement, many companies wanted to show to those within and outside their organisations that they took privacy issues seriously and to ensure proper protection of their data in the hands of third parties.

The Current Position [15.33]

The original ICC model contract clauses set out some core principles to be followed by parties to the model contract, and those principles are very similar to those being cited by the Article 29 Working Party, but were not precisely the same. Rather than set those out in full, which would be lengthy, as well as all the other provisions that ought to appear in a model contract such as addressing what happens if the contract is to terminate, the ICC concluded that the shorter (but equally effective) approach would be to provide for the importer of data overseas to follow, as if it were its own, the law of the exporter. This would by definition satisfy (it was assumed) the requirements of the *Directive*, because if the export was from any EEA Member State the exporter's law must be adequate protection for personal data, because it follows the *Directive*.

That is therefore the approach to the revised ICC model contract adopted.

The first draft was produced by the International Chamber of Commerce International Working Party on Data Protection Privacy in Spring 1998, for consultation with ICC members.

In the light of ICC members' feedback for many different jurisdictions, the ICC Working Party produced a redraft of the clauses.

At the same time as those clauses were first sent to the ICC national committees, a copy was sent to a couple of European data protection registrars, on an informal basis, for some 'feedback'. That feedback itself was very helpful.

Thereafter, the Working Party concluded that the best way forward would be to submit the clauses to the European Commission, asking them to seek approval for them in accordance with the mechanism set up under *Article 31* of the *Directive* (thereby - if so approved providing a contractual solution under *Article 26(4)* of the Directive). This happened in September 1998. A meeting took place with the Commission on 4 November 1998, in Brussels, at which the ICC explained its position.

It became fairly clear from the meeting that there were one or two problems with model contract clauses. A major concern is that the individual data subject is unable (or may be unable) to enforce terms in the model contract, although they are in his favour or for his benefit.

More importantly, the structure of the ICC Model Contract Clauses is such that, in situations where the exporter of the data remains the or a data controller (and therefore could be fined or sanctioned in its home state should its data importer overseas abuse the personal data), this should be more than sufficient as an incentive to protect the personal data. The data controller in the EU would enforce the contract against the overseas importer or face action being taken against it in its home state. This might not work in circumstances where the data controller ceases to control the data and, therefore, after the export cannot be made liable at all by the data controller's local data protection authority. The ICC is not currently suggesting that its model contract is to be used to address outright sale situations.

The ICC acknowledges that there maybe a slight concern in the 'sale' case, but as regards enforceability by data subjects is confident that there is not really an issue with the laws in the EEA (particularly now that the UK has changed its privity of contract law) preventing a data subject enforcing its rights, under a contract it is not a party to, in the unlikely event that the parties to the contract did not enforce it.

The Safe Harbor Agreement [15.34]

Consultation has been taking place in the US on the terms of the 'safe harbor' principles. Some essential principles of the safe harbor provisions (although they are more extensive than this) are:

O   Notice – to the data subject about what information is collect on them and show it is processed and used;

O   Choice – this covers the ability for consumers to 'opt-out', especially from direct marketing;

O   Onward Transfer – choice for individuals about the way in which a third party could use their data;

O   Security – the taking of reasonable measures to protect data from loss, misuse, etc.

O   Data Integrity – data to be kept accurate, current and complete, etc.

O   Access – individuals to have reasonable access to information about them derived from non-public sources.

O   Enforcement – mechanisms for assuring compliance with the principles: recourse for individuals and consequences for the organisation when the principles are not followed. The mechanisms have to include readily available and affordable independent recourse mechanisms by which individuals' complaints and disputes can be resolved, amongst other things.

The proposed way forward is that there will be a set of safe harbor principles and also a set of Frequently Asked Questions (FAQs) about privacy matters, with their answers, and it is intended that the FAQs will be part of the safe harbor arrangement and will have the same binding force as the principles.

The US government consulted widely with relevant US bodies for comment on the guiding principles.

At the end of November 1998, Member States (the Article 31 Committee) concluded that the US proposals designed to give personal data sent from the EU equivalent levels of protection were inadequate. This view was repeated in Spring 1999, Summer 1999 and November/December 1999.

The two main sticking points cited were a concern the arrangements for ensuring that individuals could obtain information about the nature and use of personal data held by companies, and the provision of systems of redress when individuals complain about how personal data has been used.

In July 1999, the Article 29 Working Party adopted a paper called 'Working document on the current state of play of the ongoing discussions between the European Commission and the United States Government concerning the 'international safe harbor principles'. This has reference number 5075/99/EN/Final.

The document was not a formal opinion of the Working Party. Whilst, strictly speaking, the working party is an advisory body only, clearly their 'opinion' will hold great sway with the European Commission and also with the separate committee set up under Article 31 of the Directive to look at (and to vote upon) data protection matters. The importance of the Article 31 Committee is that it has power to vote in relation to data protection matters such as approval of model contracts for the export of data to countries which do not provide adequate protection for personal data and also the safe harbor principles. Were they to vote in favour of the safe harbor principles, this would mean that those principles would be approved and ultimately recognised by all Member States and data could be exported to US entities adopting those principles. The Article 31 Committee is made up of representatives of all EU governments.

The Working Document referred back to previous remarks made by the working party in opinions in January, February and April 1999. Helpfully, the previous three opinions of the Working Party are annexed to the current 'working document'.

Working Party's Observations [15.35]

The working party made the following observation in the July paper, drawing them to the attention, in particular, of the Article 31 Committee. The observations are detailed below.

Legal Basis [15.36]

The Working Party recommended that both parties ensure that 'Article 25 of the directive is a solid legal basis'. That is a rather interesting (or worrying) statement and perhaps one that should have been made earlier in the day.

One assumes that what this is getting at is that *Article 25(1)(2)* provides that 'the adequacy of the level of protection afforded by a third country shall be assessed in the light of all the circumstances surrounding a data transfer operation or set of data transfer operations; particular consideration shall be given to the nature of the data, the purpose and duration of the proposed processing operation or operations, the country of origin and country of final destination, the rules of law, both general and sectoral, in force the third country in question and the professional rules and security measures which are complied with in that country.

A question to ask oneself is whether the safe harbor principles are adequate on their own, given that particular consideration has not necessarily been given to the nature of the data or the purpose and duration of a proposed operation or operations (because the principles have been drafted in general terms and not in relation to any particular types of transfers and *Article 25* does not mention, for example, voluntary codes being adopted). However, transfers are to be assessed 'in the light of all the circumstances surrounding a data transfer' and certainly one relevant factor must be the fact that the safe harbor principles have been created.

Scope of the Safe Harbor Arrangement [15.37]

The July Working Party/Working Document stated that the following should be addressed:

O whether any sectors might be excluded from the scope of the safe harbor mechanism on account of specific provisions which give specific protection or, perhaps, due to the absence of a public monitoring body with responsibility to deal with the subject matter;

O whether a company, in notifying its adherence to the principles, would be able to exclude certain activities of its own business (e.g. on-line services) and how any exclusions would be made public/notified to national supervisory authorities;

O the working party believed the current level of protection for employee data was not satisfactory. They suggested two possible solutions — to reinforce overall the level of protection awarded by the principles or to exclude employee data from them and give it reinforced protection — this was particularly so because there is no independent public body which reviews matters arising in relation to this type of data; and

O the working party remained concerned that the US authorities may derogate from the principles through regulation without giving proper weight to the interests of privacy protection.

Conditions of Implementation and Enforcement [15.38]

The Working Party raised a number of queries in relation to enforcement such as what the relationship would be between investigations by national supervisory authorities in the US and investigations by national supervisory authorities in the European Union? What if there were simultaneous and successive US and European procedures looking at a complaint which led to contradictory results?

The principles included a verification procedure and the Working Party recommended that that should be independent and carried out by a third party, failing which any report on the verification procedure should be made available to the national supervisory authorities, if necessary.

Contents of the Principles [15.39]

The Working Party acknowledged that the content of the principles (then current version 1 June 1999) had improved over the previous April draft but it did not yet provide adequate protection.

The working party flagged a number of issues for the Article 31 Committee, for example, in the principle regarding access by data subjects to information, the working party considered that the exemptions from access described in the FAQs were too broad. It also flagged that any data processed in violation of the principles should be corrected or deleted.

In September and October, further pronouncements were made by David Aaron, the Under-secretary at the Department of Commerce in Washington who was responsible for the data privacy dialogue. He indicated that the European Commission was moving away from emphasis on a self-regulatory regime and had come up with a new suggestion. This was that the United States should have responsibility for the enforcement of data protection. Consumer complaints from EU nationals would be referred from national EU data protection commissioners straight to the US courts. Currently, in the US, in the event that personal information is misused or passed to unauthorised third parties, the principles of self regulation in the US would be enforced by the Federal Trade Commission and the Attorneys General of the relevant States under existing laws based on 'deceptive business practices'. Clearly, what was being done with data has to be established as being such a practice, before an action could be brought. These different approaches have been causing a problem in negotiations between the US and the EU, particularly as the US did not relish the prospect of allowing some sort of enforcement role in the US for data protection agencies from EU Member States.

Some groups quickly spoke out against the suggested approach. It has been said that, for smaller companies, trying to defend privacy disputes in the US courts could be costly. Some consumer groups have expressed concern that that process would be 'too long and cumbersome' for individuals to pursue their rights through the US courts.

It remains to be seen whether this change in approach may be successful, but the proposal (which was discussed between David Aaron and John Mogg, the Director General of the European Commission's internal market directorate, has not been ratified by the Article 31 committee). There has been no formal approval of the proposal, though, as yet. Clearly, if the EU Member States do commit that all enforcement action under the safe harbor agreement takes place in the US, they will need to be satisfied that the US courts can take jurisdiction for such disputes and see what sort of procedures would be entailed for EU consumers to bring such an action.

Indeed, it would appear that it is intended that industry – led privacy groups like BBB On-line and TRUSTe would effectively be in charge of enforcement, with the Federal Trade Commission as a back-up. Given the views of the article 29 Working Party, and their concerned that a self-regulatory system will not really provide for effective enforcement procedures, there still seemed to be some work to be done for the EU to satisfy itself of what is proposed.

Press comment in Autumn 1999 indicated that both the EU and the US had agreed to this approach. Gerard de Graff, the First Secretary for Trade at the EU's Washington headquarters has said that the EU and the US agreed in principle on the enforcement policy in July and the EU Member States agreed to this in mid-September. However, it does still leave some work. De Graff has said "it will only work if the enforcement system is credible and effective". He also pointed out "it will continue to be a difficult area as we progress ... what are the sanctions for companies that do not comply, or abuse personal data? How often do they need to breach the safe harbor (before they're kicked out)?"

Both the *Directive* and *Schedule 4* of *DPA 1998* contemplate the use of model contract clauses in situations where there may not be an adequate level of protection for personal data in a country to which that data is being sent.

The use of model contracts is therefore potentially very important in the international business community and would be particularly beneficial for transfers of data between members of the same group of companies.

The Working Party issued an opinion on the safe harbor principles in December 1999.

Perhaps one could have guessed what the conclusion of the Working Party was going to be, when one read, right at the beginning of the opinion:

> 'The Working Party regrets that, on such an important issue, the time left for taking a position was so short. It also notes that none of the documents is considered "final" and therefore reserves its positions as regards any further developments on the texts.
>
> The Working Party note that some progress had been made but deplored that some of the comments made in its previous position papers do not seem to have been addressed in the latest version of the US documents. The Working Party therefore confirms its general concerns'.

After such an introduction, the Working Party did indeed confirm that it still does not regard the safe harbor arrangements as satisfactory.

The Working Party Opinion gives a reasonable amount of detail as to the various issues which make the solution unsatisfactory and set out below are their conclusions.

The Working Party concludes, in the light of the above observations and recommendations, that the proposed 'Safe Harbor' arrangements as reflected in the current versions of the various documents remain unsatisfactory. The Working Party invites the Commission to urge the US side to make a number of key improvements, notably:

O to clarify the scope of the 'Safe Harbor' and in particular to remove any possible misunderstandings that US organisations can choose to rely on the 'Safe Harbor' principles in circumstances when the Directive itself applies;

O to provide more reliable arrangements allowing 'Safe Harbor' participants to be identified with certainty and avoiding the risk that 'Safe Harbor' status has, for one reason or another, been lost;

O to make it absolutely clear that enforcement by an appropriately empowered public body is in place for all participants in the 'Safe Harbor';

O to make it the rule that private sector dispute resolution bodies must refer unresolved complaints to such a public body;

O to make the allowed exceptions and exemptions less sweeping and less open-ended, so that exceptions are precisely that – that is, they apply only where and to the extent necessary, and are not general invitations to override the principles; this is particularly important as regards the right of access;

○ to strengthen the Choice principle, which is the linchpin of the US approach.

At the very end of March, the European Commission Internal Market Commissioner, Frits Bolkestein, was given permission by the European Commission to approach Member States to seek their approval to the proposed safe harbor arrangement.

16 – Technology

Introduction [16.1]

Under *DPA 1998*, processing (of the automated variety) is not now limited to processing 'by reference to the data subject'. On that basis, it appears to cover the processing of any data relating to a person who is a data subject. If so, that means that businesses would need to consider implementing word search facilities in their computer systems, rather than simply going and locating, if there is a request for subject access, the specifically identified file for that particular identified individual as they might have done under *DPA 1984*.

Whilst most modern computer systems have a word searching facility like this, it is important that businesses understand the ramifications of this particular twist in the new legislation.

That is why the transitional provisions in *Schedule 8* are very important, as they provide an opportunity for data controllers, where the transitional provisions apply to their processing arrangements, to plan ahead, as they have until October 2001 to make sure they can comply with the wider subject access ramifications of *DPA 1998*.

Subject Access [16.2]

The subject access provisions enable a data controller to ask for information to satisfy itself as to the details of the person making the request and the location of the information which the person seeks (*section 7(3)*), but *DPA 1998* could still require the data controller to make a wider search than previously. If a data subject could only say that his name is 'X', then the data controller might be obliged to carry out a full search in the name of Mr X. If it can limit its search in time or to a product database, even better, but the search will still be for all relevant references to Mr X in that period.

The main balancing factor for data controllers is that *section 7* does have the concept of not being required to provide a copy in intelligible form if to do so would require a 'disproportionate effort'. Therefore, data controllers can surely not be expected to upgrade their existing systems (if relevant) to provide a word searching facility where one did not previously exist.

Transitional Relief [16.3]

The transitional provisions, described in some detail in **Chapter 14**, are going to be very important in the context of a company's review of its technology. If an automated system was already processing personal data in an automated way as at 24 October 1998 (making it 'eligible personal data'), then most of the new provisions of *DPA 1998* do not apply to that data. For example, the new requirements of the First Data Protection Principle, that require notification and satisfaction of the conditions in *Schedules 2* and *3* do not apply, nor does the new requirement under the Seventh Data Protection Principle (in relation to security) which requires provisions that relate to security to be included in contracts with third party processors.

That said, it would be prudent for businesses which can take advantage of the transitional provisions but which have processing contracts which may be renewed during the transitional period to include relevant provisions at the time of renewal.

It is important to note that the subject access provisions (effectively those as existed under *DPA 1984* for computer records only) still apply to computer records even where the transitional provisions also apply. The only difference is that if the transitional relief applies to a system to which a data subject seeks subject access, in giving subject access, the data controller is entitled to restrict the search to apply the old test under *DPA 1984* that it is only looking for files that are processed 'by reference to the data subject'. Therefore, for example, a full word search to provide all references to new elements of data about the data subject should not be required.

However, businesses will need to be thinking, now, about what they do when this concession runs out in October 2001.

Data controllers will also need to consider what happens if they have systems created after 24 October 1998, in which event *DPA 1998* will apply to that processing in full from day one. This will require a systems audit to be carried out to establish what systems exist and how long they have been in existence.

It is important to note the need to monitor whether new manual filing systems or new types of automated processing have been set up since 24 October 1998 or may be set up before 24 October 2001 by the organisation. If so, no transitional relief is available in respect of that information. This was made absolutely clear when the transitional relief provisions were introduced into the House of Lords in March 1998.

This could mean that an organisation may have some systems to which the enhanced subject access rights do not apply and in respect of which consent does not need to be obtained from data subjects for processing, nor does the data controller have to give any notifications as to the uses of that data in excess of any notification that would have been required by the First Data Protection Principle under *DPA 1984*. It could also, at the same time, have newer systems to which *DPA 1998* applies in full.

Data Security [16.4]

The other major requirement of *DPA 1998*, in a technology context, is the requirement for data security.

Under *DPA 1998* (as under *DPA 1984* – but now enhanced by *DPA 1998*), there are data security requirements. These are not simply business or risk management requirements (which companies should be following to minimise such risks) but they are also legal obligations under the new Seventh Data Protection Principle.

Under the Seventh Principle, where the processing is carried out by a data processor, one of the requirements on the data controller is to agree a written contract with the processor whereby the processor only processes the data under instructions from the data controller and in accordance with the Seventh Principle.

An example of a letter to be exchanged with a data processor with which a data controller already has a relationship, seeking to impose the new requirements of the Seventh Principle is attached as **Appendix E**. This could be appropriately amended to form a clause in a contract with a new data processor or when renewing an existing processing contract.

No well advised processor should resist a clause of this type. If it does not accept such a clause, the data controller should go elsewhere. Otherwise, (transitional provisions excepted), the data controller will knowingly be in breach of a Data Protection Principle (with the ramifications that that may entail).

DPA 1998 itself does not specify the technical measures to be taken, which is absolutely correct. An Act of Parliament like this should try to be technology neutral and merely create a regulatory framework. It is left up to individual data controllers and, ultimately, to the data protection authority in that data controller's country, to decide whether or not its security measures are adequate.

Employee Responsibility [16.5]

DPA 1998 requires organisational as well as technical measures to be put in place. This has to involve the whole area of the recruitment and training of IT staff, in particular, and making them accept responsibility for ensuring that appropriate data security is applied in their relevant areas. This will include instilling proper procedures in relation to the use of passwords and security devices and even ensuring appropriate sanctions, from an employment context, if the security requirements are knowingly breached.

Balance Between Implementation and Cost [16.6]

The Directive and DPA 1998 appear to permit a balancing test between the measures to be taken to protect personal data and the cost of implementation. Article 17(1) of the Directive, states that data controllers shall have regard to the state of the art and the cost of implementation of a system and goes on to say that:

> 'such measures shall ensure a level of security appropriate to the risks represented by the processing and the nature of the data to be protected.'

This seems to be recommending that your security measures must consider a higher level of protection for more sensitive data.

Guidance [16.7]

Data Protection – Everybody's Business which was published by the British Computer Society in response to DPA 1998, points out that the only UK national standard available in the information security area is the Code of Practice for Information Security Management (BS 7799), issued by the British Standard Institution (BSI). This lists a number of controls available in the main areas of IT security. It also specified ten key controls in that field. Every organisation which uses computers in any shape or form should consider all the controls listed in the BS 7799 document and should, as a minimum, implement the ten key controls.

A risk analysis in relation to a company's own systems would also assist it in establishing which controls are most relevant and would provide factual evidence of the consideration of appropriate security measures.

BS 7799 was first published in February 1995 and was then published as BS 7799-1 in February 1998, with the current version having come into effect on 15 May 1999.

The Commissioner has suggested that compliance with BS 7799 may be a benchmark to apply to determine the adequacy of security procedures. Organisations' systems are reviewed and their compliance with BS 7799 is certified and the procedure also involves periodic internal reviews. Compliance is reviewed by independent auditors and is therefore objectively assessed.

Opting Out   [16.8]

There is potentially an issue about the design of marketing databases in the light of the various provisions in *DPA 1998* and the regulations to give effect to the *Data Protection Telecoms Directive* (see **Chapter 22**) in relation to opting out. Consideration should be given to designing marketing databases so that they can handle the possible situations where data subjects opt-out of direct marketing by different marketing techniques – mail/fax/telephone call/E-mail. It should enable a company to suppress the parties in question, say, for marketing telephone calls but not for direct mailing.

Back-up Data   [16.9]

Under *DPA 1984*, there was a general exemption in relation to back-up data. Personal data were exempt under *DPA 1984* from subject access if they were kept only for the purpose of replacing other data in the event of the other data being lost, destroyed or impaired. This exemption covered duplicate records which were held purely for security purposes but the information held on the original files must be made available. If the data were kept so that they might be consulted (however infrequently) whether or not the original files had been damaged, then the exemption would not apply. Thus, archived data were not completely exempted. This is broadly continued by *DPA 1998*, because *Schedule 8* contains specific provisions in relation to back-up data.

Schedule 8, para 12 provides that eligible automated data which are processed only for the purpose of replacing other data in the event of the latter being lost, destroyed or impaired are exempt from *section 7* (subject access) during the first transitional period (i.e. until 23 October 2001). However, this does not necessarily mean that all the other provisions in *DPA 1998* do apply to back-up data. This could prove a practical nightmare for businesses and it is hoped that, in many circumstances, one will be able to argue legitimately that this data is not personal data for the purposes of *DPA 1998* because, particularly if it is on old back-up tapes, it may not be possible to identify living individuals from that data. However, it is alarming if back-up data could be caught by *DPA 1998*, because that would mean that the Data Protection Principles about keeping it up-to-date etc. will also apply.

When subject access does apply to back-up tapes it is hoped that the 'disproportionate effort' test will often apply, particularly with older data. Businesses should perhaps also reconsider why they hold back-up tapes and how long they need to hold them for. If they are not necessary, consideration should be given to deleting them.

It is understood that guidance will be forthcoming from the Commissioner's Office about this.

It should be noted that the exemption for back-up data only applies to automated data which is 'eligible automated data' and therefore back-up tapes made since 24 October 1998 may be subject to *DPA 1998* in full.

Discovery Bundles [16.10]

One technological issue will be of particular relevance to lawyers. Increasingly, during the course of complex litigation, technology is being used during the litigation process. In previous years, personal data held in a discovery bundle was not something that could be made the focus of a subject access request, because it was not automated data within *DPA 1984*.

Solicitors now increasingly use sophisticated technology to assist them in litigation, particularly in preparation for complex trials. Indeed, some such systems might have been capable of being made the focus of a subject access request under *DPA 1984*, once the data was searchable for key words, etc.

The use of a subject access request, to destabilise litigation, seems to be something that will increasingly be available to data subjects and, unless the electronically held information is privileged (in which event one of the miscellaneous exemptions in *Schedule 7, para 10* (legal professional privilege) will obviate the requirement for disclosure) or one of the other exemptions applies to that data the information will have to be disclosed if personal data can be identified. This would apply even though the usual disclosure procedures of the Court would not require disclosure until a later date.

In fact, this point is going to be even more useful to vexatious litigants because *DPA 1998* may now allow access even to disclosure bundles in manual form since they may well be relevant filing systems for the purpose of *DPA 1998*.

Automated Decision Taking [16.11]

It is important that companies look at the systems they use for making automated decisions such as credit scoring to ascertain whether the decision is an automated one or whether it has a manual element involved or the ultimate decision is, in fact, taken by an individual. This assessment should be part of a company's systems audit investigations in relation to *DPA 1998*.

17 – The Internet

Introduction [17.1]

Data protection laws are also equally applicable in cyberspace.

It would be interesting to see whether companies that currently allow respondents to direct mailings etc. to opt-out of direct marketing by ticking a box, will also do the same thing with their websites.

Taking a slightly cynical approach, websites could be seen by some to be slightly more controlled by the technical people within the organisation rather than by the compliance officers or lawyers and therefore there are, or may be, a number of websites which are not as 'data protection compliant' as they could be.

Whereas, over the years, many companies have set up internal procedures so that, automatically, any newspaper advert or broadcasting campaign has to be approved by an internal compliance procedure, there are companies where the establishment of a new website and the vetting of its content falls outside this longstanding procedure. Also, it might well be that a website started life as a fairly simple site containing basic information about the company, which may not have required a complex legal checking procedure to be gone through, but the website could well have matured from that situation to one where complex legal rules about, say, advertising need to be complied with.

It is a nonsense to say that the Internet is an unregulated environment. Many regulators have made it quite clear that they oversee the activities of their regulated bodies however they choose to deliver and advertise their products.

The Advertising Standards Authority (ASA), to take one example, has made it clear that they regard advertising on websites as no different to newspaper or television advertisements and that they are, therefore, subject to their rules and regulations, including the British Codes of Advertising and of Sales Promotion.

The Commissioner's Views [17.2]

The Commissioner (and previously the DPR) has been looking at data protection in the context of the Internet for a number of years.

Comments in the DPR's 1995 Annual Report [17.3]

The DPR's first detailed statement on this is probably the one published in her annual report for 1995. Even at that time, her office observed that 'the protection of privacy and information is a key consideration in the development of the information superhighway'.

At that time, the DPR commented on the 'intrinsically insecure nature of the Internet environment' and pointed out that there are:

> '...risks too for individuals who access services on the Internet. Every time you access a service, whether it is to make a contribution to a news group or to make a commercial transaction, you are at risk of leaving an electronic trace which could be used to develop a profile of your personal interests and tastes. And who knows through which countries your data has passed and by whom the data may have been captured in transit?'

The 1995 Annual Report encouraged users to be aware of the risks involved in using an inherently insecure and open system.

Internet E-mail [17.4]

The 1995 Annual Report recommended that data users (now data controllers) should point out the fact that ordinary Internet E-mail is not secure and should draw this to the attention of visitors to their site, if they were otherwise encouraging them to send personal data. Such a clause could be very simple and, if the system in question uses encryption for messages including personal data, may not even be necessary. An example could be:

> 'Please note that this facility to send E-mail is not a secure medium, and should not be used to send confidential/ sensitive information.'

Some such statements go on to say that if a customer wishes to send details of a credit card or financial details, to use a separate secure facility available on the website.

Fairly Obtaining and Processing [17.5]

In 1995, the DPR also reminded data users of their obligations under the First Data Protection Principle, to fairly obtain and fairly process personal data. She said:

> 'If you are collecting personal data on users of a service to which you are providing access over the Internet, it has to be clear to them who is to use the data and what the purposes are for which the data are to be used or disclosed. This may well mean giving notification on the screen. If you are providing access to personal data which you hold, for example by publishing biographical details of your staff, you have to make sure that those individuals understand the global nature of that access. The safe course is to publish only with their consent'.

That advice remains equally valid now.

Comments in the DPR's 1998 Annual Report [17.6]

In her 1998 Annual Report, the DPR looked at two issues:

○ websites relating to the financial services and insurance sectors; and
○ on-line application forms.

Financial Services and Insurance Sectors [17.7]

Given that the financial services and insurance sectors are such big users of technology and, increasingly, are big users of the Internet, the DPR's staff had looked at a small number of websites in the financial services and insurance sectors and, as a result of that survey, found that there was some cause for concern.

The DPR said that in some cases, there were apparently no particular security measures taken to protect an individual's personal data from being intercepted, down loaded and used for other purposes – use of encryption technology (scrambling the data) would be one example of what could have been done to improve the level of security. It is clear, therefore, that the new Seventh Data Protection Principle in *DPA 1998* will be taken seriously.

The DPR pointed out that even basic information such as a name and address is capable of being misused, and that it is usual for more detailed, and potentially sensitive, information to be requested before, for example, an insurance quotation is granted. Clearly, such data could include health details or details of criminal convictions, which would now be subject to the special requirements for the processing of sensitive data (*Schedule 3* of *DPA 1998*) (See further **Chapter 12** and details of *Data Protection (Processing of Sensitive Personal Data) Order 2000 (SI 2000/417)* are given in **Chapter 23** and set out in full in the **Legislation Annex**).

The DPR was disappointed as she felt that it was unusual to see on financial services sites a notification of the uses and disclosures to be made of personal data, but she went on to say that perhaps this 'may be because in the majority of cases the information is only to be used for the obvious purpose, that is, to permit further direct contact by the organisation concerned'. In other words, she was hinting that perhaps the data was being used for non–obvious purposes such as direct marketing.

On-Line Application Forms [17.8]

The other Internet-related area which the DPR mentioned in her 1998 Annual Report is the whole area of on-line applications i.e. job applications, applications for a loan, etc.

The DPR made the point that, traditionally, when you have completed an application form, any data protection wording to protect the consumer is normally at the end of the form, near the signature. This is not a universal approach, but it is a pretty common one. Therefore, if someone decides that they do not want to apply for the product, because of the uses that might be made of their data, then they would simply fail to sign and return the application form.

The difference with the Internet is the fact that when visitors are given advice of the non-obvious uses and disclosures of the personal data at the end of an on-line application form, it may not be adequate. The DPR said that:

'…when information is input on to a form on a website it is immediately capable of being processed as personal data. Notifications of the uses and disclosures of the data should therefore be given at the beginning of the form, so that the individual could decide, on the basis of full information, whether or not to proceed with the transaction'.

At the time, the DPR indicated that her office might be producing some guidance in this area, but nothing has emerged to date.

It is questionable whether the DPR is completely right on this issue. Often, visitors to a website will download the application form onto their own computer's hard drive, completing it on screen (without printing it out) with the result that at that stage, nothing has been submitted to the website of the provider of the form. Only when the visitor transmits the completed form to the website, does the recipient receive the information. However, it is very clear that the DPR was looking closely at such issues.

Article 29 Working Party [17.9]

The role of the Article 29 Working Party has been described at **2.31** above. They have an advisory function, as far as the European Commission and EU Member States are concerned, to opine on matters of importance in data protection matters, but, clearly, given the intellectual fire power and collective experience on that Working Party, although their role is advisory only, their opinions will clearly be given careful consideration.

In February 1999, the Working Party published their views on *Invisible and Automatic Processing of Personal Data on the Internet performed by Software and Hardware*. The introduction to the Working Party's paper encourages the software and hardware industry to work on Internet privacy-compliant products that provide the necessary tools to comply with the European data protection laws. That could mean, perhaps, that tools would be available to anonymise data completely, taking it outside the ambit of the legislation or, alternatively, software would be designed with boxes enabling a potential customer or customers to click on an icon to opt-out of (say) direct marketing.

Invisible Processing [17.10]

The Working Party also noted, with concern, the fact that all kinds of processing operations could be performed by hardware and software on the Internet without the knowledge of the data subject (invisible processing).

They give several examples of invisible processing such as:

○ the 'chattering' at the HTTP level (i.e. this means that they could send data in the HTTP requests which is excessive to the information simply necessary to contact a server – and the person to whom the data relates would not necessarily know this);
○ automatic hyperlinks to third parties (it is possible to put a link in place to someone's website without their permission); and
○ active content on the Internet (like Java, ActiveX or other client based scripting technology).

HTTP is the 'hypertext transfer protocol' (the language in which websites are written). HTTP is the protocol that forms the basis of the World Wide Web, allowing the exchange of multimedia documents on the Web.

Cookies   [17.11]

The other cause for concern is the use of 'cookies' as currently implemented in even the common Internet browsers.

The Working Party is strongly of the opinion that 'secret' information should not be collected using the technologies available for the Internet. Users should be fully informed about the uses of their data. In the case of browser software, the user should be informed, when establishing a connection with a web server (sending a request or receiving a web page) what the information being sent is intended to be used for and where it might be transferred.

In the case of hypertext links sent by a website to a user by whatever means, it would mean that the user's browser should screen the use of all hypertext links to the user and in the case of a 'cookie', the user should be informed when a cookie is intended to be received, stored or sent by the Internet software. The message should specify, in generally understandable language, which information is intended to be stored in the cookie, and for what purpose, as well as the period of validity of the cookie. Cookies are, described at their simplest, a smallish software application sent from a website to the user which would reside on the user's hard drive. The cookie 'wakes up' when the hard drive is powered up and when contact is made with the web site from which it originated, it can send information to that web site. There is clearly a security issue in sending such an item to another organisation.

The Working Party paper also encourages freedom for data subjects as to how their data is used, which might include browser software providing options so that the user could configure the browser. In the case of cookies, this should mean that the user should have the ability to accept or reject the sending or storage of a cookie. The Working Party even recommends that the user should be given options to determine which pieces of information should be kept or removed from a cookie depending on, for example, the period of validity of the cookie or the sending and receiving websites.

Data Matching [17.12]

In summer 1997, the DPR's office produced *A Guide to Developing Data Protection Codes of Practice on Data Matching*. Whilst this Guide was not specifically aimed at the Internet, clearly information collected via the Internet could be matched by data controllers against data collected by other methods. In addition, data collected by different parts of a website for different products could also be matched to build a profile of a visitor.

Admittedly the guide was produced whilst *DPA 1984* was still in force, but it is unlikely that the guidance will change vastly under *DPA 1998*.

The guide tries to define the term 'data matching' as meaning a comparison of data collected by different data users (or by the same data user in different guises/in different contexts) which are put together. The aim of such a comparison is not merely to create a larger file of information about a data subject but significantly, to identify anomalies and inconsistencies and, by pooling the information, to build a larger profile than the case otherwise.

The guide is intended to introduce or encourage the introduction of Codes of Practice to govern the use of these techniques, rather than any legislation or cases before the Data Protection Tribunal.

Jurisdiction [17.13]

Businesses will need to decide whether *DPA 1998* applies to their website or not. Broadly speaking, the conclusions, when considering jurisdiction, would be as follows.

○   If the equipment upon which personal data are being processed by a data controller, where the data has been collected via a website, is located in the UK, then that equipment will be subject to *DPA 1998*. So, for example, data can be collected from a website outside the UK but if that data is transferred to the UK, subsequently, for processing, then *DPA 1998* will apply.

○   If a website is hosted on a server in the UK, then jurisdiction would apply to that website if it processes personal data.

○   If a website is hosted in the UK, even if the data controller is overseas, *DPA 1998* will still apply if the website processes personal data.

○   If a website is hosted on an overseas server, but controlled by a UK data controller, then it is possible that *DPA 1998* might apply. *Section 5(1)* states that it applies to a data controller:
    '...in respect of any data only if:
    (i)   the data controller is established in the United Kingdom and the data are processed in the context of that establishment.'
    So, for example, if the website overseas is hosted by a provider of internet services who acts only on the instructions of the data controller, then they are probably a simple processor, the data controller is the UK entity, and *DPA 1998* will apply. The only proviso to this is that the processing overseas must also be taking place 'in the context of' the UK business' UK establishment.

○   A more difficult issue is if a website is located overseas, but, say, advertises products of a UK company in the same group on part of the website (and the UK company provides text for that section of the website) but the data that is collected by the overseas website is used by other group companies, too.

In those circumstances, a number of companies in the group could potentially be data controllers, as regards the particular website or the information collected from it. *DPA 1998* could apply to any data processed for the UK company to the extent that it is a data controller and that data is processed in the context of its UK establishment – presumably, even if others could also use it. The section talks of it applying to 'a' data controller rather than 'the' data controller.

Practical Issues in Designing Websites [17.14]

Fair Processing of Data [17.15]

As has been seen from **Chapters 11** and **12**, there is an obligation to give notice to data subjects about the uses of their data and, in certain circumstances fulfilling of one of the conditions in *Schedule 2* or *3* depending on whether the personal data is sensitive or not (see **Chapter 11**).

This means that website designers should consider whether or not they need first of all a privacy statement which gives all visitors to the website the information required under *Schedule 1, para 3*.

Notification [17.16]

Schedule I, Part II sets out the notification requirements and these differ depending upon whether or not the data is obtained directly from a data subject. For the purposes of considering websites, it is likely that a large proportion of the data will be collected direct from data subjects. In that case, the notification *must* be given, with no derogation possible from this requirement.

In order to satisfy the notice requirements, the best way forward would be an icon, prominently placed on the home page, which clearly draws the attention of the visitor to the privacy statement and stresses the importance of reading it. This would in all probability be sufficient to show that the website controller has 'made readily available' this information as required by *Schedule 1*. If the visitor does not choose to read the statement, at least the website controller will have discharged its obligation under the Fair Processing Code.

Collecting Personal Data otherwise than from the Data Subject [17.17]

If a website requires a visitor to provide details about third parties, such as members of their family, then the notification requirements are tempered somewhat. For example, the notifications need not be given if that would require a disproportionate effort on the part of the data controller (see generally **Chapter 11**).

Clearly, in the case of information collected about a third party, once that information is collected and used by a data controller, the third party becomes a data subject, as regards that data controller. Whilst it is of course possible to have a purpose statement on the website, this will only be relevant for visitors. Third parties whose personal data may be held may never visit the site and, therefore, other steps will need to be taken if they are to be notified.

The factor of 'disproportionate effort' (see **5.11**) needs to be looked at. In the case of information collected to a website, it may, indeed, be impossible to notify the third party, because all the website controller has to go on is an E-mail address of the provider of the information.

On the other hand, the data subject who is directly inputting their own information may also be filling out an application form which includes information about a third party – e.g. an application for a second credit card for a spouse.

Even if asked to do so, it would be pretty difficult to verify whether or not two separate entities have entered their own details unless some sort of digital signatures system is adopted the provision of which might amount to disproportionate effort for data controllers, in itself.

The alternative might be for the data controller, at least to require the data subject, by contract, to warrant and undertake that it has obtained or will obtain any appropriate consents or has given or will give all appropriate notifications to third parties mentioned in the application and/or the data controller should pass a second copy of, say, the relevant insurance cover note/policy wording, with a request that it be passed to the other insured parties. None of these solutions are particularly satisfactory, but they must all be possibilities.

The issue is addressed, in part, by *Data Protection (Conditions Under Paragraph 3 of Part II of Schedule 1) Order 2000 (SI 2000/185)*. When data is obtained about a third party, not directly from that third party, the notification required under *para 2(1)(b)* does not apply where there is a disproportionate effort and any other conditions imposed by the Secretary of State apply. In cases where disproportionate effort may apply, and to disapply the notification requirement in *Schedule 1, Part II, para 2(1)(b)*, requires that the data controller must record the reasons for the view that they believe that it would be a disproportionate effort so that they could show this to the Commissioner if necessary. This is an important point to remember and appropriate records should be kept when such decisions are made.

The more formal the contact with the data subject who is providing information on third parties, (where the data controller could impose obligations to notify e.g. in a contract) it is likely that the more onus there is on the data controller to try and do something with a view to notifying the third party.

Other Considerations in Relation to Notification [17.18]

The particular notification requirement which is going to have an impact in the context of the Internet is the requirement set out in *Schedule 1, Part II, para (3)(d)* which provides that subjects must be given:

'Any further information which is necessary, having regard to the specific circumstances in which the data are or are to be processed, to enable processing in respect of the data subject to be fair.'

In the Internet context, two examples spring to mind. Firstly, where personal data about the data subject may be transferred to a country outside the EEA. In such a case, the Commissioner's Office has advised that a notification ought to be given that an individual's data may be transferred to such jurisdiction. This is a relevant factor for them to know before deciding whether they wish to give the data. Clearly, given the global nature of the Internet, it may increasingly be the case that data may be transferred in this way. Secondly, visitors to a website should be told where cookies are used (for a description of these see **17.11** above).

Privacy Policies [17.19]

There are a number of privacy organisations emerging, primarily US driven, such as BBB-On Line, the On-Line Privacy Alliance, and TRUSTe. The last of these is now setting up in Europe, to be based in Denmark initially. These bodies aim to encourage controllers of websites to introduce public, transparent and fair procedures in relation to the processing of data collected by their websites. More and more businesses are contemplating joining such groups, and complying with their rules, to show to the public that they respect their privacy.

Various of these organisations require businesses to put in place a privacy policy which explains to consumers the uses to which their data are put. The rules of some of these organisations also, for example:

O   provide that consumers should be offered choice (whether they wish their data to be used for certain purposes (with an ability to opt out); and

O   require data controllers to keep information up-to-date, and impose similar good practices.

This is particularly interesting, in the light of the current debate between the EU and the US, because in fact many US companies voluntarily adopt very far reaching private policies and honour them, notwithstanding there is no Federal or State privacy law requiring them to do so.

EEA businesses may think that since they have to honour the *Directive* in any event, privacy organisations such as those described above are unnecessary. However, they certainly seem to have a value because, for example, TRUSTe even has a privacy 'wizard' on its website which enables businesses to build a specimen privacy policy without commitment and without becoming a (paying) licensee of TRUSTe (which carries with it certain obligations such as the management of your website and a requirement of an independent audit of privacy practices before being accepted as a licensee).

Many of the notification requirements of the *Directive* and *DPA 1998* can be, in fact, met to a large degree by some of the questions asked in building a privacy policy using the TRUSTe privacy wizard.

These groups place great store by the clear notification of visitors to websites about the uses of their data. TRUSTe, for example, has some draft wording one can adopt about the use of cookies and how they work. Given previous comments about the concept of fair processing of data in the UK, the approach of these organisations could be appropriate for European companies as well.

It is also worth noting that the OECD (the Organisation for Economic Cooperation and Development) has also created a privacy policy generator (http://www.oecd.org/dsti/sti) as have Microsoft with the Electronic Frontiers Foundation (http://privacy.linkexchange.com).

Consent in Cyberspace [17.20]

The issue in cyberspace, in regard to when consent to process and/or transfer personal data is needed, is how consent is manifested when the person you are dealing with is not physically present and cannot 'sign' a consent form in the traditional sense.

Consent maybe required from a data subject:

○   as one of the possible conditions to satisfy to justify processing of a data subject's personal data;
○   in regard to sensitive personal data since, consent is quite likely, particularly in the context of a website, to be the only condition that can be satisfied to enable the processing of such data under *Schedule 3*; and
○   where it is the only condition that can be satisfied under *Schedule 4* to enable the export of data to a country outside the EEA which does not provide adequate protection for personal data.

Obtaining Consent [17.21]

There are various ways in which consent could be obtained.

Wording could be included in the privacy policy that says something along the lines 'by visiting this website, you are consenting the use of your data for the above purposes'. This has certain drawbacks, for example, how can a data controller be sure that the data subject has actually viewed the privacy policy and a lot will therefore depend on how the privacy policy is brought to the individual's attention in the first place. There could well be situations, unless it is mandatory to view the privacy policy, where this will not be an adequate consent because visitors may not actually read the privacy statement.

At the time personal data is collected from a data subject, or prospective data subject, businesses may use some sort of registration procedure which should include a clear reminder to the data subject of the existence of the privacy policy and provide for that privacy policy to be accepted and consent given to the stated uses of the data (which should, if appropriate, include a notification of the fact that the data may be transferred outside the EEA to a country which may not provide adequate protection for personal data).

At the stage where personal data is collected from individuals, the privacy policy should be repeated (or at least the section of it regarding the purposes for which the data are going to be used and, in the light of that statement, visitors to the website should expressly give consent by clicking on some sort of 'I accept' or 'I consent' icon with appropriate consent wording on the website as well. Such a consent icon should certainly be adequate for consent under *Schedule 2*, to the extent that the processing in question is not permitted by the satisfaction of one of the other conditions in *Schedule 2* (such as the processing being necessary for the performance of a contract to which the data subject is a party).

Sensitive Data [17.22]

For sensitive data, the question of consent is perhaps more difficult, because it has to be 'explicit'. Consent is not defined in *DPA 1998* but it is defined in the *Directive* as being any:

> '...freely given specific and informed indication of his wishes by which the data subject signifies his agreement to the personal data relating to him being processed'.

One does not see why a 'click consent' is not enough for the purposes of 'explicit consent' under *Schedule 3*, as long as the data subject is fully informed about the uses of that data.

18 – Direct Marketing

Introduction [18.1]

A survey in July 1999 commissioned by the DPR revealed that 86% of the population are concerned that direct marketers may purchase a copy of the electoral register for their mailing purposes.

The survey also revealed that 70% of those interviewed do not want to receive unsolicited marketing calls and faxes. The Telephone Preference Service and the Fax Preference Service, which enable individuals to opt-out of direct marketing using those methods, now have statutory force (for further information tel: 020 7766 4410).

The DPR said in the survey results:

> 'the majority of people find unsolicited marketing faxes a nuisance but they do not know how to stop them. The opt-out registers run by the Director General of OFTEL provide this service and, as Registrar, I will use my enforcement powers to ensure business uses them.'

Clearly, direct marketing is a 'hot' data protection topic. This Chapter looks first at the position as it was under *DPA 1984* in relation to direct marketing and then as it currently is under *DPA 1998*.

Position under DPA 1984 [18.2]

The DPR produced a paper on the issue of direct marketing which is, perhaps, a little long in the tooth, given that it was produced in 1995, but it is still a useful indication of the attitude of the DPR to direct marketing under *DPA 1984* and, in all probability, the attitude to a number of aspects of fair processing under *DPA 1998* insofar as they relate to direct marketing.

It is particularly useful because it contains some examples of hypothetical situations with the DPR's view as to whether or not what a company wished to do in the hypothetical was feasible within the then current data protection regime. It is quite possible that much of this will remain valid (or useful at least) under *DPA 1998*. Copies may still be available from the Commissioner's Office.

Position Under DPA 1998 [18.3]

The requirements for collecting personal data for marketing purposes are substantially the same as under *DPA 1984*, although the requirements are now more detailed. It is also important to be aware of the provisions of the new regulations on direct marketing by fax and by telephone (see **Chapter 22**).

Section 4 requires all data controllers to comply with the Data Protection Principles, which are an expanded version of those in *DPA 1984*. However, there are now a number of specific conditions attaching to the processing of any personal data (*Schedule 2* − see **12.1**) and there are additional conditions attaching to the processing of sensitive personal data (*Schedule 3* − see **12.3**).

In practice it is very likely that the main condition in *Schedule 2* and the only condition in *Schedule 3* which is definitely applicable to direct marketing is that the data subject has given their consent or, in the case of sensitive data, their explicit consent to the processing.

The *Directive* requires consent to be 'unambiguously' given which suggests that the data subject has to be given enough information to understand what processing is envisaged. There is nothing to suggest that consent cannot be oral or even implied, nor is there any indication that it would no longer be enough simply to offer an opt-out (although perhaps a literal interpretation of the *Directive* might suggest that an opt-in is more appropriate).

The argument is that, on an application form, for example, if you give someone a simple and clear way to say no to direct marketing, such as simply ticking a box on a form which they are going to send back anyway, then if they choose not to tick the box this is an implied consent to direct marketing. Businesses could probably make it a condition − a very clear one accompanied by a very clear purpose statement which extends to explaining all uses of the relevant data for marketing purposes − that, if the data subject chooses, having read the purpose statement, to proceed with entering into a contract or visiting a website, this act will constitute a consent by conduct. The user always has the option not to proceed. Initial discussions with the Commissioner's office have suggested that these approaches would comply with the consent requirement.

For direct marketers the new interpretation of fair processing is particularly important. The provisions are fairly complex but in essence the interpretation provides that processing would be deemed to be unfair unless certain information is given to the individual when the data is obtained, and where the data is obtained from a third party, that information has to be provided (broadly speaking) as soon as reasonably practicable after it is obtained. So where a company buys or rents a mailing list, it should give the prescribed information to all individuals on that list in a timely fashion. Maybe the practical solution is, on the first mailing to those on the new mailing list, to give them a very clear opt out from marketing by the purchaser of that mailing list − maybe accompanied by a prepaid envelope and/or a freephone telephone number.

These provisions do not apply (by virtue of *Schedule 1, para 3(2)*), in relation to data on data subjects where the data have been collected *from third parties* and where giving the information would require 'disproportionate effort' or any conditions set by the Secretary of State are met or where the information has to be recorded by the data controller to comply with any legal obligation to which the data controller is subject, other than an obligation imposed by contract.

Right to Prevent Processing for Purposes of Direct Marketing [18.4]

Section 11 incorporates an important new right, namely the right for the individual at any time by way of written notice to a data controller to ask it to cease (within a reasonable time) or not to begin, processing, for the purposes of direct marketing of personal data in respect of which they are the data subject.

For the purposes of this section, 'direct marketing' means:

> 'the communication (by whatever means) of any advertising or marketing material which is directed to particular individuals'.

This wording goes considerably further than the wording of *DPA 1984* and is required by virtue of the *Directive* although it is very close to the practices that had emerged under *DPA 1984*. In fact, the Commissioner has said that *section 11* adds nothing to the 'fair obtaining' obligation under the First Data Protection Principle of *DPA 1984* – but perhaps that is a slight exaggeration.

It would appear that this right is exercisable at any time, even if there is a prior consent to direct marketing in place. This differs from *section 10* (right to prevent processing likely to cause damage or distress) where, if there is a prior consent in place, the prior consent appears to prevail. Direct marketing organisations and, indeed, all businesses that adopt direct marketing techniques, must be aware of this and realise they cannot assume that, once a consent to marketing is in place, it overrides a subsequent request under *section 11*. Direct marketers also have to be aware of the possibility that individuals, (and in some cases companies), have rights to opt-out of unsolicited faxes or phone calls for direct marketing purposes (see **Chapter 22**).

Implications [18.5]

The fact that individuals can call for their data to be blocked for direct marketing purposes, may have certain implications e.g. the design of computer databases (see **Chapter 16**). Companies will need to be satisfied they can suppress this data in their databases, if necessary. Thankfully, many companies which use direct marketing techniques already give data subjects the ability to opt out of direct marketing, so are already able to suppress data in this way for those who opt-out.

However, it may be necessary, in the light of the new opt-out provisions in relation to unsolicited marketing calls by telephone and fax, to redesign databases to be able to suppress marketing by these various different methods, rather than to impose in a database a general suppression for mailing. There is also discussion at European level, of creating an opt out for individuals from junk E-mail in the future. This is currently embodied in *Article 7(2)* of the draft *Electronic Commerce Directive* which states:

> 'Without prejudice to Directive 97/7/EC and Directive 97/66/EC, Member States shall take measures to ensure that service providers undertaking unsolicited commercial communications by e-mail consult regularly and respect the opt-out registers in which natural persons not wishing to receive such commercial communications can register themselves.'

Data Protection Principles [18.6]

The requirements for collecting personal data for marketing purposes are substantially the same as arose relating to *DPA 1984* although the requirements are now more detailed. Also, the requirements are now spelt out in *DPA 1998* itself, as opposed to in written guidance from the DPR or in decisions of the Data Protection Tribunal.

Fair Processing [18.7]

One of the other aspects of fair obtaining, which direct marketers will have to bear in mind is the fact that they are now required to comply with the Fair Processing Code (see **Chapter 11**).

For direct marketers the new interpretation of fair processing is particularly important. The provisions are fairly complex but in essence the interpretation provides that processing will be deemed to be unfair unless certain information is given to the individual when the data is obtained, and where the data is obtained from a third party, that information has to be provided as soon as reasonably practicable after it is obtained or if, when obtained, it was intended that those data were going to be disclosed to a third party, on or as soon as practicable thereafter. So where a company buys or rents a mailing list, it may have to give the prescribed information to all individuals on that list almost immediately.

Is Consent to Direct Marketing Required? [18.8]

As has been explained elsewhere in this book (see **Chapters 11** and **12**) there are now a number of specific conditions attaching to the processing of any personal data (*Schedule 2*) and there are additional conditions attaching to the processing of sensitive personal data (*Schedule 3*).

Schedule 2 [18.9]

In the case of *Schedule 2*, the only conditions likely to be applicable to direct marketing are consent or perhaps *para 6(1)* which applies where the processing is:

'necessary for the purposes of legitimate interests pursued by the data controller or by the third party or parties to whom the data are disclosed, except where the processing is unwarranted in any particular case by reason of prejudice to the rights and freedoms or legitimate interests of the data subject'.

It may be possible to argue that direct marketing falls within this provision rather than having to obtain consent, perhaps supported by the fact that data subjects now have the right to opt-out of direct marketing at any time. However, the current practice of using clear opt-out boxes for direct marketing is, in reality a form of implied consent, so the existing practice already goes beyond mere notification.

Many companies are now switching to opting-in for direct marketing.

Customer Profiling [18.10]

Customer profiling – using items of information from a number of sources to build an overall picture – is becoming increasingly common, particularly in the direct marketing industry. However the core principle to bear in mind, in considering whether one can build a profile in this way is the First Data Protection Principle. It is crucial that data is obtained fairly before it can be used for profiling. This will require compliance with the Fair Processing Code (see **Chapter 11**). This could mean making it clear the purpose for which the data is collected and particularly any non-obvious purposes, including profiling; that a profile will be built and using what sources.

Whilst the Commissioner's office has indicated that purpose statements should be reasonably full, there is also a suggestion, in the Commissioner's *Introduction*, that purpose statements need not include statements of the glaringly obvious, but must include details of non obvious uses/purposes.

Data Matching [18.11]

There is a degree of unease as far as the Commissioner's current views go, in relation to data matching. This involves matching information from different databases, perhaps collected at different times and for different purposes (and perhaps even by different companies in the same group), to build a profile.

In summer 1997, the DPR's office produced a document entitled *Guide to Developing Data Protection Codes of Practice on Data Matching*. Some of the concepts in that Guide will continue to be relevant to direct marketers using various different sources of data to build customer profiles, notwithstanding that it was written under *DPA 1984*.

International Matters   [18.12]

Those in the direct marketing area need to keep in touch with European developments. For example, the Opinion Number 1/2000 of the Article 29 Working Party expresses opinions about the use of E-mail for marketing (and spamming – unsolicited commercial E-mails) and makes recommendations about data collection in the context of web sites.

It also discusses the pro's and con's of opting-in and opting-out. The direct marketing industry needs to keep abreast of the Working Party's efforts and to respond if it is felt that their approach is over-zealous. The Working Party intends to produce recommendations in the future regarding 'technical measures related to spamming' and the 'validation of web sites according to a common European checklist based on the data protection directives'.

Clearly, the Working Party's opinions will have a persuasive effect on the European Commission and the Article 31 Committee.

Other Data Protection Legislation Affecting Direct Marketing   [18.13]

DPA 1998 is not the only legislation to consider in relation to direct marketing and data protection.

Chapter 23 expands on the new secondary legislation (which implements most of the Data Protection in Telecommunications Directive in relation to direct marketing by fax and phone. The new legislation creates new opt-out registers in relation to direct marketing by fax and phone and it is unlawful to call any number that has been registered under the Preference Schemes for more than 28 days. The Commissioner has been given the power to enforce this legislation.

Practical Pointers [18.14]

DPA 1998 will require direct marketers, at the very least, to re-visit the way that they currently use data for direct marketing purposes and, at worse, they will have to revise their procedures. Some issues to consider are detailed below.

✓ Those the organisation writes to must be given purpose statements. These must include the fact that data can be used for direct marketing. This was already the position under *DPA 1984*.

✓ It would appear that a very clear and easily effected opt-out for direct marketing will still satisfy the requirements of *DPA 1998*, according to the Commissioner Office.

✓ It is quite likely that, to process data for direct marketing purposes, consent may be required, unless it can be argued that, applying the 'balancing test' set out *Schedule 2, para 6(1)*, the use of data for direct marketing would be permitted. It is unlikely that *DPA 1998* would be interpreted more liberally than *DPA 1984* so consideration should be given at least to putting an opt-opt box into literature but also perhaps consider including an express consent provision instead.

✓ If any of the data being collected is sensitive, it is reasonably certain that to use that data in a direct marketing context 'explicit' consent will be required and direct marketers will need to consider this.

✓ In the light of the provisions in the direct marketing regulations permitting opting-out, (in addition to the right to opt out of direct marketing in *section 11* – see **18.4** above), in relation to the use of the telephone and fax for direct marketing to consumers, it may well be that databases may need to be set up in a more sophisticated way, to contemplate the possibility that a customer might be happy to receive direct mailing but would not wish to receive junk faxes.

✓ Since there is the possibility that customers may want to opt-out of some but not all methods of direct marketing, opt-out boxes could/should become more sophisticated or, alternatively, one must ensure that any consent obtained is not merely a consent to direct marketing by mail but also by other media.

19 – Employment

Introduction [19.1]

Data protection has far reaching implications for human resources departments in many areas. This Chapter looks at a few general issues relating to employment and data protection as well as focusing on the:

- difficulty of finding out about employees' criminal records;
- regulation of the recording of telephone calls; and
- rules surrounding the storing of personal information about employees.

New Employees [19.2]

From now on, the procedures for the recruitment of all new employees should contemplate compliance with *DPA 1998* in full. This is notwithstanding the fact that those provisions may not be necessary as yet, for some existing employees, given the transitional provisions in *DPA 1998*. However, it must be prudent to try and adopt the new provisions of *DPA 1998* for new employees as soon as possible. Otherwise, businesses will merely be postponing the inevitable so that, at the relevant future time, all employees employed prior to 24 October 1998 and all employees recruited since that date but before 24 October 2001 (if the transitional relief applies) will still have to be notified in the future. Surely, it makes sense to minimise the number of future notifications and start putting systems in place now.

Notification [19.3]

All existing employees will have to be given a purpose statement, at some stage, and (assuming that a company could satisfy itself that its existing databases already had processing under way at 24 October 1998), employers will have to decide what future notifications need to be given to comply with *DPA 1998*.

Uses of Data [19.4]

Employers will have to get to grips with their obligations to notify their employees about the uses of their data (although hopefully this is not too onerous, because many employers already make this sort of data available. They will have to notify:

O   their identity (a must in the context of their employment relationship); and

O   any other information about the processing necessary to make it fair to the particular individual in question (e.g. where the data maybe exported outside the EEA to a country which may not provide adequate protection for personal data).

Data Obtained from Third Parties [19.5]

There is a provision that, where personal data are obtained from a third party, notification need not be made if this would involve 'disproportionate effort'. This might include where an employee provides details of next of kin in case of accidents and this is kept on their employment file. Employers will need to consider if that person should be notified.

In the case of employee data, in any event, most of the data will have been obtained direct from the data subject, so any relaxation of the obligation to give notice is not applicable.

Employees may, in their capacity as holders of a pension or of personal health insurance, for example, provide data about their family. If so, as regards the family members, the obligation to inform need not be complied with if this might constitute a disproportionate effort (see **5.11** above).

Employers must look at all third parties about whom they hold data and consider whether notification is practicable.

Employees' Rights and Obligations [19.6]

How an organisation goes about notifying employees of their rights and obligations under *DPA 1998* will vary from case to case. For any organisation which takes on new employees, any new consents required to comply with *DPA 1998* can be included in their employment contract at the time of the appointment. Any notifications can be given at that time too, so that no employee could argue that they have been employed under any false premise. Notification could be in the employment contract or in a separate notice or in a staff manual, provided it is stressed that the staff manual should be read by all employees because it contains important information about the employer's relationship in the firm.

For existing employees, it is clear that the notification provisions need to be complied with, although perhaps the current view appears to be that only the non obvious uses of data need to be notified. Employees should, if there is any doubt, be required to sign a consent to the uses of their data for purposes expressly given to them. The consent requirements of *DPA 1998* must also be followed, as appropriate, which may mean sending a notification and consent form to them all.

Consent [19.7]

In addition to the notification requirements under *DPA 1998*, there are also obligations to obtain consent in certain circumstances, possibly under *Schedule 2* (where the data are not sensitive) and also under *Schedule 3*, if the data are sensitive).

It is almost certain that employee files will contain sensitive data (e.g. details of when and why an employee was off sick and trade union membership etc.). The much more rigorous 'explicit' consent requirements of *Schedule 3* will need to be complied with as regards such data.

It is important to note that there is a narrow condition in *Schedule 3, para 9* which has been drafted in the light of the fact that certain information which may be held by an employer is maybe held by it in connection with its compliance with employment law.

Schedule 3, para 9(1), provides that consent is not required where the processing of personal data:

'(a) is of sensitive personal data consisting of information as to racial or ethnic origin,

(b) is necessary for the purpose of identifying or keeping under review the existence or absence of equality of opportunity or treatment between persons of different racial or ethnic origins, with a view to enabling such equality to be promoted or maintained' and

(c) is carried out with appropriate safeguards for the rights and freedoms of data subjects.'

In the above case, employers can monitor their compliance with various statutes which prohibit discrimination of any kind, without being required to obtain the data subject's consent.

Prospective Employees   [19.8]

Employers also need to consider what they say to applicants for jobs. As a result of an application, data subjects will provide employers with information about themselves, even if they are not ultimately interviewed or offered a job. Therefore, application forms will need to contain a statement of purposes to which the information on the form may be put (even if there is a wider and subsequent purpose statement delivered to employees if and when they start work). The processing of the preliminary data on the application form needs to be carried out lawfully.

Any notification should also include a statement regarding any non-obvious uses of that data. If the employer, for example, will hold on to an application form and the accompanying CV, even if the applicant is not even interviewed, then perhaps the applicants should know this.

If details about applicants may be shared around group companies, this should also be notified, particularly if they are outside the EEA.

Finally, it is very likely job applicants will provide data which may be sensitive and, therefore, it is recommended that any application forms should include clear wording by which the applicant consents to the uses of their data and signs the application form accordingly. If this is done in an internet context, there needs to be a clear act showing their agreement (e.g. clicking on a clearly designated icon against a notification of the prospective employer's purposes and a statement that clicking on the icon will constitute consent).

References   [19.9]

One area of concern is the rather unclear situation of the law in relation to employment (and other) references under *Schedule 7*. It is suggested that there are no hard and fast rules, as yet, to cover this sort of processing and that a lot of guidance will be needed from the Commissioner's Office on this point.

As was seen at **7.17**, the exemption from subject access in relation to references only applies to references given by a data controller which is still on the data controller's file and the subject of the reference attempts to have access to it.

The exemption does not apply to references given to the data controller by, say, a previous employer.

Information Relates to Another Individual [19.10]

Section 7(4) states that where a data controller cannot comply with a subject access request without disclosing information relating to another individual who can be identified from that information, he is not obliged to comply with the request unless:

○   the other individual has consented to a disclosure; or
○   it is reasonable in all the circumstances to comply with the request without the consent of the other individual.

Information Identifies Another Individual as the

Source [19.11]

Where a reference to information relating to another individual includes a reference to information identifying that individual as the source of the information sought by the request, it could be argued that the identity of a referee cannot be revealed since that would mean disclosing information about another individual.

However, on the assumption that the referee has not consented to the disclosure, the employer faced with the subject access request has to decide whether or not it should comply without the consent of the referee.

If it would mean disclosing the identity of the individual who has given the reference, then it may not be necessary to disclose the reference but *section 7(5)* goes on to say that this:

'...is not to be construed as excusing a data controller from communicating so much of the information sought by the request as can be communicated without disclosing the identity of the other individual concerned, whether by the omission of names or other identifying particulars or otherwise'.

So, for example, one might have to reveal an incoming reference provided that the writer's reference on the letter is deleted and also the name of the person giving the reference.

Guidance [19.12]

Section 7(6) seeks to give some assistance as to how data controllers can decide whether it is reasonable in all the circumstances to comply with the request to disclose a reference without the consent of the other individual concerned and regard will be had, in particular, to:

'(a) any duty of confidentiality owed to the other individual,
(b) any steps taken by the data controller with a view to seeking the consent of the other individual,
(c) whether the other individual is capable of giving consent, and
(d) any express refusal of consent by the other individual.'

Considerations [19.13]

All this put together suggests that most businesses will need to rethink their current procedures on taking references if it was their intention to hold such references but not to disclose them to data subjects because, say, they are marked as confidential or in asking for the reference the (then prospective) employer had said that the reference would be held in confidence. To protect themselves, the obvious thing would be, in the letter requesting a reference, to state that, in giving the reference, the referee is consenting to any future disclosure of the reference to the data subject, if the new employer is asked for subject access. Alternatively, this could perhaps say that it may be disclosed if the new employer is required by law to do so.

If a referee would object strongly to a reference that they have intended only to give in confidence being disclosed, then the giver of the reference could expressly state that they do not consent to its disclosure in the reference itself (relevant under *section 7(6)(d)* above). This is, again, a relevant fact to take into account, as would be the fact that an incoming reference is marked as 'confidential', because the confidential nature of information is also one of the factors to consider (*section 7(6)(a)* above).

The fact remains that this particular situation is unsatisfactory.

Businesses need to ask themselves why references are hold on the file. If somebody is taken on, then it is assumed that the reference was probably not adverse. Employers should consider, in some situations, simply saying on the file that a satisfactory reference was, or was not, received, and then there is really no need to hold the reference on the file.

If somebody is taken on, subject to references, and a reference is received that he or she is not very good, then that is a likely situation where an employee whose employment is not continued would wish to see the reference.

The approach of simply putting on record that a reference was satisfactory (and destroying the original) will not work in some industries such as parts of the financial services industry, where references on certain members of staff, particularly if they are recognised by certain regulatory bodies, must be kept.

It is worth remembering, that if a disclosure is made in breach of a duty of confidence, then that breach could be actionable against the person making the disclosure unless that disclosure is required by operation of law. The concern for data controllers here is that they are left in a difficult position as to whether they can say the disclosure is required by law, particularly when there is a level of discretion, seemingly, introduced by *section 7*.

Criminal Records [19.14]

Every employer will be concerned to know about prospective employees' backgrounds and many employers are particularly concerned to check whether job applicants have a criminal record. This is particularly important in certain industries.

Here the position as it was under *DPA 1984* and the position as it is under *DPA 1998* are examined.

Position under DPA 1984 [19.15]

Under *DPA 1984*, an individual could apply for a copy of information held about them on police computerised records. This included the individual's criminal record where it is computerised. However, the access of prospective employers to an individual's criminal record is severely limited and tightly regulated – criminal record checks are only available to certain employers. This led a number of employers to require job applicants to use their right of access under *DPA 1984* to obtain their criminal records and to pass these on to their prospective employer. This practice is known as 'enforced subject access'.

Enforced subject access under *DPA 1984* was not, of itself, unlawful. However, it has been strongly criticised in the past as being an abuse of an individual's rights. It also undermines *Rehabilitation of Offenders Act 1974 (ROA 1974)*.

ROA 1974 allows some criminal convictions to become 'spent' after a certain period. It is unlawful for an employer to ask about spent convictions or to let the fact that a job applicant or employee has a spent conviction influence them in their decision to employ or to continue to employ the individual. If a candidate with a spent conviction is asked about their criminal record, *ROA 1974* entitles them to assume that the question does not relate to spent convictions.

Furthermore, if an employer makes it a condition of employment that prospective employees provide a written statement of any past criminal record, it must be taken as read that that condition does not require the inclusion of any spent convictions in the statement.

Since police records do not normally distinguish between spent and unspent convictions, the risk with enforced subject access is that the employer will (perhaps unwittingly) commit an unlawful act by taking into account a conviction disclosed on an individual's criminal record when it is in fact spent.

By contrast, an employer was free to ask about unspent convictions and to choose not to employ an applicant on account of any unspent conviction they may have. However, it is important to note that candidates are not under a duty to volunteer information about unspent convictions.

Position under DPA 1998 [19.16]

Now that *DPA 1998* has come into force, an individual's criminal record will be regarded as 'sensitive personal data'. *DPA 1998* makes it clear that, in general, sensitive personal data can only be processed by an employer with the employee's 'explicit consent'. This is likely to mean an informed and possibly written consent (the highest level of consent *DPA 1998* can require) and employers should, therefore, consider including appropriate wording in their application forms.

More importantly, *section 56* (which is not yet in force) will make it an offence for an employer to require the data subject to produce their criminal record. Therefore, it will still be legitimate for a potential employer to ask a job applicant for details of their criminal record but it will be a criminal offence for the employer to require provision of that information through the individual's right (as a data subject) to access their criminal record. *Section 56* even extends to cover a statement from the police that an individual has no criminal record.

Furthermore, *section 57* will mean that any term or condition of a contract will be void if it requires an individual to provide a copy of their criminal record to a prospective employer.

The only exception to this is where the employer can show that their requirement that the individual obtain and disclose a copy of his criminal record is:

O   required or authorised by law (or a court order); or
O   that in the particular circumstances the imposition of the requirement is justified as being in the public interest.

Unfortunately for employers, *DPA 1998* makes it quite clear that an employer's requirement that the individual disclose his criminal record (or a criminal record certificate under *Police Act 1997* when it comes into force) is not to be regarded as justified as being in the public interest on the grounds that it would assist in the prevention or detection of crime.

Part V of *Police Act 1997* will eventually introduce a new regime in respect of criminal records, but this is unlikely to greatly help employers. The new criminal convictions certificates will only be made available to the individual in question. The more detailed criminal record certificate may be made available directly to an employer but only if that employer is a registered person. In order to be registered, employers will have to apply for inclusion and satisfy the Secretary of State that they are likely to recruit to one of the jobs or professions excluded from *ROA 1974* (e.g. accountants, police, prison service workers, those in certain social services).

The final grade of certificate, the enhanced criminal record certificate, will also only be issued to a registered person (and then only in special circumstances) and will include all the information on a criminal record certificate together with, for example, information on failed prosecutions.

Recording Telephone Calls and E-mails [19.17]

An employer may wish to record some of their employees' telephone calls for a variety of wholly legitimate reasons. These include performance assessment, quality control and fraud prevention. There are, however, certain restrictions on the freedom of employers to do this. This is a fast developing area of the law and there appear to be at least three different legislative threads:

O   telecommunications law;
O   data protection; and
O   human rights.

Telecommunications Law [19.18]

Telecommunications Act 1984 and its subordinate Regulations govern telecommunications apparatus. In essence, the recording of calls is permitted under telecommunications 'class licences' provided that the licensees make every reasonable effort to inform the parties to a telephone call before recording, silent monitoring or intruding into that call i.e. the employer needs to notify both parties to the call, the caller and the called.

In practice, this is best achieved by notification on letterheads, fax frontsheets, advertising, purchase orders or invoices, or any general literature which the employer sends to those with whom he deals. As far as its own employees are concerned, an employer should notify employees by (for example) a note to all his staff or by an amendment to the staff handbook (which should be notified to all the employees in any case where their calls may be recorded). For potential employees, notification might be set out in a 'starter pack' or perhaps included in all new contracts of employment.

Data Protection Legislation [19.19]

The class licences do not require that a purpose for the recording or monitoring of calls be notified, although previous regulations in this area did require this. It is, however, best to do so and indeed, if tapes of telephone conversations falls within the definition of personal data under *DPA 1998* and the information is then processed by an automated system, there will be a requirement to notify the individuals to whom that data relates of the purposes of the processing, in any event. Now *DPA 1998* is in force, this notification requirement will also apply to certain manual records (if the transitional provisions in *Schedule 8* do not apply) which have, for example, been transcribed from taped telephone calls. Employees' E-mails may also be personal data, in which case they will also be subject to the data protection rules.

The situation will become more complicated when the provisions on recording and monitoring calls under *European Telecoms Data Protection Directive* are brought into force as required by October 2000. This will require Member States to ensure (by appropriate regulations) that communications by means of public telecommunications networks are confidential, and it specifically requires Member States to prohibit listening, taping, storage or other kinds of interception or surveillance of communications without the consent of the users concerned. Furthermore, consent is required from both users, i.e. both parties to the call.

The *Telecoms Data Protection Directive* is subject to an exemption that recording is permitted without consent where it is to tape commercial transactions for business purposes. However, many employers who make use of call centres or telephone marketing monitor the calls as part of staff training, or to assess the quality of staff performance. The exemptions to the *Telecoms Data Protection Directive* will not apply in these cases and consent from both users would therefore be required. This clearly has significant practical implications and consultation has taken place regarding implementation. This area is now addressed in the draft Regulation of Investigatory Powers Bill, Clause 4, which is currently before Parliament.

Human Rights [19.20]

On the human rights front there has been publicity surrounding both the recent European Court of Human Rights case, *Halford v UK*, which established that the interception of a person's office telephone without their consent can constitute an interference with the right to respect for private life established under *Article 8* of the *Convention on Human Rights*, and the implementation of the Convention in the UK (*Human*

Rights Act 1998) which will come into force in October 2000. As a result, OFTEL has, at the request of the Home Office, published new guidance on recording phone calls which it has based on guidance produced by the Home Office for public bodies such as the police.

In order to avoid being in breach of the Convention, OFTEL recommends that companies which routinely record their employees' calls must ensure that their employees are aware of this and they must be given the facility to make unrecorded personal calls if they wish to do so. Strictly speaking, the *Human Rights Act 1998* does not directly apply to non-public bodies but, since the Courts are a public body they will have to consider human rights principles in their decisions – recommendations like this could well, in due course, accurately reflect the way that privacy law is developing.

The Commissioner has already commissioned a study from the Personnel Policy Research Unit (produced in January 1999) on the question of interception/monitoring of employee communications which contains various conclusions and some comments on access to employee E-mails. The study is available from the Commissioner's website.

The Commissioner's Office is going to produce some guidelines soon, drawing on the findings of the above study, on employers' access to employee E-mails which is an area of particular concern. The Commissioner's Office are indicating that this will be produced in September 2000. Similar principles of fairness apply in the context of the interception of E-mails generally in a company's system (i.e. not on the public network) which may in some circumstances breach the fair processing code.

Details of Third Parties held on Human Resources

Databases [19.21]

Almost all employers will hold a wide variety of personal information about their employees on databases. Furthermore, employers are also likely to hold personal information in various manual records.

The subject access application form on which this personal information is requested from and submitted by employees should make quite clear all the purposes for which the information is required (for example, the administration of the employment relationship between the employer and the individual). The form should also consider requesting the employee's consent to the processing by his employer of personal data about him for the purposes set out in the form. It is very likely that the data held in an employee context will include sensitive personal data, so explicit consent to process that data is likely to be required. There is, however, a common difficulty. Most employers will require details of an employee's next of kin (for example for the purposes of private health insurance) or emergency contact details. This information will very often constitute 'personal data' about third parties to the employment relationship, and it is therefore highly likely that the third parties will be data subjects in their own right. They will, therefore, enjoy the protection of *DPA 1998* for both manual and computerised records.

Third party data subjects should be notified of the purposes for which personal data about them will be processed and their consent to that processing should be sought. However, this presents obvious practical difficulties (not only for employers but also for the administrators of pension schemes or, for example, insurance companies). The view of the Commissioner's office at present appears to be that, although the strict legal requirement is for consent of the third party data subject, it might be acceptable in practice to be enough to include wording of the sort set out below:

> 'I, [insert employee's name] consent, for myself and those named in this form, to the processing by [name of employer] of the above personal data for the purposes set out above.'

Where the third party data subject is a minor the difficulty of consent should not really arise as it is likely that the parent in question can validly give consent on their child's behalf.

However, such an approach must surely be appropriate only where the personal data in question is uncontroversial (for example, name, address and telephone number). Where the personal data about the third party constitutes 'sensitive personal data' within the meaning of *DPA 1998*, then (as with any other data subject) the third party's explicit consent will be required (or the information will have to be anonymised).

This practical problem has been recognised by the Commissioner's Office and by the Home Office and the regulations on the processing of sensitive personal data include an exemption for processing in certain insurance or occupational pension scheme contexts, where details of particular relatives of the insured or member are required. The data controller must not process these data to make decisions or take action with respect to the relatives, nor if the data controller is aware of the relative withholding his consent concerning the processing. If employers are unsure whether this exemption is wide enough to cover them then application forms should be amended so that both potential employees and their next of kin give their express consent to the processing of personal data.

Data Protection (Conditions under Paragraph 3 of Part II of Schedule 1) Order 2000 (SI 2000/185) generally provides for further conditions in cases where the disproportionate effort condition for the disapplication of the fair processing code is relied upon. *SI 2000/185* provides that any data controller claiming the benefit of the disapplication of the information requirements must still provide the relevant information to any individual who requests it.

Further, if a data controller cannot readily determine whether he is processing information about the individual concerned because of a lack of identifying information, that data controller must write to the individual explaining the position. In the former case only (disproportionate effort), the Order provides for a further condition to be met – the data controller must keep a record of the reasons why he believes the disapplication of the information requirements is necessary).

Another possible approach, in some cases, might be to pass on an extra copy of an employer's purpose statement explaining their uses of personal data to the employee, with a request for it to be passed to the next of kin. A prudent employer might even, in any consent wording obtained from an employee as set out above, include a statement that the employee in question has made their next of kin (for example) aware of the disclosure of their personal data to the employer.

Transitional Provisions [19.22]

The transitional arrangements in *DPA 1998* are remarkably complicated but it should be remembered that they could apply to human resources files which were already been processed on or before 24 October 1998.

Practical Pointers [19.23]

✓ Prepare a purpose statement for all staff, although this may vary for different categories of staff.

✓ Consider how best to provide this to existing staff (e.g. a circular).

✓ Consider how best to provide this to prospective staff (e.g. staff manual or in their contracts of employment.

✓ Consider altering all job application forms to include a purpose statement and probably a consent to process − particularly if asking for sensitive data (Note: It must particularly make non-obvious uses clear e.g. if an employer keeps all application forms even if someone is not offered an interview or where the application might be passed to another member of the same group.)

✓ Consider who is to be tasked with keeping the purpose statement for employees up-to-date.

✓ Are you going to obtain consent to process employees' data. If the data is not sensitive, consider if the processing is permitted by one of the other conditions in *Schedule 2* (e.g. necessary to perform the employment contract). Paying salaries might well fall into this category.

✓ Does the data you hold on employees include sensitive data such as medical information? Consider obtaining explicit consent to process such data.

✓ Do the transitional provisions apply to your employee files?

✓ Consider if there any files to which subject access does not apply for example because of the transitional provisions in *Schedule 8*.

✓ What are your procedures to give subject access?

✓ Consider 'weeding' any files to facilitate subject access and keep down the cost of providing a copy of personal data e.g. remove drafts of letters that are not required or information that is no longer necessary to be held.

✓ Consider guidance to your HR department not to 'clutter' files with unnecessary information to keep the cost of subject access down.

✓ Consider guidance to your HR department as to what should and should not be disclosed following a subject access request.

✓ Do you hold any information about third parties on your employment files which should not be disclosed if subject access is sought? Consider details on family members, next of kin etc.

20 – Medical Records and the Pharmaceutical Industry

Introduction [20.1]

This Chapter looks at some key data protection implications for the medical profession and the pharmaceutical industry arising from *DPA 1998*. It does not look at the wider issues in relation to the law relating to pharmaceutical data, save for the important *Source Informatics* case which, although a case regarding confidentiality, has data protection implications as well.

Medical Records [20.2]

There are a number of specific provisions in *DPA 1998* which have been considered in previous chapters, in so far as the Act relates to medical records. Indeed, subject access to medical records is wider than in the case of other sensitive data.

Under *section 68*, 'an accessible record' includes a health record, that being any record which:

O consists of information relating to the physical or mental health or condition of an individual; and
O has been made by or on behalf of a health professional in connection with the care of that individual.

So, for example, although such a record may not be part of a relevant filing system, nor may it necessarily be held on equipment operating automatically in response to instructions given for that purpose (or recorded with the intention it should be so processed), nevertheless such data can be eligible data for the purposes of *DPA 1998*. If that data is also personal data, then subject access will apply to it even though the files may not be structured sufficiently to fall within the definition of a 'relevant filing system', if the records are held in manual form.

These provisions acknowledge the fact that medical data is clearly the most sensitive of all the sensitive data covered by *DPA 1998* and reflects the fact that access to manual health records was allowed even during the time of *DPA 1984* (although access was not by virtue of that Act, which only legislated in relation to computerised/automated records).

Transitional Relief [20.3]

Transitional relief under *Schedule 8* applies to accessible records and they will also enjoy an exemption from the Data Protection Principles and *Part II* of *DPA 1998* (except insofar as these provisions relate to subject access or the rights of the data subject provided for in *sections 12A* or *15*), until 23 October 2001.

This acknowledges the existing law which already created greater accessibility for medical records. Data held in an accessible record will also have a further limited exemption from some of the Data Protection Principles until October 2007.

Notification [20.4]

The obligation to notify data subjects in relation to uses of their personal data applies equally in the context of medical data as it does for any other personal data.

This has particular relevance where, for example, individuals may participate in clinical trials and provide data about themselves or, perhaps, blood samples or other medical information which may be used for a range of medical purposes and even, possibly, disclosed to external laboratories or agencies or organisations which prepare databases showing prescribing trends or levels of resistance to certain drugs.

Non-obvious Uses or Purposes [20.5]

Whilst it is surely the case that most pharmaceutical companies already notify data subjects who participate directly in their trials about the uses of their data, this is now a legal requirement. In addition, if there is anything about the use of their data that is not obvious, then that information must be provided under *Schedule 1, Part II, para 3*.

Transfer Outside the EU [20.6]

In the case of pharmaceutical companies, for example, data about English patients might be passed to other members of their group of companies outside the EEA, in which event it may be necessary to notify the trial participants of this fact if the recipient country may be one which does not provide an adequate level of protection for personal data.

Obtaining Data From a Third Party [20.7]

Where personal data is initially collected by a doctor, say, and then disclosed to a pharmaceutical company which includes that person in a database, as far as the pharmaceutical company is concerned, it has obtained the data from a third party, rather than directly. If so, there may be instances where notification by the pharmaceutical company to the data subject is not necessary, as being a disproportionate effort. However, if the doctor knows that the data are going to such a recipient, the fair processing code probably requires that the data subject knows of this use of their data, in any event, so the doctor would be obliged to notify the data subject of this use.

It is quite common, of course, when visiting your doctor, particularly if a possible illness might be a hereditary one, to disclose detail of, for example, heart disease or diabetes within the same family. Some of the information disclosed might be personal data. Also, when being admitted to hospital, it is common to be required to give details of family/next of kin.

This is therefore data which is collected otherwise than direct from the data subject, in which event, whether or not that data subject needs to be notified of the information required to be given under *Schedule 1, Part II, para 3* depends upon whether or not the provision of that information would involve a disproportionate effort.

Probably the most important point, as regards this sort of information, is that the Commissioner says that:

> '...a relevant consideration would be the likelihood that/ extent to which the data subject already knows about the processing of their personal data by the data controller'.

In some cases, particularly where details of next of kin are given, it may well be a widely known practice. Also, it must surely be the case that anyone who has ever visited a doctor knows that questions about the health of other members of the family is crucial information in trying to diagnose a patient and that this sort of information is held on file.

Finally, it is hoped that it would be a balancing factor in favour of the doctor or hospital that the data would be held on confidential files, in any event, given the doctor's duties to his patient so it is difficult to see how the third party data subject could suffer any harm as a result of such data being held.

Consent – When is it Required? [20.8]

The issue of consent has been addressed in a number of places in this book. However, it is worth noting that medical data is sensitive data, and therefore particular rules apply. Usually, the processing of sensitive data will require *explicit* consent.

One specific provision in *Schedule 3*, in relation to sensitive data, which may be relevant for doctors and hospitals when dealing with patient data, may mean that explicit consent from the data subject may not be necessary provided that the condition in *Schedule 3, para 8* can be satisfied which provides:

'(1)   The processing is necessary for medical purposes and is undertaken by –
(a)   a health professional, or
(b)   a person who in the circumstances has a duty of confidentiality which is equivalent to that which would arise if that person were a health professional.
(2)   In this paragraph "medical purposes" includes the purposes of preventative medicine, medical diagnosis, medical research, the provision of care and treatment and the management of health care services.'

'Health professional' is defined in *section 69* with a comprehensive list including registered medical practitioners, dentists, opticians, pharmaceutical chemists, nurses, midwives or health visitors (to name but a few). It also extends to a scientist employed by a health service body as a head of department.

This exemption is actually quite wide and would certainly include the use of prescription data, within a hospital, and its day-to-day running of blood tests, and other diagnostic procedures. It might also include sending data to certain specialist laboratories for analysis if it is the only laboratory which is capable of performing a necessary specialist test needed in respect of a particular patient and the test is carried out by an appropriate person described in *Schedule 3, para 8.*

What is slightly more difficult is the situation where a hospital, for example, discloses to its external caterers the special dietary requirements of certain patients – which could indicate something about their medical condition or even their religious beliefs. It could be said that this is processing necessary for medical purposes because medical purposes includes 'the management of health care services' and that is surely what is happening.

However, the exemption is possibly quite narrow in so far as it states that the processing must not only be necessary for medical purposes but also undertaken by 'a health professional' or 'a person who in the circumstances has a duty of confidentiality which is equivalent to that which would arise if that person were a health professional'. What is unclear is precisely what that latter provision is intended to cover. Is it enough if the duty of confidentiality is imposed by contract or because the person holding the data is the data controller's agent?

So, the condition may not extend to outside agencies like caterers. However, it could apply if an external agency is in fact a data processor who processes a hospital's data and acts solely on the instructions of a medical professional. In that situation, perhaps all that is required should be that a data processing contract with the data processor, providing a high level of security for that data, in accordance with the requirements of the Seventh Data Protection Principle is put in place by the hospital. After all, the hospital or medical practitioner remains the data controller. The Commissioner's views on this would be very welcome.

Third Party Data Subjects [20.9]

This Chapter has considered the extent to which third party data subjects about whom data are held need to be notified of certain information as required by *DPA 1998* (see **20.4** *et seq.* above).

As a separate issue, one needs to consider whether those data subjects may have to give their consent to their data being processed. It may not be sensitive data, in which case only *Schedule 2* applies to the processing of that data (e.g. the data is only a name and address held in case a member of family has to be notified of somebody's illness). Alternatively, a doctor may hold on file the fact that a member of the family is a diabetic. That would be sensitive data, and the requirements of *Schedule 3* would apply.

For non-sensitive data it is possible that *Schedule 2, para 6* might apply to such processing, in which event consent would not need to be obtained.

In the case of sensitive data, however, one of the conditions in *Schedule 3* also has to be complied with. However, it would be expected that *para 8* (described at **20.8** above) should apply, because this is processing that is necessary for medical purposes and is undertaken by a health professional. Since medical purposes includes holding information for the purposes of medical diagnosis, preventative medicine and the provision of care and treatment, one would expect this to fall within the ambit of *para 8*. Consent would not, therefore, be required.

Source Informatics Case [20.10]

There is case law regarding the confidential nature of medical data and the doctor's duty of care to his patient. This book is not the place to consider it, save for the very important *Source Informatics* case, where it could be said that the laws of confidence and data protection collide.

First Instance [20.11]

R v Department of Health ex parte Source Informatics Limited [1999] All ER (D) 563 arose out of a Department of Health policy document issued to health authorities in July 1997 and it may develop the law on duty of confidentiality and its links to data protection laws. This is the first time that the issue of the duty of confidence between doctor or pharmacist and patient and the status of anonymised data has been considered in litigation. The case has important ramifications in a data protection context.

The Department of Health policy document in question was circulated in response to a request from a data collecting agency to general practitioners and pharmacists for their consent to obtain certain information relating to the treatment of their patients. The information would be provided to the data collecting agency in a form which would ensure the anonymity of patients. However, the Department of Health policy document advised health authorities that information given in confidence could not be disclosed without the consent of the provider of the information. The Department of Health regarded both patients and GPs as providers of the data and stated that:

> 'Anonymisation...does not, in our view, remove the duty of confidence towards the patients who are the subject of the data. Apart from the risk of identification of a patient despite anonymisation, the patient would not have entrusted the information to the GP or the pharmacist for it to be provided to the data company. The patient would not be aware of or have consented to the information being given to the data company but would have given it to be used in connection with his care and treatment and wider NHS purposes.'

The policy document recommended that any GP or pharmacist interested in providing the information to the data collecting agency should seek legal advice.

It also said, which is where the possible data protection link becomes clear:

> 'You may be aware that the Department published guidance – The Protection and Use of Patient Information – March 1996. The guidance makes it clear that under common law and Data Protection Act principles, the general rule is that information given in confidence may not be disclosed without the consent of the provider of the information. In this instance both patients and GPs may be regarded as providers of the data in question.'

At the time the policy document was issued, another data collecting company, Source Informatics Limited (SI Ltd), a subsidiary of IMS Health, was trying to persuade GPs and pharmacists to allow it to collect data about the prescribing habits of GPs, also confirming that there would be nothing in that data to identify patients.

Under SI Ltd's proposed scheme, pharmacists were to be paid a fee to obtain the consent of GPs to download the GP's name and the identity and quantity of drugs prescribed onto disc using software provided by SI Ltd. The patient who the prescription related to would not be identifiable from the data. SI Ltd intended to sell the prescribing data to pharmaceutical companies with a commercial interest in monitoring GP prescribing patterns. However, in light of the Department of Health policy document, most GPs and pharmacists refused to take part in SI Ltd's project.

SI Ltd unsuccessfully tried to persuade the Department of Health to change its guidance and agreed to exclude rare drugs or rare drug combinations from the scheme as an additional safeguard against patient identification. SI Ltd applied to the Court for a declaration that the guidance set out in the Department of Health's policy document was wrong in law on the basis that disclosure by GPs and pharmacists to a third party of anonymous information did not amount to a breach of confidentiality. This was therefore a judicial review case. It did not, however, address the data protection issue directly (namely that the Department said what was proposed could breach the Data Protection Principles).

Judgment [20.12]

In a judgment by Mr Justice Latham on 28 May 1999, the High Court ruled that SI Ltd's proposal to GPs and pharmacists involved a potential breach of confidence as patients would not have given consent to disclosure by their GPs or pharmacists of prescribing information to the company. This entitled the Department of Health to give guidance in the form of the policy document it had issued. Patients could not be said to have given implied consent to the commercial use of the prescribing data. In addition, the Court held that in the circumstances there was a public interest in ensuring that confidences were kept.

The Judge also said:

> 'It is a curious fact that this issue has never before been the subject matter of litigation, either in the context of the relationship of a doctor and his patient, or any other similar relationship which carries with it the duty of confidence. I say that it is curious because it is common knowledge that material gleaned from patients records is routinely used, as has been pointed out on behalf of the applicants, for the purposes of medical literature and research, and to obtain relevant statistics.'

Wider Implications [20.13]

This case has an importance beyond the pharmaceutical industry, and it is not only companies within that sector which will be affected by the appeal ruling. A number of industry sectors, particularly the financial services industry, share anonymised information and statistical information derived from such personal data will also be affected.

If an action in confidence can be established, it is not an action available only to individuals, as would a remedy under data protection laws. Businesses may have an actionable right for breach of confidence which could entitle them to damages for breach of that duty or to an injunction to prevent further disclosure.

Within the general law of confidence, a number of specific examples have emerged where the relationship between the holder of the information and the subject of the information lends itself to a duty of confidence. Three obvious examples are the relationship between:

○   doctor and patient;
○   solicitor and client; and
○   banker and customer.

It would be interesting to see how the *Source Informatics* case fits with an older case, *Tournier v National Provincial and Union Bank of England [1924] 1 KB 461*. In that case, which is the leading case on confidentiality as it affects banks, Bankes LJ said:

> 'At the present day I think it may be asserted with confidence that the duty (of secrecy) is a legal one arising out of contract in that the duty is not absolute but qualified. It is not possible to frame any exhaustive definitions of the duty. The most that can be done is to classify the qualification, and to indicate its limits...on principle, I think that the qualifications can be classified under four heads:
> (a)   where disclosure is under compulsion of law;
> (b)   where there is a duty to the public to disclose;
> (c)   where the interest of the Bank requires disclosure;
> (d)   where the disclosure is made by the express or complied consent of the customer.'

Looking at the heads in *Tournier*, if disclosure of anonymised data is a breach of confidence, it is quite difficult to see how any of the exceptions to *Tournier* may apply (other than consent). In theory (c) could perhaps apply, but that exception should surely be narrowly construed. It is worth going back a little in history to look at the Jack Report of 1989 on *Banking Service: Law and Practice Report by the Review Committee*. It looked at many aspects of the banker/customer relationship.

The Jack Report looked at the banker's duty of confidentiality and in particular the exception in (c). The Jack Report indicated that this exception offered few problems of interpretation in the 'simpler world of the 1920s'. At that time there are likely to have been few calls on banks to disclose confidential information about a customer without at least invoking his implied consent, except in the case of litigation. However, the Jack Report expressed concerns firstly in relation to the growing perception by some banks, at least, that they are entitled to release confidential information about customers, without those customers' express consent, to other members of their group. This concern seems to have been addressed by the Banking Code subsequently.

The second major area of concern was in relation to credit reference agencies and the possible disclosure of confidential information to them by banks. Again, subsequent developments have probably dealt with that concern.

At the time of the Jack Report, the recommendation was made that the extent of permitted disclosure 'in the interest of the bank' without customer consent should be clearly limited by statute to particular circumstances but that otherwise:

> 'we in general respect the consultee view already cited that
> a customer expects his affairs to be kept confidential within
> his own bank'.

It should be noted that the Jack Report was never implemented, but its findings are nonetheless interesting. It does indicate that exception (c) is not really to be used other than in the narrowest of situations.

This therefore left a bank disclosing information in a SI Ltd type of situation, after the decision at first instance, having to obtain consent or needing to be satisfied that it is able to imply it. To what extent could a bank argue that a customer knew or ought to have known of this use of their data, to justify arguing for implied consent? One suspects consent could not be implied in such circumstances.

So, the *Source Informatics* decision at first instance had ramifications beyond the pharmaceutical and medical sector.

Relationship Between the Decision and Data

Protection Laws   [20.14]

An important consideration is that under *DPA 1984*, the First Data Protection Principle required that personal data must be obtained and processed fairly and lawfully.

Obtaining data in breach of confidence or processing data in breach of confidence could arguably be unlawful. The *Source Informatics* case, therefore, if not overturned, could have caused data protection implications for the collection of data that is going to be anonymised.

This would be the case even though, strictly speaking, the disclosure of anonymised data (if it is truly anonymised so that the subject cannot be identified in any circumstances) is not a disclosure of personal data for the purposes of *DPA 1984* (or indeed, *DPA 1998*) and even though, in the hands of the recipient, that data is clearly not personal data and the data protection legislation should not apply to it, unless the recipient has some way of using other information in its possession to identify the subjects of that anonymised data.

Appeal [20.15]

SI Ltd lodged an appeal and this was heard at the end of November 1999. The Association of the British Pharmaceutical Industry (ABPI), the National Pharmaceutical Association (NPA), the General Medical Council and the Medical Research Council were given leave to intervene in the appeal proceedings. Clearly, the wide ramifications of the case had been realised.

The High Court's decision was overturned by the Court of Appeal so one hopes that the significant practical and administrative hurdles for schemes of the type proposed by SI Ltd have been overturned.
The central issue raised on the appeal was:

> 'What duty of confidence is owed by pharmacists to patients to whom they dispense prescribed drugs? In particular, provided always that the patient's anonymity is fully protected, does their duty of confidence to patients prevent pharmacists from using the material contained in the GP's prescription forms for whatever purpose they wish?'

Decision [20.16]

The Court of Appeal considered existing case law relating to the law of confidence and noted that a clear and consistent theme emerged – confidants (here, pharmacists) owe a duty of good faith to confiders (patients) and the scope of such duty should be judged by the pharmacists' consciences. The Court held that pharmacists' consciences ought not reasonably to be troubled by co-operation with SI Ltd's proposed scheme. A reasonable pharmacist would not think that by participating in SI Ltd's proposed scheme they were breaking their customers' confidence and therefore pharmacists' duty of confidence would not be breached by their participation in it.

The Court of Appeal concluded that:

> 'Participation in Source's scheme by doctors and pharmacists would not in my judgment expose them to any serious risk of successful breach of confidence proceedings by a patient (any more than were a prescribing doctor, asked by a manufacturer's representative what medicine he ordinarily prescribes for a given condition, to answer candidly on the basis of his current practice).'

The Court further held that:

> 'If the Department continued to view such schemes as operating against the public interest, then they must take further powers in this already heavily regulated area to control or limit their effect. The law of confidence cannot be distorted for that purpose.'

The Court of Appeal's decision means that, provided prescribing data is sufficiently anonymised to protect patients' identities, such data can be made available by pharmacists (or doctors, presumably) in certain circumstances without involving any breach of confidence. This has important implications for data collecting companies and the pharmaceutical industry in relation to wide-ranging areas including marketing, medical research, fulfilment of regulatory obligations and adverse event monitoring.

It is also good news for other industries which make regular use of anonymised data in their businesses.

The Court of Appeal also touched upon the data protection analysis of the Source scheme. They said:

> 'I turn to deal altogether more briefly with the remaining issues debated before us. First, there is the Directive 95/46/ EC on the protection of individuals with regard to the processing of personal data and on the free movement of such data, which fell to be implemented by 24 October 1998

and which the United Kingdom will finally implement on 1 March 2000 when the relevant provisions of the Data Protection Act 1998 come into force. Although all this post-dates the Department's policy guidance and, indeed, attracted no consideration in the court below, we cannot, I fear, entirely ignore it. The Directive was first raised in these proceedings by Lord Lester QC on behalf of the General Medical Council (GMC), another intervening party. His argument (much over-simplified) is that, even if Source's proposal would involve a breach of confidence under domestic law, it does not offend the Directive and so should be held compatible also with domestic law, the latter being read down if necessary for the purpose. By a linked submission, he further argues that the policy guidance (and/or any ruling by the court in support of it) would violate Article 10 of ECHR, there being on the facts no countervailing interest in privacy to protect under Article 8, and that domestic common law and, indeed, the scope of the Directive itself (see the reference to ECHR in recital 1) should accordingly be determined as he contends so as to avoid such violation.

These arguments encouraged Mr Sales to advance mirror submissions on behalf of the Department, namely that even if Source's proposal would not offend the common law (as I would hold) it should nevertheless be recognised to fall foul of the Directive (and eventually the 1998 Act) so that domestic law ought accordingly to be read up for the purpose.
Let me put aside further complications such as whether or not Source are entitled to invoke the transitional provisions in Article 32(2) of the Directive, and whether or not the Directive is directly effective pending its implementation, and turn to those of its Articles upon which Mr Sales principally relies.

Article 2 (the definition Article) by paragraph (a) defines "personal data" as meaning:

> "any information relating to an identified or identifiable natural person ("data subject")...and by paragraph (b) defines "processing of personal data" ("processing") as meaning: "any operation or set of operations which is performed upon personal data, whether or not by automatic means, such as collection, recording, organisation, storage, adaptation or alteration, retrieval, consultation, use, disclosure by transmission,

dissemination or otherwise making available, alignment or combination, blocking, erasure or destruction."

Article 8.1, requires that:

"Member states shall prohibit ... the processing of data concerning health ... ."

Article 8.2(a) disapplies Article 8.1 where:

"...the data subject has given his explicit consent to the processing of those data ..." (a provision to which I shall briefly return later in this judgment)

Article 8.3, disapplies Article 8.1:

"...where processing of the data is required for the purposes of preventive medicine, medical diagnosis, the provision of care or treatment or the management of health-care services, and where those data are processed by a health professional [which includes, all parties agree, a pharmacist]..."

Mr Sales' argument put at its simplest is that the proposed anonymisation of the information contained in a prescription form will – under the very wide definition of "processing" set out in Article 2(b) – constitute the processing of data concerning the patient's health, and that this is impermissible under Article 8.1, such processing not being required for any of the stipulated purposes allowed for by Article 8.3.

Lord Lester's best answer to this submission (and he is joined in it by Source) is that the Directive can have no more application to the operation of anonymising data than to the use or disclosure of anonymous data (which, of course, by definition is not "personal data" and to which, therefore, it is conceded that the Directive has no application). He points to the several recitals emphasising the right to privacy as the principal concern underlying this Directive, and he places great reliance on recital 26:

"Whereas the principles of protection must apply to any information concerning an identified or identifiable person; whereas, to determine whether a person is identifiable, account should be taken of all the means likely reasonably to be used either by the controller or by any other person to identify the said person; whereas the principles of protection shall not apply to data rendered anonymous in such a way that the data subject is no longer identifiable; whereas codes of conduct within the meaning of Article 27 may be a useful instrument for providing guidance as to the ways in which data may be rendered anonymous and retained in a form in which identification of the data subject is no longer possible."

Although this is clearly not the appropriate occasion to attempt a definitive ruling on the scope of the Directive – and still less of the impending legislation – I have to say that common-sense and justice alike would appear to favour the GMC's contention. By the same token that the anonymisation of data is in my judgment unobjectionable here under domestic law, so too, I confidently suppose, would it be regarded by other Member States. Of course the processing of health data requires special protection and no doubt the "erasure or destruction" of such data is included in the definition of processing for good reason: on occasion it could impair the patient's own health requirements. It by no means follows, however, that the process envisaged here should be held to fall within the definition: on the contrary, recital 26 strongly suggests that it does not.'

This last paragraph is the most important, as far as data protection considerations are concerned.

The Current Position [20.17]

The Department of Health was initially refused leave to appeal to the House of Lords. However, it has applied directly to the House of Lords for leave to appeal. That application may take some weeks to be heard. If they are given leave to appeal, we are looking at it being some months before this issue is finally clarified – so this may not be the end of the story. All that can be said is that such use of anonymised data is currently legal.

It will be interesting to see whether leave is given and, if it is, whether the House of Lords will be required to address their attention to the data protection issues.

Practical Pointers [20.18]

✓ Even if consent is not required, in all circumstances a very clear statement of purposes will need to be given to all data subjects from whom data is collected direct. This must stress all non-obvious uses or disclosures of that data.

✓ Does the processing carried out fall within *Schedule 3, para 8*?

✓ If not, consider obtain 'explicit consent' as it is unlikely any other condition could be satisfied in respect of that data in a medical context.

✓ If you do currently seek consent, check that your current procedures are adequate to satisfy the Fair Processing Code and the requirements of *Schedule 3*

✓ Do you obtain sensitive personal data other than directly from data subjects? If so, consider if you need to notify them of this and, in particular, consider whether it would be a disproportionate effort to do so.

✓ In a medical context, individuals quite often provide details of their family and/or next of kin. Those collecting this information must consider whether or not they need to notify these third party data subjects, or whether to do so would constitute a 'disproportionate effort' and therefore this would not be required by *Schedule 1, Part II*.

✓ Consider anonymising data before disclosure and, if this done, that data should not be personal data in the hands of the recipient and, therefore, *DPA 1998* does not apply to the recipient as regards that data.

✓ Even in the case where data is anonymised before disclosure, the act of anonymising the data and using and disclosing it in its anonymised form should probably be notified to the data subject at the time it is obtained because of the fair processing code.

21 – Financial Services

Introduction [21.1]

There is no attempt made in this Chapter to flag (yet again) the general data protection issues for financial services companies because they have been dealt with in earlier chapters e.g. notification requirements and the circumstances in which financial services companies should be obtaining consent.

Section 12 particularly affects financial services companies in relation to automated decision-taking. This is referred to in **Chapter 5** and is reviewed in this Chapter in some detail.

The Right to Prevent Automated Decision-taking [21.2]

Section 12(1) provides that:

> 'An individual is entitled at any time, by notice in writing to a data controller, to require the data controller to ensure that no decision taken by or on behalf of the data controller which significantly affects that individual is based solely on the processing by automatic means of personal data in respect of which that individual is the data subject for the purpose of evaluating matters relating to him such as, for example, his performance at work, his creditworthiness, his reliability or his conduct'.

This covers a number of areas including, obviously, credit scoring (a very popular activity with financial services organisations) but also covers some other automated processes such as, for example, equipment which can automatically scan CV's of individuals and reject them unless certain information appears in certain boxes on the scanned application forms.

Set out below is a detailed analysis of *section 12(1)* because it will be important for financial services companies using credit scoring and similar techniques.

Notice [21.3]

Section 12(1) provides that by a notice in writing to a data controller, an individual can require that no decision made by or on behalf of a data controller which *significantly affects* the data subject may be based *solely* on the processing *by automatic means* of personal data in respect of which he is the data subject. This applies to a non-exhaustive list of areas, which includes information supplied for the purposes of evaluating matters relating to them such as performance at work, their creditworthiness (crucial in the financial services sector), their reliability or conduct. Receipt of such a notice might cause a data controller, as a result, to introduce a manual element into the decision-making process for that individual, rather than relying on *solely* automated procedures – effectively, a person will make the credit decision.

The data controller must also tell data subjects (who have not given notice preventing automated decision-taking) if such a decision was made about them on an automated basis and they are entitled, within 21 days of notification, to require the decision to be reconsidered or to be taken other than on an automated basis (*section 12(2)*).

Exempt Decisions [21.4]

Importantly, the restrictions on automatic processing in *section 12(1)* and *(2)* do not apply to 'exempt decisions'. If a decision is an 'exempt decision', then a notice from a data subject under *section 12(1)* does not require the data controller to take any specific action and the obligation to notify data subjects under *section 12(2)* does not apply (see **21.3** above).

An exempt decision is a decision which firstly (under *section 12(6)*):

'(a) is taken in the course of steps taken –
  (i) for the purpose of considering whether to enter into a contract with the data subject,
  (ii) with a view to entering into such a contract, or
  (iii) in the course of performing such a contract, or
(b) are authorised or required by or under any enactment.'

and secondly (under *section 12(7)*) either:

'(a) the effect of granting the decision is to grant a request of the data subject, or

    (b)   steps have been taken to safeguard the legitimate interests of the data subject (for example, by allowing him to make representations).'

The most obvious category of exempt decision will be a positive decision taken in response to an application for a product or service. Individuals will not be able to prevent, say, a lender from applying credit scoring techniques to an application for credit or object to a decision taken on this basis. This is because the application is a request of the data subject and the decision is taken in the course of steps taken for the purpose of considering whether to enter into a contract with the data subject. This fulfils the first requirement of the section. If the second requirement is also satisfied - with a positive answer to the application – the request of the data subject has been granted and, therefore, the second requirement of the section as regards that data subject is also satisfied.

Looking at the various tests that have to be fulfilled in relation to *section 12*, it would appear that an exempt decision is one where the data controller's automated decision is taken for the purposes of considering whether to enter into a contract with the data subject (one condition that has to be satisfied to make this an exempt decision) accompanied by *either* the fact that the effect of the decision is to grant a request of the data subject (they get that loan they have asked for or the mortgage they have asked for) or steps have been taken to safeguard the legitimate interests of the data subject (for example, by allowing them to make representations).

Presumably, provided that a decision is made in the course of steps taken to decide whether to enter into a contract with the data subject and the proposed terms and conditions of contract contain a right to make representations (if the applicant is rejected), then the requirement to act on the notice from data subjects under *section 12* does not apply. Financial services companies should, therefore, revisit their terms and conditions to consider a right of representation and perhaps to structure the application for the relevant product accordingly.

Practical Pointers [21.5]

This new right implies the need for significant advance preparation on the part of data controllers in order to put in place the necessary systems and procedures.

✓   In the first place it is essential to identify decisions which fall within *section 12*. Data controllers must review their processes to see whether any decisions are taken solely by automated means which *significantly affect* their data subjects. The refusal of a mortgage or loan would surely fall into that category.

✓ Having identified what decisions are caught by *section 12*, it will be necessary to maintain a register of them so that:

    ○ no such decisions are made automatically in relation to any customer who has given a notice under *section 12*; and

    ○ where automated decisions are made, the mailing which is based on that decision contains a statement to that effect.

✓ Where a customer has given notice under *section 12*, and the decision is not an exempt decision, financial services companies must make sure that no decisions affecting a customer are taken on an automated basis. This implies system changes. Depending on numbers of data subjects likely to be affected by this, another solution might be to have an appropriate flag on the system to identify customers who have given a *section 12* notice so a human element can be introduced to the process. The decision would not then be based solely on processing by automatic means and would therefore fall outside the scope of *section 12*.

✓ Data controllers will have to establish a procedure for handling notices given under *section 12*. As mentioned above this could be extremely onerous for large institutions managed in separate divisions, in separate locations and especially if with separate computer systems.

✓ It will also be necessary to implement a procedure for registering and acting upon notices received from data subjects asking the data controller to reconsider the automated decision or take a new decision not on an automated basis. The data controller has twenty one days to respond to a data subject notice under *section 12* with details of the action they intend to take to comply with the notice.

✓ Data Controllers should review their terms and conditions with applicants for their products and include the necessary protections for data subjects, so that the resulting decision will be an exempt decision.

Guidance [21.6]

The *Introduction* contains a section which looked at the rights of individuals in relation to automated decision-taking. The text is somewhat disappointing because all it really does is paraphrase *section 12* and does not seek to give any guidance on some of the more knotty issues described above.

The only item of information which the *Introduction* gives in relation to *section 12* is that, no order detailing other circumstances in which an automated decision may qualify as an exempt decision, is currently proposed.

Transitional Provisions [21.7]

DPA 1998 contains transitional provisions (see further **Chapter 14**) which, effectively, provide a three year exemption from the requirements of *section 12* for all existing automated or manual files which were already in existence and undergoing processing prior to 24 October 1998. Financial services companies will clearly need to look at their automated and manual filing systems to see whether their files can benefit from this exemption and, if they do, it gives UK companies some time to plan how they are going to implement *DPA 1998* in this particular area.

It would be prudent to make any necessary changes to documentation now for all new customers, to minimise the level of future notifications.

Miscellaneous Matters [21.8]

The Banking Code [21.9]

The Banking Code and the Council of Mortgage Lenders' Code of Mortgage Lending Practice both already contain references to *DPA 1984* and exhort signatories to these Codes to notify customers of their right of subject access under that Act.

The next edition of these Codes (due in July 2000) may well address data protection in the light of *DPA 1998*.

Application Forms [21.10]

Financial services companies will need to revisit their existing application forms (e.g. for loans), to see if notifications need to be expanded and, where appropriate, consents obtained. They must be particularly aware of the processing of sensitive data which will almost certainly require 'explicit' consent (e.g. medical information or details of previous convictions given for insurance purposes).

Banks which subscribe to the Banking Code may already have adequate wording that covers consent for their purposes because they already have to obtain express consent to pass personal data to any company, including other companies in the same group, for marketing purposes and many banks already address various other consents at the same time, such as passing personal data to credit reference agencies and using it for statistical analysis.

Card Transaction Data [21.11]

There is a line of argument that card transaction data could, in certain circumstances, be held to be sensitive data, if it showed, for example, that someone pays trade union membership fees, pays a parking fine or buys a magazine subscription which suggests that they may be (say) of a particular ethnic origin or have particular religious or political beliefs.

Insurance Related Issues [21.12]

Certain types of insurance products would require a data subject from whom data are collected directly to give data about other people, who will thereafter become data subjects of the data controller. An example would be where someone applies for car insurance and the insurance is to cover other named drivers. A further example might be some types of life insurance cover, where details of next of kin are disclosed or, perhaps, private health insurance where details of a whole family and their health records may be disclosed.

The problems with this type of situation have been described in previous chapters, namely that one needs to consider whether notification needs to be made to those third parties, or whether that would constitute a disproportionate effort (see **5.11 above**). Unfortunately, there is no hard and fast rule and one suspects that this will have to be looked at on a case by case basis.

Data Protection (Processing of Sensitive Personal Data) Order 2000 (SI 2000/ 417) seeks to address this issue in the context of insurance and pensions where, in certain circumstances (notwithstanding that the information about a member of the family may be sensitive) it may not be necessary to notify the family member that this data is held (see *paras 5* and *6* of the Order). However, this is related specifically to certain insurance and pensions business whereas, one suspects, that several examples will emerge in other areas of financial services where information is collected on third parties (such as for a second card holder for a store card.)

Employees [21.13]

Financial services companies are particularly sensitive to matters such as their employees' criminal records (or potential criminal records) because of the ability of their employees to have access to means to defraud or rob members of the public. They will therefore be likely to hold details about criminal records (and wish to obtain information about criminal records) both being areas previously indicated as ones to be treated with great care (see **4.20** above).

Data Matching [21.14]

Banks and financial services groups are likely to be companies which would wish to take advantage of data matching techniques as they will often collect details about individuals when they apply for various different financial products, which they would like to match to build a profile of the individual.

It is crucial that financial services companies ensure that they, and the members of their group, comply with the requirements of *Schedule 1, Part II, para 3* in relation to processing such data – so they should probably indicate that they may use information collected in conjunction with other information that they hold to profile their customers with a view to providing tailored and selective marketing, for example.

Security Matters [21.15]

Almost more than for any other industry, security is crucial for financial services companies. It is likely that the level of security that such companies may have to provide will be higher than that of those in other industries, since they must have a level of security 'appropriate to the harm that might result from unauthorised or unlawful processing'.

Financial services companies will need to be particularly sensitive to the requirements of the Seventh Principle and must ensure that, for any new technology projects, the invitation to tender or request for proposal must require tenderers to provide full details of their security procedures. They must also insist on a right of audit/inspection of their processor's security operations, during the life of any contractual relationship with the processor, however much the processor may not like this.

Recording Telephone Calls/Monitoring E-mails [21.16]

The recording of telephone calls is something financial services companies do almost as a matter of course, particularly in a case of dealing rooms, for example. Indeed, the Bank of England positively recommends the recording of calls in certain circumstances. Financial services companies must be particularly sensitive to the law relating to the recording of telephone calls which is itself in a state of flux (see particularly **Chapters 19** and **22**).

There is new legislation before Parliament which may require consent from data subjects to the recording or monitoring of live speech in certain circumstances. The Relevant Bill is the Regulation of Investigatory Powers Bill, expected to become law in the year 2000.

22 – The Telecommunications Data Protection Directive

Introduction [22.1]

The *Telecoms Data Protection Directive* (97/66/EC) concerns the processing of personal data and the protection of privacy in the telecommunications sector, in particular, in the integrated services digital network (ISDN) and in the public digital mobile networks.

The primary focus of the *Telecoms Data Protection Directive* is, by its preamble, to ensure that the new advanced digital technologies that are being introduced into public telecommunications networks will not adversely affect the protection of personal data and privacy of the users of those services. It is also aimed at new telecommunications services and the successful cross border development of those services within the parameters of data protection laws. The sort of services mentioned include video on demand and interactive television. Clearly, it addresses much more than 'telecommunications'.

It recognises in its preamble the existence of the *Data Protection Directive* and points out that, in the telecommunications sector, in particular for all matters concerning protection of fundamental rights and freedoms which are not specifically covered by the provisions of the *Telecoms Data Protection Directive*, the *Data Protection Directive* applies, as it did already to non-publicly available telecommunications services.

It nevertheless indicates that specific protections for personal data and privacy may be required in the telecommunications networks, in particular with regard to the increasing risk connected with automated storage and processing of data relating to subscribers and users and in the use of methods such as calling line identification and automatic call forwarding.

Article 15 provides for implementation of the *Telecoms Data Protection Directive* by no later than 24 October 1998, save for *Article 5* (confidentiality of communications, see **22.10** below), which shall be introduced no later than 24 October 2000. The main body has been implemented as of 1 March 2000 in the UK.

Object and Scope [22.2]

The *Telecoms Data Protection Directive* is to provide harmonisation of the laws of Member States to ensure an equivalent level of protection of fundamental rights and freedoms, and in particular the right to privacy, with respect to the processing of personal data in the telecommunications sector. Its provisions 'particularise and complement' the *Data Protection Directive* and provide that protection for the 'legitimate interests' of subscribers who are 'legal persons'.

Definitions [22.3]

Subscriber [22.4]

A subscriber is any 'natural or legal' person, which does not just include individuals but can include companies. A subscriber is a person who or which is party to a contract with the provider of publicly available telecommunications services for the supply of such services.

User [22.5]

A user is any natural person using a publicly available telecommunications service, for private or business purposes, without necessarily having subscribed to this service.

Public Telecommunications Networks [22.6]

Public telecommunications networks are transmission systems and other equipment which permit the conveyance of signals between defined termination points which are used, in whole or in part, for the provision of publicly available telecommunications services.

Telecommunications Service [22.7]

Telecommunications service means a service consisting wholly or partly in the transmission and routing of signals on telecommunications networks, with the exception of radio and television broadcasting.

Services Concerned [22.8]

Under *Article 3*, the *Telecoms Data Protection Directive* applies to the processing of personal data in connection with the provision of publicly available telecommunications services in a public telecommunications network, in particular via the public switched network and public digital mobile networks.

Security [22.9]

The provider of a publicly available telecommunications service has to take 'appropriate technical and organisational measures to safeguard security of its services', if necessary in conjunction with the provider of the public telecommunications network with respect to network security. 'Having regard to the state of the art and the cost of their implementation', these measures shall ensure a level of security appropriate to the risk presented. This mirrors *Article 17* of the *Data Protection Directive* which imposes duties to safeguard personal data.

Article 4(2) requires the provider of a publicly available telecommunications service, if it is aware of a particular risk of a breach of security of the network, to inform subscribers concerning such risk and any possible remedies of such risk, including the costs involved.

Confidentiality of the Communications [22.10]

Article 5 provides:

> 'Member States shall ensure via national regulations the confidentiality of communications by means of public telecommunications network and publicly available telecommunications services. In particular, they shall prohibit listening, taping, storage or other kinds of interception or surveillance of communications, by others than users, without the consent of the users concerned, except when legally authorised.'

The first exception to requiring consent of the users is where the phone tap or surveillance is 'legally authorised', in accordance with *Article 14(1)*. This provides that Member States may adopt legislative measures to restrict the scope of the obligations and rights provided for in *Article 5* when such restriction constitutes a necessary measure to safeguard national security, defence, public security, prevention, investigation, detection and prosecution of criminal offences or of unauthorised use of the telecommunications system as is referred to in *Article 13(1)* of the *Data Protection Directive*.

Practical Problems [22.11]

The requirement to obtain consent of users is going to be difficult and impractical in some sectors such as the financial services industry. At the moment, the legal requirement in relation to the use of devices for recording telephone conversations under English law is that the parties to the call should be made aware that recording may take place. This requirement is contained, currently, in the UK in two telecommunications class licences (the 'Self-Provision Licence' and the 'Telecommunication Services Licence').

This could often be done, for example, by ensuring that, in an advertisement which suggests that you should telephone a particular telephone number for a service, it says that the call may be recorded for 'the protection of the caller' or 'to avoid misunderstandings'. The two class licences do not require a purpose to be notified, but clearly *Schedule 1* of *DPA 1998* would. In the case of employees, the notification could be in their contract of employment or by a notice to all employees.

The *Telecoms Data Protection Directive* goes much further because it requires consent and also consent from both 'users' (the person making the call and the person receiving it) unless the general exemption for recording commercial transactions applies (as it would in many cases).

This could have quite impractical results for those who use call centres or telephone marketing techniques. They often monitor telephone calls as part of staff training for call centre operatives or, alternatively, randomly sample the quality of their staff's performance. As long as staff were made aware that they may be recorded or monitored at any time, English law did not previously require their consent.

Legally Authorised Recording [22.12]

Article 5(2) says that *para 1* shall not affect any legally authorised recording of communications:

'in the course of lawful business practice for the purpose of providing evidence of a commercial transaction or of any other business communication'.

Fortunately, it is to be hoped that *Article 5(2)* would permit the UK to continue recording telephone calls in the way that it does at present. However, it is not quite clear how the staff training example given above would fit within *Article 5(2)*. It is not really being recorded, under those circumstances, to provide 'evidence' of a 'business communication' – it is really for other purposes. Hopefully, however, *Article 5(2)* would largely permit 'business as usual' in the UK business community as regards telephone recording for evidential purposes. However, the *Telecoms Data Protection Directive* could narrow, in theory, the areas where recording without consent currently takes place.

To give an example where recording should be able to continue by virtue of *Article 5(2)*, telephone calls are recorded in the financial services field to avoid future disputes or to assist in handling queries. The Bank of England, for example, recommends that calls of many kinds should be recorded. It would be totally impractical for busy dealers to have to carry out a consent procedure for each call (and, supposedly, to give his or her own consent).

Article 5 applies only to users who are natural persons, as opposed to corporations.

Article 5 will be implemented into English law by the draft Regulation of Investigatory Powers Bill. The Bill is intended to be passed in the Year 2000 and not only addresses interception of communications on public telecommunication systems (which had been regulated for some time) but also seeks to create offences in relation to the interception of private telecommunication systems, other than with a lawful reason. The lawful reasons are intended to reflect provisions such as *Article 5*.

Traffic and Billing Data [22.13]

Traffic Data relating to subscribers and users processed to establish calls and stored by the provider of the public telecommunications network and/or publicly available telecommunications service has to be erased or made anonymous upon termination of the call.

Notwithstanding *Article 6(1)*, where the purpose of the processing is for subscriber billing and calculation of interconnection payments, as indicated in the *Annex* to the *Telecoms Data Protection Directive*, certain data can be processed without requiring consent but only up to the end of the period during which the bill may lawfully be challenged or payment may be perused. The *Annex* extends to data containing the:

- number of identification of the subscriber station;
- address of the subscriber and the type of station;
- total number of units to be charged for the accounting period;
- called subscriber number;
- type, starting time and duration of the calls made and/or the data volume transmitted;
- date of the call/service;
- other information concerning payments such as advance payment, payments by instalments, disconnection and reminders.

The provider of a publicly available telecommunications service (although the Article is silent whether this also applies to the provider of a public telecommunications network) can process the data referred to above for the purpose of marketing its own telecommunications services provided the subscriber has given its consent. A subscriber in this context includes a legal as well as a natural person. Some have argued that this is an insidious way of giving companies data protection rights and is unwelcome.

The only circumstances where processing of traffic and billing data can take place other than by the provider of a public telecommunications network and/or a publicly available telecommunications service is where the processing of that information is solely necessary for handling billing and traffic management, customer enquiries, fraud detection and marketing of the provider's own telecommunications services and is done by persons acting with the authority of the provider of the network/services. Such activities, particularly fraud detection, are clearly for the general good.

Itemised Billing [22.14]

Subscribers (which includes corporate subscribers) shall have the right to receive non itemised bills and, in creating national law to give effect to the *Telecoms Data Protection Directive*, Member States have to reconcile the rights of subscribers receiving itemised bills with the right to privacy of calling users and called subscribers, for example, by ensuring that sufficient alternative methods of communications or payments are available to such users and subscribers.

Presentation and Restriction of Calling and
Connected Line Identification [22.15]

Article 8 expressly addresses calling-line identification (CLI). Where presentation of the CLI is offered, the calling user has to have the ability via a simple means and free of charge to eliminate the presentation of the calling-line identification, on a per-call basis. The calling subscriber has also to have this possibility on a per-line basis. This applies with regard to calls to third countries originating in the EU.

Where presentation of the CLI is offered, the called subscriber also has to have the possibility, in such circumstances, via a simple means and free of charge for 'reasonable' use of such a function, to prevent the presentation of the CLI of in-coming calls. Presumably, *Article 8* implicitly leaves it open that some charge can be made for extensive use. This shall apply to incoming calls originating in third countries.

Where presentation of CLI is offered and where the CLI is presented prior to the call being established, the called subscriber has to have the ability, via a 'simple means', to reject in-coming calls where the presentation of the CLI has been eliminated by the calling user or subscriber. This paragraph does not mention 'free of charge'. This shall apply to incoming calls originating in third countries.

Where presentation of connected line identification is offered, the called subscriber has to have the possibility via a 'simple means', free of charge, to eliminate the presentation of the connected line identification to the calling user. This shall apply to incoming calls originating in third countries.

Article 8 has other requirements regarding the use of CLI. Where CLI is offered, the providers of publicly available telecommunications services has to inform the public thereof and of the various possibilities available to them.

Exceptions [22.16]

Member States have to ensure that there are transparent procedures governing the way in which a provider of a public telecommunications network and/or a publicly available telecommunications service may override the elimination of the presentation of CLI.

CLI elimination use can be overridden on a temporary basis or, for example, on the application of a subscriber requesting the tracing of malicious or nuisance calls in order to identify the calling subscriber and on a per-line basis for organisations dealing with emergency calls (as recognised as such by a Member State) which could include ambulance services and fire brigades, where CLI elimination is overcome for the purpose of answering such emergency calls.

Automatic Call Forwarding [22.17]

Member States shall ensure that any subscriber (including corporate ones) is provided, free of charge, and via a simple means, with the possibility to stop automatic call forwarding by a third party to the subscriber's terminal. For 'terminal', here, read individual telephone.

Directories of Subscribers [22.18]

Personal data containing printed or electronic directories of subscribers available to the public or which could be obtained through the Directory Enquiries services has to be limited to what is necessary to identify a particular subscriber, unless the subscriber has given his unambiguous consent to the publication of additional personal data. Subscribers shall be entitled to be omitted from a printed electronic directory at their request, free of charge, to indicate that their personal data may not be used for the purpose of direct marketing, to have their address omitted in part and not to have a reference revealing their sex, where this is applicable linguistically.

Unsolicited Calls [22.19]

Article 12 provides that use of automated calling systems without human intervention (automatic calling machines), or facsimile machines, for the purpose of direct marketing may only be allowed in respect of subscribers who have given their prior consent. This is clearly going to have a ramification for direct marketing organisations (see **Chapter 18**).

In addition, Member States are required to take appropriate measures to ensure that, free of charge, unsolicited calls for purposes of direct marketing by means other than those referred to above, are not allowed either without the consent of the subscribers concerned or in respect of subscribers who have made it clear they do not wish to receive these calls, the choice between these options is to be determined by national legislation.

The rights described above shall apply to subscribers who are natural persons (i.e. not to companies). However, *Article 12(3)* provides that Member States shall also guarantee, in the framework of Community Law and applicable national legislation, that the legitimate interests of subscribers other than natural persons with regard to unsolicited calls are sufficiently protected – although what exactly this entails is unclear.

Clearly, this is aimed at junk mail by fax and random calling by automated calling systems but covers *all* unsolicited calls for the purposes of direct marketing, even if they are not by the two means mentioned.

Technical Features and Standardisation [22.20]

In implementing the *Telecoms Data Protection Directive*, Member States are called upon to ensure, subject to the provisions of *Article 13*, that no mandatory requirements for specific technical features are imposed on terminal or other telecommunications equipment which could impede the placing of such equipment on the open market and the free circulation of such equipment in and between Member States.

Where provisions of the *Telecoms Data Protection Directive* can only be implemented by requiring specific technical features, Member States have to inform the European Commission according to pre-existing procedures for the provision of information in the field of technical standards and regulations.

The European Commission will, if appropriate, ensure the drawing-up of common European standards for the implementation of specific technical features along the lines set out in existing legislation (existing directives) for mutual recognition, etc. of telecommunications terminal equipment and on standardisation in the information technology and telecommunications fields.

Consent [22.21]

Consent is not required under *Article 6(3)* (provisions of certain billing and interconnection data for marketing purposes with consent) for a provider of a publicly available telecommunications service to process data for the purposes of marketing its own telecommunications services where such processing is already under way at the date the national provisions adopted pursuant to the *Telecoms Data Protection Directive* entered into force. In those cases, subscribers shall be informed of this processing and if they do not express their dissent within a period to be determined by the Member State, they shall been deemed to have given consent. This makes an interesting contrast to the requirement of the *Data Protection Directive* and the *Telecoms Data Protection Directive* as regards consent. In all other circumstances, consent cannot be deemed given unless that consent is indicated by some positive act by the person giving that consent – so a non-response to a leaflet, for example, would not usually be an adequate consent.

Article 11, with its requirement that only certain information can appear within an electronic or printed directory without consent of the data subject, shall not apply to editions of directories which have been published before the national provisions adopted pursuant to the *Telecoms Data Protection Directive* enter into force.

UK Consultation [22.22]

A consultation paper on the *Telecoms Data Protection Directive* was published in April 1998. It noted that the *Telecoms Data Protection Directive* gave Member States a number of choices, in terms of implementation, and sought views from interested parties on these.

The key issues considered in the consultation paper for international business related to direct marketing and are set out below:

Directories [22.23]

Article 11(1) of the *Telecoms Data Protection Directive* gives subscribers rights to say that their personal data in a publicly available directory may not be used for direct marketing. Comment was sought on how subscribers who do not wish their personal data to be used like this should be identified in directories and how this fits with the provisions of that Directive on unsolicited calling by facsimile and telephone.

Unsolicited Calls and Faxes [22.24]

Article 12(1) states that automatic calling machines and fax machines may only be used for direct marketing purposes if the subscriber receiving the call or fax has given prior consent. This compares to *section 11* of *DPA 1998* which gives individuals a general right to opt-out from use of their personal data for direct marketing.

Article 12(2) is different. It relates to all other types of unsolicited calls for direct marketing (which could include, for example, unsolicited telemarketing calls) and requires Member States to choose between one of two options. These options relate to all types of unsolicited calls for direct marketing other than faxed calls and calls from automatic calling machines. The Consultation Paper suggested that either such calls would not be allowed:

O   without the recipient's consent – an 'opt-in' system; or
O   in respect of recipient subscribers who do not wish to receive such calls – an 'opt-out' system.

This latter option is consistent with the approach in *DPA 1998*.

Whichever option the Member State chose, it had to be free of charge to subscribers.

If an opt-in system was adopted by any Member State, it would make it unlawful to make calls to subscribers who had not consented. If this route was chosen, the UK Government suggested there might be merit in establishing a scheme whereby subscribers could notify a single body which would pass lists of such subscribers to industry. The Government's initial view was that whilst it would not preclude such a system being developed, the proposed regulations would be unlikely to prescribe this.

The likely approach was expressed to be that the implementing regulations would make it unlawful for calls to be made to subscribers who have registered an objection. Therefore some procedure needed to be created to enable subscribers not wishing to receive such calls to register their objection (opt-out).

The Government wondered if it is possible to have a system whereby subscribers could chose to consent to receive unsolicited direct marketing calls from certain types of organisations – the example given was calls from charities. The consultation paper also noted that the

Distance Selling Directive (97/7/EC) has similar provisions to *Article 12(2)* – but the *Distance Selling Directive* covers a wider range of means of communication, including E-mails.

The *Distance Selling Directive* has to be implemented in the UK by June 2000. It is likely, however, that whatever scheme was chosen for one Directive would also be adopted in the case of the other. Indeed, consultation is ongoing on the implementation of the *Distance Selling Directive*, including draft regulations attached to a November 1999 consultation paper. The treatment of unsolicited E-mail is one of the specific areas for consultation.

The Government noted that an effective opt-in scheme would have to have certain characteristics.

O   All subscribers would need to be aware of its existence.
O   It would have to be simple and free to join.
O   It would have to be effective within a reasonable time of joining.
O   It had to require companies engaged in telemarketing to update their lists regularly.
O   It should have an adequate complaints procedure.

There already existed a Telephone Preference Scheme (TPS) run by the Direct Marketing Association. This allowed residential subscribers to register their objection to receiving unsolicited direct marketing calls through their telephone operator which passed this information on to the TPS and the list was licensed to direct marketing companies on payment of a fee. The Government asked what scheme should be set up and who should run it. One advantage of using the TPS was the short time frame for implementation because the TPS was already fully operational.

Natural Persons   [22.25]

Rights under *Articles 12(1)* and *12(2)* apply only to natural persons, but *Article 12(3)* of the *Telecoms Data Protection Directive* requires Member States to guarantee the protection of the legitimate interests of all subscribers with regard to unsolicited calls and faxes. The Government sought comments as to whether the existing law sufficiently protected companies, for example, with regard to unsolicited calls and/or faxes or whether some form of scheme contemplated by *Articles 12(1)* and/ or *12(2)* should extend to legal persons. If so, should it be to all legal persons, or certain categories only?

General Observations [22.26]

A number of business organisations responded to the consultation, such as the British Bankers' Association and the London Investment Banking Association, since direct marketing is particularly relevant in the financial services sector which regards itself as already heavily and adequately regulated in this regard and unwilling to accept further onerous and/or unnecessary restrictions.

The business community's response to the consultation was strongly in favour of an opt-out approach under *Article 12(2)* although this would involve a greater burden for businesses than at present (compared to some responses from consumer bodies in favour of an opt-in approach).

Issues that still needed clarifying were identified as, for example, the relationship between a general opt-out which is registered by an individual and positive consent. This would allow for an individual who has opted out in general terms to opt back for the purpose of a relationship it wishes to establish with a specific supplier.

Businesses also suggested that the regulations should make it clear that they would be able to rely on the data in a list of opted out individuals. If the information was provided by a database which could be accessed by businesses, they should not be required to search continuously but should, say, be able to rely on a search once a month.

There was a strong feeling in the business community that legal persons should not have the protections under *Articles 12(1)* and *12(2)*, particularly as existing UK telecommunications class licences already provided some protection by allowing companies to prevent advertisers from sending advertising and solicitation messages without consent. To breach this would entitle the Director General of Telecommunications to proceed against the licensee. It had done this, in May 1998, against a company trading as The British Fax Directory which was using an automated system which rang telephone numbers at random for the purpose of establishing whether or not there was a fax on the other end and, if there was, sent unsolicited faxes.

One of the UK class licences required that this could only be done where the person receiving the calls had consented in writing to receive them. The British Fax Directory was unable to produce evidence that it had received written consents and was therefore in breach of its licence. The Director General of Telecommunications forbade that licensee to continue unless it first obtained consent in writing from each called party to receive the calls and that consent had to be identified by reference to the telephone number which was used to make the call.

Regulations to Implement the Telecoms Data Protection Directive [22.27]

The key regulations initially passed to implement this Directive were the *Telecommunications (Data Protection and Privacy) (Direct Marketing) Regulations 1998* ('the 1998 Regulations'). The Regulations gave effect only to the direct marketing provisions of the *Telecoms Data Protection Directive* and were published on 17 December 1998. The Regulations came into force on 1 May 1999.

The *Telecommunications (Data Protection and Privacy) Regulations 1999* ('the 1999 Regulations') were subsequently made on the 22 July 1999, laid before Parliament on the 26 July 1999, and made some variations to the 1998 Regulations with effect from 16 August 1999. The 1999 Regulations also implemented all of the *Telecoms Data Protection Directive* save for the provisions in relation to monitoring/recording telephone calls. So, the 1998 Regulations remained in force (as varied) until 1 March 2000. The 1999 Regulations then replaced the 1998 Regulations for all purposes with effect from 1 March 2000. The 1999 Regulations, therefore, address matters such as the use of traffic and billing data, CLI, directories of subscribers, etc., and are now in force. The 1999 Regulations were themselves subject to minor changes by an order dated 25 January 2000, the *Telecommunications (Data Protection and Privacy) (Amendment) Regulations 2000 (SI 2000/157)*. The provisions regarding the recording and monitoring of calls have been included in the Regulation of Investigatory Powers Bill.

Key Provisions [22.28]

Key provisions of the 1999 Regulations (in the direct marketing context):

○ a ban on sending unsolicited direct marketing faxes to individual subscribers;
○ the ability for corporate subscribers to opt-out from receiving unsolicited direct marketing faxes;
○ the ability for individual subscribers to opt-out from receiving unsolicited direct marketing telephone calls; and

O   enforcement by the Data Protection Commissioner, who will be advised on technical matters by the Office of the Director General of Telecommunications.

Most importantly, *Article 12* of the *Telecoms Data Protection Directive* is implemented by *Part V* of the 1999 Regulations on unsolicited calls and faxes for direct marketing purposes.

Traffic and Billing Data   **[22.29]**

Part II of the 1999 Regulations deals with traffic and Billing Data

Limitation on Processing Certain Traffic Data   **[22.30]**

Regulation 6 of the 1999 Regulations relates to data which:

O   are in respect of traffic handled by a telecommunications network provider or a telecommunications service provider;
O   are processed to secure the connection of a call and held by the provider of the network/service; and
O   are personal data relating to a subscriber or, in the case of a corporate subscriber, would be personal data if that subscriber were an individual.

With some exceptions, *Regulation 6* provides that on termination of the call in question the data shall be erased or depersonalised.

Limitation on Processing Certain Billing Data   **[22.31]**

Regulation 7 of the 1999 Regulations relates to limitations on processing certain billing data. The types of data are listed in *Schedule 2* which include the number or other identification of the subscriber's station and the subscriber's address and the type of station, as well as the total number of units used and a number of other facts. These data are to be stored for a limited period.

This is connected with the payment of sums falling to be paid by a subscriber or by way of interconnection charges. This Regulation governs how long such data may be held and for what purposes.

Processing of Billing Data for Certain Marketing Purposes [22.32]

Regulation 8 relates to the processing of billing data for certain marketing purposes of telecommunications service providers. They provide that the relevant data may be processed by the provider of the PATS concerned for the purposes of marketing telecommunication services which he provides if, but only if, the subscriber concerned has given his consent in this context, subscriber includes a company.

Other Provisions [22.33]

Regulation 9 restricts what may be held by telecommunications network providers and permits processing for certain limited purposes such as customer enquiries and the detection of fraud.

Regulation 10 permits the provision of billing or traffic data to a person who is a competent authority for that purpose in the context of settling of disputes contained in, or made by virtue of, an enactment.

Caller or Connected Line Identification [22.34]

Part III of the 1999 Regulations deals with Caller or Connected Line Identification (CLI).

Prevention of CLI – Outgoing Calls [22.35]

This Regulation relates to outgoing calls and CLI. The relevant telecommunication services provider is required to ensure that a user originating a call has, (subject to *Regulations 13* and *14* – see **22.37** and **22.38** below) as respects that call, a simple means to prevent, without charge, presentation of the identity of the calling line on the connected line.

He must also ensure that his subscriber has, (subject to *Regulations 13* and *14* – see **22.37** and **22.38** below) as respects his line and all calls originating from his line, a simple means to prevent, without charge, presentation of the identity of his line on any connected line.

Prevention of CLI – Incoming Calls [22.36]

Regulation 12 addresses this area. Where the presentation on the connected line of the identity of the calling line is available, the relevant telecommunications service provider shall ensure that the subscriber has, in respect of their line, the simple means to prevent such presentation of the identity of a calling line. This facility must be without charge for the reasonable use of such facility. The Regulation expands further on this.

999 or 112 Calls [22.37]

Regulation 13 addresses 999 or 112 calls. In order to facilitate responses to such calls, they are excluded from *Regulation 11*, for example.

Tracing of Malicious or Nuisance Calls [22.38]

Regulation 14 addresses the tracing of malicious or nuisance calls.

Facility for CLI to be Publicised [22.39]

Regulation 15 requires a telecommunication service provider who offers CLI facilities to take reasonable steps to publicise such service.

Directories of Subscribers [22.40]

Entries Relating to Individuals [22.41]

Regulation 18 consists of entries relating to individuals and requires that directories shall not, unless the subscriber in question consents, contain any personal data about him other than data necessary to identify him and his number. The regulation expands on other matters related to directory entries for individuals.

Entries relating to Corporate Subscribers [22.42]

Regulation 19 addresses entries in directories relating to corporate subscribers who might not want to be included in directories.

Supplementary Provisions [22.43]

Regulation 20 contains supplementary provisions relating to directory enquiry services as the mechanics of dealing with a subscriber.

Use of Telecommunications Services for Direct Marketing Purposes [22.44]

Part V applies in relation to the use of PATS for direct marketing. This means the communication of any advertising or marketing material on a particular 'line'. 'Line' is not defined.

'Caller' is defined as a person using PATS for direct marketing purposes, except that where PATS are used at the instigation of another person, that other person then being the 'caller'.

Use of Automated Calling Systems for Direct Marketing Purposes [22.45]

Regulation 22 addresses the use of automated calling systems (i.e. systems which operate to make calls without human intervention) for direct marketing purposes on lines of individual or corporate subscribers. It provides that a subscriber to a PATS will not permit their line to be used for direct marketing purposes except where the line is that of a subscriber who has previously notified the caller that, for the time being, they consent to such communications being made by or at the instigation of the caller.

The definition of 'automated calling system' is not sufficiently detailed and the DTI has indicated that they are seeking clarification from the EC. If it means an automated system which delivers a pre-recorded message to the subscriber, then this regulation is unlikely to affect many organisations. If, however, it means an automated dialling system then the implications are more significant. These systems are commonly used by organisations for their efficiency savings.

Use of Fax for Direct Marketing Purposes [22.46]

Regulation 23 addresses use of fax for direct marketing purposes – unsolicited communications on lines of individual or corporate subscribers. Such systems cannot be used where the called line is that of a subscriber who has previously notified the caller that such unsolicited communications should not be made on that line or the number allocated is that of a subscriber whose name is listed on a record to be kept by the Director General of Telecommunications of all those subscribers who have said they do not wish to be contacted in this way.

The Director will charge a fee (of an amount approved by the Secretary of State) for giving out information from the record and this fee may vary depending on the type and frequency of information requested. The Director will also have the power to delegate the task of maintaining and administering the record (and, indeed, has done so to the Direct Marketing Association).

Material is not to be treated as unsolicited where the called line is that of a subscriber who has notified the caller that it does not object to receiving such communications. This could be done, for example, by having ticked a box or agreed to this in standard terms and conditions.

Regulation 24 addresses calls on PATS for direct marketing purposes by means of fax on lines of subscribers who are individuals. In those circumstances, PATS cannot be used for calls for marketing purposes by means of fax except where the subscriber in question has previously notified the caller that he consents to such communications being made on that line.

Unsolicited Calls for Direct Marketing Purposes [22.47]

Regulation 25 addresses unsolicited calls on PATS for direct marketing purposes on lines of subscribers who are individuals in situations other than those described in *Regulation 24*. In those circumstances, PATS cannot be used for unsolicited calls for marketing purposes where the subscriber in question has previously notified the caller that such unsolicited calls should not be made on that line or his number is on a list maintained by the Director General of Telecommunications of those who do not wish to receive unsolicited calls for direct marketing purposes. Again, the Director General has power to delegate the maintenance of such a list.

Regulation 25 provides that callers may use publicly available telecommunications services for direct marketing *unless* the relevant subscriber has previously notified the caller that he did not consent to such communications or the subscriber's name appears on a list maintained by the Director General of numbers allocated to subscribers who do not wish to receive marketing calls. This opt-out system is regarded by the government as a balanced way, with suitable publicity and statutory backing, of providing a proper level of consumer protection. The government has stated, however, that it reserves the right, if an opt-out scheme is not working, to adopt an opt-in approach, as used in *Regulation 24*.

The position is, therefore, that direct marketing companies, for example, could make unsolicited calls without consent unless and until the subscriber gives notice to the contrary but will have to make regular checks against the list maintained by the Director General before doing so. Callers are charged fees for searching.

It is also not entirely clear what is meant by 'previously notified'. This is important for institutions which do or might market their products or services by fax or automated calling. 'Notify' suggests something less than consent. It may be necessary to include a form of notice which the subscriber must see.

There are no specific requirements under *DPA 1998* or the 1999 Regulations to draw these new rights to the attention of data subjects in a manner which might have an impact on drafting customer documentation, for example.

Notifications for the Purposes of Regulations 23(4)(a) or 25(4)(a) [22.48]

Regulation 26 provides that if a telecommunications service provider or the producer of a directory of subscribers comes into possession of a copy or record of a notification stating that a subscriber wishes to be added to the statutory 'opt-out' list, then this notification should be passed on to the Director General without delay and its receipt acknowledged.

'Producer' means the person who publishes or prepares the directory.

Supplementary Provisions [22.49]

Regulation 27 contains supplementary provisions to various Regulations in particular Regulations 22–25. It provides that the person calling for marketing purposes has to include, in the material communicated, his name and either an address or a freephone telephone number where he could be reached.

It also provides that the producer of a directory must ensure that it contains a statement bringing Regulations 22–25 to the attention of subscribers.

It adds that a caller will not be held to have breached Regulations 23 or 25 by making a call and a subscriber will not be held to have breached Regulations 23 or 25 by permitting his line to be used for making a call, notwithstanding that the number of the line is one listed on the Director General's record, if the number is not listed on the record at any time within the 28 days preceding that on which the call is made.

Miscellaneous Provisions [22.50]

Part VI deals with miscellaneous provisions including those to deal with security (Regulation 28) and termination of unwanted automatic forwarding (Regulation 31).

Compensation and Enforcement [22.51]

Regulation 35 gives a person who suffers damage by reason of a breach of any of the Regulations by any other person a right to be entitled to compensation from that other person for that damage. In proceedings brought under this Regulation, it would be a defence to prove that the defendant had taken such care as is reasonable in all the circumstances to comply with the Regulation concerned.

Where a breach of the Regulations has been alleged, either the Director General of Telecommunications or a person aggrieved by the alleged contravention may request the Commissioner to exercise his enforcement functions in respect of that contravention. In addition, the Commissioner has the ability to exercise his enforcement functions, even if he has not been so requested (*Regulation 37*).

The Director General of Telecommunications is required to comply with any reasonable requests made by the Data Protection Commissioner in connection with his enforcement functions, for advice on technical and similar matters relating to telecommunications (*Regulation 38*).

Regulation of Investigatory Powers Bill [22.52]

What is the Bill About? [22.53]

It introduces a new statutory framework for the interception of communications and covert surveillance by public bodies. It also contains new provisions obliging internet service providers (ISPs) and others to assist the authorities in decrypting information.

The Bill is controversial. Jack Straw presents it as a striking blow for human rights by ensuring that the relevant investigatory powers will be 'properly regulated by law'. Civil liberties groups, however, have expressed concerns that it gives the authorities too wide powers and will lead to greater government surveillance of communications, whilst ISPs have voiced fears that it may threaten the security of E-commerce and damage Britain's competitiveness in cyberspace.

Why Has it Been Introduced Now? [22.54]

The government wants it on the statute book before the *Human Rights Act* comes into force in October 2000. This is to address concerns that the current law does not comply with *Article 8* of the *European Convention on Human Rights (ECHR)* – respect for private life and correspondence. 'Correspondence' here includes telephone and E-mail.

Under the *ECHR* any interference by a public authority with *Article 8* rights must be 'in accordance with the law'. This means there must be laws allowing the interference and in the context of secret interception the law must be 'sufficiently clear in its terms to give citizens an adequate indication as to the circumstances in and conditions on which public authorities are empowered to resort to such measures' (*Halford v UK* [1997] 24 ECHR 523). The interference must also be 'necessary in a democratic society' for certain defined purposes, for example, national security, the prevention of crime or the economic well-being of the country. A measure will not be 'necessary' unless it is proportional.

That current UK laws are wanting in this area was illustrated recently in the case of *Halford v UK* in which we were found to be in breach of *Article 8* because there is no law controlling interception on private telephone networks. The *Bill* aims to bring the UK into compliance with the ECHR by plugging this and other gaps in a way that accords with human rights principles 'permitting interception in closely defined circumstances to protect national security and fight serious crime whilst resolutely ensuring that the citizen's privacy is safeguarded' (Home Secretary, launching the bill on 9 February 2000).

In addition to human rights concerns there is a need to bring the law in this area up to date with the modern communications market.

Interception of Communications [22.55]

The Bill repeals the *Interception of Communications Act 1985* (*ICA 1985*) replacing it with an updated regime. Under the Bill, as under *ICA 1985*, it is an offence intentionally to intercept communications on a public postal or telecommunications system. Under the Bill it is also an offence intentionally to intercept communications on a private telecommunications system. A private system means a non-public system that is attached to a public system, for example an office or hotel switchboard or an internal E-mail system that connects to the internet. A completely self-contained system such as a secure intranet or purely internal E-mail system is not caught.

Recording Business Calls [22.56]

The *Bill* implements *Article 5* of *Telecommunications Data Protection Directive 97/66/EC* aimed at ensuring the confidentiality of communications. Reflecting the exceptions in the Directive, it provides that calls may be recorded if both sender and recipient have consented. Industry responses to the initial consultation paper for the Bill made it quite clear that express consent is impracticable in many situations. Fortunately, therefore, the Bill also permits recording without consent under regulations to be published by the Secretary of State where it appears to the Secretary of State that recording would constitute a legitimate business practice. Taking a fairly liberal view of the exceptions in the Directive, such regulations may permit recording not only for the purpose of evidencing transactions but also for other purposes, for example, monitoring for quality control or fraud prevention. Regulations are being prepared by the DTI after consultation with industry and are expected to be available by the summer. The government has indicated in committee that (reflecting current provisions in the relevant class licences under *Telecommunications Act 1984*) the regulations are likely to include obligations to make every reasonable effort to inform the parties that monitoring is taking place. In response to *Halford* there will be provisions relating to the privacy of those being monitored. This might take the form of an obligation to provide unmonitored telephones for employees' private use, reflecting Oftel's current recommendations.

Practical Pointers [22.57]

The details of the new facsimile preference scheme, for example, are available from the Facsimile Preference Service, 5th Floor, Haymarket House, 1 Oxenden Street, London SW1Y 4EE, tel 0171 766 4422 or fax 0171 976 1886.

The literature sets out, for example, the fees which direct marketing companies must pay to search that register – £3,750 for unlimited access for a full year. The data file of the Register needs to be taken every 28 days at least. If a person is marketed to whose name has been on the register for more than 28 days, this is unlawful.

23 – Regulations Implementing DPA 1998

Introduction [23.1]

The relevant orders and regulations are detailed below.

- Data Protection (International Co-operation) Order 2000 (SI 2000/190);
- Data Protection (Subject Access) (Fees and Miscellaneous Provisions) Regulations 2000 (SI 2000/191);
- Data Protection (Subject Access Modification) (Education) Order 2000 (SI 2000/414);
- Data Protection (Subject Access Modification) (Social Work) Order 2000 (SI 2000/415);
- Data Protection (Miscellaneous Subject Access Exemptions) Order 2000 (SI 2000/419);
- Data Protection (Crown Appointments) Order 2000 (SI 2000/416);
- Data Protection (Functions of Designated Authority) Order 2000 (SI 2000/186);
- Data Protection (Fees under section 19(7)) Regulations 2000 (SI 2000/187);
- Data Protection (Conditions under Paragraph 3 of Part II of Schedule 1) Order 2000 (SI 2000/185);
- Data Protection (Subject Access Modification) (Health) Order 2000 (SI 2000/413);
- Data Protection (Processing of Sensitive Personal Data) Order 2000 (SI 2000/417);
- Data Protection Tribunal (Enforcement Appeals) Rules 2000 (SI 2000/189);
- Data Protection (Corporate Finance Exemption) Order 2000 (SI 2000/184);
- Data Protection (Notification and Notification Fees) Regulation 2000 (SI 2000/188);
- Data Protection Tribunal (National Security Appeals) Rules 2000 (SI 2000/206);
- Data Protection Act 1998 (Commencement) Order 2000 (SI 2000/183);
- Data Protection (Designated Codes of Practice) Order 2000, which list

designated codes of practice issued by various media organisations, namely:

- The Code on Fairness and Privacy from the Broadcasting Standards Commission,
- The ITC Programme Code from the Independent Television Commission,
- The Code of Practice from the Press Complaints Commission,
- The Producers' Guidelines from the British Broadcasting Corporation, and
- The Programme Code from the Radio Authority.

Data Protection (International Co-operation) Order 2000 [23.2]

This Order is concerned with data being transferred to countries outside the EEA where protection may be inadequate and the data controller is likely be in contravention of the Eighth Data Protection Principle in *Schedule 1*.

This Order gives effect to the provisions of *Directive 95/46/EC* on the protection to individuals with regards to the processing of personal data and on the free movement of such data between countries.

Article 3(3) obliges the Commissioner to give the European Commission and supervisory authorities his reasons for being satisfied a transfer or proposed transfer has involved or would involve a transfer to a country outside the EEA with inadequate protection for the rights and freedoms of data subjects in relation to the processing of personal data.

Article 4 allows the Commissioner to object to the European Commission, where another Member State with supervisory authority has authorised a transfer to such a third country.

Article 5 extends enforcement powers of the Commissioner under *Part V* of *DPA 1998* so that they can be exercised in relation to certain data controllers who are processing data in the UK but to whom *DPA 1998* does not apply by virtue of *section 5*.

Article 6 allows the Commissioner to make requests for assistance where a data controller within the scope of the Commissioner's functions is processing data in another EEA State.

Article 7 permits the Commissioner to supply other information to the European Commission or supervisory authorities where that information is necessary for the discharge of their data protection function.

Data Protection (Subject Access) (Fees and Miscellaneous Provisions) Regulations 2000 [23.3]

These Regulations define the extent of subject access requests under *section 7(1)* and impose a maximum fee that can be charged by a data controller for the access to that information. It limits requests for subject access where the data controller is a credit referral agency. Furthermore, it clarifies subject access in respect of educational records and provides transitional provisions for certain subject access for health records.

The Regulations, whose purpose includes giving effect to *Directive 95/46/EC*, make provisions for the exercise of the right of access to personal data conferred in *section* 7.

Extent of Request [23.4]

Regulation 2 provides that a request for access to information under any provision of *section 7(1)(a)–(c)* is to be treated as extending to all such information. However, a request is not to be taken to extend to information about the logic of automated decision-taking under *section 7(1)(d)* unless an express intention appears, and where there is such an express intention, the request is to be treated as limited to that information unless an express contrary intention appears.

Charge for Access [23.5]

Regulation 3 provides that, except in the special cases set out in *Regs 4, 5* and *6*, the maximum fee which a data controller may charge for access to data under *section 7(2)* is £10.
The regulations make special provision as to fees and time limits in relation to three particular types of subject access request which are detailed below.

Limited Requests Under Section 7, DPA 1998 [23.6]

In respect of limited requests as provided in *section 9*, the maximum fee which may be charged by the data controller for access is prescribed as £2.

The period within which a data controller must comply with the request is prescribed as seven working days rather than the forty day period which, by virtue of *section 7(10)*, otherwise applies (*Regulation 4*).

Requests Relating to Educational Records [23.7]

In respect of subject access requests relating to accessible records which are educational records (as defined in *section 68(1)* and *Schedule 11*), no access fee may be charged unless a permanent copy of the information is to be provided, in which case the maximum fee which may be charged for access is as set out in the Schedule to the Regulations, and varies according to the type and volume of copies in question. The prescribed period for compliance with these requests is set at fifteen school days in England and Wales (*Regulation 5*).

Requests Relating to Health Records [23.8]

In respect of subject access requests relating to accessible records which are health records (as defined in *section 68*), and which are not exclusively automated or intended for automation within the meaning of the first two paragraphs of the definition of 'data' in *section 1(1)*, the Regulations create transitional provisions in respect of certain requests made before 24 October 2001.

Firstly, where a permanent copy of the information is to be provided, the maximum fee which may be charged by the data controller for access in the case of such requests is prescribed as £50.

Secondly, where the request is restricted solely to data which form part of a health record, and that record has been at least partially created within the forty days preceding the request, and no permanent copy of the information is to be provided, no fee may be charged. Provision is made for requests to be specifically limited to conform to these circumstances (*Regulation 6*).

Data Protection (Subject Access Modification)

(Education) Order 2000 [23.9]

This Order applies to an 'educational record' as defined in *Schedule 11, para 1* and provides exemptions from the subject information provisions and *section 7* (Right of Access to Personal Data). It also provides modifications to *section 7*, including modifications relating to the 'principal reporter'.

The Order provides for the partial exemption from the provisions of *DPA 1998*, which confer rights on data subjects to gain access to data held about them, of certain data where the exercise of those rights as they apply to certain educational records would be likely to cause serious harm to the physical or mental health or condition of the data subject or another person, or, in some circumstances, (except in the case of Scotland) would disclose information as to whether the data subject is or has been the subject of or at risk from child abuse which disclosure would not be in the best interests of that data subject. Note that the Order does not apply to any data to which *Data Protection (Subject Access Modification) (Health) Order 2000 (SI 2000/413)* or any order made under *section 38(1)* applies.

In the case of court reports in certain proceedings where information in the report may be withheld by the court, there is a complete exemption from both *section 7* and the First Data Protection Principle to the extent to which it requires compliance with *Schedule 1, Part II, para 2* of *DPA 1998*. For other personal data to which the Order applies, there is an exemption from *section 7*.

The Order also modifies *section 7* such that a data controller cannot refuse access on the grounds that the identity of a third party would be disclosed in cases where the third party is a relevant person.

In the case of data controllers which are education authorities in Scotland who receive certain data from the principal reporter, the Order requires such data controllers to obtain the principal reporter's opinion on whether the disclosure of the information might cause serious harm to anyone before complying with any *section 7* request.

This Order gives effect to *Directive 95/46/EC* on the protection of individuals with regard to the processing of personal data and on the free movement of such data.

Data Protection (Subject Access Modification)

(Social Work) Order 2000 [23.10]

The Order applies to personal data listed in the schedule to the Order with some exceptions. Personal data in *para 1* of the *Schedule* is exempt from *section 7* (right of access to personal data) and *para 2* is exempt from the subject information provisions. It also provides modifications to *section 7*, including modifications relating to the principal reporter.

This Order provides for a partial exemption from the provisions of *DPA 1998* which confer rights on data subjects to gain access to data held about them of certain data where the exercise of those rights would be likely to prejudice the carrying out of social work by causing serious harm to the physical or mental health or condition of the data subject or another person. The Order does not apply to any data to which *Data Protection (Subject Access Modification) (Health) Order 2000 (SI 2000/413*; *Data Protection (Subject Access Modification) (Education) Order 2000 (SI 2000/414)* or any order made under *section 38(1)* applies.

In the case of court reports in certain proceedings where information in the report may be withheld by the court, there is a complete exemption from *section 7* and also a complete exemption from the First Data Protection Principle to the extent to which it requires compliance with *Schedule 1, Part II, para 2* to *DPA 1998*. In all other cases, the Order confers an exemption from *section 7(1)(b)–(d)*, leaving the right of the data subject to be informed by any data controller whether data about him are being processed by or on behalf of that data controller.

The Order also expands upon *section 7* such that a data controller cannot refuse access on the grounds that the identity of a third party would be disclosed in cases where the third party is a relevant person, unless serious harm to that relevant person's physical or mental health or condition is likely to be caused by giving access such that the exemption in *Article 5(1)* applies.

A further exemption from the subject access provisions is conferred in certain circumstances where a third party is making the request for access on behalf of the data subject and the data subject does not wish that information to be disclosed to that third party.

The Order principally applies to data processed by local authorities, in relation to their social services and education welfare functions, and health authorities to whom such data are passed and by probation committees and the National Society for the Prevention of Cruelty to Children. The Order also applies to data processed for similar purposes by the corresponding bodies in Northern Ireland. Data processed by government departments for certain purposes connected with social work and by officers such as guardians at litem and (in Scotland) the principal reporter of the Scottish Children's Reporter Administration are also within the scope of the Order.

Provision is made enabling other voluntary organisations or other bodies to be added to the list of bodies whose data are subject to the provisions of the Order where the data are processed for purposes similar to the social services functions (or in Scotland social work functions) of local authorities.

In the case of social work authorities in Scotland who receive certain data from the principal reporter, the Order requires such data controllers to obtain the principal reporter's approval before complying with any *section 7* request.

This Order gives effect to *Directive 95/46/EC* on the protection of individuals with regard to the processing of personal data and on the free movement of such data.

Data Protection (Miscellaneous Subject Access Exemptions) Order 2000 [23.11]

This Order exempts from *section 7* (which entitles individuals to gain access to personal data held about them) data the disclosure of which is prohibited or restricted by certain enactments and subordinate instruments, in the interests of safeguarding the interests of the data subject himself or the rights and freedoms of some other individual.

The data which are exempted by the Order concern:

O   human fertilisation and embryology information in the UK;
O   information contained in adoption and parental order records and reports and statements and records of the special educational needs of children in England or Wales, Scotland and Northern Ireland; and
O   in Scotland only, information provided by reporters for the purposes of a children's hearing.

Data Protection (Crown Appointments) Order 2000

[23.12]

DPA 1998 imposes certain obligations on data controllers to give data subjects information about the processing of personal data, to give access to personal data. By virtue of *section 27(2)*, the provisions imposing these obligations are referred to as the 'subject information provisions'.

This Order exempts from the subject information provisions processing for the purposes of assessing any person's suitability for certain offices to which appointments are made by Her Majesty.

Data Protection (Functions of Designated Authority) Order 2000 [23.13]

Section 54(1) provides that the Commissioner shall continue to be the designated authority in the UK for the purposes of Article 13 of the Convention for the Protection of Individuals with regard to Automatic Processing of Personal Data which was opened for signature on 28th January 1981 (the Convention). It also provides that the Secretary of State may by Order make provision as to the functions to be discharged by the Commissioner in that capacity.

This Order specifies those functions. In particular, *Article 3* requires the Commissioner to furnish particular information to the designated authorities in other Convention countries and also provides that she may request such authorities to furnish her with information.

Article 4 requires the Commissioner to assist persons resident outside the UK in exercising certain of their rights under *Part II* of *DPA 1998*. It also requires her in specific circumstances to notify a resident outside the UK of certain of the rights and remedies available under *Part II* and, again in specific circumstances, to treat any request made to him by such a resident as a request for an assessment to be dealt with under *section 42(1)*.

Article 5 provides that if a request for assistance in exercising, *inter alia*, rights of access to personal data in a Convention country is made by a person resident in the UK and submitted to the Commissioner, the Commissioner will send the request to the designated authority in that country.

Data Protection (Fees under Section 19(7))

Regulations 2000 [23.14]

The Regulations prescribe a fee of £2 to be paid to the Commissioner for the supply of a duly certified copy of any data controller's entry on the register.

Consumer Credit (Credit Reference Agency)

Regulations 2000 [23.15]

These Regulations revoke (with a saving) the *Consumer Credit (Credit Reference Agency) Regulations 1977 (SI 1977/329)* (the 1977 Regulations). They supplement *sections 157–160 of Consumer Credit Act 1974 (CCA 1974)* and *section 9(3) of DPA 1998*, which relate to the disclosure to consumers of information about their financial standing held by credit reference agencies and the correction of such information where it is found to be incorrect.

Section 157 of *CCA 1974* requires a creditor, owner or negotiator to disclose to a debtor or hirer on request the name and address of any credit reference agency he has consulted about the debtor's or hirer's financial standing, and these Regulations prescribe a period of seven working days during which such a request must be complied with (*Regulation 3*).

Sections 158(1) and *160(3)* of *CCA 1974* (as amended by *section 62* of *DPA 1998*) require credit reference agencies to give specified information to partnerships and other unincorporated bodies of persons (not consisting entirely of bodies corporate) on request, and these Regulations prescribe a period of seven working days during which such requests must be complied with (*Regulation 3*).

Sections 158(2) and *160(3)* of *CCA 1974* (as amended) require accompanying statements of rights to be given and these Regulations prescribe the form of such statements (*Regulation 4(2)* and *(3)* and *Schedules 2* and *3*).

Section 9(3) of *DPA 1998* requires credit reference agencies to give individuals statements of their rights under *section 159* of *CCA 1974* (as amended by *section 62* of *DPA 1998*) when complying with requests to disclose information. These Regulations prescribe the form of such statements (*Regulation 4(1)* and *Schedule 1*). The prescribed form incorporates a statement of certain rights under *DPA 1998*.

Finally, these Regulations prescribe the manner in which applications under *section 159(5)* of *CCA 1974* (as amended by *section 62* of *DPA 1998*) must be made (*Regulation 5*). Two sorts of applications are made under this section:

○ applications by individuals and other consumers to the Commissioner or the Director General of Fair Trading (the relevant authority) for an order where a credit reference agency has not given notice that it intends to include a notice of correction drawn up by the consumer on its files; and
○ applications by credit reference agencies to the relevant authority where they think it would be improper to include such a notice of correction on their files.

Data Protection (Conditions under Paragraph 3 of Part II of Schedule 1) Order 2000 [23.16]

Schedule 1, Part II, para 2 to *DPA 1998* provides that personal data will not be treated as processed fairly unless certain requirements are met relating to the provision to the data subject of information about the processing (the information requirements). As previously explained in this book, different provisions apply where data have been obtained from the data subject and where data have been obtained from some other source.

Schedule 1, Part II, para 3 to *DPA 1998* sets out conditions which, if met, allow the data controller to disregard the information requirements in cases where the data have been obtained from a source other than the data subject. Power is given to the Secretary of State to prescribe further conditions which must be met before the information requirements can be disregarded in this way.

This Order prescribes further conditions for cases where the 'disproportionate effort' ground is being relied upon (where data is obtained from a third party and not directly from a data subject), or where the disclosure or recording of the data is necessary for compliance with a legal obligation, other than one imposed by contract or an obligation imposed expressly by or under an enactment. In both cases, the Order provides that an individual may request any data controller to provide him with the relevant information if the data controller at any time claims the benefit of the disapplication of the information requirements. Further, if a data controller cannot readily determine whether he is processing information about the individual concerned because of a lack of identifying information, that data controller must write to the individual explaining the position.

In the former case only (disproportionate effort), the Order provides for a further condition to be met: the data controller must keep a record of the reasons why the disapplication of the information requirements is necessary.

This Order gives effect to certain provisions of *Directive 95/46/EC* on the protection of individuals with regard to the processing of personal data and on the free movement of such data.

Data Protection (Subject Access Modification)

(Health) Order 2000 [23.17]

This Order provides for the partial exemption from the provisions of *DPA 1998*, which confer rights on data subjects to gain access to data held about them, of data relating to the physical or mental health or condition of the data subject.

An exemption from *section 7* is conferred only to the extent to which to supply the data subject with particulars of the information constituting the data would be likely to cause serious harm to his or any other person's physical or mental health or condition. Before deciding whether this exemption applies (and, accordingly, whether to grant or withhold subject access) a data controller who is not a health professional is obliged by the Order to consult the health professional responsible for the clinical care of the data subject or, if there is more than one, the most suitable available health professional or, if there is none available or the data controller is the Secretary of State exercising his functions relating to social security, child support or war pensions, a health professional who has the necessary experience and qualifications to advise on the matters to which the information which is requested relates. This obligation to consult does not apply where the data subject has already seen or knows about the information which is the subject of the request, nor in certain limited circumstances where consultation has been carried out prior to the request being made.

A further exemption from *section 7* is conferred in certain circumstances where a third party is making the request for access on behalf of the data subject and the data subject does not wish that information to be disclosed to that third party.

In the case of court reports in certain proceedings where information in the report may be withheld by the court, there is a complete exemption from *section* 7 and also a complete exemption from the first data protection principle to the extent to which it requires compliance with *Schedule 1, Part II, para 2* to *DPA 1998*.

The Order also modifies *section* 7 such that a data controller cannot refuse access on the grounds that the identity of a third party would be disclosed in cases where the information is contained in a health record and the third party is a health professional who has compiled or contributed to that health record or has been involved in the care of the data subject in his capacity as a health professional, unless serious harm to that health professional's physical or mental health or condition is likely to be caused by giving access such that the exemption in *Article 5(1)* applies.

This Order gives effect to some of the provisions of *Directive 95/46/EC* on the protection of individuals with regard to the processing of personal data and on the free movement of such data.

Data Protection (Processing of Sensitive Personal Data) Order 2000 [23.18]

This is a particularly important Order for many organisations, containing ten varying situations where processing of 'sensitive' personal data can take place without, for example, obtaining the data subject's consent. Otherwise, the conditions for processing personal data which is 'sensitive' rarely permit such data to be used without the relevant person's permission especially if it is sensitive personal data.

The First Data Protection Principle prohibits the processing of sensitive personal data unless one of the conditions in *Schedule 3* is met. The condition set out in *Schedule 3, para 10* is that the processing of sensitive personal data is carried out in circumstances specified by the Secretary of State. The *Schedule* to this Order specifies ten such circumstances.

This Order gives effect to some of the provisions of *Directive 95/46/EC* on the protection of individuals with regard to the processing of personal data and on the free movement of such data.

Prevention or Detection of any Unlawful Act [23.19]

Para 1 of the *Schedule* covers certain processing for the purposes of the prevention or detection of any unlawful act, where seeking the explicit consent of the data subject to the processing would prejudice those purposes (where such processing is in the public interest). This might cover certain types of checking where there is a very strong likelihood that a serious crime is being committed and the processing may prove this.

Protection of Members of the Public [23.20]

Para 2 of the *Schedule* is a similar provision for cases where the processing is required to discharge functions designed to protect members of the public from certain conduct which may not constitute an unlawful act, such as incompetence or mismanagement. This must clearly be of assistance to certain regulators and supervisory bodies.

Para 3 of the *Schedule* covers very similar ground to *para 2* but where the disclosures are for journalistic, artistic or literary purposes and the disclosure is made with a view to publication of those data by any person as the data controller reasonably believes that such publication would.

Substantial Public Interest [23.21]

Para 4 of the *Schedule* covers processing in the substantial public interest required to discharge functions involving the provision of services such as confidential counselling and advice, in circumstances where the consent of the data subject is not obtained for one of the specified reasons set out in that paragraph.

Certain Insurance or Occupational Pension Scheme Contexts [23.22]

Para 5 of the *Schedule* covers processing in certain insurance or occupational pension scheme contexts, where details of particular relatives of the principal insured or member are required (e.g. health details of relatives used to calculate the life expectancy of the insured).

The data controller must not process these data to make decisions or take action with respect to the relatives, nor if he is aware of the relative withholding his consent concerning the processing.

Para 6 of the Schedule covers the processing of sensitive data in certain insurance contexts which were already being processed before 24 October 1998. Like the provision in para 5, the data controller must not continue to process these data if he is aware of the data subject withholding his consent to the processing. Alternatively, in the case of group schemes, the data controller may continue processing without explicit consent if it is necessary to avoid prejudice to the scheme as a whole.

Monitoring of Equality [23.23]

Schedule 3, para 9 of DPA 1998 provides as a condition relevant for the purposes of the First Data Protection Principle that the processing is of personal data relating to racial or ethnic origin for the purposes of ethnic monitoring. Para 7 of the Schedule to this Order makes similar provision in relation to the monitoring of equality between persons with different religious beliefs or between persons with differing physical disabilities or mental conditions.

Political Opinions [23.24]

Para 8 of the Schedule relates to the processing of political opinions by registered political parties, provided such processing does not cause substantial damage or distress to any person.

Other Exemptions [23.25]

Para 9 of the Schedule covers, for example, archives where the sensitive personal data are not used to take decisions about any person without their consent and no substantial damage or distress is caused to any person by the keeping of those data.

Para 10 of the Schedule covers processing by the police in the exercise of their common law powers.

Data Protection Tribunal (Enforcement Appeals)

Rules 2000 [23.26]

These Rules, which have been prepared after consultation with the Council on Tribunals regulate the exercise of the rights of appeal against decisions of the Data Protection Commissioner conferred by *section 48* and the practice and procedure of the Data Protection Tribunal in such cases.

Rule 3 requires an appeal to be made by notice of appeal served on the Tribunal, stating the grounds of appeal and other specified particulars, with provision for including a request with reasons for an early hearing. An appeal against an information notice may also include representations against a hearing by the Chairman or deputy sitting alone.

The notice must, under *Rule 4*, be served within 28 days of the date on which the Commissioner's decision was served on the appellant, but in special circumstances appeals may be accepted out of time. *Rule 5* provides for acknowledgment of the notice of appeal, and for service of a copy on the Commissioner except in the case of certain appeals to be heard ex parte. *Rule 6* provides for a reply by the Commissioner.

Rule 7 allows the Commissioner to apply for an appeal to be struck out in limited circumstances. *Rule 8* provides for the parties to amend their pleadings, in some cases with leave only, and *Rule 9* makes provision in respect of the withdrawal of an appeal. Provision is made as to the consolidation of appeals (*Rule 10*).

Rule 11 provides for the giving of directions by the Tribunal, of its own motion or on the application of a party. This power may be exercised in the absence of the parties, and any party may apply to set aside or vary directions. Provision is made by *Rule 12* for the ordering of persons in occupation of premises to permit entry for the testing of equipment or material connected with the processing of personal data.

The Tribunal must as a general rule proceed by way of a hearing but in certain circumstances it may determine an appeal without one (*Rule 13*). Provision is made as to:

○ the appointment of time and place of a hearing (*Rule 14*);
○ summoning of witnesses to attend a hearing (*Rule 15*);
○ representation at a hearing (*Rule 16*); and
○ default of appearance at a hearing (*Rule 17*).

Rule 18 makes provision for the constitution of the Tribunal for hearing certain appeals against an information notice.

Hearings by the Tribunal must generally be in public, but special provision is made for private hearings in limited circumstances (*Rule 19*).

The Rules include provision as to:

O the conduct of proceedings at a hearing (*Rule 20*);
O powers of the chairman to act for the Tribunal (*Rule 21*);
O evidence (*Rule 23*);
O the determination of appeals (*Rule 24*); and
O costs (*Rule 25*).

In all proceedings, other than those relating to the inclusion of a statement of urgency in a Commissioner's notice, the onus is placed on the Commissioner of satisfying the Tribunal that his decision should be upheld (*Rule 22*).

These Rules give effect to some of the provisions of *Directive 95/46/ EC* on the protection of individuals with regard to the processing of personal data and on the free movement of such data.

Data Protection (Corporate Finance Exemption)

Order 2000 [23.27]

DPA 1998 imposes certain obligations on data controllers to give data subjects information about the processing of personal data, and to give access to personal data. By virtue of *section 27(2)*, the provisions imposing these obligations are referred to as 'the subject information provisions'. *Schedule 7, para 6* creates an exemption from the subject information provisions where, inter alia, the exemption is required for the purpose of safeguarding an important economic or financial interest of the UK.

This Order provides that the fact that a prejudicial effect on the orderly functioning of financial markets or the efficient allocation of capital will result from the occasional or regular application of the subject information provisions to certain data is to be taken into account in determining whether the corporate finance exemption is required for the purpose of safeguarding an important economic or financial interest of the UK. The data in question are data to which the application of the subject information provisions could, in the reasonable belief of the data controller, affect decisions whether to deal in, subscribe for or issue instruments or decisions which are likely to affect any business activity.

Data Protection (Notification and Notification Fees)

Regulations 2000 [23.28]

These Regulations contributes to the implementation of *Directive 95/46/EC* on the Protection of individuals with regard to the processing of personal data and on the free movement of such data. They set out several arrangements for the giving of notifications to the Commissioner by data controllers under *Part III* of *DPA 1998*.

The Regulations set out the exemptions from notification, the form of giving notification such as in respect of partnerships or a governing body. It specifies the fee to accompany notification, date of entry in the register, acknowledgment of receipt of notification and confirmation of register entries by the Commissioner. Furthermore, it specifies the obligation to notify changes to the information held in registered entries. The *Schedule* to the Regulations sets out exemptions from notification.

Notification [23.29]

Regulation 3 exempts data controllers carrying out certain processing from the need to notify. The descriptions of the exempt processing operations are set out in the *Schedule* to the Regulations, and cover:

O   processing operations involving staff administration;
O   advertising, marketing and public relations;
O   accords and record keeping; and
O   certain processing operations carried out by non profit-making organisations.

Exemption from notification is lost if the processing falls within any description of assessable processing specified by the Secretary of State under *section 22* of *DPA 1998*.

Regulation 4 makes general provision for the form of all such notifications to be determined by the Commissioner. *Regulations 5* and *6* make special provision in two cases where there is more than one data controller in respect of personal data. *Regulation 5* provides for notification by business partners to be in the name of the partnership, and *Regulation 6* for notification by the governing body and head teacher of a school to be in the name of the school.

Regulation 7 prescribes fees to accompany a notification under *section 18*. A fee of £35 is prescribed.

Regulation 8 provides that an entry in the register of notifications maintained by the Commissioner under *section 19* is to be taken to have been made, for the purposes of avoiding the prohibition in *section 17* on processing without a register entry, in the case of a notification sent by registered post or recorded delivery service on the day after the day it was received by the Post Office, and in any other case on the day it was received by the Commissioner.

Requirement of Commissioner to Give Notice   [23.30]

Regulation 9 requires the Commissioner to give written notice to a data controller acknowledging receipt of any notification which she considers relates to assessable processing within the meaning of *section 22*. The notice must indicate the date of receipt and the processing considered to be assessable.

Regulation 10 requires the Commissioner to give notice to a data controller confirming the register entry. The notice must be given as soon as practicable and in any event within 28 days of making a register entry under *section 19* or of amending it under *section 20*.

It must contain the date on which the entry is deemed by *Regulation 8* to have been made or as the case may be the date of alteration, the particulars entered or amended, and, in the case of a notification under *section 18*, the date on which the fee provided for by *Regulation 14* falls due.

Additional Entries in the Register   [23.31]

Regulation 11 authorises the Commissioner to include certain matters in a register entry additional to the registerable particulars set out in *section 16*. Those matters are:

○   a registration number;
○   the deemed date of the entry provided by *Regulation 8*;
○   the date on which the entry may lapse under *Regulation 14* or *15*; and
○   additional information for the purpose of assisting communication about data protection matters between persons consulting the register and the data controller.

Changes to Register Entries [23.32]

Regulation 12 imposes on everyone who has a register entry a duty to notify the Commissioner of any respect in which the entry becomes an inaccurate or incomplete statement of his current registrable particulars or in which the latest description of security matters given under *section 18(2)(b)* of *DPA 1998* becomes inaccurate or incomplete. The notification must set out the changes which need to be made to ensure accuracy and completeness, and be given as soon as practicable and in any event within 28 days from the time when the inaccuracy or incompleteness arises.

Regulation 12 is modified by *Regulation 13* in its application to persons who have a register entry by virtue of the manner in which *DPA 1998*'s transitional provisions operate on entries in the register maintained under *section 4* of *DPA 1984*. In these cases, the duty under *Regulation 12* varies according to the extent to which the entry relates to data subject to processing which was already under way immediately before 24 October 1998. In respect of such data, the notification must specify certain aspects of processing which are not from time to time included in the existing register entry; in other cases it must specify any respect in which the entry becomes inaccurate or incomplete in certain respects, and set out the changes needed to ensure accuracy and completeness.

Other Provisions [23.33]

Regulation 14 provides that, other than in the transitional circumstances addressed in *Regulation 15*, the fee to be paid annually to secure retention of a register entry is £35. *Regulation 15* provides for the retention of register entries included by virtue of the manner in which the *DPA 1998*'s transitional provisions operate on entries in the register maintained under *section 4* of *DPA 1984*. These are to be retained until the end of the defined registration period, or 24 October 2001, or the date on which notification is given under *section 18* of *DPA 1998*, whichever occurs first.

Data Protection Tribunal (National Security Appeals) Rules 2000 [23.34]

These Rules regulate the exercise of the rights of appeal conferred by *section 28* (relating to Ministerial certification that exemption from provisions of the Act is or was required for the purpose of safeguarding national security), and the practice and procedure of the Data Protection Tribunal (the Tribunal) in such cases.

Rule 3 places a general duty on the Tribunal in such cases to secure that information is not disclosed contrary to the interests of national security, and limits the ex parte jurisdiction of the Tribunal to matters concerning the summary disposal of appeals under *Rule 11*.

Rule 4 requires an appeal to be made by notice of appeal served on the Tribunal, stating the grounds of appeal and other specified particulars, and *Rule 5* makes provision as to the time limits for appealing. *Rule 6* provides for acknowledgment of the notice of appeal, and for service of copies. *Rule 7* provides for a notice in reply by the Minister who signed the certificate, and *Rule 8* for a reply by the data controller in *section 28(6)* cases (where a data controller is claiming an exemption from various provisions of *DPA 1998* because it is in the interest of national security) who is claiming the application of a certificate. *Rule 9* provides for the parties to amend their pleadings, in some cases with leave only. *Rule 10* allows the Minister or the data controller to apply for an appeal to be struck out in limited circumstances.

Rule 11 enables the Tribunal to dismiss an appeal on the basis of consideration of the notice of appeal, the Minister's notice, and any reply by a data controller, where it considers it proper to do so, but it must first allow the appellant to make representations, written and oral, against a proposal to deal with the appeal under this procedure.

Rule 12 permits the Minister to object, on national security grounds, to the disclosure of his notice in reply, or any data controller's reply, to a party (or the Commissioner). Where he does so, he must give reasons and if possible supply a version of the notice which can be disclosed, and the procedure set out in *Rule 17* applies to the objection.

Rules 13 and *14* make provision in respect of the withdrawal of an appeal and the consolidation of appeals. *Rule 15* provides for the giving of directions by the Tribunal, of its own motion or on the application of a party; this power may be exercised in the absence of the parties, and any party may apply to set aside or vary directions.

Rule 16 provides for the Minister to be able to apply, on national security grounds, for the Tribunal to reconsider proposals to exercise certain of its powers (including giving directions, issuing a witness summons or publishing a determination). The procedure in *Rule 17* applies to such an application.

Rule 17 provides for the Tribunal to adjudicate on objections and applications of the Minister made on national security grounds.

Other than in cases to which *Rule 11* applies, the Tribunal must as a general rule proceed by way of a hearing but in certain additional circumstances it may determine an appeal without a hearing (*Rule 18*). Provision is made as to the appointment of time and place of a hearing (*Rule 19*), summoning of witnesses to attend a hearing (*Rule 20*), representation at a hearing (*Rule 21*) and default of appearance at a hearing (*Rule 22*).

Hearings by the Tribunal must generally be in private, but provision is made for public hearings, and the admission of other persons, in limited circumstances (*Rule 23*). The Rules include provision as to the conduct of proceedings at a hearing (*Rule 24*), powers of the president to act for the Tribunal (*Rule 25*), evidence (*Rule 26*), the determination of appeals (*Rule 27*) and costs (*Rule 28*).

These Rules contribute to the implementation of *Directive 95/46/EC* on the protection of individuals with regard to the processing of personal data and on the free movement of such data.

Data Protection Act 1998 (Commencement) Order

2000 [23.35]

The Order provided for *DPA 1998* to come into force on 1 March 2000, except for *sections 75(2)* (already in force) and *56* (Prohibition of requirements as to production of certain records) which must not be brought into force before *sections 112, 113* and *115* of *Police Act 1997* are all in force.

24 – Related Legislation

Human Rights Legislation [24.1]

Article 8 (the right to privacy) and *Article 10* (the right to freedom of expression) of the *European Convention for the Protection of Human Rights and Fundamental Freedoms* (the *Convention*) and their interplay have already been the subject of considerable debate and analysis, particularly by the media in the context of whether individuals will have greater rights to prevent the publication of private information. However, these Articles have significant commercial implications going well beyond this albeit important debate.

'Article 8
Right to respect for private and family life
1.   Everyone has the right to respect for his private and family life, his home and his correspondence.
2.   There shall be no interference by a public authority with the exercise of this right except such as is in accordance with the law and is necessary in a democratic society in the interests of national security, public safety or the economic well-being of the country, for the prevention of disorder or crime, for the protection of health or morals, or for the protection of the rights and freedoms of others.

Article 10
Freedom of expression
1.   Everyone has the right to freedom of expression. This right shall include freedom to hold opinions and to receive and impart information and ideas without interference by public authority and regardless of frontiers. This Article shall not prevent States from requiring the licensing of broadcasting, television or cinema enterprises.
2.   The exercise of these freedoms, since it carries with it duties and responsibilities, may be subject to such formalities, conditions, restrictions or penalties as are prescribed by law and are necessary in a democratic

313

society, in the interests of national security, territorial integrity or public safety, for the prevention of disorder or crime, for the protection of health or morals, for the protection of the reputation or rights of others, for preventing the disclosure of information received in confidence, or for maintaining the authority and impartiality of the judiciary.'

It can be immediately seen that these Articles each prescribe the basic human rights, privacy and freedom of expression, but equally each may yield to the other and to other stipulated public interests, but only when this is democratically necessary. An objective 'balancing' exercise will always be required to decide what amounts to democratic necessity on the facts of each case and in view of the societal conditions at the relevant time.

In addition, both Articles, on their face, only apply to interferences by 'public authority'. However, dangers to privacy stem not only from unnecessary governmental interference, but also from the activities of private persons and bodies, such as newspaper publishing companies and commercial broadcasting companies. It would be anomalous, however, if a public service broadcaster, such as the BBC, could not under the *Convention* unjustifiably invade privacy, whereas a commercial broadcasting company, such as Granada, could.

The European Commission and Court of Human Rights (ECtHR) have held, in answer, that to ensure the effective protection of Convention rights the state may have to adopt measures, even in relationships between private individuals. There are those who will argue that *Human Rights Act 1998* (*HRA 1998*) merely has 'vertical' effect i.e. can only be enforced against 'public authorities'. However, despite any such limitations which may be imposed by *HRA 1998*, it seems inevitable that a general right of privacy with 'horizontal' effect, i.e. between private parties, will gradually develop at common law.

Importance of Free Speech [24.2]

The ECtHR in a number of cases has held that freedom of expression: 'constitutes one of the essential foundations in a democratic society' and accords particular importance to political expression (see, for example, *Lingens v Austria (1986) 8 EHRR 407*, ECtHR). Companies are entitled to free speech as much as individuals and *Article 10* of the *Convention* is of crucial importance to newspaper, broadcasting, multimedia, book publishing and Internet service providing companies.

From the *Sunday Times Thalidomide* case *(1979) EHRR 245*, ECtHR, resulting in the *Contempt of Court Act 1981*, to the *Spycatcher* case (*Sunday Times v UK (No 2) (1991) EHRR 229*), when the UK Government was condemned for continuing to 'gag' the British press when the book had been published, the following principles emerge. Given the importance of free speech as a primary cornerstone of democracy, any restriction can be imposed only if 'strictly necessary' and must always be 'proportionate' to the pursuit of a 'legitimate aim'.

Governmental censorship must be particularly scrutinised. In *Autronic AG v Switzerland (1990) 12 EHRR 485*; [*1991*] *FSR 55*, ECtHR, the ECtHR held that the refusal of the Swiss Government to grant permission to receive uncoded television programmes from a Russian satellite violated *Article 10* of the *Convention*. Also, in *Informationsverein Lentia v Austria (1993) 17 EHRR 93*, ECtHR and *Radio ABC v Austria (1997) 25 EHRR 185*, ECtHR the Austrian Government's prohibition on setting up and operating television and radio stations, given the State monopoly, was held to breach *Article 10*.

The ECtHR has, however, been reluctant to grant full *Article 10* protection to advertising. In *Casado Coca v Spain (1994) 18 EHRR 1*, ECtHR it held that advertising, while necessary and useful, can be restricted if the rights of others or the 'special circumstances of particular business activities' so demand. A ban on advertising professional services was upheld on this basis. However, in *Hetel v Switzerland (25 August 1998, unreported)*, although the ECtHR held that the national authorities had a wide margin of appreciation, i.e. discretion, to decide whether there is a pressing social need for a restriction on commercial speech, that discretion was reduced when what was at stake was not purely commercial statements but a debate affecting the public interest, for example over public health. The advertisement in question, concerning the safety of microwaves, should not have been restricted. Several tobacco companies are now challenging the lawfulness of the EU Directive banning tobacco advertising alleging, amongst other matters, a breach of *Article 10*.

Public employees have complained of a restriction on their *Article 10* rights due to their employment status. Strasbourg has consistently held that the State may curtail its employees' rights to free speech in relation to their duties and job functions. For example, in a case involving the UK, it was held that the State could forbid a teacher in a non-denominational school from expressing certain beliefs. In 1995, however, the ECtHR found in *Vogt v Germany (1995) 21 EHRR 205*, ECtHR that the dismissal of a language teacher on grounds of her membership of the German Communist Party breached *Article 10*. An individual may, therefore, contract to limit his/her freedom of expression, but if an issue of public interest is involved such limitation may still be found to breach *Article 10*.

Privacy and the Media [24.3]

Article 8 of the *Convention* guarantees respect for privacy, family life, home and correspondence. During the Bill's Parliamentary passage, the media greatly feared that *Article 8* would empower judges to prevent them publishing information in breach of privacy. This was despite the fact that in *William Stanley Winer v UK (1986) 48 DR 154*, EComHR it was held by the ECtHR that:

> 'the absence of an actionable right to privacy under English law [did not] show a lack of respect for...private life'.

Similarly, although for different reasons, Earl and Countess Spencer's breach of privacy complaint failed in January 1998.

It seems that, when deciding what level of privacy protection is adequate, Strasbourg will accord States a wide margin of appreciation, particularly against non-public authorities such as commercial publishers and broadcasters.

Surveillance and Data Collection [24.4]

Article 8 of the *Convention* is also of relevance to surveillance and data collection. In *Malone v UK (1984) 7 EHRR 14*, the applicant successfully contended that the police intercepting telephone calls in the course of a criminal investigation violated *Article 8*, leading to the *Interception of Communications Act 1985*. More recently, in *Halford v UK (1997) 24 EHRR 523* where the police secretly recorded an employee's calls from police headquarters, a violation of *Article 8* was found. This was also found in *Kopp v Switzerland (1998)* where a lawyer's telephone calls from his office were unlawfully tapped by a Post Office official without any judicial supervision. Similarly if an employer company were to vet E-mails and other correspondence or use closed circuit TV without notifying employees, this could also amount to a breach of *Article 8*. Guidance will be forthcoming from the Commissioner's office on the issues of CCTV and of employers' access to employee E-mails.

The requirements of *DPA 1998* are a legislative attempt to protect the privacy of collected data. A question arose as to whether the provisions might be too onerous for journalists, given the free speech guarantee of *Article 10*. This was overcome by the 'media exemption' provided by *section 32* of *DPA 1998*.

Human Rights Act 1998 [24.5]

Consistent with the Government's commitment to human rights, *HRA 1998* will, when effective, directly incorporate the *Convention* into our own domestic law. *HRA 1998* will not come into force until 2 October 2000, so that judicial training can be given and governmental and public bodies have time to adapt to the new regime.

Businesses and individuals will be able to secure their rights from misuse of State and public authority power directly from any court or tribunal in the UK. No longer will it be necessary first to take the long, slow and often expensive trek to the ECtHR in Strasbourg. A culture of awareness of rights and how they can effectively be enforced should develop here.

Businesses will be able to claim the benefits of *HRA 1998*. However, concern has been expressed that it may be relied upon too heavily by commerce as a legal tool, with rich and powerful businesses using it to protect their interests against progressive State action. Such concerns are misplaced. Businesses have always been able to claim their rights in Strasbourg, as described below. However, the *Convention* has hardly become a 'boardroom charter'. In addition, companies who are likely to fall under the definition of 'public authorities' in *HRA 1998*, may indeed perceive that Act to be more of a threat than an opportunity, as they will be obliged to act compatibly with the *Convention*.

In line with considering *HRA 1998*, data controllers should consider their obligations under *DPA 1998*. An activity relating to personal data which is carried out covertly may not only be in breach of *HRA 1998* but also of the First Data Protection Principle. In many cases, the two Acts could in future, be used together by data subjects to great effect.

Freedom of Information Bill [24.6]

The UK *Freedom of Information Bill*, was introduced into the House of Commons in November 1999. It is primarily about enabling citizens to participate:

'in the discussion of policy issues, and so improve the quality of government decision making', and holding 'government and other bodies to account'.

The Bill will apply to public authorities in England, Wales and Northern Ireland. It will not apply to the Scottish Parliament, the Scottish Administration or Scottish public authorities with mixed functions or no reserved functions. The relevant authorities are listed at the end of this Chapter.

On first reading the Bill appears to give effective protection to confidential business information while promising the release of more government information. The common law duty of confidence will be unchanged and the test for the exemption of commercial information seems an easy one to meet.

Areas of Concern [24.7]

Looking at the Bill more closely there are some real areas of concern for business:

O   the Bill is retrospective. It applies to information that is 'held' by a public authority at the time a request is received;

O   a public authority will have discretion to release commercial information that is properly exempt within the terms of the Act once passed, in the light of its own judgement of all the circumstances and the balance of the public interest;

O   a company will have no statutory right to advance notice when a public authority plans to release information that the company has claimed to be confidential (the provision for advance notice will be merely in a non-statutory code of practice); and

O   a requester who is refused company information that is claimed to be confidential will have an easy appeal process to the Information Commissioner and the Tribunal. A company that disagrees with a decision to release its information has no appeal process. Its only recourse is to the High Court.

Importance for Business [24.8]

The Bill will create new risks and provide new opportunities for business. The risks are that confidential information may become more easily available to competitors, customers, suppliers and interest groups. In addition to the risks inherent in the features of the Bill outlined above, the context in which it is being introduced and the practicalities of implementation add to these risks.

Decisions about what qualifies as confidential, and when discretion should be exercised will be taken by many officials in many different authorities. Also the overall effect may well be larger than a close reading of the provisions of the Bill would imply. If one considers the likely combined effect of a promised drive to make the culture more open, the requirement for publication schemes, the role of the Information Commissioner as a public one, and the clear legal provisions, it would be prudent for business to anticipate a larger change from the status quo than most commentators expect.

Practical Pointers [24.9]

The business community should give immediate attention to actions to protect confidential information. The key actions to be taken could include the following:

✓ Review information given to public authorities. Who provides what information to which public authority on what basis? Which of this information definitely is, or could become, confidential?

✓ Design and apply suitable processes for this information. These should clarify who is required to approve submissions, to claim confidentiality and to negotiate with the authority about release, track the handling of the information by the authority, and alert senior management and the legal department to the need for action.

✓ Establish clear policies and processes for claiming confidentiality and ensuring that these claims are effective. This could include taking care to segregate confidential information, ensure that it is carefully marked and reasons are given to the authority that make it clear that exemptions are being claimed and for which reasons that are in line with the terms of the Bill.

The actions to obtain information that will be valuable are likely to be less urgent, but should be considered before too long. Priorities will depend upon circumstances, but companies should be aware that many companies with US experience will be expected to grasp the new opportunity to gain a competitive edge. The actions that one should consider taking can be summarised as follows.

✓   Review the information that is held by public authorities that could be valuable to the company. The nature of this will vary according to the market, and priorities of the company.

✓   Focus upon those areas that are most important.

✓   Consider what can be obtained now. In some cases a company may decide the value is so great that it adopts a leading edge position in arguing for release in advance of the Freedom of Information Act. Some Ministers may decide they do not need to wait for the Act to come into force to release some information within their own discretion, which would be released later anyway.

Appendix A

A Comparison Between the Sections in *DPA 1984* and *DPA 1998*

Data Protection Act 1984	Data Protection Act 1998
s1(2) Definition of 'data'.	*s1(1)* Definition of 'data' extended to include 'relevant filing systems'.
s1(3) Definition of 'personal data'.	*s1(1)* Definition extended to include information 'likely to come into the possession of' the data controller and to include not only expressions of opinion about an individual (as per *DPA 1984*) but also 'any indication of the intentions of the data controller or any other person in respect of the individual'.
s1(5) Definition of 'data user'.	*s1(1)* Replaced by definition of 'data controller', which is wider.
s1(6) Definition of 'computer bureau'.	*s1(1)* Replaced by definition of 'data processor'.
s1(7) Definition of 'processing'.	*s1(1)* Definition is much wider and covers just about any activity involving data. It no longer has to take place 'by reference to data subject'.
s1(9) Definition of 'disclosing'.	*s1(2)* Expanded to include 'obtaining' or 'recording' and 'using' or 'disclosing'.
ss4–9 Registration procedure.	*ss16–26* Notification procedure.
s5 Prohibition of unregistered holding etc. of personal data.	*s17* Prohibition on processing without registration – note *s17(3)*.
s5(6)–(11) Any breach of terms of registration is a criminal offence.	s21 Breaches could be the subject of an enforcement notice, but are not automatically criminal offences.

s8 Duration and renewal of registration – need to reapply for registration every three years.	*s19* No need to reapply for registration - data controller would remain registered so long as pays annual fee.
ss10–12 Enforcement, de-registration de-registration and transfer prohibition notices.	*ss40–44* Types of enforcement notice changed – enforcement notices, information notices and special information notices.
s13 Rights of appeal.	*s48* Rights of appeal.
s14 Determination of appeals.	*s49* Determination of appeals.
s19 Prosecutions and penalties.	*s60* Prosecutions and penalties.
s20 Liability of directors.	*s61* Liability of directors.
s21 Data subject's right of access to personal data.	*s7* Data subject's right of access to personal data – information to be supplied slightly expanded to include not only a copy of the information held, but also the purposes for which it is being processed and to whom it may be disclosed. A new provision (*s7(1)(c)*) also includes the obligation to reveal information as to the 'source' of the data.
s21(4)(b) Data user needs consent from other individual, if compliance with a request to supply information relating to one individual, would include information about another.	*s7(4)(b)* This allows the data controller to comply with the request without this consent if it is 'reasonable in all the circumstances.' *s7(6)* Gives guidance as to what is 'reasonable.'
s21(6) Time limit for data user to comply with request to supply information runs from day of request.	*s7(8)* Time limit for compliance did not start running until fee paid, although the prescribed period remains the same (40 days).
ss22–23 Compensation provisions.	*s13* Compensation provisions – an extension of the data subject's rights.
s24 Rectification and erasure rights of data subject.	*s14* Rectification and erasure rights of data subject – slightly wider.
ss26–35 Exemptions from Act provisions.	*ss27–39* Exemptions from Act provisions – some new provisions:

	s32 Journalism, literature and art
	s38 Power of Secretary of State to make further exemptions by order.
s36 General duties of the Registrar.	*s51* General duties of the Commissioner.
s38 Application to government departments and police.	*s63* Application to Crown.
No special treatment of 'sensitive personal data'.	*s2* Definition of 'sensitive personal data'.
No definition of 'special purposes' for the treatment of data.	*s3* Definition of 'special purposes' (particularly relevant for the media exemption).
No relevant provision.	*s8(2)* Prescribed form of the copy of any information supplied.
No relevant provision.	*s9* Where the data controller is a credit reference agency.
No relevant provision.	*s10* Right to prevent processing likely to cause damage or distress.
No relevant provision.	*s11* Right to prevent processing for the purposes of direct marketing.
No relevant provision.	*s12* Restrictions on automated decision-taking.
No relevant provision.	*s64* Transmission of notices by electronic or other means.
Schedule 1: The Data Protection Principles	*Schedule 1*: The Data Protection Principles – note the changes: 1st Reference to 'obtaining' data removed and principle now subject to meeting conditions in *Schedules 2 and 3*; 2nd new Principle now encompasses the Second and Third Principles from *DPA 1984*; Sixth new Principle simplifies and replaces the old Seventh Principle; 7th

	Formerly the old Eighth Principle; Eighth new Principle. Important to read new principles in conjunction with their interpretation in *Schedule 1, Part II.*
No relevant provision.	*Schedule 2* Conditions relevant for purposes of the First Principle: processing of any personal data.
No relevant provision.	*Schedule 3* Conditions relevant for purposes of the First Principle: processing of sensitive personal data.
No relevant provision.	*Schedule 4* Cases where the Eighth Principle did not apply.
No relevant provision.	*Schedule 14* Transitional provisions and savings – deals with the relationship between 'Registration' under *DPA 1984* and 'Notification' under *DPA 1998.*

Appendix B

Bibliography

Listed below are some of the core materials which would be useful to those interested in this area.

Data Protection Act 1998

This is available from The Stationery Office Limited, price £10. It is available from the Publications Centre (Mail, Telephone and Fax orders only) PO Box 276, London SW8 5DT, order through the Parliamentary Hotline LONDON-call 0345 02 34 74. Faxed orders could be sent to 020 7873 8200. The publication is also available from Stationery Office Bookshops. The cost is £10.00. It is also available at: www.legislation.hmso.gov.uk/acts/acts1998/19980029.htm.

Data Protection Act 1984, Chapter 35

This is available from the Stationery Office.

Data Protection Act 1998, an Introduction

This publication is available, free of charge, from the Data Protection Registrar's Office and the current version is version 1, October 1998. It is available from the Office of the Data Protection Registrar, Wycliffe House, Water Lane, Wilmslow, Cheshire SK9 5AF. The Data Protection Registrar's Information Line is 01625 545710. E-mail: data@Wycliffe.demon.co.uk. The ISDN No is 1 870 466 21 7.

Consultation Paper on the EC Data Protection Directive (95/ 46/EC)

This Consultation Paper was produced by the Home Office in March 1996 and is available from Graham Sutton, Data Protection Section,

Home Office, Room 1181, 50 Queen Anne's Gate, London SW1H
9AT. Fax: 020 7273 3205.

Directive 95/46/EC of the European Parliament and of the Council of 24 October 1995 on 'The protection of individuals with regard to the processing of personal data and on the free movement of such data'.

This could be found in the Official Journal of the European
Communities where it appeared on 23 November 1995 with number
L 281/31. The footnotes to the final version of the Directive published
in the Official Journal also contain references to a number of other
useful papers produced by the Commission with regard to the Directive.
(See also http://europa.eu.int/eur-lex/eu/lif/dat/1995/en-
395L0046.html). European Commission contact for the Directive is
Mr Ulf Brühann, DGXV - D1 (CORT 107), Commission of the
European Communities, Rue de la Loi 200, B1049, Brussels, Belgium.

The Guidelines - The Data Protection Act 1984 (Third series, November 1994)

These are available free of charge from the DPR's Office as described
above. Guidelines were first produced some years ago and have evolved as
the DPR's Office became more familiar with *DPA 1984*. Separate guidance
has also been produced on certain specific areas particularly in relation to
the financial services industry and in relation to direct marketing.

Also available on the Data Protection website: http://wood.ccta.gov.uk/
dpr/dpdoc.nsf.

Data Protection Registrar's website

It is worth visiting the Data Protection Registrar's home page at http://
www.open.gov.uk/dpr/dprhome.htm

Data Protection - Everybody's business – A practical guide for professionals & business managers

This publication is available from The British Computer Society from
their Marketing Department, British Computer Society, 1 Sanford Street,
Swindon, Wiltshire SN1 1HJ, telephone number 01793 417424. This

was first printed in October 1998 with ISBN No 1 902 505 04 2. It is available to be purchased from them.

Working Party on the protection of individuals with regard to the processing of personal data – 2nd annual report

This document has been produced by the European Commission and is the second annual report of the Working Party on the Protection of Individuals with regard to the Processing of Personal Data. The report was adopted by the above Working Party on 30 November 1998. It is available from the European Commission, DG XV (see further http://europa.eu.int/eclas/cgi/squery.pl?=en). Its reference is DG XV DXV/5047/98 final. This report analyses, inter alia, the position that countries in the EU have reached with regard to the implementation of the *Data Protection Directive*. Author: Yves Poullet, publication: Luxembourg: EUR-OP, 1998 ISBN 9 282 84304 1.

Final Report – Application of a methodology designed to assess the adequacy of the level of protection of individuals with regard to processing personal data: test of the method on several categories of transfer

This is a report that was produced for the European Commission Tender No XV/97/18/T and has been presented by the University of Edinburgh and others in September 1998.

Author: Charles D Raab, publication: Luxembourg: EUR-OP, 1999. ISBN 9 282 85638 0. (See further: http://europa.eu.int/eclas/cgi/squery.pl?lang=en.

This report tests a methodology for assessing the adequacy of the level of protection of individuals with regard to processing personal data in connection with *Article 25* of the *Data Protection Directive*. The report describes 30 cases of data transfer from six countries. Five categories of transfer are reviewed – human resources data; sensitive data in airline reservations; medical/epidemiological data; data in electronic commerce; and sub-contracted data processing.

All change for Europe? – The Data Protection Act 1998 *by Dr Ian Walden*

Published in Tolley's Communications Law, Vol 3 No 6.

The New Data Protection Act – BBA Guidance

This publication is available for purchase. ISBN 1 874185 10 7. It is available from the British Bankers' Association at Pinners Hall, 105–108 Old Broad Street, London EC2N 1EX.

Other Papers Available from the DPR

The additional papers which have been produced by the DPR on the new data protection law so far are:

○ EU Data Protection Directive – Preparing for the New Law.
○ EU Data Protection Directive – Implementing the New Law.
○ New Data Protection Law – Initial comments from the Data Protection Registrar:
  ● Cost of Implementing the EU Data Protection Directive,
  ● Transferring Data to Third Countries,
  ● Criminal Disclosures by the Commissioner's Staff,
  ● Notification Requirements,
  ● Media Exemptions.
○ Data Protection: The Governments Proposals – Comments of the Data Protection Registrar.
○ House of Commons Second Reading of the Data Protection Bill – Comments of the Registrar 20/4/98.
○ House of Commons Third Reading of the Data Protection Bill – Comments of the Registrar 26/6/98.
○ House of Commons Committee Stage Data Protection Bill – Comments of the Registrar – Exemption.
○ 'Questions to Answer' – The EU Directive and Data Protection (papers from the Data Protection Registrar, April 1996).
○ 'Our Answers' – from the Data Protection Registrar (relating to the above entry).
○ 97/66/EC Directive – Processing of Personal Data in Connection with Telecommunication Services (DTI Consultation Paper).

The above publications from the DPR's Office are available via the DPR's website (http://www.open.gov.uk/dpr/dprhome.htm) or on request by writing to the Office of the DPR.

The Office of The Data Protection Registrar, Wycliffe House, Water Lane, Wilmslow, Cheshire SK9 5AF. The DPR's recorded message line (01625 545737) outlines the latest information available from the Office.

The Fourteenth Annual Report of the Data Protection Registrar – June 1998

Price £21.30. It contains a useful Appendix 10 looking at some of the issues in relation to transfers of personal data outside the EEA to countries which may not provide adequate protection for personal data. Available at http://www.dataprotection.gov.uk/99arcontents.htm.

The Fifteenth Annual Report of the Data Protection Registrar (June 1998)

http://www.dataprotection.gov.uk/99arcontents.htm.

Home Office News Release Data Protection Act – Consultation on Notification

This news release was published on 24 August 1998 and is available from the Home Office at 50 Queen Anne's Gate, London SW1H 9AT on telephone number 020 7273 4640.

Home Office Consultation Paper: 'Data Protection Act 1998, Subordinate Legislation'

This was published by the Home Office in August 1998 and is available from the address above.

Model clauses for use in contracts involving transborder data flows – *produced by the International Chamber of Commerce, Paris*

This document is available from the International Chamber of Commerce, Paris, website at: www.iccwbo.org.

Data Protection Act 1998 – Subordinate Legislation; Notification Regulations

This consultation paper is available from the Home Office as above.

Convention for the Protection of Individuals with regard to the Automatic Processing of Personal Data European Treaty Series, No 108 of 1981 Strasbourg.

OECD Recommendation of 23 September 1980 The Recommendation concerning Guidelines governing the protection of privacy and transborder flows of personal data.

Data Protection Act 1984: a consultation paper on the Registrar's proposals for simplifying and restructuring the registration system – available from the Registrar's Office, Wycliffe House (see above) 23 September 1980

The European Directive concerning the processing of personal data and the protection of privacy in the telecommunications sector and in particular in the integrated services digital network and in the public digital mobile network

This Directive has official reference 97/66/EC and is now referred to more commonly as the Telecoms Data Protection Directive.

DTI Consultation Paper on the Telecoms Data Protection Directive (published in April 1998). Contact the DTI either by telephone: 020 7215 5000, or by post: The Enquiry Unit, DTI, 1 Victoria Street, London, SW1H 0ET.

Telecommunications (Data Protection and Privacy) (Direct Marketing) Regulations 1998 (SI 1998/3170)

Those regulations came into force on 1 May 1999 and are available from the Stationery Office (tel: 020 7873 9090) and either the HMSO website (http://www.hmso.gov.uk) or the DTI website (http://www.dti.gov.uk/cii/tdpd/regs/). They were repealed on 1 March 2000.

Adopted documents of the Article 29 Working Party set up under the Directive

O   **WP 3 (5025/97)**. First Annual Report. Adopted 25 June 1997 (in 11 languages).
O   **WP 4 (5020/97)**. First orientations on Transfers of Personal Data to Third Countries – Possible Ways Forward in Assessing Adequacy. Adopted 26 June 1997 (in 11 languages).
O   **WP 6 (5022/97)**: Recommendation 3/97. Anonymity on the Internet. Adopted 3 December 1997 (in 11 languages).
O   **WP 7 (5057/97)**: Working Document. *Judging industry self-regulation: when does it make a meaningful contribution to the level of*

data protection in a third country? Adopted 14 January 1998 (in 11 languages).

○ **WP 9 (5005/98)**: Working Document: Preliminary views on the use of contractual provisions in the context of transfers of personal data to third countries. Adopted 22 April 1998 (in 11 languages).

○ **WP 12 (5025/98)**: Working Document. *Transfers of personal data to third countries: Applying Articles 25 and 26 of the EU Data Protection Directive*. Adopted 24 July 1998 (in 11 languages).

○ **WP 14 (5047/98)**: Second Annual Report. Adopted by the Working Party on 30 November 1998 (in 11 languages).

○ **WP 16 (5013/99)**: Working document. *Processing of Personal Data on the Internet*. Adopted on 23 February 1999 (in 11 languages).

○ **WP 17 (5093/98)**: Recommendation 1/99 on Invisible and Automatic Processing of Personal Data on the Internet Performed by Software and Hardware. Adopted on 23 February 1999 (in 11 languages).

○ **WP 23 (5075/99)**: Working document on the current state of play of the ongoing discussions between the European Commission and the United States Government concerning the 'International Safe Harbor Principles' issued by the US Department of Commerce on 1st June 1999. Adopted on 7 July 1999 (in English and French).

○ **WP 27 (5146/99)**: Opinion 7/99 on the level of Data Protection provided by the 'Safe Harbor' Principles as published together with the Frequently Asked Questions (FAQs) and other related documents on 15 and 16 November 1999 by the US Department of Commerce. Adopted on 3 December 1999.

○ **WP 5007/00/EN/Final**: Opinion 1/200 on certain data protection aspects of electronic commerce. Presented by the Internet Task Force. Adopted on 3 February 2000.

○ **WP 5009/00/EN/Final**: Opinion 2/2000 concerning the general review of the telecommunications legal framework. Presented by the Internet Task Force. Adopted on 3 February 2000.

○ **WP 5139/99/EN/Final**: Recommendation 1/2000 on the Implementation of Directive 95/46/EC. Adopted on 3 February 2000.

Appendix C

Countries Where the Data Protection Directive is to be Implemented

O   Austria
O   Belgium
O   Denmark
O   Finland
O   France
O   Germany
O   Greece
O   Iceland (EEA)
O   Italy
O   Liechtenstein (EEA)
O   Luxembourg
O   The Netherlands
O   Norway (EEA)
O   Portugal
O   Republic of Ireland
O   Spain
O   Sweden
O   United Kingdom

Note

For the purposes of implementation of the Directive, the 'United Kingdom' means Great Britain and Northern Ireland, exclusive of the Channel Islands and the Isle of Man. 'Great Britain' means England, Wales and Scotland. This means that the Channel Islands and the Isle of Man are outside the EU for data protection purposes such as transfers of data outside the EU.

Guernsey, Jersey and the Isle of Man are all looking at whether their laws need to be amended to ensure that those laws provide an adequate level of protection for personal data for the purposes of *Article 25* of the *Directive*.

Status of Implementation by Member States (as at February 2000)

Country	Status of Implementing Legislation	Next Step
Belgium	The implementation law was passed by the Parliament and published on the Official Journal of 3 February 1999.	
Denmark	Partial implementation by a law amending the Civil Registration Act which came into force on 1 October 1998. A bill has been introduced twice to Parliament.	Current Bill published December 1999. Should be law by July.
Germany	Legislation passed in relation to data protection in the context of telecommunications. Draft general data protection law exists but is not yet before Parliament. Legislation will be needed at the Laender level as well.	Consideration by Parliament. No Parliamentary work as yet.
Spain	The Government adopted a Bill in July. It consisted of minor changes to the existing "Ley Organica". Implementation Law (Ley Organica 15/99) came into force in January 2000 to ensure, for example, that data can be exported outside the EU if, inter alia, the data subject's consent is obtained, Before that, there was some concern that export could not take place even with consent.	Parliamentary adoption.
France	A bill is before Parliament.	Parliament to discuss in Spring 2000.
Greece	Implementation Law 2472 adopted on 10 April 1997.	
Italy	Law 675 of 31.12.1996. Completed by secondary legislation.	
Ireland	Draft bill presented to Government in July 1998.	Bill to be approved by Government and submitted to Parliament.

Luxembourg	Bill being finalised by Ministry of Justice.	Formal adoption and Parliamentary discussions.
The Netherlands	Draft bill adopted by the Second Chamber on 23 November 1999.	Discussion and adoption by First Chamber (Senate).
Austria	Directive has been implemented by the Data Protection Act 2000. Entered into force 1 January 2000.	
Portugal	Directive has been implemented by Law 67/98 of 26 October 1998.	
Sweden	SFS 1998: 204 of 29 April 1998 and Regulation SFS 1998: 1191 of 3 September 1998, all of which came into force on 25 October 1998.	
Finland	The law was enacted by the Finnish Parliament on 10 February 1999 and entered into force on 1 June 1999.	
UK	*Data Protection Act 1998* received Royal Assent on 16 July 1998. Secondary legislation (18 orders) all adopted on 1 March 2000. *DPA 1998* came into force 1 March 2000. UK in a position to notify the EC Commission of that fact.	

Appendix D

An Example of a Data Protection Implementation Checklist

Note. This checklist is written as a general guide only. It should not be relied upon as a substitute for specific legal advice.

Data protection – are you ready for the new regime?

The following checklist is intended to remind you about the requirements of *Data Protection Act 1998* (*DPA 1998*). These will apply to you either:

О   from 1 March 2000; or
О   by 24 October 2001, if you qualify for transitional relief.

Some of these are the same as (or very similar to) existing data protection requirements.

Answering the questions in the checklist will give you a good idea of how prepared you are and what changes you may need to make to your documentation, systems and procedures but remember this is a complex area.

Checklist

Answer Yes or No to the following questions.

	Yes	No

1. **Do you hold information manually or electronically about living individuals ('personal data')?**
If yes, *DPA 1998* applies to you. ☐ ☐

2. **Are you registered?**
If no, you need to register – it is an offence to process personal data for any purpose unless you are registered for that purpose. ☐ ☐

3. **Have you recently reviewed your registration?**
Regular review is necessary to avoid committing an offence. Registrations can quickly become out of date. ☐ ☐

4. **Was your processing already under way before 24 October 1998?**
If yes, then you should have the benefit of the transitional provisions and be exempt from some parts of *DPA 1998*. Remember you can lose transitional relief. ☐ ☐

5. **Are you intending to alter, upgrade, replace or add to your systems or the processing you are carrying out before 24 October 2001?**
If the answer to any of these is Yes, you may not be entitled to transitional relief in relation to the new processing. In practice this might prevent you from relying on the relief for all your processing. ☐ ☐

You must comply with the fair processing code[1] and have correct data subject consents

6. **Do you use personal data only for purposes which will be obvious[2] to the data subject?**
If no, to comply with the fair processing code, as the Data Protection Commissioner is describing it, you need to tell the data subject about all the non-obvious uses (perhaps in a purpose statement) and get his consent. ☐ ☐

7. **Do you use sensitive personal data[3]?**
If yes, you will probably need explicit consent[4]. ☐ ☐

8. **Do you buy mailing lists?**
If yes, you need to work out how you will comply with the fair processing code[5]. ☐ ☐

		Yes	No

9. **Do you sell mailing lists?** □ □
If yes, you need to avoid problems with sales in the
future by including passing the data to prospective
purchasers of your mailing lists in consents you obtain.

10. **Do you, or might you, transfer personal data outside
the European Economic Area?** □ □
If yes, you must make sure:
○   the receiving country has an adequate level of
protection for an individual's rights and
freedoms, or
○   obtain the data subject's consent to the transfer, or
○   (assuming regulatory approval of model contract
clauses) impose data protection requirements on
the recipient of the data by contract, or
○   the transfer is permitted because it is necessary
for certain specific reasons.

11. **Do you keep personal data in manual and
automated form?** □ □
Manual records held in a relevant filing system[6] fall
within the ambit of *DPA 1998*.
If you hold such records you need to:
○   introduce a system for locating the records easily
○   review the records bearing in mind that all
information (e.g. manuscript notes) will have to
be disclosed unless an exemption applies.

12. **On receipt of a request from a data subject, can
you tell them[7]:**
○   whether you are processing their data; □ □
○   a description and copy of the personal data; □ □
○   the purposes for which you use it; □ □
○   the source of the data; □ □
○   who you might disclose it to; and □ □
○   if you are processing by automatic means the
logic involved in any decision taking process. □ □

13. **Do you engage in direct marketing by mail, fax
or telephone[8]?** □ □

14. **If your answer to question 13 is yes, can you:**
○   record on your system which data subjects
have asked you to stop processing their
personal data for direct marketing? □ □
○   distinguish between those who do not want to
receive marketing faxes, telephone calls or other
communications? □ □

If you answered no to either of these you will need to adapt your system.

15. **Do you take decisions which significantly affect a data subject based solely on automatic means?** ☐   ☐
(**Note:** *you need to review your systems to answer this question taking account of exemptions.*)
If the answer is yes, you need to be able to:
- O   inform data subjects that decisions are made in this way;
- O   put in place a procedure which allows data subjects to ask you to reconsider the decision on a non-automated basis; and
- O   flag on your system data subjects who have requested that you do not take automated decisions about them.

16. **Do you use data processors?** ☐   ☐

If yes, you must vet their data security provisions and have a written contract requiring the data processor to keep your data secure and only act on your instructions. The contract should also include a right to vet the processor's security measures.

17. **In order to comply with the Data Protection Principles you need to do the following. Do you:**
- O   keep data secure;
- O   keep data protected against unauthorised or unlawful processing; ☐   ☐
- O   keep data protected against accidental loss, destruction or damage; ☐   ☐
- O   regularly review the data to ensure that it is adequate, relevant and not excessive; ☐   ☐
- O   keep the data up-to-date and destroy it after a reasonable period? ☐   ☐

NOTES

1. To comply with the 'fair processing code' (the First Data Protection Principle) you must tell the data subject your identity, what you are going to use the data for and any other information necessary to make the processing fair before you obtain the data.
2. Use will be obvious if it is directly required for the primary reason for holding data.
3. Sensitive personal data is information about ethnic or racial origin, political opinions, religious beliefs, health, sexual life, trade union membership and the commission of, or proceedings in relation to, criminal offences.

4. Explicit consent may be written or verbal and you must clearly specify what sensitive personal data will be used and why.

5. You must tell individuals on a mailing list the information necessary to comply with the code before you start processing their data (i.e. before you enter it into your systems).

6. Any filing system where information is grouped together by reference to individuals or by reference to criteria relating to individuals in such a way that specific information relating to an individual is easily accessible.

7. There are exemptions which you need to be aware of.

8. *Telecommunications (Data Protection and Privacy) (Direct Marketing) Regulations 1998* regulated direct marketing by fax and telephone ('cold calling') and came into force on 1 May 1999. They were replaced in full on 1 March 2000 by regulations covering similar ground but which are much more extensive and cover other areas, the *Telecommunications (Data Protection and Privacy) Regulations 1999*. The 1999 Regulations were varied by *Telecommunications (Data Protection and Privacy) (Amendment) Regulations 2000* which also came into force on 1 March 2000.

Appendix E

An Example of a Draft Letter from a Data Controller to a Data Processor

[appropriate officer of Data Processor]
[address of Data Processor]

[For the attention of: [appropriate representative of Data Processor]]

Dear [**Sir**] [ ]

Processing contract between [Data Processor] and [Data Controller]

We refer to the processing contract between us dated [   ] ("the Contract") under which you have undertaken to provide certain processing services ("Services") on our behalf.

In July 1998, the Data Protection Act 1998 ("the Act") received Royal Assent and it became law in March 2000. Under that document, by virtue of the seventh data protection principle contained in Schedule 1 of the Act, "data controllers" (in the case of our relationship with you, that will be [full name],) are obliged to impose certain obligations of security in relation to personal data upon their "data processors" which, in the context of the Contract, is you.

Since it is our legal requirement to include such a provision in our Contract, we would be grateful if you would undertake to us as set out below. [In consideration of that undertaking, we would be prepared to contemplate continuing future relationships with you.] If you are unable to give such an undertaking, then we may [be forced to seek services elsewhere in the future] [will not renew the Contract] [on expiry of the Contract] since, if we are unable to obtain appropriate assurances from you, we will be in breach of our legal obligations under the Act.

343

The assurance that we seek from you is that you undertake to us to comply with the obligations of a "data controller" under the provisions of the Seventh Data Protection Principle, as set out in Schedule I, Part II of the Act when it comes into force as regards any personal data you process in providing the Services. In addition, you:

(a)   Warrant and undertake that you have and will at all times during the term of the Contract appropriate technical and organisational measures in place acceptable to us to protect any personal data accessed or processed by you against unauthorised or unlawful processing of personal data and against accidental loss or destruction of, or damage to, personal data held or processed by you [(such measures as at the date of this letter being described in the attached Annex)] and that you have taken all reasonable steps to ensure the reliability of any of your staff which will have access to personal data processed as part of the Services;

(b)   Undertake that you will act only on our instructions in relation to the processing of any personal data provided to you by us, [or] on our behalf, [or] by our employees [or former employees];

(c)   Undertake [to provide the Services at least to the level of security set out in the Annex to this Letter and] to allow us (or our representative) access to any relevant premises owned or controlled by you on reasonable notice to inspect your procedures described at (a) above and will, on our request from time to time, prepare a report for us as to your then current technical and organisational measures used to protect any such personal data.

[(d)   Undertake to consider all [reasonable] suggestions which we may put to you to ensure that the level of protection you provide for personal data is in accordance with this Letter and to make changes suggested unless you can prove to our reasonable satisfaction that they are not necessary to ensure ongoing compliance with your warranty and undertaking at (a) above.]

Breach of any of the above warranties or undertakings will entitle us to terminate the Contract forthwith.

Any terms defined in the Act will have the same meaning in this letter.

Please indicate your agreement to the provisions set out above by signing and returning the attached copy of this letter.

Yours faithfully

....
For and on behalf of [Data Controller]

....
Accepted and Agreed
[Data Processor]

....

Annex

The Current Security Procedures

Legislation
Annex

Data Protection Act 1998

1998 Chapter 29

An Act to make new provision for the regulation of the processing of information relating to individuals, including the obtaining, holding, use or disclosure of such information.

[16th July 1998]

BE IT ENACTED by the Queen's most Excellent Majesty, by and with the advice and consent of the Lords Spiritual and Temporal, and Commons, in this present Parliament assembled, and by the authority of the same, as follows:–

PART I
PRELIMINARY

1. – Basic interpretative provisions

(1) In this Act, unless the context otherwise requires –

"data" means information which –

(a) is being processed by means of equipment operating automatically in response to instructions given for that purpose,

(b) is recorded with the intention that it should be processed by means of such equipment,

(c) is recorded as part of a relevant filing system or with the intention that it should form part of a relevant filing system, or

(d) does not fall within paragraph (a), (b) or (c) but forms part of an accessible record as defined by section 68;

"data controller" means, subject to subsection (4), a person who (either alone or jointly or in common with other persons) determines the purposes for which and the manner in which any personal data are, or are to be, processed;

"data processor", in relation to personal data, means any person (other than an employee of the data controller) who processes the data on behalf of the data controller;

"data subject" means an individual who is the subject of personal data;

"personal data" means data which relate to a living individual who can be identified –

(a) from those data, or

(b) from those data and other information which is in the possession of, or is likely to come into the possession of, the data controller,

and includes any expression of opinion about the individual and any indication of the intentions of the data controller or any other person in respect of the individual;

"processing", in relation to information or data, means obtaining, recording or holding the information or data or carrying out any operation or set of operations on the information or data, including –

(a) organisation, adaptation or alteration of the information or data,

(b) retrieval, consultation or use of the information or data,

(c) disclosure of the information or data by transmission, dissemination or otherwise making available, or

(d) alignment, combination, blocking, erasure or destruction of the information or data;

"relevant filing system" means any set of information relating to individuals to the extent that, although the information is not processed by means of equipment operating automatically in response to instructions given for that purpose, the set is structured, either by reference to individuals or by reference to criteria relating to individuals, in such a way that specific information relating to a particular individual is readily accessible.

(2) In this Act, unless the context otherwise requires –

(a) "obtaining" or "recording", in relation to personal data, includes obtaining or recording the information to be contained in the data, and

(b) "using" or "disclosing", in relation to personal data, includes using or disclosing the information contained in the data.

(3) In determining for the purposes of this Act whether any information is recorded with the intention –

(a) that it should be processed by means of equipment operating automatically in response to instructions given for that purpose, or

(b) that it should form part of a relevant filing system,

it is immaterial that it is intended to be so processed or to form part of such a system only after being transferred to a country or territory outside the European Economic Area.

(4) Where personal data are processed only for purposes for which they are required by or under any enactment to be processed, the person on whom the obligation to process the data is imposed by or under that enactment is for the purposes of this Act the data controller.

2. In this Act "sensitive personal data" means personal data consisting of information as to –
(a) the racial or ethnic origin of the data subject,
(b) his political opinions,
(c) his religious beliefs or other beliefs of a similar nature,
(d) whether he is a member of a trade union (within the meaning of the Trade Union and Labour Relations (Consolidation) Act 1992,
(e) his physical or mental health or condition,
(f) his sexual life,
(g) the commission or alleged commission by him of any offence, or
(h) any proceedings for any offence committed or alleged to have been committed by him, the disposal of such proceedings or the sentence of any court in such proceedings.

3. In this Act "the special purposes" means any one or more of the following –
(a) the purposes of journalism,
(b) artistic purposes, and
(c) literary purposes.

4. – (1) References in this Act to the data protection principles are to the principles set out in Part I of Schedule 1.

(2) Those principles are to be interpreted in accordance with Part II of Schedule 1.

(3) Schedule 2 (which applies to all personal data) and Schedule 3 (which applies only to sensitive personal data) set out conditions applying for the purposes of the first principle; and Schedule 4 sets out cases in which the eighth principle does not apply.

(4) Subject to section 27(1), it shall be the duty of a data controller to comply with the data protection principles in relation to all personal data with respect to which he is the data controller.

5. – (1) Except as otherwise provided by or under section 54, this Act applies to a data controller in respect of any data only if –
(a) the data controller is established in the United Kingdom and

the data are processed in the context of that establishment, or

(b) the data controller is established neither in the United Kingdom nor in any other EEA State but uses equipment in the United Kingdom for processing the data otherwise than for the purposes of transit through the United Kingdom.

(2) A data controller falling within subsection (1)(b) must nominate for the purposes of this Act a representative established in the United Kingdom.

(3) For the purposes of subsections (1) and (2), each of the following is to be treated as established in the United Kingdom –

(a) an individual who is ordinarily resident in the United Kingdom,

(b) a body incorporated under the law of, or of any part of, the United Kingdom,

(c) a partnership or other unincorporated association formed under the law of any part of the United Kingdom, and

(d) any person who does not fall within paragraph (a), (b) or (c) but maintains in the United Kingdom—

(i) an office, branch or agency through which he carries on any activity, or

(ii) a regular practice;

and the reference to establishment in any other EEA State has a corresponding meaning.

6. – (1) The office originally established by section 3(1)(a) of the Data Protection Act 1984 as the office of Data Protection Registrar shall continue to exist for the purposes of this Act but shall be known as the office of Data Protection Commissioner; and in this Act the Data Protection Commissioner is referred to as "the Commissioner".

(2) The Commissioner shall be appointed by Her Majesty by Letters Patent.

(3) For the purposes of this Act there shall continue to be a Data Protection Tribunal (in this Act referred to as "the Tribunal").

(4) The Tribunal shall consist of –

(a) a chairman appointed by the Lord Chancellor after consultation with the Lord Advocate,

(b) such number of deputy chairmen so appointed as the Lord Chancellor may determine, and

(c) such number of other members appointed by the Secretary of State as he may determine.

(5) The members of the Tribunal appointed under subsection (4)(a) and (b) shall be –

(a) persons who have a 7 year general qualification, within the meaning of section 71 of the Courts and Legal Services Act 1990,

(b) advocates or solicitors in Scotland of at least 7 years' standing, or

(c) members of the bar of Northern Ireland or solicitors of the Supreme Court of Northern Ireland of at least 7 years' standing.

(6) The members of the Tribunal appointed under subsection (4)(c) shall be –

(a) persons to represent the interests of data subjects, and

(b) persons to represent the interests of data controllers.

(7) Schedule 5 has effect in relation to the Commissioner and the Tribunal.

PART II
RIGHTS OF DATA SUBJECTS AND OTHERS

7. – (1) Subject to the following provisions of this section and to sections 8 and 9, an individual is entitled –

(a) to be informed by any data controller whether personal data of which that individual is the data subject are being processed by or on behalf of that data controller,

(b) if that is the case, to be given by the data controller a description of –

(i) the personal data of which that individual is the data subject,

(ii) the purposes for which they are being or are to be processed, and

(iii) the recipients or classes of recipients to whom they are or may be disclosed,

(c) to have communicated to him in an intelligible form –

(i) the information constituting any personal data of which that individual is the data subject, and

(ii) any information available to the data controller as to the source of those data, and

(d) where the processing by automatic means of personal data of which that individual is the data subject for the purpose of evaluating matters relating to him such as, for example, his performance at work, his creditworthiness, his reliability or his conduct, has constituted or is likely to constitute the sole basis for any decision significantly affecting him, to be informed by the data controller of the logic involved in that decision-taking.

(2) A data controller is not obliged to supply any information under subsection (1) unless he has received –
(a) a request in writing, and
(b) except in prescribed cases, such fee (not exceeding the prescribed maximum) as he may require.

(3) A data controller is not obliged to comply with a request under this section unless he is supplied with such information as he may reasonably require in order to satisfy himself as to the identity of the person making the request and to locate the information which that person seeks.

(4) Where a data controller cannot comply with the request without disclosing information relating to another individual who can be identified from that information, he is not obliged to comply with the request unless –
(a) the other individual has consented to the disclosure of the information to the person making the request, or
(b) it is reasonable in all the circumstances to comply with the request without the consent of the other individual.

(5) In subsection (4) the reference to information relating to another individual includes a reference to information identifying that individual as the source of the information sought by the request; and that subsection is not to be construed as excusing a data controller from communicating so much of the information sought by the request as can be communicated without disclosing the identity of the other individual concerned, whether by the omission of names or other identifying particulars or otherwise.

(6) In determining for the purposes of subsection (4)(b) whether it is reasonable in all the circumstances to comply with the request without the consent of the other individual concerned, regard shall be had, in particular, to –
(a) any duty of confidentiality owed to the other individual,
(b) any steps taken by the data controller with a view to seeking the consent of the other individual,
(c) whether the other individual is capable of giving consent, and
(d) any express refusal of consent by the other individual.

(7) An individual making a request under this section may, in such cases as may be prescribed, specify that his request is limited to personal data of any prescribed description.

(8) Subject to subsection (4), a data controller shall comply with a

request under this section promptly and in any event before the end of the prescribed period beginning with the relevant day.

(9) If a court is satisfied on the application of any person who has made a request under the foregoing provisions of this section that the data controller in question has failed to comply with the request in contravention of those provisions, the court may order him to comply with the request.

(10) In this section –
> "prescribed" means prescribed by the Secretary of State by regulations;

> "the prescribed maximum" means such amount as may be prescribed;

> "the prescribed period" means forty days or such other period as may be prescribed;

> "the relevant day", in relation to a request under this section, means the day on which the data controller receives the request or, if later, the first day on which the data controller has both the required fee and the information referred to in subsection (3).

(11) Different amounts or periods may be prescribed under this section in relation to different cases.

8. – (1) The Secretary of State may by regulations provide that, in such cases as may be prescribed, a request for information under any provision of subsection (1) of section 7 is to be treated as extending also to information under other provisions of that subsection.

(2) The obligation imposed by section 7(1)(c)(i) must be complied with by supplying the data subject with a copy of the information in permanent form unless –
> (a) the supply of such a copy is not possible or would involve disproportionate effort, or
> (b) the data subject agrees otherwise;

and where any of the information referred to in section 7(1)(c)(i) is expressed in terms which are not intelligible without explanation the copy must be accompanied by an explanation of those terms.

(3) Where a data controller has previously complied with a request made under section 7 by an individual, the data controller is not obliged to comply with a subsequent identical or similar request under that

section by that individual unless a reasonable interval has elapsed between compliance with the previous request and the making of the current request.

(4)   In determining for the purposes of subsection (3) whether requests under section 7 are made at reasonable intervals, regard shall be had to the nature of the data, the purpose for which the data are processed and the frequency with which the data are altered.

(5)   Section 7(1)(d) is not to be regarded as requiring the provision of information as to the logic involved in any decision-taking if, and to the extent that, the information constitutes a trade secret.

(6)   The information to be supplied pursuant to a request under section 7 must be supplied by reference to the data in question at the time when the request is received, except that it may take account of any amendment or deletion made between that time and the time when the information is supplied, being an amendment or deletion that would have been made regardless of the receipt of the request.

(7)   For the purposes of section 7(4) and (5) another individual can be identified from the information being disclosed if he can be identified from that information, or from that and any other information which, in the reasonable belief of the data controller, is likely to be in, or to come into, the possession of the data subject making the request.

9. – (1) Where the data controller is a credit reference agency, section 7 has effect subject to the provisions of this section.

(2)   An individual making a request under section 7 may limit his request to personal data relevant to his financial standing, and shall be taken to have so limited his request unless the request shows a contrary intention.

(3)   Where the data controller receives a request under section 7 in a case where personal data of which the individual making the request is the data subject are being processed by or on behalf of the data controller, the obligation to supply information under that section includes an obligation to give the individual making the request a statement, in such form as may be prescribed by the Secretary of State by regulations, of the individual's rights –
(a)   under section 159 of the Consumer Credit Act 1974 , and
(b)   to the extent required by the prescribed form, under this Act.

10. – (1) Subject to subsection (2), an individual is entitled at any time by notice in writing to a data controller to require the data controller at the end of such period as is reasonable in the circumstances to cease, or not to begin, processing, or processing for a specified purpose or in a specified manner, any personal data in respect of which he is the data subject, on the ground that, for specified reasons –

(a) the processing of those data or their processing for that purpose or in that manner is causing or is likely to cause substantial damage or substantial distress to him or to another, and

(b) that damage or distress is or would be unwarranted.

(2) Subsection (1) does not apply –

(a) in a case where any of the conditions in paragraphs 1 to 4 of Schedule 2 is met, or

(b) in such other cases as may be prescribed by the Secretary of State by order.

(3) The data controller must within twenty-one days of receiving a notice under subsection (1) ("the data subject notice") give the individual who gave it a written notice –

(a) stating that he has complied or intends to comply with the data subject notice, or

(b) stating his reasons for regarding the data subject notice as to any extent unjustified and the extent (if any) to which he has complied or intends to comply with it.

(4) If a court is satisfied, on the application of any person who has given a notice under subsection (1) which appears to the court to be justified (or to be justified to any extent), that the data controller in question has failed to comply with the notice, the court may order him to take such steps for complying with the notice (or for complying with it to that extent) as the court thinks fit.

(5) The failure by a data subject to exercise the right conferred by subsection (1) or section 11(1) does not affect any other right conferred on him by this Part.

11. – (1) An individual is entitled at any time by notice in writing to a data controller to require the data controller at the end of such period as is reasonable in the circumstances to cease, or not to begin, processing for the purposes of direct marketing personal data in respect of which he is the data subject.

(2) If the court is satisfied, on the application of any person who has given a notice under subsection (1), that the data controller has failed to comply with the notice, the court may order him to take such steps for complying with the notice as the court thinks fit.

(3) In this section "direct marketing" means the communication (by whatever means) of any advertising or marketing material which is directed to particular individuals.

12. – (1) An individual is entitled at any time, by notice in writing to any data controller, to require the data controller to ensure that no decision taken by or on behalf of the data controller which significantly affects that individual is based solely on the processing by automatic means of personal data in respect of which that individual is the data subject for the purpose of evaluating matters relating to him such as, for example, his performance at work, his creditworthiness, his reliability or his conduct.

(2) Where, in a case where no notice under subsection (1) has effect, a decision which significantly affects an individual is based solely on such processing as is mentioned in subsection (1) –

(a) the data controller must as soon as reasonably practicable notify the individual that the decision was taken on that basis, and

(b) the individual is entitled, within twenty-one days of receiving that notification from the data controller, by notice in writing to require the data controller to reconsider the decision or to take a new decision otherwise than on that basis.

(3) The data controller must, within twenty-one days of receiving a notice under subsection (2)(b) ("the data subject notice") give the individual a written notice specifying the steps that he intends to take to comply with the data subject notice.

(4) A notice under subsection (1) does not have effect in relation to an exempt decision; and nothing in subsection (2) applies to an exempt decision.

(5) In subsection (4) "exempt decision" means any decision –

(a) in respect of which the condition in subsection (6) and the condition in subsection (7) are met, or

(b) which is made in such other circumstances as may be prescribed by the Secretary of State by order.

(6) The condition in this subsection is that the decision –

(a) is taken in the course of steps taken –

(i) for the purpose of considering whether to enter into a contract with the data subject,

(ii) with a view to entering into such a contract, or

(iii) in the course of performing such a contract, or

(b) is authorised or required by or under any enactment.

(7) The condition in this subsection is that either –
(a) the effect of the decision is to grant a request of the data subject, or
(b) steps have been taken to safeguard the legitimate interests of the data subject (for example, by allowing him to make representations).

(8) If a court is satisfied on the application of a data subject that a person taking a decision in respect of him ("the responsible person") has failed to comply with subsection (1) or (2)(b), the court may order the responsible person to reconsider the decision, or to take a new decision which is not based solely on such processing as is mentioned in subsection (1).

(9) An order under subsection (8) shall not affect the rights of any person other than the data subject and the responsible person.

13. – (1) An individual who suffers damage by reason of any contravention by a data controller of any of the requirements of this Act is entitled to compensation from the data controller for that damage.

(2) An individual who suffers distress by reason of any contravention by a data controller of any of the requirements of this Act is entitled to compensation from the data controller for that distress if –
(a) the individual also suffers damage by reason of the contravention, or
(b) the contravention relates to the processing of personal data for the special purposes.

(3) In proceedings brought against a person by virtue of this section it is a defence to prove that he had taken such care as in all the circumstances was reasonably required to comply with the requirement concerned.

14. – (1) If a court is satisfied on the application of a data subject that personal data of which the applicant is the subject are inaccurate, the court may order the data controller to rectify, block, erase or destroy those data and any other personal data in respect of which he is the data controller and which contain an expression of opinion which appears to the court to be based on the inaccurate data.

(2) Subsection (1) applies whether or not the data accurately record information received or obtained by the data controller from the data subject or a third party but where the data accurately record such information, then –

(a) if the requirements mentioned in paragraph 7 of Part II of Schedule 1 have been complied with, the court may, instead of making an order under subsection (1), make an order requiring the data to be supplemented by such statement of the true facts relating to the matters dealt with by the data as the court may approve, and

(b) if all or any of those requirements have not been complied with, the court may, instead of making an order under that subsection, make such order as it thinks fit for securing compliance with those requirements with or without a further order requiring the data to be supplemented by such a statement as is mentioned in paragraph (a).

(3)   Where the court—

(a) makes an order under subsection (1), or

(b) is satisfied on the application of a data subject that personal data of which he was the data subject and which have been rectified, blocked, erased or destroyed were inaccurate,

it may, where it considers it reasonably practicable, order the data controller to notify third parties to whom the data have been disclosed of the rectification, blocking, erasure or destruction.

(4)   If a court is satisfied on the application of a data subject –

(a) that he has suffered damage by reason of any contravention by a data controller of any of the requirements of this Act in respect of any personal data, in circumstances entitling him to compensation under section 13, and

(b) that there is a substantial risk of further contravention in respect of those data in such circumstances,

the court may order the rectification, blocking, erasure or destruction of any of those data.

(5)   Where the court makes an order under subsection (4) it may, where it considers it reasonably practicable, order the data controller to notify third parties to whom the data have been disclosed of the rectification, blocking, erasure or destruction.

(6)   In determining whether it is reasonably practicable to require such notification as is mentioned in subsection (3) or (5) the court shall have regard, in particular, to the number of persons who would have to be notified.

15. – (1) The jurisdiction conferred by sections 7 to 14 is exercisable by the High Court or a county court or, in Scotland, by the Court of Session or the sheriff.

(2) For the purpose of determining any question whether an applicant under subsection (9) of section 7 is entitled to the information which he seeks (including any question whether any relevant data are exempt from that section by virtue of Part IV) a court may require the information constituting any data processed by or on behalf of the data controller and any information as to the logic involved in any decision-taking as mentioned in section 7(1)(d) to be made available for its own inspection but shall not, pending the determination of that question in the applicant's favour, require the information sought by the applicant to be disclosed to him or his representatives whether by discovery (or, in Scotland, recovery) or otherwise.

PART III
NOTIFICATION BY DATA CONTROLLERS

16. − (1) In this Part "the registrable particulars", in relation to a data controller, means −

(a) his name and address,

(b) if he has nominated a representative for the purposes of this Act, the name and address of the representative,

(c) a description of the personal data being or to be processed by or on behalf of the data controller and of the category or categories of data subject to which they relate,

(d) a description of the purpose or purposes for which the data are being or are to be processed,

(e) a description of any recipient or recipients to whom the data controller intends or may wish to disclose the data,

(f) the names, or a description of, any countries or territories outside the European Economic Area to which the data controller directly or indirectly transfers, or intends or may wish directly or indirectly to transfer, the data, and

(g) in any case where −

(i) personal data are being, or are intended to be, processed in circumstances in which the prohibition in subsection (1) of section 17 is excluded by subsection (2) or (3) of that section, and

(ii) the notification does not extend to those data,

a statement of that fact.

(2) In this Part −

"fees regulations" means regulations made by the Secretary of State under section 18(5) or 19(4) or (7);

"notification regulations" means regulations made by the Secretary of State under the other provisions of this Part;

"prescribed", except where used in relation to fees regulations, means prescribed by notification regulations.

(3)   For the purposes of this Part, so far as it relates to the addresses of data controllers —
(a) the address of a registered company is that of its registered office, and
(b) the address of a person (other than a registered company) carrying on a business is that of his principal place of business in the United Kingdom.

17. — (1) Subject to the following provisions of this section, personal data must not be processed unless an entry in respect of the data controller is included in the register maintained by the Commissioner under section 19 (or is treated by notification regulations made by virtue of section 19(3) as being so included).

(2)   Except where the processing is assessable processing for the purposes of section 22, subsection (1) does not apply in relation to personal data consisting of information which falls neither within paragraph (a) of the definition of "data" in section 1(1) nor within paragraph (b) of that definition.

(3)   If it appears to the Secretary of State that processing of a particular description is unlikely to prejudice the rights and freedoms of data subjects, notification regulations may provide that, in such cases as may be prescribed, subsection (1) is not to apply in relation to processing of that description.

(4)   Subsection (1) does not apply in relation to any processing whose sole purpose is the maintenance of a public register.

18. — (1) Any data controller who wishes to be included in the register maintained under section 19 shall give a notification to the Commissioner under this section.

(2)   A notification under this section must specify in accordance with notification regulations —
(a) the registrable particulars, and
(b) a general description of measures to be taken for the purpose of complying with the seventh data protection principle.

(3)   Notification regulations made by virtue of subsection (2) may provide for the determination by the Commissioner, in accordance with any requirements of the regulations, of the form in which the

registrable particulars and the description mentioned in subsection (2)(b) are to be specified, including in particular the detail required for the purposes of section 16(1)(c), (d), (e) and (f) and subsection (2)(b).

(4) Notification regulations may make provision as to the giving of notification –
> (a) by partnerships, or
> (b) in other cases where two or more persons are the data controllers in respect of any personal data.

(5) The notification must be accompanied by such fee as may be prescribed by fees regulations.

(6) Notification regulations may provide for any fee paid under subsection (5) or section 19(4) to be refunded in prescribed circumstances.

19. – (1) The Commissioner shall –
> (a) maintain a register of persons who have given notification under section 18, and
> (b) make an entry in the register in pursuance of each notification received by him under that section from a person in respect of whom no entry as data controller was for the time being included in the register.

(2) Each entry in the register shall consist of –
> (a) the registrable particulars notified under section 18 or, as the case requires, those particulars as amended in pursuance of section 20(4), and
> (b) such other information as the Commissioner may be authorised or required by notification regulations to include in the register.

(3) Notification regulations may make provision as to the time as from which any entry in respect of a data controller is to be treated for the purposes of section 17 as having been made in the register.

(4) No entry shall be retained in the register for more than the relevant time except on payment of such fee as may be prescribed by fees regulations.

(5) In subsection (4) "the relevant time" means twelve months or such other period as may be prescribed by notification regulations; and different periods may be prescribed in relation to different cases.

(6) The Commissioner –
> (a) shall provide facilities for making the information contained in the entries in the register available for inspection (in visible

and legible form) by members of the public at all reasonable hours and free of charge, and

(b) may provide such other facilities for making the information contained in those entries available to the public free of charge as he considers appropriate.

(7) The Commissioner shall, on payment of such fee, if any, as may be prescribed by fees regulations, supply any member of the public with a duly certified copy in writing of the particulars contained in any entry made in the register.

20. – (1) For the purpose specified in subsection (2), notification regulations shall include provision imposing on every person in respect of whom an entry as a data controller is for the time being included in the register maintained under section 19 a duty to notify to the Commissioner, in such circumstances and at such time or times and in such form as may be prescribed, such matters relating to the registrable particulars and measures taken as mentioned in section 18(2)(b) as may be prescribed.

(2) The purpose referred to in subsection (1) is that of ensuring, so far as practicable, that at any time –

(a) the entries in the register maintained under section 19 contain current names and addresses and describe the current practice or intentions of the data controller with respect to the processing of personal data, and

(b) the Commissioner is provided with a general description of measures currently being taken as mentioned in section 18(2)(b).

(3) Subsection (3) of section 18 has effect in relation to notification regulations made by virtue of subsection (1) as it has effect in relation to notification regulations made by virtue of subsection (2) of that section.

(4) On receiving any notification under notification regulations made by virtue of subsection (1), the Commissioner shall make such amendments of the relevant entry in the register maintained under section 19 as are necessary to take account of the notification.

21. – (1) If section 17(1) is contravened, the data controller is guilty of an offence.

(2) Any person who fails to comply with the duty imposed by notification regulations made by virtue of section 20(1) is guilty of an offence.

(3) It shall be a defence for a person charged with an offence under

subsection (2) to show that he exercised all due diligence to comply with the duty.

22. − (1) In this section "assessable processing" means processing which is of a description specified in an order made by the Secretary of State as appearing to him to be particularly likely −
(a) to cause substantial damage or substantial distress to data subjects, or
(b) otherwise significantly to prejudice the rights and freedoms of data subjects.

(2) On receiving notification from any data controller under section 18 or under notification regulations made by virtue of section 20 the Commissioner shall consider −
(a) whether any of the processing to which the notification relates is assessable processing, and
(b) if so, whether the assessable processing is likely to comply with the provisions of this Act.

(3) Subject to subsection (4), the Commissioner shall, within the period of twenty-eight days beginning with the day on which he receives a notification which relates to assessable processing, give a notice to the data controller stating the extent to which the Commissioner is of the opinion that the processing is likely or unlikely to comply with the provisions of this Act.

(4) Before the end of the period referred to in subsection (3) the Commissioner may, by reason of special circumstances, extend that period on one occasion only by notice to the data controller by such further period not exceeding fourteen days as the Commissioner may specify in the notice.

(5) No assessable processing in respect of which a notification has been given the Commissioner as mentioned in subsection (2) shall be carried on unless either −
(a) the period of twenty-eight days beginning with the day on which the notification is received by the Commissioner (or, in a case falling within subsection (4), that period as extended under that subsection) has elapsed, or
(b) before the end of that period (or that period as so extended) the data controller has received a notice from the Commissioner under subsection (3) in respect of the processing.

(6) Where subsection (5) is contravened, the data controller is guilty of an offence.

(7) The Secretary of State may by order amend subsections (3), (4) and (5) by substituting for the number of days for the time being specified there a different number specified in the order.

23. – (1) The Secretary of State may by order –
(a) make provision under which a data controller may appoint a person to act as a data protection supervisor responsible in particular for monitoring in an independent manner the data controller's compliance with the provisions of this Act, and
(b) provide that, in relation to any data controller who has appointed a data protection supervisor in accordance with the provisions of the order and who complies with such conditions as may be specified in the order, the provisions of this Part are to have effect subject to such exemptions or other modifications as may be specified in the order.

(2) An order under this section may –
(a) impose duties on data protection supervisors in relation to the Commissioner, and
(b) confer functions on the Commissioner in relation to data protection supervisors.

24. – (1) Subject to subsection (3), where personal data are processed in a case where –
(a) by virtue of subsection (2) or (3) of section 17, subsection (1) of that section does not apply to the processing, and
(b) the data controller has not notified the relevant particulars in respect of that processing under section 18,
the data controller must, within twenty-one days of receiving a written request from any person, make the relevant particulars available to that person in writing free of charge.

(2) In this section "the relevant particulars" means the particulars referred to in paragraphs (a) to (f) of section 16(1).

(3) This section has effect subject to any exemption conferred for the purposes of this section by notification regulations.

(4) Any data controller who fails to comply with the duty imposed by subsection (1) is guilty of an offence.

(5) It shall be a defence for a person charged with an offence under subsection (4) to show that he exercised all due diligence to comply with the duty.

25. – (1) As soon as practicable after the passing of this Act, the Commissioner shall submit to the Secretary of State proposals as to the provisions to be included in the first notification regulations.

(2) The Commissioner shall keep under review the working of notification regulations and may from time to time submit to the Secretary of State proposals as to amendments to be made to the regulations.

(3) The Secretary of State may from time to time require the Commissioner to consider any matter relating to notification regulations and to submit to him proposals as to amendments to be made to the regulations in connection with that matter.

(4) Before making any notification regulations, the Secretary of State shall –

  (a) consider any proposals made to him by the Commissioner under subsection (1), (2) or (3), and

  (b) consult the Commissioner.

26. – (1) Fees regulations prescribing fees for the purposes of any provision of this Part may provide for different fees to be payable in different cases.

(2) In making any fees regulations, the Secretary of State shall have regard to the desirability of securing that the fees payable to the Commissioner are sufficient to offset –

  (a) the expenses incurred by the Commissioner and the Tribunal in discharging their functions and any expenses of the Secretary of State in respect of the Commissioner or the Tribunal, and

  (b) to the extent that the Secretary of State considers appropriate –

    (i) any deficit previously incurred (whether before or after the passing of this Act) in respect of the expenses mentioned in paragraph (a), and

    (ii) expenses incurred or to be incurred by the Secretary of State in respect of the inclusion of any officers or staff of the Commissioner in any scheme under section 1 of the Superannuation Act 1972.

PART IV
EXEMPTIONS

27. – (1) References in any of the data protection principles or any provision of Parts II and III to personal data or to the processing of personal data do not include references to data or processing which by virtue of this Part are exempt from that principle or other provision.

(2) In this Part "the subject information provisions" means –
(a) the first data protection principle to the extent to which it requires compliance with paragraph 2 of Part II of Schedule 1, and
(b) section 7.

(3) In this Part "the non-disclosure provisions" means the provisions specified in subsection (4) to the extent to which they are inconsistent with the disclosure in question.

(4) The provisions referred to in subsection (3) are –
(a) the first data protection principle, except to the extent to which it requires compliance with the conditions in Schedules 2 and 3,
(b) the second, third, fourth and fifth data protection principles, and
(c) sections 10 and 14(1) to (3).

(5) Except as provided by this Part, the subject information provisions shall have effect notwithstanding any enactment or rule of law prohibiting or restricting the disclosure, or authorising the withholding, of information.

28. – (1) Personal data are exempt from any of the provisions of –
(a) the data protection principles,
(b) Parts II, III and V, and
(c) section 55,
if the exemption from that provision is required for the purpose of safeguarding national security.

(2) Subject to subsection (4), a certificate signed by a Minister of the Crown certifying that exemption from all or any of the provisions mentioned in subsection (1) is or at any time was required for the purpose there mentioned in respect of any personal data shall be conclusive evidence of that fact.

(3) A certificate under subsection (2) may identify the personal data to which it applies by means of a general description and may be expressed to have prospective effect.

(4) Any person directly affected by the issuing of a certificate under subsection (2) may appeal to the Tribunal against the certificate.

(5) If on an appeal under subsection (4), the Tribunal finds that, applying the principles applied by the court on an application for judicial review, the Minister did not have reasonable grounds for

issuing the certificate, the Tribunal may allow the appeal and quash the certificate.

(6) Where in any proceedings under or by virtue of this Act it is claimed by a data controller that a certificate under subsection (2) which identifies the personal data to which it applies by means of a general description applies to any personal data, any other party to the proceedings may appeal to the Tribunal on the ground that the certificate does not apply to the personal data in question and, subject to any determination under subsection (7), the certificate shall be conclusively presumed so to apply.

(7) On any appeal under subsection (6), the Tribunal may determine that the certificate does not so apply.

(8) A document purporting to be a certificate under subsection (2) shall be received in evidence and deemed to be such a certificate unless the contrary is proved.

(9) A document which purports to be certified by or on behalf of a Minister of the Crown as a true copy of a certificate issued by that Minister under subsection (2) shall in any legal proceedings be evidence (or, in Scotland, sufficient evidence) of that certificate.

(10) The power conferred by subsection (2) on a Minister of the Crown shall not be exercisable except by a Minister who is a member of the Cabinet or by the Attorney General or the Lord Advocate.

(11) No power conferred by any provision of Part V may be exercised in relation to personal data which by virtue of this section are exempt from that provision.

(12) Schedule 6 shall have effect in relation to appeals under subsection (4) or (6) and the proceedings of the Tribunal in respect of any such appeal.

29. – (1) Personal data processed for any of the following purposes –
    (a) the prevention or detection of crime,
    (b) the apprehension or prosecution of offenders, or
    (c) the assessment or collection of any tax or duty or of any imposition of a similar nature,
are exempt from the first data protection principle (except to the extent to which it requires compliance with the conditions in Schedules 2 and 3) and section 7 in any case to the extent to which the application of those provisions to the data would be likely to prejudice any of the matters mentioned in this subsection.

(2) Personal data which –

(a) are processed for the purpose of discharging statutory functions, and

(b) consist of information obtained for such a purpose from a person who had it in his possession for any of the purposes mentioned in subsection (1),

are exempt from the subject information provisions to the same extent as personal data processed for any of the purposes mentioned in that subsection.

(3) Personal data are exempt from the non-disclosure provisions in any case in which –

(a) the disclosure is for any of the purposes mentioned in subsection (1), and

(b) the application of those provisions in relation to the disclosure would be likely to prejudice any of the matters mentioned in that subsection.

(4) Personal data in respect of which the data controller is a relevant authority and which –

(a) consist of a classification applied to the data subject as part of a system of risk assessment which is operated by that authority for either of the following purposes –

(i) the assessment or collection of any tax or duty or any imposition of a similar nature, or

(ii) the prevention or detection of crime, or apprehension or prosecution of offenders, where the offence concerned involves any unlawful claim for any payment out of, or any unlawful application of, public funds, and

(b) are processed for either of those purposes,

are exempt from section 7 to the extent to which the exemption is required in the interests of the operation of the system.

(5) In subsection (4) –

"public funds" includes funds provided by any Community institution;

"relevant authority" means –

(a) a government department,

(b) a local authority, or

(c) any other authority administering housing benefit or council tax benefit.

30. – (1) The Secretary of State may by order exempt from the subject information provisions, or modify those provisions in relation to, personal data consisting of information as to the physical or mental health or condition of the data subject.

(2) The Secretary of State may by order exempt from the subject information provisions, or modify those provisions in relation to –

(a) personal data in respect of which the data controller is the proprietor of, or a teacher at, a school, and which consist of information relating to persons who are or have been pupils at the school, or

(b) personal data in respect of which the data controller is an education authority in Scotland, and which consist of information relating to persons who are receiving, or have received, further education provided by the authority.

(3) The Secretary of State may by order exempt from the subject information provisions, or modify those provisions in relation to, personal data of such other descriptions as may be specified in the order, being information –

(a) processed by government departments or local authorities or by voluntary organisations or other bodies designated by or under the order, and

(b) appearing to him to be processed in the course of, or for the purposes of, carrying out social work in relation to the data subject or other individuals;

but the Secretary of State shall not under this subsection confer any exemption or make any modification except so far as he considers that the application to the data of those provisions (or of those provisions without modification) would be likely to prejudice the carrying out of social work.

(4) An order under this section may make different provision in relation to data consisting of information of different descriptions.

(5) In this section –

"education authority" and "further education" have the same meaning as in the Education (Scotland) Act 1980 ("the 1980 Act"), and

"proprietor" –

(a) in relation to a school in England or Wales, has the same meaning as in the Education Act 1996,

(b) in relation to a school in Scotland, means –

(i) in the case of a self-governing school, the board of management within the meaning of the Self-Governing Schools etc (Scotland) Act 1989,

(ii) in the case of an independent school, the proprietor within the meaning of the 1980 Act,

(iii) in the case of a grant-aided school, the managers within the meaning of the 1980 Act, and

(iv) in the case of a public school, the education authority within the meaning of the 1980 Act, and

(c) in relation to a school in Northern Ireland, has the same meaning as in the Education and Libraries (Northern Ireland) Order 1986 and includes, in the case of a controlled school, the Board of Governors of the school.

31. – (1) Personal data processed for the purposes of discharging functions to which this subsection applies are exempt from the subject information provisions in any case to the extent to which the application of those provisions to the data would be likely to prejudice the proper discharge of those functions.

(2) Subsection (1) applies to any relevant function which is designed –

(a) for protecting members of the public against –

(i) financial loss due to dishonesty, malpractice or other seriously improper conduct by, or the unfitness or incompetence of, persons concerned in the provision of banking, insurance, investment or other financial services or in the management of bodies corporate,

(ii) financial loss due to the conduct of discharged or undischarged bankrupts, or

(iii) dishonesty, malpractice or other seriously improper conduct by, or the unfitness or incompetence of, persons authorised to carry on any profession or other activity,

(b) for protecting charities against misconduct or mismanagement (whether by trustees or other persons) in their administration,

(c) for protecting the property of charities from loss or misapplication,

(d) for the recovery of the property of charities,

(e) for securing the health, safety and welfare of persons at work, or

(f) for protecting persons other than persons at work against risk to health or safety arising out of or in connection with the actions of persons at work.

(3) In subsection (2) "relevant function" means –

(a) any function conferred on any person by or under any enactment,

(b) any function of the Crown, a Minister of the Crown or a government department, or

(c) any other function which is of a public nature and is exercised in the public interest.

(4) Personal data processed for the purpose of discharging any function which —

(a) is conferred by or under any enactment on —
(i) the Parliamentary Commissioner for Administration,
(ii) the Commission for Local Administration in England, the Commission for Local Administration in Wales or the Commissioner for Local Administration in Scotland,
(iii) the Health Service Commissioner for England, the Health Service Commissioner for Wales or the Health Service Commissioner for Scotland,
(iv) the Welsh Administration Ombudsman,
(v) the Assembly Ombudsman for Northern Ireland, or
(vi) the Northern Ireland Commissioner for Complaints, and
(b) is designed for protecting members of the public against —
(i) maladministration by public bodies,
(ii) failures in services provided by public bodies, or
(iii) a failure of a public body to provide a service which it was a function of the body to provide,

are exempt from the subject information provisions in any case to the extent to which the application of those provisions to the data would be likely to prejudice the proper discharge of that function.

(5) Personal data processed for the purpose of discharging any function which —

(a) is conferred by or under any enactment on the Director General of Fair Trading, and
(b) is designed —
(i) for protecting members of the public against conduct which may adversely affect their interests by persons carrying on a business,
(ii) for regulating agreements or conduct which have as their object or effect the prevention, restriction or distortion of competition in connection with any commercial activity, or
(iii) for regulating conduct on the part of one or more undertakings which amounts to the abuse of a dominant position in a market,

are exempt from the subject information provisions in any case to the extent to which the application of those provisions to the data would be likely to prejudice the proper discharge of that function.

32. — (1) Personal data which are processed only for the special purposes are exempt from any provision to which this subsection relates if —

(a) the processing is undertaken with a view to the publication by any person of any journalistic, literary or artistic material,
(b) the data controller reasonably believes that, having regard in particular to the special importance of the public interest in freedom of expression, publication would be in the public interest, and
(c) the data controller reasonably believes that, in all the circumstances, compliance with that provision is incompatible with the special purposes.

(2) Subsection (1) relates to the provisions of –
(a) the data protection principles except the seventh data protection principle,
(b) section 7,
(c) section 10,
(d) section 12, and
(e) section 14(1) to (3).

(3) In considering for the purposes of subsection (1)(b) whether the belief of a data controller that publication would be in the public interest was or is a reasonable one, regard may be had to his compliance with any code of practice which –
(a) is relevant to the publication in question, and
(b) is designated by the Secretary of State by order for the purposes of this subsection.

(4) Where at any time ("the relevant time") in any proceedings against a data controller under section 7(9), 10(4), 12(8) or 14 or by virtue of section 13 the data controller claims, or it appears to the court, that any personal data to which the proceedings relate are being processed –
(a) only for the special purposes, and
(b) with a view to the publication by any person of any journalistic, literary or artistic material which, at the time twenty-four hours immediately before the relevant time, had not previously been published by the data controller,
the court shall stay the proceedings until either of the conditions in subsection (5) is met.

(5) Those conditions are –
(a) that a determination of the Commissioner under section 45 with respect to the data in question takes effect, or
(b) in a case where the proceedings were stayed on the making of a claim, that the claim is withdrawn.

(6) For the purposes of this Act "publish", in relation to journalistic, literary or artistic material, means make available to the public or any

section of the public.

33. – (1) In this section –
"research purposes" includes statistical or historical purposes;

"the relevant conditions", in relation to any processing of personal data, means the conditions –
(a) that the data are not processed to support measures or decisions with respect to particular individuals, and
(b) that the data are not processed in such a way that substantial damage or substantial distress is, or is likely to be, caused to any data subject.

(2) For the purposes of the second data protection principle, the further processing of personal data only for research purposes in compliance with the relevant conditions is not to be regarded as incompatible with the purposes for which they were obtained.

(3) Personal data which are processed only for research purposes in compliance with the relevant conditions may, notwithstanding the fifth data protection principle, be kept indefinitely.

(4) Personal data which are processed only for research purposes are exempt from section 7 if –
(a) they are processed in compliance with the relevant conditions, and
(b) the results of the research or any resulting statistics are not made available in a form which identifies data subjects or any of them.

(5) For the purposes of subsections (2) to (4) personal data are not to be treated as processed otherwise than for research purposes merely because the data are disclosed –
(a) to any person, for research purposes only,
(b) to the data subject or a person acting on his behalf,
(c) at the request, or with the consent, of the data subject or a person acting on his behalf, or
(d) in circumstances in which the person making the disclosure has reasonable grounds for believing that the disclosure falls within paragraph (a), (b) or (c).

34. – Personal data are exempt from –
(a) the subject information provisions,
(b) the fourth data protection principle and section 14(1) to (3), and
(c) the non-disclosure provisions,
if the data consist of information which the data controller is obliged

by or under any enactment to make available to the public, whether by publishing it, by making it available for inspection, or otherwise and whether gratuitously or on payment of a fee.

35. – (1) Personal data are exempt from the non–disclosure provisions where the disclosure is required by or under any enactment, by any rule of law or by the order of a court.

(2) Personal data are exempt from the non–disclosure provisions where the disclosure is necessary –
> (a) for the purpose of, or in connection with, any legal proceedings (including prospective legal proceedings), or
> (b) for the purpose of obtaining legal advice,

or is otherwise necessary for the purposes of establishing, exercising or defending legal rights.

36. Personal data processed by an individual only for the purposes of that individual's personal, family or household affairs (including recreational purposes) are exempt from the data protection principles and the provisions of Parts II and III.

37. Schedule 7 (which confers further miscellaneous exemptions) has effect.

38. – (1) The Secretary of State may by order exempt from the subject information provisions personal data consisting of information the disclosure of which is prohibited or restricted by or under any enactment if and to the extent that he considers it necessary for the safeguarding of the interests of the data subject or the rights and freedoms of any other individual that the prohibition or restriction ought to prevail over those provisions.

(2) The Secretary of State may by order exempt from the non–disclosure provisions any disclosures of personal data made in circumstances specified in the order, if he considers the exemption is necessary for the safeguarding of the interests of the data subject or the rights and freedoms of any other individual.

39. Schedule 8 (which confers transitional exemptions) has effect.

PART V
ENFORCEMENT

40. – (1) If the Commissioner is satisfied that a data controller has contravened or is contravening any of the data protection principles, the Commissioner may serve him with a notice (in this Act referred to as "an enforcement notice") requiring him, for complying with the principle or principles in question, to do either or both of the following –

    (a) to take within such time as may be specified in the notice, or to refrain from taking after such time as may be so specified, such steps as are so specified, or

    (b) to refrain from processing any personal data, or any personal data of a description specified in the notice, or to refrain from processing them for a purpose so specified or in a manner so specified, after such time as may be so specified.

(2) In deciding whether to serve an enforcement notice, the Commissioner shall consider whether the contravention has caused or is likely to cause any person damage or distress.

(3) An enforcement notice in respect of a contravention of the fourth data protection principle which requires the data controller to rectify, block, erase or destroy any inaccurate data may also require the data controller to rectify, block, erase or destroy any other data held by him and containing an expression of opinion which appears to the Commissioner to be based on the inaccurate data.

(4) An enforcement notice in respect of a contravention of the fourth data protection principle, in the case of data which accurately record information received or obtained by the data controller from the data subject or a third party, may require the data controller either –

    (a) to rectify, block, erase or destroy any inaccurate data and any other data held by him and containing an expression of opinion as mentioned in subsection (3), or

    (b) to take such steps as are specified in the notice for securing compliance with the requirements specified in paragraph 7 of Part II of Schedule 1 and, if the Commissioner thinks fit, for supplementing the data with such statement of the true facts relating to the matters dealt with by the data as the Commissioner may approve.

(5) Where –

    (a) an enforcement notice requires the data controller to rectify, block, erase or destroy any personal data, or

    (b) the Commissioner is satisfied that personal data which have been rectified, blocked, erased or destroyed had been processed in contravention of any of the data protection principles,

an enforcement notice may, if reasonably practicable, require the data controller to notify third parties to whom the data have been disclosed of the rectification, blocking, erasure or destruction; and in determining whether it is reasonably practicable to require such notification regard shall be had, in particular, to the number of persons who would have to be notified.

(6) An enforcement notice must contain –
(a) a statement of the data protection principle or principles which the Commissioner is satisfied have been or are being contravened and his reasons for reaching that conclusion, and
(b) particulars of the rights of appeal conferred by section 48.

(7) Subject to subsection (8), an enforcement notice must not require any of the provisions of the notice to be complied with before the end of the period within which an appeal can be brought against the notice and, if such an appeal is brought, the notice need not be complied with pending the determination or withdrawal of the appeal.

(8) If by reason of special circumstances the Commissioner considers that an enforcement notice should be complied with as a matter of urgency he may include in the notice a statement to that effect and a statement of his reasons for reaching that conclusion; and in that event subsection (7) shall not apply but the notice must not require the provisions of the notice to be complied with before the end of the period of seven days beginning with the day on which the notice is served.

(9) Notification regulations (as defined by section 16(2)) may make provision as to the effect of the service of an enforcement notice on any entry in the register maintained under section 19 which relates to the person on whom the notice is served.

(10) This section has effect subject to section 46(1).

41. – (1) If the Commissioner considers that all or any of the provisions of an enforcement notice need not be complied with in order to ensure compliance with the data protection principle or principles to which it relates, he may cancel or vary the notice by written notice to the person on whom it was served.

(2) A person on whom an enforcement notice has been served may, at any time after the expiry of the period during which an appeal can be brought against that notice, apply in writing to the Commissioner for the cancellation or variation of that notice on the ground that, by reason of a change of circumstances, all or any of the provisions of that notice need not be complied with in order to ensure compliance with the data protection principle or principles to which that notice relates.

42. – (1) A request may be made to the Commissioner by or on behalf of any person who is, or believes himself to be, directly affected by any processing of personal data for an assessment as to whether it is likely or unlikely that the processing has been or is being carried out in compliance with the provisions of this Act.

(2) On receiving a request under this section, the Commissioner shall make an assessment in such manner as appears to him to be appropriate, unless he has not been supplied with such information as he may reasonably require in order to –
(a) satisfy himself as to the identity of the person making the request, and
(b) enable him to identify the processing in question.

(3) The matters to which the Commissioner may have regard in determining in what manner it is appropriate to make an assessment include –
(a) the extent to which the request appears to him to raise a matter of substance,
(b) any undue delay in making the request, and
(c) whether or not the person making the request is entitled to make an application under section 7 in respect of the personal data in question.

(4) Where the Commissioner has received a request under this section he shall notify the person who made the request –

(a) whether he has made an assessment as a result of the request, and
(b) to the extent that he considers appropriate, having regard in particular to any exemption from section 7 applying in relation to the personal data concerned, of any view formed or action taken as a result of the request.

43. – (1)   If the Commissioner –
(a) has received a request under section 42 in respect of any processing of personal data, or
(b) reasonably requires any information for the purpose of determining whether the data controller has complied or is complying with the data protection principles,
he may serve the data controller with a notice (in this Act referred to as "an information notice") requiring the data controller, within such time as is specified in the notice, to furnish the Commissioner, in such form as may be so specified, with such information relating to the request or to compliance with the principles as is so specified.

(2) An information notice must contain –
(a) in a case falling within subsection (1)(a), a statement that the Commissioner has received a request under section 42 in relation to the specified processing, or
(b) in a case falling within subsection (1)(b), a statement that the Commissioner regards the specified information as relevant for the purpose of determining whether the data controller has complied, or is complying, with the data protection principles and his reasons for regarding it as relevant for that purpose.

(3) An information notice must also contain particulars of the rights of appeal conferred by section 48.

(4) Subject to subsection (5), the time specified in an information notice shall not expire before the end of the period within which an appeal can be brought against the notice and, if such an appeal is brought, the information need not be furnished pending the determination or withdrawal of the appeal.

(5) If by reason of special circumstances the Commissioner considers that the information is required as a matter of urgency, he may include in the notice a statement to that effect and a statement of his reasons for reaching that conclusion; and in that event subsection (4) shall not apply, but the notice shall not require the information to be furnished before the end of the period of seven days beginning with the day on which the notice is served.

(6) A person shall not be required by virtue of this section to furnish the Commissioner with any information in respect of –
(a) any communication between a professional legal adviser and his client in connection with the giving of legal advice to the client with respect to his obligations, liabilities or rights under this Act, or
(b) any communication between a professional legal adviser and his client, or between such an adviser or his client and any other person, made in connection with or in contemplation of proceedings under or arising out of this Act (including proceedings before the Tribunal) and for the purposes of such proceedings.

(7) In subsection (6) references to the client of a professional legal adviser include references to any person representing such a client.

(8) A person shall not be required by virtue of this section to furnish the Commissioner with any information if the furnishing of that information would, by revealing evidence of the commission of any

offence other than an offence under this Act, expose him to proceedings for that offence.

(9) The Commissioner may cancel an information notice by written notice to the person on whom it was served.

(10) This section has effect subject to section 46(3).

44. If the Commissioner —

(a) has received a request under section 42 in respect of any processing of personal data, or

(b) has reasonable grounds for suspecting that, in a case in which proceedings have been stayed under section 32, the personal data to which the proceedings relate —

    (i) are not being processed only for the special purposes, or

    (ii) are not being processed with a view to the publication by any person of any journalistic, literary or artistic material

    which has not previously been published by the data controller,

he may serve the data controller with a notice (in this Act referred to as a "special information notice") requiring the data controller, within such time as is specified in the notice, to furnish the Commissioner, in such form as may be so specified, with such information as is so specified for the purpose specified in subsection (2).

(2) That purpose is the purpose of ascertaining —

(a) whether the personal data are being processed only for the special purposes, or

(b) whether they are being processed with a view to the publication by any person of any journalistic, literary or artistic material which has not previously been published by the data controller.

(3) A special information notice must contain —

(a) in a case falling within paragraph (a) of subsection (1), a statement that the Commissioner has received a request under section 42 in relation to the specified processing, or

(b) in a case falling within paragraph (b) of that subsection, a statement of the Commissioner's grounds for suspecting that the personal data are not being processed as mentioned in that paragraph.

(4) A special information notice must also contain particulars of the rights of appeal conferred by section 48.

(5) Subject to subsection (6), the time specified in a special information notice shall not expire before the end of the period within which an

appeal can be brought against the notice and, if such an appeal is brought, the information need not be furnished pending the determination or withdrawal of the appeal.

(6) If by reason of special circumstances the Commissioner considers that the information is required as a matter of urgency, he may include in the notice a statement to that effect and a statement of his reasons for reaching that conclusion; and in that event subsection (5) shall not apply, but the notice shall not require the information to be furnished before the end of the period of seven days beginning with the day on which the notice is served.

(7) A person shall not be required by virtue of this section to furnish the Commissioner with any information in respect of –

(a) any communication between a professional legal adviser and his client in connection with the giving of legal advice to the client with respect to his obligations, liabilities or rights under this Act, or

(b) any communication between a professional legal adviser and his client, or between such an adviser or his client and any other person, made in connection with or in contemplation of proceedings under or arising out of this Act (including proceedings before the Tribunal) and for the purposes of such proceedings.

(8) In subsection (7) references to the client of a professional legal adviser include references to any person representing such a client.

(9) A person shall not be required by virtue of this section to furnish the Commissioner with any information if the furnishing of that information would, by revealing evidence of the commission of any offence other than an offence under this Act, expose him to proceedings for that offence.

(10) The Commissioner may cancel a special information notice by written notice to the person on whom it was served.

45. – (1) Where at any time it appears to the Commissioner (whether as a result of the service of a special information notice or otherwise) that any personal data –

(a) are not being processed only for the special purposes, or

(b) are not being processed with a view to the publication by any person of any journalistic, literary or artistic material which has not previously been published by the data controller,

he may make a determination in writing to that effect.

(2) Notice of the determination shall be given to the data controller;

and the notice must contain particulars of the right of appeal conferred by section 48.

(3) A determination under subsection (1) shall not take effect until the end of the period within which an appeal can be brought and, where an appeal is brought, shall not take effect pending the determination or withdrawal of the appeal.

46. – (1) The Commissioner may not at any time serve an enforcement notice on a data controller with respect to the processing of personal data for the special purposes unless –
  (a) a determination under section 45(1) with respect to those data has taken effect, and
  (b) the court has granted leave for the notice to be served.

(2) The court shall not grant leave for the purposes of subsection (1)(b) unless it is satisfied –
  (a) that the Commissioner has reason to suspect a contravention of the data protection principles which is of substantial public importance, and
  (b) except where the case is one of urgency, that the data controller has been given notice, in accordance with rules of court, of the application for leave.

(3) The Commissioner may not serve an information notice on a data controller with respect to the processing of personal data for the special purposes unless a determination under section 45(1) with respect to those data has taken effect.

47. – (1) A person who fails to comply with an enforcement notice, an information notice or a special information notice is guilty of an offence.

(2) A person who, in purported compliance with an information notice or a special information notice –
  (a) makes a statement which he knows to be false in a material respect, or
  (b) recklessly makes a statement which is false in a material respect,
is guilty of an offence.

(3) It is a defence for a person charged with an offence under subsection (1) to prove that he exercised all due diligence to comply with the notice in question.

48. – (1) A person on whom an enforcement notice, an information

notice or a special information notice has been served may appeal to the Tribunal against the notice.

(2) A person on whom an enforcement notice has been served may appeal to the Tribunal against the refusal of an application under section 41(2) for cancellation or variation of the notice.

(3) Where an enforcement notice, an information notice or a special information notice contains a statement by the Commissioner in accordance with section 40(8), 43(5) or 44(6) then, whether or not the person appeals against the notice, he may appeal against –
(a) the Commissioner's decision to include the statement in the notice, or
(b) the effect of the inclusion of the statement as respects any part of the notice.

(4) A data controller in respect of whom a determination has been made under section 45 may appeal to the Tribunal against the determination.

(5) Schedule 6 has effect in relation to appeals under this section and the proceedings of the Tribunal in respect of any such appeal.

49. – (1) If on an appeal under section 48(1) the Tribunal considers –
(a) that the notice against which the appeal is brought is not in accordance with the law, or
(b) to the extent that the notice involved an exercise of discretion by the Commissioner, that he ought to have exercised his discretion differently,
the Tribunal shall allow the appeal or substitute such other notice or decision as could have been served or made by the Commissioner; and in any other case the Tribunal shall dismiss the appeal.

(2) On such an appeal, the Tribunal may review any determination of fact on which the notice in question was based.

(3) If on an appeal under section 48(2) the Tribunal considers that the enforcement notice ought to be cancelled or varied by reason of a change in circumstances, the Tribunal shall cancel or vary the notice.

(4) On an appeal under subsection (3) of section 48 the Tribunal may direct –
(a) that the notice in question shall have effect as if it did not contain any such statement as is mentioned in that subsection, or

(b) that the inclusion of the statement shall not have effect in relation to any part of the notice,

and may make such modifications in the notice as may be required for giving effect to the direction.

(5) On an appeal under section 48(4), the Tribunal may cancel the determination of the Commissioner.

(6) Any party to an appeal to the Tribunal under section 48 may appeal from the decision of the Tribunal on a point of law to the appropriate court; and that court shall be –

(a) the High Court of Justice in England if the address of the person who was the appellant before the Tribunal is in England or Wales,
(b) the Court of Session if that address is in Scotland, and
(c) the High Court of Justice in Northern Ireland if that address is in Northern Ireland.

(7) For the purposes of subsection (6) –

(a) the address of a registered company is that of its registered office, and
(b) the address of a person (other than a registered company) carrying on a business is that of his principal place of business in the United Kingdom.

50.   Schedule 9 (powers of entry and inspection) has effect.

PART VI
MISCELLANEOUS AND GENERAL
Functions of Commissioner

51. – (1) It shall be the duty of the Commissioner to promote the following of good practice by data controllers and, in particular, so to perform his functions under this Act as to promote the observance of the requirements of this Act by data controllers.

(2) The Commissioner shall arrange for the dissemination in such form and manner as he considers appropriate of such information as it may appear to him expedient to give to the public about the operation of this Act, about good practice, and about other matters within the scope of his functions under this Act, and may give advice to any person as to any of those matters.

(3) Where –

(a) the Secretary of State so directs by order, or

(b) the Commissioner considers it appropriate to do so,
the Commissioner shall, after such consultation with trade associations,
data subjects or persons representing data subjects as appears to him to
be appropriate, prepare and disseminate to such persons as he considers
appropriate codes of practice for guidance as to good practice.

(4)   The Commissioner shall also —
(a) where he considers it appropriate to do so, encourage trade
associations to prepare, and to disseminate to their members, such
codes of practice, and
(b) where any trade association submits a code of practice to him
for his consideration, consider the code and, after such consultation
with data subjects or persons representing data subjects as appears
to him to be appropriate, notify the trade association whether in
his opinion the code promotes the following of good practice.

(5)   An order under subsection (3) shall describe the personal data or
processing to which the code of practice is to relate, and may also
describe the persons or classes of persons to whom it is to relate.

(6)   The Commissioner shall arrange for the dissemination in such
form and manner as he considers appropriate of —
(a) any Community finding as defined by paragraph 15(2) of
Part II of Schedule 1,
(b) any decision of the European Commission, under the
procedure provided for in Article 31(2) of the Data Protection
Directive, which is made for the purposes of Article 26(3) or (4)
of the Directive, and
(c) such other information as it may appear to him to be
expedient to give to data controllers in relation to any personal
data about the protection of the rights and freedoms of data subjects
in relation to the processing of personal data in countries and
territories outside the European Economic Area.

(7)   The Commissioner may, with the consent of the data controller,
assess any processing of personal data for the following of good practice
and shall inform the data controller of the results of the assessment.

(8)   The Commissioner may charge such sums as he may with the
consent of the Secretary of State determine for any services provided
by the Commissioner by virtue of this Part.

(9)   In this section —
"good practice" means such practice in the processing of personal
data as appears to the Commissioner to be desirable having regard

to the interests of data subjects and others, and includes (but is not limited to) compliance with the requirements of this Act;

"trade association" includes any body representing data controllers.

52. – (1) The Commissioner shall lay annually before each House of Parliament a general report on the exercise of his functions under this Act.

(2) The Commissioner may from time to time lay before each House of Parliament such other reports with respect to those functions as he thinks fit.

(3) The Commissioner shall lay before each House of Parliament any code of practice prepared under section 51(3) for complying with a direction of the Secretary of State, unless the code is included in any report laid under subsection (1) or (2).

53. – (1) An individual who is an actual or prospective party to any proceedings under section 7(9), 10(4), 12(8) or 14 or by virtue of section 13 which relate to personal data processed for the special purposes may apply to the Commissioner for assistance in relation to those proceedings.

(2) The Commissioner shall, as soon as reasonably practicable after receiving an application under subsection (1), consider it and decide whether and to what extent to grant it, but he shall not grant the application unless, in his opinion, the case involves a matter of substantial public importance.

(3) If the Commissioner decides to provide assistance, he shall, as soon as reasonably practicable after making the decision, notify the applicant, stating the extent of the assistance to be provided.

(4) If the Commissioner decides not to provide assistance, he shall, as soon as reasonably practicable after making the decision, notify the applicant of his decision and, if he thinks fit, the reasons for it.

(5) In this section –
(a) references to "proceedings" include references to prospective proceedings, and
(b) "applicant", in relation to assistance under this section, means an individual who applies for assistance.

(6) Schedule 10 has effect for supplementing this section.

54. – (1) The Commissioner –
(a) shall continue to be the designated authority in the United Kingdom for the purposes of Article 13 of the Convention, and
(b) shall be the supervisory authority in the United Kingdom for the purposes of the Data Protection Directive.

(2) The Secretary of State may by order make provision as to the functions to be discharged by the Commissioner as the designated authority in the United Kingdom for the purposes of Article 13 of the Convention.

(3) The Secretary of State may by order make provision as to co-operation by the Commissioner with the European Commission and with supervisory authorities in other EEA States in connection with the performance of their respective duties and, in particular, as to –
(a) the exchange of information with supervisory authorities in other EEA States or with the European Commission, and
(b) the exercise within the United Kingdom at the request of a supervisory authority in another EEA State, in cases excluded by section 5 from the application of the other provisions of this Act, of functions of the Commissioner specified in the order.

(4) The Commissioner shall also carry out any data protection functions which the Secretary of State may by order direct him to carry out for the purpose of enabling Her Majesty's Government in the United Kingdom to give effect to any international obligations of the United Kingdom.

(5) The Commissioner shall, if so directed by the Secretary of State, provide any authority exercising data protection functions under the law of a colony specified in the direction with such assistance in connection with the discharge of those functions as the Secretary of State may direct or approve, on such terms (including terms as to payment) as the Secretary of State may direct or approve.

(6) Where the European Commission makes a decision for the purposes of Article 26(3) or (4) of the Data Protection Directive under the procedure provided for in Article 31(2) of the Directive, the Commissioner shall comply with that decision in exercising his functions under paragraph 9 of Schedule 4 or, as the case may be, paragraph 8 of that Schedule.

(7) The Commissioner shall inform the European Commission and the supervisory authorities in other EEA States –
(a) of any approvals granted for the purposes of paragraph 8 of Schedule 4, and

(b) of any authorisations granted for the purposes of paragraph 9 of that Schedule.

(8) In this section –
"the Convention" means the Convention for the Protection of Individuals with regard to Automatic Processing of Personal Data which was opened for signature on 28th January 1981;

"data protection functions" means functions relating to the protection of individuals with respect to the processing of personal information.

Unlawful obtaining etc of personal data

55. – (1) A person must not knowingly or recklessly, without the consent of the data controller –
(a) obtain or disclose personal data or the information contained in personal data, or
(b) procure the disclosure to another person of the information contained in personal data.

(2) Subsection (1) does not apply to a person who shows –
(a) that the obtaining, disclosing or procuring –
(i) was necessary for the purpose of preventing or detecting crime, or
(ii) was required or authorised by or under any enactment, by any rule of law or by the order of a court,
(b) that he acted in the reasonable belief that he had in law the right to obtain or disclose the data or information or, as the case may be, to procure the disclosure of the information to the other person,
(c) that he acted in the reasonable belief that he would have had the consent of the data controller if the data controller had known of the obtaining, disclosing or procuring and the circumstances of it, or
(d) that in the particular circumstances the obtaining, disclosing or procuring was justified as being in the public interest.

(3) A person who contravenes subsection (1) is guilty of an offence.

(4) A person who sells personal data is guilty of an offence if he has obtained the data in contravention of subsection (1).

(5) A person who offers to sell personal data is guilty of an offence if –
(a) he has obtained the data in contravention of subsection (1), or

(b) he subsequently obtains the data in contravention of that subsection.

(6)   For the purposes of subsection (5), an advertisement indicating that personal data are or may be for sale is an offer to sell the data.

(7)   Section 1(2) does not apply for the purposes of this section; and for the purposes of subsections (4) to (6), "personal data" includes information extracted from personal data.

(8)   References in this section to personal data do not include references to personal data which by virtue of section 28 are exempt from this section.

Records obtained under data subject's right of access

56. – (1) A person must not, in connection with –
(a) the recruitment of another person as an employee,
(b) the continued employment of another person, or
(c) any contract for the provision of services to him by another person,
require that other person or a third party to supply him with a relevant record or to produce a relevant record to him.

(2)   A person concerned with the provision (for payment or not) of goods, facilities or services to the public or a section of the public must not, as a condition of providing or offering to provide any goods, facilities or services to another person, require that other person or a third party to supply him with a relevant record or to produce a relevant record to him.

(3)   Subsections (1) and (2) do not apply to a person who shows –
(a) that the imposition of the requirement was required or authorised by or under any enactment, by any rule of law or by the order of a court, or
(b) that in the particular circumstances the imposition of the requirement was justified as being in the public interest.

(4)   Having regard to the provisions of Part V of the Police Act 1997 (certificates of criminal records etc), the imposition of the requirement referred to in subsection (1) or (2) is not to be regarded as being justified as being in the public interest on the ground that it would assist in the prevention or detection of crime.

(5)   A person who contravenes subsection (1) or (2) is guilty of an offence.

(6) In this section "a relevant record" means any record which –
    (a) has been or is to be obtained by a data subject from any data controller specified in the first column of the Table below in the exercise of the right conferred by section 7, and
    (b) contains information relating to any matter specified in relation to that data controller in the second column,
and includes a copy of such a record or a part of such a record.

TABLE

Data controller	Subject-matter
1. Any of the following persons – (a) a chief officer of police of a police force in England and Wales. (b) a chief constable of a police force in Scotland. (c) the Chief Constable of the Royal Ulster Constabulary. (d) the Director General of the National Criminal Intelligence Service. (e) the Director General of the National Crime Squad.	(a) Convictions. (b) Cautions.
2. The Secretary of State.	(a) Convictions. (b) Cautions. (c) His functions under section 53 of the Children and Young Persons Act 1933, section 205(2) or 208 of the Criminal Procedure (Scotland) Act 1995 or section 73 of the Children and Young Persons Act (Northern Ireland) 1968 in relation to any person sentenced to detention. (d) His functions under the Prison Act 1952, the Prisons (Scotland) Act 1989 or the Prison Act (Northern Ireland) 1953 in relation to any person imprisoned or detained. (e) His functions under the Social Security Contributions and Benefits Act 1992, the Social Security

	Administration Act 1992 or the Jobseekers Act 1995. (f) His functions under Part V of the Police Act 1997.
3. The Department of Health and Social Services for Northern Ireland.	Its functions under the Social Security Contributions and Benefits (Northern Ireland) Act 1992, the Social Security Administration (Northern Ireland) Act 1992 or the Jobseekers (Northern Ireland) Order 1995.

(7) In the Table in subsection (6) —
"caution" means a caution given to any person in England and Wales or Northern Ireland in respect of an offence which, at the time when the caution is given, is admitted;

"conviction" has the same meaning as in the Rehabilitation of Offenders Act 1974 or the Rehabilitation of Offenders (Northern Ireland) Order 1978.

(8) The Secretary of State may by order amend —
(a) the Table in subsection (6), and
(b) subsection (7).

(9) For the purposes of this section a record which states that a data controller is not processing any personal data relating to a particular matter shall be taken to be a record containing information relating to that matter.

(10) In this section "employee" means an individual who —
(a) works under a contract of employment, as defined by section 230(2) of the Employment Rights Act 1996, or
(b) holds any office,
whether or not he is entitled to remuneration; and "employment" shall be construed accordingly.

57. – (1) Any term or condition of a contract is void in so far as it purports to require an individual —
(a) to supply any other person with a record to which this section applies, or with a copy of such a record or a part of such a record, or
(b) to produce to any other person such a record, copy or part.
(2) This section applies to any record which —

(a) has been or is to be obtained by a data subject in the exercise of the right conferred by section 7, and

(b) consists of the information contained in any health record as defined by section 68(2).

Information provided to Commissioner or Tribunal

58. No enactment or rule of law prohibiting or restricting the disclosure of information shall preclude a person from furnishing the Commissioner or the Tribunal with any information necessary for the discharge of their functions under this Act.

59. – (1) No person who is or has been the Commissioner, a member of the Commissioner's staff or an agent of the Commissioner shall disclose any information which –

(a) has been obtained by, or furnished to, the Commissioner under or for the purposes of this Act,

(b) relates to an identified or identifiable individual or business, and

(c) is not at the time of the disclosure, and has not previously been, available to the public from other sources,

unless the disclosure is made with lawful authority.

(2) For the purposes of subsection (1) a disclosure of information is made with lawful authority only if, and to the extent that –

(a) the disclosure is made with the consent of the individual or of the person for the time being carrying on the business,

(b) the information was provided for the purpose of its being made available to the public (in whatever manner) under any provision of this Act,

(c) the disclosure is made for the purposes of, and is necessary for, the discharge of –

(i) any functions under this Act, or

(ii) any Community obligation,

(d) the disclosure is made for the purposes of any proceedings, whether criminal or civil and whether arising under, or by virtue of, this Act or otherwise, or

(e) having regard to the rights and freedoms or legitimate interests of any person, the disclosure is necessary in the public interest.

(3) Any person who knowingly or recklessly discloses information in contravention of subsection (1) is guilty of an offence.

General provisions relating to offences

60. – (1) No proceedings for an offence under this Act shall be instituted –

(a) in England or Wales, except by the Commissioner or by or with the consent of the Director of Public Prosecutions;

(b) in Northern Ireland, except by the Commissioner or by or with the consent of the Director of Public Prosecutions for Northern Ireland.

(2) A person guilty of an offence under any provision of this Act other than paragraph 12 of Schedule 9 is liable –

(a) on summary conviction, to a fine not exceeding the statutory maximum, or

(b) on conviction on indictment, to a fine.

(3) A person guilty of an offence under paragraph 12 of Schedule 9 is liable on summary conviction to a fine not exceeding level 5 on the standard scale.

(4) Subject to subsection (5), the court by or before which a person is convicted of –

(a) an offence under section 21(1), 22(6), 55 or 56,

(b) an offence under section 21(2) relating to processing which is assessable processing for the purposes of section 22, or

(c) an offence under section 47(1) relating to an enforcement notice,

may order any document or other material used in connection with the processing of personal data and appearing to the court to be connected with the commission of the offence to be forfeited, destroyed or erased.

(5) The court shall not make an order under subsection (4) in relation to any material where a person (other than the offender) claiming to be the owner of or otherwise interested in the material applies to be heard by the court, unless an opportunity is given to him to show cause why the order should not be made.

61. – (1) Where an offence under this Act has been committed by a body corporate and is proved to have been committed with the consent or connivance of or to be attributable to any neglect on the part of any director, manager, secretary or similar officer of the body corporate or any person who was purporting to act in any such capacity, he as well as the body corporate shall be guilty of that offence and be liable to be proceeded against and punished accordingly.

(2) Where the affairs of a body corporate are managed by its members subsection (1) shall apply in relation to the acts and defaults of a member in connection with his functions of management as if he were a director of the body corporate.

(3) Where an offence under this Act has been committed by a Scottish partnership and the contravention in question is proved to have occurred with the consent or connivance of, or to be attributable to any neglect on the part of, a partner, he as well as the partnership shall be guilty of that offence and shall be liable to be proceeded against and punished accordingly.

Amendments of Consumer Credit Act 1974

62. — (1) In section 158 of the Consumer Credit Act 1974 (duty of agency to disclose filed information) —
    (a) in subsection (1) —
        (i) in paragraph (a) for "individual" there is substituted "partnership or other unincorporated body of persons not consisting entirely of bodies corporate", and
        (ii) for "him" there is substituted "it",
    (b) in subsection (2), for "his" there is substituted "the consumer's", and
    (c) in subsection (3), for "him" there is substituted "the consumer".

(2) In section 159 of that Act (correction of wrong information) for subsection (1) there is substituted —
    "(1) Any individual (the "objector") given —
        (a) information under section 7 of the Data Protection Act 1998 by a credit reference agency, or
        (b) information under section 158,
who considers that an entry in his file is incorrect, and that if it is not corrected he is likely to be prejudiced, may give notice to the agency requiring it either to remove the entry from the file or amend it.".

(3) In subsections (2) to (6) of that subsection —
    (a) for "consumer", wherever occurring, there is substituted "objector", and
    (b) for "Director", wherever occurring, there is substituted "the relevant authority".

(4) After subsection (6) of that section there is inserted —
    "(7) The Data Protection Commissioner may vary or revoke any order made by him under this section.

    (8) In this section "the relevant authority" means —
        (a) where the objector is a partnership or other unincorporated body of persons, the Director, and
        (b) in any other case, the Data Protection Commissioner.".

(5) In section 160 of that Act (alternative procedure for business consumers) −

(a) in subsection (4) −

    (i) for "him" there is substituted "to the consumer", and

    (ii) in paragraphs (a) and (b) for "he" there is substituted "the consumer" and for "his" there is substituted "the consumer's", and

(b) after subsection (6) there is inserted −

    "(7) In this section "consumer" has the same meaning as in section 158.".

General

63. − (1) This Act binds the Crown.

(2) For the purposes of this Act each government department shall be treated as a person separate from any other government department.

(3) Where the purposes for which and the manner in which any personal data are, or are to be, processed are determined by any person acting on behalf of the Royal Household, the Duchy of Lancaster or the Duchy of Cornwall, the data controller in respect of those data for the purposes of this Act shall be −

(a) in relation to the Royal Household, the Keeper of the Privy Purse,

(b) in relation to the Duchy of Lancaster, such person as the Chancellor of the Duchy appoints, and

(c) in relation to the Duchy of Cornwall, such person as the Duke of Cornwall, or the possessor for the time being of the Duchy of Cornwall, appoints.

(4) Different persons may be appointed under subsection (3)(b) or (c) for different purposes.

(5) Neither a government department nor a person who is a data controller by virtue of subsection (3) shall be liable to prosecution under this Act, but section 55 and paragraph 12 of Schedule 9 shall apply to a person in the service of the Crown as they apply to any other person.

64. − (1) This section applies to

(a) a notice or request under any provision of Part II,

(b) a notice under subsection (1) of section 24 or particulars made available under that subsection, or

(c) an application under section 41(2),

but does not apply to anything which is required to be served in accordance with rules of court.

(2) The requirement that any notice, request, particulars or application to which this section applies should be in writing is satisfied where the text of the notice, request, particulars or application –
    (a) is transmitted by electronic means,
    (b) is received in legible form, and
    (c) is capable of being used for subsequent reference.

(3) The Secretary of State may by regulations provide that any requirement that any notice, request, particulars or application to which this section applies should be in writing is not to apply in such circumstances as may be prescribed by the regulations.

65. – (1) Any notice authorised or required by this Act to be served on or given to any person by the Commissioner may –
    (a) if that person is an individual, be served on him –
        (i) by delivering it to him, or
        (ii) by sending it to him by post addressed to him at his usual or last-known place of residence or business, or
        (iii) by leaving it for him at that place;
    (b) if that person is a body corporate or unincorporate, be served on that body –
        (i) by sending it by post to the proper officer of the body at its principal office, or
        (ii) by addressing it to the proper officer of the body and leaving it at that office;
    (c) if that person is a partnership in Scotland, be served on that partnership –
        (i) by sending it by post to the principal office of the partnership, or
        (ii) by addressing it to that partnership and leaving it at that office.

(2) In subsection (1)(b) "principal office", in relation to a registered company, means its registered office and "proper officer", in relation to any body, means the secretary or other executive officer charged with the conduct of its general affairs.

(3) This section is without prejudice to any other lawful method of serving or giving a notice.

66. – (1) Where a question falls to be determined in Scotland as to the legal capacity of a person under the age of sixteen years to exercise any right conferred by any provision of this Act, that person shall be taken to have that capacity where he has a general understanding of what it means to exercise that right.

(2) Without prejudice to the generality of subsection (1), a person of twelve years of age or more shall be presumed to be of sufficient age and maturity to have such understanding as is mentioned in that subsection.

67. – (1) Any power conferred by this Act on the Secretary of State to make an order, regulations or rules shall be exercisable by statutory instrument.

(2) Any order, regulations or rules made by the Secretary of State under this Act may –
    (a) make different provision for different cases, and
    (b) make such supplemental, incidental, consequential or transitional provision or savings as the Secretary of State considers appropriate;
and nothing in section 7(11), 19(5), 26(1) or 30(4) limits the generality of paragraph (a).

(3) Before making –
    (a) an order under any provision of this Act other than section 75(3),
    (b) any regulations under this Act other than notification regulations (as defined by section 16(2)),
the Secretary of State shall consult the Commissioner.

(4) A statutory instrument containing (whether alone or with other provisions) an order under –
    section 10(2)(b),
    section 12(5)(b),
    section 22(1),
    section 30,
    section 32(3),
    section 38,
    section 56(8),
    paragraph 10 of Schedule 3, or
    paragraph 4 of Schedule 7,
shall not be made unless a draft of the instrument has been laid before and approved by a resolution of each House of Parliament.

(5) A statutory instrument which contains (whether alone or with other provisions) –
    (a) an order under –
        section 22(7),

section 23,
section 51(3),
section 54(2), (3) or (4),
paragraph 3, 4 or 14 of Part II of Schedule 1,
paragraph 6 of Schedule 2,
paragraph 2, 7 or 9 of Schedule 3,
paragraph 4 of Schedule 4,
paragraph 6 of Schedule 7,
  (b) regulations under section 7 which –
    (i) prescribe cases for the purposes of subsection (2)(b),
    (ii) are made by virtue of subsection (7), or
    (iii) relate to the definition of "the prescribed period",
  (c) regulations under section 8(1) or 9(3),
  (d) regulations under section 64,
  (e) notification regulations (as defined by section 16(2)), or
  (f) rules under paragraph 7 of Schedule 6,
and which is not subject to the requirement in subsection (4) that a draft of the instrument be laid before and approved by a resolution of each House of Parliament, shall be subject to annulment in pursuance of a resolution of either House of Parliament.

(6) A statutory instrument which contains only –
  (a) regulations prescribing fees for the purposes of any provision of this Act, or
  (b) regulations under section 7 prescribing fees for !he purposes of any other enactment,
shall be laid before Parliament after being made.

68. – (1) In this Act "accessible record" means –
  (a) a health record as defined by subsection (2),
  (b) an educational record as defined by Schedule 11, or
  (c) an accessible public record as defined by Schedule 12.

(2) In subsection (1)(a) "health record" means any record which –
  (a) consists of information relating to the physical or mental health or condition of an individual, and
  (b) has been made by or on behalf of a health professional in connection with the care of that individual.

69. – (1) In this Act "health professional" means any of the following –
  (a) a registered medical practitioner,
  (b) a registered dentist as defined by section 53(1) of the Dentists Act 1984,
  (c) a registered optician as defined by section 36(1) of the Opticians Act 1989,

(d) a registered pharmaceutical chemist as defined by section 24(1) of the Pharmacy Act 1954 or a registered person as defined by Article 2(2) of the Pharmacy (Northern Ireland) Order 1976,
(e) a registered nurse, midwife or health visitor,
(f) a registered osteopath as defined by section 41 of the Osteopaths Act 1993,
(g) a registered chiropractor as defined by section 43 of the Chiropractors Act 1994,
(h) any person who is registered as a member of a profession to which the Professions Supplementary to Medicine Act 1960 for the time being extends,
(i) a clinical psychologist, child psychotherapist or speech therapist,
(j) a music therapist employed by a health service body, and
(k) a scientist employed by such a body as head of a department.

(2) In subsection (1)(a) "registered medical practitioner" includes any person who is provisionally registered under section 15 or 21 of the Medical Act 1983 and is engaged in such employment as is mentioned in subsection (3) of that section.

(3) In subsection (1) "health service body" means –
(a) a Health Authority established under section 8 of the National Health Service Act 1977,
(b) a Special Health Authority established under section 11 of that Act,
(c) a Health Board within the meaning of the National Health Service (Scotland) Act 1978,
(d) a Special Health Board within the meaning of that Act,
(e) the managers of a State Hospital provided under section 102 of that Act,
(f) a National Health Service trust first established under section 5 of the National Health Service and Community Care Act 1990 or section 12A of the National Health Service (Scotland) Act 1978,
(g) a Health and Social Services Board established under Article 16 of the Health and Personal Social Services (Northern Ireland) Order 1972,
(h) a special health and social services agency established under the Health and Personal Social Services (Special Agencies) (Northern Ireland) Order 1990, or
(i) a Health and Social Services trust established under Article 10 of the Health and Personal Social Services (Northern Ireland) Order 1991.

70. – (1) In this Act, unless the context otherwise requires –

"business" includes any trade or profession;

"the Commissioner" means the Data Protection Commissioner;

"credit reference agency" has the same meaning as in the Consumer Credit Act 1974;

"the Data Protection Directive" means Directive 95/46/EC on the protection of individuals with regard to the processing of personal data and on the free movement of such data;

"EEA State" means a State which is a contracting party to the Agreement on the European Economic Area signed at Oporto on 2nd May 1992 as adjusted by the Protocol signed at Brussels on 17th March 1993;

"enactment" includes an enactment passed after this Act;

"government department" includes a Northern Ireland department and any body or authority exercising statutory functions on behalf of the Crown;

"Minister of the Crown" has the same meaning as in the Ministers of the Crown Act 1975;

"public register" means any register which pursuant to a requirement imposed –
    (a) by or under any enactment, or
    (b) in pursuance of any international agreement,
is open to public inspection or open to inspection by any person having a legitimate interest;

"pupil" –
    (a) in relation to a school in England and Wales, means a registered pupil within the meaning of the Education Act 1996,
    (b) in relation to a school in Scotland, means a pupil within the meaning of the Education (Scotland) Act 1980, and
    (c) in relation to a school in Northern Ireland, means a registered pupil within the meaning of the Education and Libraries (Northern Ireland) Order 1986;

"recipient", in relation to any personal data, means any person to whom the data are disclosed, including any person (such as an employee or agent of the data controller, a data processor or an employee or agent of a data processor) to whom they are disclosed in the course of processing the data for the data controller, but does not include any person to whom disclosure is or may be made as a result of, or with a view to, a particular inquiry by or on behalf of that person made in the exercise of any power conferred by law;

"registered company" means a company registered under the enactments relating to companies for the time being in force in the United Kingdom;

"school" –
(a) in relation to England and Wales, has the same meaning as in the Education Act 1996,
(b) in relation to Scotland, has the same meaning as in the Education (Scotland) Act 1980, and
(c) in relation to Northern Ireland, has the same meaning as in the Education and Libraries (Northern Ireland) Order 1986;

"teacher" includes –
(a) in Great Britain, head teacher, and
(b) in Northern Ireland, the principal of a school;

"third party", in relation to personal data, means any person other than –
(a) the data subject,
(b) the data controller, or
(c) any data processor or other person authorised to process data for the data controller or processor;

"the Tribunal" means the Data Protection Tribunal.

(2) For the purposes of this Act data are inaccurate if they are incorrect or misleading as to any matter of fact.

71. The following Table shows provisions defining or otherwise explaining expressions used in this Act (other than provisions defining or explaining an expression only used in the same section or Schedule) –

accessible record	section 68
address (in Part III)	section 16(3)
business	section 70(1)
the Commissioner	section 70(1)

credit reference agency	section 70(1)
data	section 1(1)
data controller	sections 1(1) and (4) and 63(3)
data processor	section 1(1)
the Data Protection Directive	section 70(1)
data protection principles	section 4 and Schedule 1
data subject	section 1(1)
disclosing (of personal data)	section 1(2)(b)
EEA State	section 70(1)
enactment	section 70(1)
enforcement notice	section 40(1)
fees regulations (in Part III)	section 16(2)
government department	section 70(1)
health professional	section 69
inaccurate (in relation to data)	section 70(2)
information notice	section 43(1)
Minister of the Crown	section 70(1)
the non-disclosure provisions (in Part IV)	section 27(3)
notification regulations (in Part III)	section 16(2)
obtaining (of personal data)	section 1(2)(a)
personal data	section 1(1)
prescribed (in Part III)	section 16(2)

processing (of information or data)	section 1(1) and paragraph 5 of Schedule 8
public register	section 70(1)
publish (in relation to journalistic, literary or artistic material)	section 32(6)
pupil (in relation to a school)	section 70(1)
recipient (in relation to personal data)	section 70(1)
recording (of personal data)	section 1(2)(a)
registered company	section 70(1)
registrable particulars (in Part III)	section 16(1)
relevant filing system	section 1(1)
school	section 70(1)
sensitive personal data	section 2
special information notice	section 44(1)
the special purposes	section 3
the subject information provisions (in Part IV)	section 27(2)
teacher	section 70(1)
third party (in relation to processing of personal data)	section 70(1)
the Tribunal	section 70(1)
using (of personal data)	section 1(2)(b).

72. During the period beginning with the commencement of this section and ending with 23rd October 2007, the provisions of this Act shall have effect subject to the modifications set out in Schedule 13.

73. Schedule 14 (which contains transitional provisions and savings) has effect.

74. – (1) Schedule 15 (which contains minor and consequential amendments) has effect.

(2) The enactments and instruments specified in Schedule 16 are repealed or revoked to the extent specified.

75. – (1) This Act may be cited as the Data Protection Act 1998.

(2) The following provisions of this Act –
  (a) sections 1 to 3,
  (b) section 25(1) and (4),
  (c) section 26,
  (d) sections 67 to 71,
  (e) this section,
  (f) paragraph 17 of Schedule 5,
  (g) Schedule 11,
  (h) Schedule 12, and
  (i) so much of any other provision of this Act as confers any power to make subordinate legislation,
shall come into force on the day on which this Act is passed.

(3) The remaining provisions of this Act shall come into force on such day as the Secretary of State may by order appoint; and different days may be appointed for different purposes.

(4) The day appointed under subsection (3) for the coming into force of section 56 must not be earlier than the first day on which sections 112, 113 and 115 of the Police Act 1997 (which provide for the issue by the Secretary of State of criminal conviction certificates, criminal record certificates and enhanced criminal record certificates) are all in force.

(5) Subject to subsection (6), this Act extends to Northern Ireland.

(6) Any amendment, repeal or revocation made by Schedule 15 or 16 has the same extent as that of the enactment or instrument to which it relates.

SCHEDULE 1
THE DATA PROTECTION PRINCIPLES
Part I
The Principles

1. Personal data shall be processed fairly and lawfully and, in particular, shall not be processed unless –
  (a) at least one of the conditions in Schedule 2 is met, and
  (b) in the case of sensitive personal data, at least one of the conditions in Schedule 3 is also met.

2. Personal data shall be obtained only for one or more specified and lawful purposes, and shall not be further processed in any manner incompatible with that purpose or those purposes.

3. Personal data shall be adequate, relevant and not excessive in relation to the purpose or purposes for which they are processed.

4. Personal data shall be accurate and, where necessary, kept up to date.

5. Personal data processed for any purpose or purposes shall not be kept for longer than is necessary for that purpose or those purposes.

6. Personal data shall be processed in accordance with the rights of data subjects under this Act.

7. Appropriate technical and organisational measures shall be taken against unauthorised or unlawful processing of personal data and against accidental loss or destruction of, or damage to, personal data.

8. Personal data shall not be transferred to a country or territory outside the European Economic Area unless that country or territory ensures an adequate level of protection for the rights and freedoms of data subjects in relation to the processing of personal data.

Part II
Interpretation of the Principles in Part I

The first principle

1. – (1) In determining for the purposes of the first principle whether personal data are processed fairly, regard is to be had to the method by which they are obtained, including in particular whether any person from whom they are obtained is deceived or misled as to the purpose or purposes for which they are to be processed.

(2) Subject to paragraph 2, for the purposes of the first principle data are to be treated as obtained fairly if they consist of information obtained from a person who –

    (a) is authorised by or under any enactment to supply it, or

    (b) is required to supply it by or under any enactment or by any convention or other instrument imposing an international obligation on the United Kingdom.

2. – (1) Subject to paragraph 3, for the purposes of the first principle personal data are not to be treated as processed fairly unless –

    (a) in the case of data obtained from the data subject, the data controller ensures so far as practicable that the data subject has, is provided with, or has made readily available to him, the information specified in sub-paragraph (3), and

    (b) in any other case, the data controller ensures so far as practicable that, before the relevant time or as soon as practicable after that time, the data subject has, is provided with, or has made readily available to him, the information specified in sub-paragraph (3).

(2) In sub-paragraph (1)(b) "the relevant time" means –

    (a) the time when the data controller first processes the data, or

    (b) in a case where at that time disclosure to a third party within a reasonable period is envisaged –

        (i) if the data are in fact disclosed to such a person within that period, the time when the data are first disclosed,

        (ii) if within that period the data controller becomes, or ought to become, aware that the data are unlikely to be disclosed to such a person within that period, the time when the data controller does become, or ought to become, so aware, or

        (iii) in any other case, the end of that period.

(3) The information referred to in sub-paragraph (1) is as follows, namely –

    (a) the identity of the data controller,

    (b) if he has nominated a representative for the purposes of this Act, the identity of that representative,

    (c) the purpose or purposes for which the data are intended to be processed, and

    (d) any further information which is necessary, having regard to the specific circumstances in which the data are or are to be processed, to enable processing in respect of the data subject to be fair.

3. – (1) Paragraph 2(1)(b) does not apply where either of the primary conditions in sub-paragraph (2), together with such further conditions as may be prescribed by the Secretary of State by order, are met.

(2) The primary conditions referred to in sub-paragraph (1) are –
   (a) that the provision of that information would involve a disproportionate effort, or
   (b) that the recording of the information to be contained in the data by, or the disclosure of the data by, the data controller is necessary for compliance with any legal obligation to which the data controller is subject, other than an obligation imposed by contract.

4. – (1) Personal data which contain a general identifier falling within a description prescribed by the Secretary of State by order are not to be treated as processed fairly and lawfully unless they are processed in compliance with any conditions so prescribed in relation to general identifiers of that description.

(2) In sub-paragraph (1) "a general identifier" means any identifier (such as, for example, a number or code used for identification purposes) which –
   (a) relates to an individual, and
   (b) forms part of a set of similar identifiers which is of general application.

The second principle

5. The purpose or purposes for which personal data are obtained may in particular be specified –
   (a) in a notice given for the purposes of paragraph 2 by the data controller to the data subject, or
   (b) in a notification given to the Commissioner under Part III of this Act.

6. In determining whether any disclosure of personal data is compatible with the purpose or purposes for which the data were obtained, regard is to be had to the purpose or purposes for which the personal data are intended to be processed by any person to whom they are disclosed.

The fourth principle

7. The fourth principle is not to be regarded as being contravened by reason of any inaccuracy in personal data which accurately record information obtained by the data controller from the data subject or a third party in a case where –

(a) having regard to the purpose or purposes for which the data were obtained and further processed, the data controller has taken reasonable steps to ensure the accuracy of the data, and

(b) if the data subject has notified the data controller of the data subject's view that the data are inaccurate, the data indicate that fact.

The sixth principle

8. A person is to be regarded as contravening the sixth principle if, but only if –

(a) he contravenes section 7 by failing to supply information in accordance with that section,

(b) he contravenes section 10 by failing to comply with a notice given under subsection (1) of that section to the extent that the notice is justified or by failing to give a notice under subsection (3) of that section,

(c) he contravenes section 11 by failing to comply with a notice given under subsection (1) of that section, or

(d) he contravenes section 12 by failing to comply with a notice given under subsection (1) or (2)(b) of that section or by failing to give a notification under subsection (2)(a) of that section or a notice under subsection (3) of that section.

The seventh principle

9. Having regard to the state of technological development and the cost of implementing any measures, the measures must ensure a level of security appropriate to –

(a) the harm that might result from such unauthorised or unlawful processing or accidental loss, destruction or damage as are mentioned in the seventh principle, and

(b) the nature of the data to be protected.

10. – The data controller must take reasonable steps to ensure the reliability of any employees of his who have access to the personal data.

11. Where processing of personal data is carried out by a data processor on behalf of a data controller, the data controller must in order to comply with the seventh principle –

(a) choose a data processor providing sufficient guarantees in respect of the technical and organisational security measures governing the processing to be carried out, and

(b) take reasonable steps to ensure compliance with those measures.

12. Where processing of personal data is carried out by a data processor on behalf of a data controller, the data controller is not to be regarded as complying with the seventh principle unless –

(a) the processing is carried out under a contract –

(i) which is made or evidenced in writing, and

(ii) under which the data processor is to act only on instructions from the data controller, and

(b) the contract requires the data processor to comply with obligations equivalent to those imposed on a data controller by the seventh principle.

The eighth principle

13. An adequate level of protection is one which is adequate in all the circumstances of the case, having regard in particular to –

(a) the nature of the personal data,

(b) the country or territory of origin of the information contained in the data,

(c) the country or territory of final destination of that information,

(d) the purposes for which and period during which the data are intended to be processed,

(e) the law in force in the country or territory in question,

(f) the international obligations of that country or territory,

(g) any relevant codes of conduct or other rules which are enforceable in that country or territory (whether generally or by arrangement in particular cases), and

(h) any security measures taken in respect of the data in that country or territory.

14. The eighth principle does not apply to a transfer falling within any paragraph of Schedule 4, except in such circumstances and to such extent as the Secretary of State may by order provide.

15. – (1) Where –

(a) in any proceedings under this Act any question arises as to whether the requirement of the eighth principle as to an adequate level of protection is met in relation to the transfer of any personal data to a country or territory outside the European Economic Area, and

(b) a Community finding has been made in relation to transfers of the kind in question,

that question is to be determined in accordance with that finding.

(2) In sub-paragraph (1) "Community finding" means a finding of the European Commission, under the procedure provided for in Article 31(2) of the Data Protection Directive, that a country or territory outside

the European Economic Area does, or does not, ensure an adequate level of protection within the meaning of Article 25(2) of the Directive.

SCHEDULE 2
CONDITIONS RELEVANT FOR PURPOSES OF THE FIRST PRINCIPLE: PROCESSING OF ANY PERSONAL DATA

1. The data subject has given his consent to the processing.

2. The processing is necessary –
(a) for the performance of a contract to which the data subject is a party, or
(b) for the taking of steps at the request of the data subject with a view to entering into a contract.

3. The processing is necessary for compliance with any legal obligation to which the data controller is subject, other than an obligation imposed by contract.

4. The processing is necessary in order to protect the vital interests of the data subject.

5. The processing is necessary –
(a) for the administration of justice,
(b) for the exercise of any functions conferred on any person by or under any enactment,
(c) for the exercise of any functions of the Crown, a Minister of the Crown or a government department, or
(d) for the exercise of any other functions of a public nature exercised in the public interest by any person.

6. – (1) The processing is necessary for the purposes of legitimate interests pursued by the data controller or by the third party or parties to whom the data are disclosed, except where the processing is unwarranted in any particular case by reason of prejudice to the rights and freedoms or legitimate interests of the data subject.

(2) The Secretary of State may by order specify particular circumstances in which this condition is, or is not, to be taken to be satisfied.

SCHEDULE 3
CONDITIONS RELEVANT FOR PURPOSES OF THE FIRST PRINCIPLE PROCESSING OF SENSITIVE PERSONNAL DATA

1. The data subject has given his explicit consent to the processing of the personal data.

411

2. – (1) The processing is necessary for the purposes of exercising or performing any right or obligation which is conferred or imposed by law on the data controller in connection with employment.

(2) The Secretary of State may by order –
  (a) exclude the application of sub-paragraph (1) in such cases as may be specified, or
  (b) provide that, in such cases as may be specified, the condition in subparagraph (1) is not to be regarded as satisfied unless such further conditions as may be specified in the order are also satisfied.

3. The processing is necessary –
  (a) in order to protect the vital interests of the data subject or another person, in a case where –
    (i) consent cannot be given by or on behalf of the data subject, or
    (ii) the data controller cannot reasonably be expected to obtain the consent of the data subject, or
  (b) in order to protect the vital interests of another person, in a case where consent by or on behalf of the data subject has been unreasonably withheld.

4. The processing –
  (a) is carried out in the course of its legitimate activities by any body or association which –
  (i) is not established or conducted for profit, and
  (ii) exists for political, philosophical religious or trade–union purposes,
  (b) is carried out with appropriate safeguards for the rights and freedoms of data subjects,
  (c) relates only to individuals who either are members of the body or association or have regular contact with it in connection with its purposes, and
  (d) does not involve disclosure of the personal data to a third party without the consent of the data subject.

5. The information contained in the personal data has been made public as a result of steps deliberately taken by the data subject.

6. The processing –
  (a) is necessary for the purpose of, or in connection with, any legal proceedings (including prospective legal proceedings),
  (b) is necessary for the purpose of obtaining legal advice, or
  (c) is otherwise necessary for the purposes of establishing, exercising or defending legal rights.

7. – (1) The processing is necessary –
(a) for the administration of justice,
(b) for the exercise of any functions conferred on any person by or under an enactment, or
(c) for the exercise of any functions of the Crown, a Minister of the Crown or a government department.

(2) The Secretary of State may by order –
(a) exclude the application of sub-paragraph (1) in such cases as may be specified, or
(b) provide that, in such cases as may be specified, the condition in subparagraph (1) is not to be regarded as satisfied unless such further conditions as may be specified in the order are also satisfied.

8. – (1) The processing is necessary for medical purposes and is undertaken by –
(a) a health professional, or
(b) a person who in the circumstances owes a duty of confidentiality which is equivalent to that which would arise if that person were a health professional.

(2) In this paragraph "medical purposes" includes the purposes of preventative medicine, medical diagnosis, medical research, the provision of care and treatment and the management of healthcare services.

9. – (1) The processing –
(a) is of sensitive personal data consisting of information as to racial or ethnic origin,
(b) is necessary for the purpose of identifying or keeping under review the existence or absence of equality of opportunity or treatment between persons of different racial or ethnic origins, with a view to enabling such equality to be promoted or maintained, and
(c) is carried out with appropriate safeguards for the rights and freedoms of data subjects.

(2) The Secretary of State may by order specify circumstances in which processing falling within sub-paragraph (1)(a) and (b) is, or is not, to be taken for the purposes of sub-paragraph (1)(c) to be carried out with appropriate safeguards for the rights and freedoms of data subjects.

10. The personal data are processed in circumstances specified in an order made by the Secretary of State for the purposes of this paragraph.

SCHEDULE 4
CASES WHERE THE EIGHTH PRINCIPLE DOES NOT APPLY

1.   The data subject has given his consent to the transfer.

2.   The transfer is necessary –
(a) for the performance of a contract between the data subject and the data controller, or
(b) for the taking of steps at the request of the data subject with a view to his entering into a contract with the data controller.

3.   The transfer is necessary –
(a) for the conclusion of a contract between the data controller and a person other than the data subject which –
(i)   is entered into at the request of the data subject, or
(ii) is in the interests of the data subject, or
(b) for the performance of such a contract.

4. – (1) The transfer is necessary for reasons of substantial public interest.

(2)   The Secretary of State may by order specify –
(a) circumstances in which a transfer is to be taken for the purposes of subparagraph (1) to be necessary for reasons of substantial public interest, and
(b) circumstances in which a transfer which is not required by or under an enactment is not to be taken for the purpose of subparagraph (1) to be necessary for reasons of substantial public interest.

5.   The transfer –
(a) is necessary for the purpose of, or in connection with, any legal proceedings (including prospective legal proceedings),
(b) is necessary for the purpose of obtaining legal advice, or
(c) is otherwise necessary for the purposes of establishing, exercising or defending legal rights.

6.   The transfer is necessary in order to protect the vital interests of the data subject.

7.   The transfer is of part of the personal data on a public register and any conditions subject to which the register is open to inspection are complied with by any person to whom the data are or may be disclosed after the transfer.

8. The transfer is made on terms which are of a kind approved by the Commissioner as ensuring adequate safeguards for the rights and freedoms of data subjects.

9. The transfer has been authorised by the Commissioner as being made in such a manner as to ensure adequate safeguards for the rights and freedoms of data subjects.

SCHEDULE 5
THE DATA PROTECTION COMMISSIONER AND THE DATA PROTECTION TRIBUNAL

Part I
The Commissioner

Status and capacity

1. – (1) The corporation sole by the name of the Data Protection Registrar established by the Data Protection Act 1984 shall continue in existence by the name of the Data Protection Commissioner.

(2) The Commissioner and his officers and staff are not to be regarded as servants or agents of the Crown.

Tenure of office

2. – (1) Subject to the provisions of this paragraph, the Commissioner shall hold office for such term not exceeding five years as may be determined at the time of his appointment.

(2) The Commissioner may be relieved of his office by Her Majesty at his own request.

(3) The Commissioner may be removed from office by Her Majesty in pursuance of an Address from both Houses of Parliament.

(4) The Commissioner shall in any case vacate his office –
    (a) on completing the year of service in which he attains the age of sixty-five years, or
    (b) if earlier, on completing his fifteenth year of service.

(5) Subject to sub-paragraph (4), a person who ceases to be Commissioner on the expiration of his term of office shall be eligible for re-appointment, but a person may not be re-appointed for a third or subsequent term as Commissioner unless, by reason of special

circumstances, the person's re-appointment for such a term is desirable in the public interest.

Salary etc

3. – (1) There shall be paid –
    (a) to the Commissioner such salary, and
    (b) to or in respect of the Commissioner such pension,
as may be specified by a resolution of the House of Commons.

(2) A resolution for the purposes of this paragraph may –
    (a) specify the salary or pension,
    (b) provide that the salary or pension is to be the same as, or calculated on the same basis as, that payable to, or to or in respect of, a person employed in a specified office under, or in a specified capacity in the service of, the Crown, or
    (c) specify the salary or pension and provide for it to be increased by reference to such variables as may be specified in the resolution.

(3) A resolution for the purposes of this paragraph may take effect from the date on which it is passed or from any earlier or later date specified in the resolution.

(4) A resolution for the purposes of this paragraph may make different provision in relation to the pension payable to or in respect of different holders of the office of Commissioner.

(5) Any salary or pension payable under this paragraph shall be charged on and issued out of the Consolidated Fund.

(6) In this paragraph "pension" includes an allowance or gratuity and any reference to the payment of a pension includes a reference to the making of payments towards the provision of a pension.

Officers and staff

4. – (1) The Commissioner –
    (a) shall appoint a deputy commissioner, and
    (b) may appoint such number of other officers and staff as he may determine.

(2) The remuneration and other conditions of service of the persons appointed under this paragraph shall be determined by the Commissioner.

(3)   The Commissioner may pay such pensions, allowances or gratuities to or in respect of the persons appointed under this paragraph, or make such payments towards the provision of such pensions, allowances or gratuities, as he may determine.

(4)   The references in sub-paragraph (3) to pensions, allowances or gratuities to or in respect of the persons appointed under this paragraph include references to pensions, allowances or gratuities by way of compensation to or in respect of any of those persons who suffer loss of office or employment.

(5)   Any determination under sub-paragraph (1)(b), (2) or (3) shall require the approval of the Secretary of State.

(6)   The Employers' Liability (Compulsory Insurance) Act 1969 shall not require insurance to be effected by the Commissioner.

5. – (1) The deputy commissioner shall perform the functions conferred by this Act on the Commissioner during any vacancy in that office or at any time when the Commissioner is for any reason unable to act.

(2)   Without prejudice to sub-paragraph (1), any functions of the Commissioner under this Act may, to the extent authorised by him, be performed by any of his officers or staff.

Authentication of seal of the Commissioner

6.   The application of the seal of the Commissioner shall be authenticated by his signature or by the signature of some other person authorised for the purpose.

Presumption of authenticity of documents issued by the Commissioner

7.   Any document purporting to be an instrument issued by the Commissioner and to be duly executed under the Commissioner's seal or to be signed by or on behalf of the Commissioner shall be received in evidence and shall be deemed to be such an instrument unless the contrary is shown.

Money

8.   The Secretary of State may make payments to the Commissioner out of money provided by Parliament.

9. – (1) All fees and other sums received by the Commissioner in the exercise of his functions under this Act or section 159 of the Consumer Credit Act 1974 shall be paid by him to the Secretary of State.

(2) Sub-paragraph (1) shall not apply where the Secretary of State, with the consent of the Treasury, otherwise directs.

(3) Any sums received by the Secretary of State under sub-paragraph (1) shall be paid into the Consolidated Fund.

Accounts

10. – (1) It shall be the duty of the Commissioner –
(a) to keep proper accounts and other records in relation to the accounts,
(b) to prepare in respect of each financial year a statement of account in such form as the Secretary of State may direct, and
(c) to send copies of that statement to the Comptroller and Auditor General on or before 31st August next following the end of the year to which the statement relates or on or before such earlier date after the end of that year as the Treasury may direct.

(2) The Comptroller and Auditor General shall examine and certify any statement sent to him under this paragraph and lay copies of it together with his report thereon before each House of Parliament.

(3) In this paragraph "financial year" means a period of twelve months beginning with 1st April.

Application of Part I in Scotland

11. Paragraphs 1(1), 6 and 7 do not extend to Scotland.

Part II
The Tribunal

Tenure of office

12. – (1) Subject to the following provisions of this paragraph, a member of the Tribunal shall hold and vacate his office in accordance with the terms of his appointment and shall, on ceasing to hold office, be eligible for re-appointment.

(2) Any member of the Tribunal may at any time resign his office by notice in writing to the Lord Chancellor (in the case of the chairman

or a deputy chairman) or to the Secretary of State (in the case of any other member).

(3)   A person who is the chairman or deputy chairman of the Tribunal shall vacate his office on the day on which he attains the age of seventy years; but this sub-paragraph is subject to section 26(4) to (6) of the Judicial Pensions and Retirement Act 1993 (power to authorise continuance in office up to the age of seventy-five years).

Salary etc

13. The Secretary of State shall pay to the members of the Tribunal out of money provided by Parliament such remuneration and allowances as he may determine.

Officers and staff

14. The Secretary of State may provide the Tribunal with such officers and staff as he thinks necessary for the proper discharge of its functions.

Expenses

15. Such expenses of the Tribunal as the Secretary of State may determine shall be defrayed by the Secretary of State out of money provided by Parliament.

Part III
Transitional Provisions

16. Any reference in any enactment, instrument or other document to the Data Protection Registrar shall be construed, in relation to any time after the commencement of section 6(1), as a reference to the Commissioner

17. Any reference in this Act or in any instrument under this Act to the Commissioner shall be construed, in relation to any time before the commencement of section 6(1), as a reference to the Data Protection Registrar.

SCHEDULE 6
APPEAL PROCEEDINGS

Hearing of appeals

1.   For the purpose of hearing and determining appeals or any matter preliminary or incidental to an appeal the Tribunal shall sit at such times and in such places as the chairman or a deputy chairman may direct and may sit in two or more divisions.

Constitution of Tribunal in national security cases

2. – (1) The Lord Chancellor shall from time to time designate, from among the chairman and deputy chairmen appointed by him under section 6(4)(a) and (b), those persons who are to be capable of hearing appeals under section 28(4) or (6).

(2) A designation under sub-paragraph (1) may at any time be revoked by the Lord Chancellor.

3. In any case where the application of paragraph 6(1) is excluded by rules under paragraph 7, the Tribunal shall be duly constituted for an appeal under section 28(4) or (6) if it consists of three of the persons designated under paragraph 2(1), of whom one shall be designated by the Lord Chancellor to preside.

Constitution of Tribunal in other cases

4. – (1) Subject to any rules made under paragraph 7, the Tribunal shall be duly constituted for an appeal under section 48(1), (2) or (4) if it consists of –
    (a) the chairman or a deputy chairman (who shall preside), and
    (b) an equal number of the members appointed respectively in accordance with paragraphs (a) and (b) of section 6(6).

(2) The members who are to constitute the Tribunal in accordance with subparagraph (1) shall be nominated by the chairman or, if he is for any reason unable to act, by a deputy chairman.

Determination of questions by full Tribunal

5. The determination of any question before the Tribunal when constituted in accordance with paragraph 3 or 4 shall be according to the opinion of the majority of the members hearing the appeal.

Ex parte proceedings

6. – (1) Subject to any rules made under paragraph 7, the jurisdiction of the Tribunal in respect of an appeal under section 28(4) or (6) shall be exercised ex parte by one or more persons designated under paragraph 2(1).

(2) Subject to any rules made under paragraph 7, the jurisdiction of the Tribunal in respect of an appeal under section 48(3) shall be exercised ex parte by the chairman or a deputy chairman sitting alone.

Rules of procedure

7. – (1) The Secretary of State may make rules for regulating the exercise of the rights of appeal conferred by sections 28(4) or (6) and 48 and the practice and procedure of the Tribunal.

(2) Rules under this paragraph may in particular make provision –
(a) with respect to the period within which an appeal can be brought and the burden of proof on an appeal,
(b) for the summoning (or, in Scotland, citation) of witnesses and the administration of oaths,
(c) for securing the production of documents and material used for the processing of personal data,
(d) for the inspection, examination, operation and testing of any equipment or material used in connection with the processing of personal data,
(e) for the hearing of an appeal wholly or partly in camera,
(f) for hearing an appeal in the absence of the appellant or for determining an appeal without a hearing,
(g) for enabling an appeal under section 48(1) against an information notice to be determined by the chairman or a deputy chairman,
(h) for enabling any matter preliminary or incidental to an appeal to be dealt with by the chairman or a deputy chairman,
(i) for the awarding of costs or, in Scotland, expenses,
(j) for the publication of reports of the Tribunal's decisions, and
(k) for conferring on the Tribunal such ancillary powers as the Secretary of State thinks necessary for the proper discharge of its functions.

(3) In making rules under this paragraph which relate to appeals under section 28(4) or (6) the Secretary of State shall have regard, in particular, to the need to secure that information is not disclosed contrary to the public interest.

Obstruction etc

8. – (1) If any person is guilty of any act or omission in relation to proceedings before the Tribunal which, if those proceedings were proceedings before a court having power to commit for contempt, would constitute contempt of court, the Tribunal may certify the offence to the High Court or, in Scotland, the Court of Session.

421

(2) Where an offence is so certified, the court may inquire into the matter and, after hearing any witness who may be produced against or on behalf of the person charged with the offence, and after hearing any statement that may be offered in defence, deal with him in any manner in which it could deal with him if he had committed the like offence in relation to the court.

SCHEDULE 7
MISCELLANEOUS EXEMPTIONS

Confidential references given by the data controller

1.   Personal data are exempt from section 7 if they consist of a reference given or to be given in confidence by the data controller for the purposes of –

(a) the education, training or employment, or prospective education, training or employment, of the data subject,

(b) the appointment, or prospective appointment, of the data subject to any office, or

(c) the provision, or prospective provision, by the data subject of any service.

Armed forces

2.   Personal data are exempt from the subject information provisions in any case to the extent to which the application of those provisions would be likely to prejudice the combat effectiveness of any of the armed forces of the Crown.

Judicial appointments and honours

3.   Personal data processed for the purposes of –

(a) assessing any person's suitability for judicial office or the office of Queen's Counsel, or

(b) the conferring by the Crown of any honour,

are exempt from the subject information provisions.

Crown employment and Crown or Ministerial appointments

4.   The Secretary of State may by order exempt from the subject information provisions personal data processed for the purposes of assessing any person's suitability for –

(a) employment by or under the Crown, or

(b) any office to which appointments are made by Her Majesty, by a Minister of the Crown or by a Northern Ireland department.

Management forecasts etc

5. Personal data processed for the purposes of management forecasting or management planning to assist the data controller in the conduct of any business or other activity are exempt from the subject information provisions in any case to the extent to which the application of those provisions would be likely to prejudice the conduct of that business or other activity.

Corporate finance

6. (1) Where personal data are processed for the purposes of, or in connection with, a corporate finance service provided by a relevant person –

(a) the data are exempt from the subject information provisions in any case to the extent to which either –

(i) the application of those provisions to the data could affect the price of any instrument which is already in existence or is to be or may be created, or

(ii) the data controller reasonably believes that the application of those provisions to the data could affect the price of any such instrument, and

(b) to the extent that the data are not exempt from the subject information provisions by virtue of paragraph (a), they are exempt from those provisions if the exemption is required for the purpose of safeguarding an important economic or financial interest of the United Kingdom.

(2) For the purposes of sub-paragraph (1)(b) the Secretary of State may by order specify –

(a) matters to be taken into account in determining whether exemption from the subject information provisions is required for the purpose of safeguarding an important economic or financial interest of the United Kingdom, or

(b) circumstances in which exemption from those provisions is, or is not, to be taken to be required for that purpose.

(3) In this paragraph –

"corporate finance service" means a service consisting in –

(a) underwriting in respect of issues of, or the placing of issues of, any instrument,

(b) advice to undertakings on capital structure, industrial strategy and related matters and advice and service relating to mergers and the purchase of undertakings, or

(c) services relating to such underwriting as is mentioned in paragraph (a);

"instrument" means any instrument listed in section B of the Annex to the Council Directive on investment services in the securities field (93/22/EEC), as set out in Schedule 1 to the Investment Services Regulations 1995;

"price" includes value;

"relevant person" means –
(a) any person who is authorised under Chapter III of Part I of the Financial Services Act 1986 or is an exempted person under Chapter IV of Part I of that Act,
(b) any person who, but for Part III or IV of Schedule 1 to that Act, would require authorisation under that Act,
(c) any European investment firm within the meaning given by Regulation 3 of the Investment Services Regulations 1995,
(d) any person who, in the course of his employment, provides to his employer a service falling within paragraph (b) or (c) of the definition of "corporate finance service", or
(e) any partner who provides to other partners in the partnership a service falling within either of those paragraphs.

Negotiations

7. Personal data which consist of records of the intentions of the data controller in relation to any negotiations with the data subject are exempt from the subject information provisions in any case to the extent to which the application of those provisions would be likely to prejudice those negotiations.

Examination marks

8. – (1) Section 7 shall have effect subject to the provisions of sub-paragraphs (2) to (4) in the case of personal data consisting of marks or other information processed by a data controller –
(a) for the purpose of determining the results of an academic, professional or other examination or of enabling the results of any such examination to be determined, or
(b) in consequence of the determination of any such results.

(2) Where the relevant day falls before the day on which the results of the examination are announced, the period mentioned in section 7(8) shall be extended until –

(a) the end of five months beginning with the relevant day, or
(b) the end of forty days beginning with the date of the announcement,
whichever is the earlier.

(3) Where by virtue of sub-paragraph (2) a period longer than the prescribed period elapses after the relevant day before the request is complied with, the information to be supplied pursuant to the request shall be supplied both by reference to the data in question at the time when the request is received and (if different) by reference to the data as from time to time held in the period beginning when the request is received and ending when it is complied with.

(4) For the purposes of this paragraph the results of an examination shall be treated as announced when they are first published or (if not published) when they are first made available or communicated to the candidate in question.

(5) In this paragraph —

"examination" includes any process for determining the knowledge, intelligence, skill or ability of a candidate by reference to his performance in any test, work or other activity;

"the prescribed period" means forty days or such other period as is for the time being prescribed under section 7 in relation to the personal data in question;

"relevant day" has the same meaning as in section 7.

Examination scripts etc

9. – (1) Personal data consisting of information recorded by candidates during an academic, professional or other examination are exempt from section 7.

(2) In this paragraph "examination" has the same meaning as in paragraph 8.

Legal professional privilege

10. Personal data are exempt from the subject information provisions if the data consist of information in respect of which a claim to legal professional privilege or, in Scotland, to confidentiality as between client and professional legal adviser, could be maintained in legal proceedings.

Self-incrimination

11. – (1) A person need not comply with any request or order under section 7 to the extent that compliance would, by revealing evidence of the commission of any offence other than an offence under this Act, expose him to proceedings for that offence.

(2) Information disclosed by any person in compliance with any request or order under section 7 shall not be admissible against him in proceedings for an offence under this Act.

SCHEDULE 8
TRANSITIONAL RELIEF

Part I
Interpretation of Schedule

1. – (1) For the purposes of this Schedule, personal data are "eligible data" at any time if, and to the extent that, they are at that time subject to processing which was already under way immediately before 24th October 1998.

(2) In this Schedule –

"eligible automated data" means eligible data which fall within paragraph (a) or (b) of the definition of "data" in section 1(1);

"eligible manual data" means eligible data which are not eligible automated data;

"the first transitional period" means the period beginning with the commencement of this Schedule and ending with 23rd October 2001;

"the second transitional period" means the period beginning with 24th October 2001 and ending with 23rd October 2007.

Part II
Eexemptions Avaiable Before 24th October 2001

Manual data

2. – (1) Eligible manual data, other than data forming part of an accessible record, are exempt from the data protection principles and Parts II and III of this Act during the first transitional period.

(2) This paragraph does not apply to eligible manual data to which paragraph 4 applies.

3. – (1) This paragraph applies to –

(a) eligible manual data forming part of an accessible record, and
(b) personal data which fall within paragraph (d) of the definition of "data" in section 1(1) but which, because they are not subject to processing which was already under way immediately before 24th October 1998, are not eligible data for the purposes of this Schedule.

(2) During the first transitional period, data to which this paragraph applies are exempt from –

(a) the data protection principles, except the sixth principle so far as relating to sections 7 and 12A,
(b) Part II of this Act, except—
(i) section 7 (as it has effect subject to section 8) and section 12A, and
(ii) section 15 so far as relating to those sections, and
(c) Part III of this Act.

4. – (1) This paragraph applies to eligible manual data which consist of information relevant to the financial standing of the data subject and in respect of which the data controller is a credit reference agency.

(2) During the first transitional period, data to which this paragraph applies are exempt from –

(a) the data protection principles, except the sixth principle so far as relating to sections 7 and 12A, and
(b) Part II of this Act, except –
(i) section 7 (as it has effect subject to sections 8 and 9) and section 12A, and
(ii) section 15 so far as relating to those sections, and
(c) Part III of this Act.

Processing otherwise than by reference to the data subject

5. During the first transitional period, for the purposes of this Act (apart from paragraph 1), eligible automated data are not to be regarded as being "processed" unless the processing is by reference to the data subject.

Payrolls and accounts

6. – (1) Subject to sub-paragraph (2), eligible automated data processed by a data controller for one or more of the following purposes –

(a) calculating amounts payable by way of remuneration or pensions in respect of service in any employment or office or making payments of, or of sums deducted from, such remuneration or pensions, or

(b) keeping accounts relating to any business or other activity carried on by the data controller or keeping records of purchases, sales or other transactions for the purpose of ensuring that the requisite payments are made by or to him in respect of those transactions or for the purpose of making financial or management forecasts to assist him in the conduct of any such business or activity,

are exempt from the data protection principles and Parts II and III of this Act during the first transitional period.

(2) It shall be a condition of the exemption of any eligible automated data under this paragraph that the data are not processed for any other purpose, but the exemption is not lost by any processing of the eligible data for any other purpose if the data controller shows that he had taken such care to prevent it as in all the circumstances was reasonably required.

(3) Data processed only for one or more of the purposes mentioned in subparagraph (1)(a) may be disclosed –

(a) to any person, other than the data controller, by whom the remuneration or pensions in question are payable,

(b) for the purpose of obtaining actuarial advice,

(c) for the purpose of giving information as to the persons in any employment or office for use in medical research into the health of, or injuries suffered by, persons engaged in particular occupations or working in particular places or areas,

(d) if the data subject (or a person acting on his behalf) has requested or consented to the disclosure of the data either generally or in the circumstances in which the disclosure in question is made, or

(e) if the person making the disclosure has reasonable grounds for believing that the disclosure falls within paragraph (d).

(4) Data processed for any of the purposes mentioned in sub-paragraph (1) may be disclosed –

(a) for the purpose of audit or where the disclosure is for the purpose only of giving information about the data controller's financial affairs, or

(b) in any case in which disclosure would be permitted by any other provision of this Part of this Act if sub-paragraph (2) were included among the non-disclosure provisions.

(5) In this paragraph "remuneration" includes remuneration in kind and "pensions" includes gratuities or similar benefits.

Unincorporated members' clubs and mailing lists

7. Eligible automated data processed by an unincorporated members' club and relating only to the members of the club are exempt from the data protection principles and Parts II and III of this Act during the first transitional period.

8. Eligible automated data processed by a data controller only for the purposes of distributing, or recording the distribution of, articles or information to the data subjects and consisting only of their names, addresses or other particulars necessary for effecting the distribution, are exempt from the data protection principles and Parts II and III of this Act during the first transitional period.

9. Neither paragraph 7 nor paragraph 8 applies to personal data relating to any data subject unless he has been asked by the club or data controller whether he objects to the data relating to him being processed as mentioned in that paragraph and has not objected.

10. It shall be a condition of the exemption of any data under paragraph 7 that the data are not disclosed except as permitted by paragraph 11 and of the exemption under paragraph 8 that the data are not processed for any purpose other than that mentioned in that paragraph or as permitted by paragraph 11, but –
    (a) the exemption under paragraph 7 shall not be lost by any disclosure in breach of that condition, and
    (b) the exemption under paragraph 8 shall not be lost by any processing in breach of that condition,
if the data controller shows that he had taken such care to prevent it as in all the circumstances was reasonably required.

11. Data to which paragraph 10 applies may be disclosed –
    (a) if the data subject (or a person acting on his behalf) has requested or consented to the disclosure of the data either generally or in the circumstances in which the disclosure in question is made,
    (b) if the person making the disclosure has reasonable grounds for believing that the disclosure falls within paragraph (a), or
    (c) in any case in which disclosure would be permitted by any other provision of this Part of this Act if paragraph 8 were included among the non-disclosure provisions.

Back-up data

12. Eligible automated data which are processed only for the purpose of replacing other data in the event of the latter being lost, destroyed or impaired are exempt from section 7 during the first transitional period.

Exemption of all eligible automated data from certain requirements

13. – (1) During the first transitional period, eligible automated data are exempt from the following provisions –
    (a) the first data protection principle to the extent to which it requires compliance with –
        (i) paragraph 2 of Part II of Schedule 1,
        (ii) the conditions in Schedule 2, and
        (iii) the conditions in Schedule 3,
    (b) the seventh data protection principle to the extent to which it requires compliance with paragraph 12 of Part II of Schedule 1;
    (c) the eighth data protection principle,
    (d) in section 7(1), paragraphs (b), (c)(ii) and (d),
    (e) sections 10 and 11,
    (f) section 12, and
    (g) section 13, except so far as relating to –
        (i) any contravention of the fourth data protection principle,
        (ii) any disclosure without the consent of the data controller,
        (iii) loss or destruction of data without the consent of the data controller, or
        (iv) processing for the special purposes.

(2) The specific exemptions conferred by sub-paragraph (1)(a), (c) and (e) do not limit the data controller's general duty under the first data protection principle to ensure that processing is fair.

Part III
Exemptions Available After 23rd October 2001 but Before 24th October 2007

14. – (1) This paragraph applies to –
    (a) eligible manual data which were held immediately before 24th October 1998, and
    (b) personal data which fall within paragraph (d) of the definition of "data" in section 1(1) but do not fall within paragraph (a) of this subparagraph,
but does not apply to eligible manual data to which the exemption in paragraph 16 applies.

(2) During the second transitional period, data to which this paragraph applies are exempt from the following provisions –
    (a) the first data protection principle except to the extent to which

it requires compliance with paragraph 2 of Part II of Schedule 1,
(b) the second, third, fourth and fifth data protection principles, and
(c) section 14(1) to (3).

Part IV
Exemptions after 23rd October 2001 for Historical Research

15. In this Part of this Schedule "the relevant conditions" has the same meaning as in section 33.

16. – (1) Eligible manual data which are processed only for the purpose of historical research in compliance with the relevant conditions are exempt from the provisions specified in sub-paragraph (2) after 23rd October 2001.

(2) The provisions referred to in sub-paragraph (1) are –
(a) the first data protection principle except in so far as it requires compliance with paragraph 2 of Part II of Schedule 1,
(b) the second, third, fourth and fifth data protection principles, and
(c) section 14(1) to (3).

17. – (1) After 23rd October 2001 eligible automated data which are processed only for the purpose of historical research in compliance with the relevant conditions are exempt from the first data protection principle to the extent to which it requires compliance with the conditions in Schedules 2 and 3.

(2) Eligible automated data which are processed –
(a) only for the purpose of historical research,
(b) in compliance with the relevant conditions, and
(c) otherwise than by reference to the data subject,
are also exempt from the provisions referred to in sub-paragraph (3) after 23rd October 2001.

(3) The provisions referred to in sub-paragraph (2) are –
(a) the first data protection principle except in so far as it requires compliance with paragraph 2 of Part II of Schedule 1,
(b) the second, third, fourth and fifth data protection principles, and
(c) section 14(1) to (3).

18. For the purposes of this Part of this Schedule personal data are not to be treated as processed otherwise than for the purpose of historical research merely because the data are disclosed –

(a) to any person, for the purpose of historical research only,

(b) to the data subject or a person acting on his behalf,

(c) at the request, or with the consent, of the data subject or a person acting on his behalf, or

(d) in circumstances in which the person making the disclosure has reasonable grounds for believing that the disclosure falls within paragraph (a), (b) or (c).

Part V
Exemption from Section 22

19. Processing which was already under way immediately before 24th October 1998 is not assessable processing for the purposes of section 22.

SCHEDULE 9
POWERS OF ENTRY AND INSPECTION

Issue of warrants

1. – (1) If a circuit judge is satisfied by information on oath supplied by the Commissioner that there are reasonable grounds for suspecting –

(a) that a data controller has contravened or is contravening any of the data protection principles, or

(b) that an offence under this Act has been or is being committed,

and that evidence of the contravention or of the commission of the offence is to be found on any premises specified in the information, he may, subject to subparagraph (2) and paragraph 2, grant a warrant to the Commissioner.

(2) A judge shall not issue a warrant under this Schedule in respect of any personal data processed for the special purposes unless a determination by the Commissioner under section 45 with respect to those data has taken effect.

(3) A warrant issued under sub-paragraph (1) shall authorise the Commissioner or any of his officers or staff at any time within seven days of the date of the warrant to enter the premises, to search them, to inspect, examine, operate and test any equipment found there which is used or intended to be used for the processing of personal data and to inspect and seize any documents or other material found there which may be such evidence as is mentioned in that sub-paragraph.

2. – (1) A judge shall not issue a warrant under this Schedule unless he is satisfied –

(a) that the Commissioner has given seven days' notice in writing to the occupier of the premises in question demanding access to the premises, and

(b) that either –

(i) access was demanded at a reasonable hour and was unreasonably refused, or

(ii) although entry to the premises was granted, the occupier unreasonably refused to comply with a request by the Commissioner or any of the Commissioner's officers or staff to permit the Commissioner or the officer or member of staff to do any of the things referred to in paragraph 1(3), and

(c) that the occupier, has, after the refusal, been notified by the Commissioner of the application for the warrant and has had an opportunity of being heard by the judge on the question whether or not it should be issued.

(2) Sub-paragraph (1) shall not apply if the judge is satisfied that the case is one of urgency or that compliance with those provisions would defeat the object of the entry.

3. A judge who issues a warrant under this Schedule shall also issue two copies of it and certify them clearly as copies.

Execution of warrants

4. A person executing a warrant issued under this Schedule may use such reasonable force as may be necessary.

5. A warrant issued under this Schedule shall be executed at a reasonable hour unless it appears to the person executing it that there are grounds for suspecting that the evidence in question would not be found if it were so executed.

6. If the person who occupies the premises in respect of which a warrant is issued under this Schedule is present when the warrant is executed, he shall be shown the warrant and supplied with a copy of it; and if that person is not present a copy of the warrant shall be left in a prominent place on the premises.

7. – (1) A person seizing anything in pursuance of a warrant under this Schedule shall give a receipt for it if asked to do so.

(2) Anything so seized may be retained for so long as is necessary in all the circumstances but the person in occupation of the premises in question shall be given a copy of anything that is seized if he so requests

and the person executing the warrant considers that it can be done without undue delay.

Matters exempt from inspection and seizure

8. The powers of inspection and seizure conferred by a warrant issued under this Schedule shall not be exercisable in respect of personal data which by virtue of section 28 are exempt from any of the provisions of this Act.

9. – (1) Subject to the provisions of this paragraph, the powers of inspection and seizure conferred by a warrant issued under this Schedule shall not be exercisable in respect of –
  (a) any communication between a professional legal adviser and his client in connection with the giving of legal advice to the client with respect to his obligations, liabilities or rights under this Act, or
  (b) any communication between a professional legal adviser and his client, or between such an adviser or his client and any other person, made in connection with or in contemplation of proceedings under or arising out of this Act (including proceedings before the Tribunal) and for the purposes of such proceedings.

(2) Sub-paragraph (1) applies also to –
  (a) any copy or other record of any such communication as is there mentioned, and
  (b) any document or article enclosed with or referred to in any such communication if made in connection with the giving of any advice or, as the case may be, in connection with or in contemplation of and for the purposes of such proceedings as are there mentioned.

(3) This paragraph does not apply to anything in the possession of any person other than the professional legal adviser or his client or to anything held with the intention of furthering a criminal purpose.

(4) In this paragraph references to the client of a professional legal adviser include references to any person representing such a client.

10. If the person in occupation of any premises in respect of which a warrant is issued under this Schedule objects to the inspection or seizure under the warrant of any material on the grounds that it consists partly of matters in respect of which those powers are not exercisable, he shall, if the person executing the warrant so requests, furnish that person with a copy of so much of the material as is not exempt from those powers.

Return of warrants

11. A warrant issued under this Schedule shall be returned to the court from which it was issued –
(a) after being executed, or
(b) if not executed within the time authorised for its execution;
and the person by whom any such warrant is executed shall make an endorsement on it stating what powers have been exercised by him under the warrant.

Offences

12. Any person who –
(a) intentionally obstructs a person in the execution of a warrant issued under this Schedule, or
(b) fails without reasonable excuse to give any person executing such a warrant such assistance as he may reasonably require for the execution of the warrant,
is guilty of an offence.

Vessels, vehicles etc

13. In this Schedule "premises" includes any vessel, vehicle, aircraft or hovercraft, and references to the occupier of any premises include references to the person in charge of any vessel, vehicle, aircraft or hovercraft.

Scotland and Northern Ireland

14. In the application of this Schedule to Scotland –
(a) for any reference to a circuit judge there is substituted a reference to the sheriff,
(b) for any reference to information on oath there is substituted a reference to evidence on oath, and
(c) for the reference to the court from which the warrant was issued there is substituted a reference to the sheriff clerk.

15. In the application of this Schedule to Northern Ireland –
(a) for any reference to a circuit judge there is substituted a reference to a county court judge, and
(b) for any reference to information on oath there is substituted a reference to a complaint on oath.

SCHEDULE 10
FURTHER PROVISIONS RELATING TO ASSISTANCE
UNDER SECTION 53

1. In this Schedule "applicant" and "proceedings" have the same meaning as in section 53.

2. The assistance provided under section 53 may include the making of arrangements for, or for the Commissioner to bear the costs of –
(a) the giving of advice or assistance by a solicitor or counsel, and
(b) the representation of the applicant, or the provision to him of such assistance as is usually given by a solicitor or counsel –
(i) in steps preliminary or incidental to the proceedings, or
(ii) in arriving at or giving effect to a compromise to avoid or bring an end to the proceedings.

3. Where assistance is provided with respect to the conduct of proceedings –
(a) it shall include an agreement by the Commissioner to indemnify the applicant (subject only to any exceptions specified in the notification) in respect of any liability to pay costs or expenses arising by virtue of any judgment or order of the court in the proceedings,
(b) it may include an agreement by the Commissioner to indemnify the applicant in respect of any liability to pay costs or expenses arising by virtue of any compromise or settlement arrived at in order to avoid the proceedings or bring the proceedings to an end, and
(c) it may include an agreement by the Commissioner to indemnify the applicant in respect of any liability to pay damages pursuant to an undertaking given on the grant of interlocutory relief (in Scotland, an interim order) to the applicant.

4. Where the Commissioner provides assistance in relation to any proceedings, he shall do so on such terms, or make such other arrangements, as will secure that a person against whom the proceedings have been or are commenced is informed that assistance has been or is being provided by the Commissioner in relation to them.

5. In England and Wales or Northern Ireland, the recovery of expenses incurred by the Commissioner in providing an applicant with assistance (as taxed or assessed in such manner as may be prescribed by rules of court) shall constitute a first charge for the benefit of the Commissioner –

(a) on any costs which, by virtue of any judgment or order of the court, are payable to the applicant by any other person in respect of the matter in connection with which the assistance is provided, and

(b) on any sum payable to the applicant under a compromise or settlement arrived at in connection with that matter to avoid or bring to an end any proceedings.

6. In Scotland, the recovery of such expenses (as taxed or assessed in such manner as may be prescribed by rules of court) shall be paid to the Commissioner, in priority to other debts –

(a) out of any expenses which, by virtue of any judgment or order of the court, are payable to the applicant by any other person in respect of the matter in connection with which the assistance is provided, and

(b) out of any sum payable to the applicant under a compromise or settlement arrived at in connection with that matter to avoid or bring to an end any proceedings.

SCHEDULE 11
EDUCATIONAL RECORDS

Meaning of "educational record"

1. For the purposes of section 68 "educational record" means any record to which paragraph 2, 5 or 7 applies.

England and Wales

2. This paragraph applies to any record of information which –

(a) is processed by or on behalf of the governing body of, or a teacher at, any school in England and Wales specified in paragraph 3,

(b) relates to any person who is or has been a pupil at the school, and

(c) originated from or was supplied by or on behalf of any of the persons specified in paragraph 4,

other than information which is processed by a teacher solely for the teacher's own use.

3. The schools referred to in paragraph 2(a) are –

(a) a school maintained by a local education authority, and

(b) a special school, as defined by section 6(2) of the Education Act 1996, which is not so maintained.

4. The persons referred to in paragraph 2(c) are –

(a) an employee of the local education authority which maintains the school,

(b) in the case of –

(i) a voluntary aided, foundation or foundation special school (within the meaning of the School Standards and Framework Act 1998), or

(ii) a special school which is not maintained by a local education authority,

a teacher or other employee at the school (including an educational psychologist engaged by the governing body under a contract for services),

(c) the pupil to whom the record relates, and

(d) a parent, as defined by section 576(1) of the Education Act 1996, of that pupil.

Scotland

5. This paragraph applies to any record of information which is processed –

(a) by an education authority in Scotland, and

(b) for the purpose of the relevant function of the authority,

other than information which is processed by a teacher solely for the teacher's own use.

6. For the purposes of paragraph 5 –

(a) "education authority" means an education authority within the meaning of the Education (Scotland) Act 1980 ("the 1980 Act") or, in relation to a self-governing school, the board of management within the meaning of the Self-Governing Schools etc (Scotland) Act 1989 ("the 1989 Act"),

(b) "the relevant function" means, in relation to each of those authorities, their function under section 1 of the 1980 Act and section 7(1) of the 1989 Act, and

(c) information processed by an education authority is processed for the purpose of the relevant function of the authority if the processing relates to the discharge of that function in respect of a person –

(i) who is or has been a pupil in a school provided by the authority, or

(ii) who receives, or has received, further education (within the meaning of the 1980 Act) so provided.

Northern Ireland

7. – (1) This paragraph applies to any record of information which –

(a) is processed by or on behalf of the Board of Governors of, or

a teacher at, any grant-aided school in Northern Ireland,
(b) relates to any person who is or has been a pupil at the school, and
(c) originated from or was supplied by or on behalf of any of the persons specified in paragraph 8,
other than information which is processed by a teacher solely for the teacher's own use.

(2) In sub-paragraph (1) "grant-aided school" has the same meaning as in the Education and Libraries (Northern Ireland) Order 1986.

8. The persons referred to in paragraph 7(1) are –
(a) a teacher at the school,
(b) an employee of an education and library board, other than such a teacher,
(c) the pupil to whom the record relates, and
(d) a parent (as defined by Article 2(2) of the Education and Libraries (Northern Ireland) Order 1986) of that pupil.

England and Wales: transitory provisions

9. – (1) Until the appointed day within the meaning of section 20 of the School Standards and Framework Act 1998, this Schedule shall have effect subject to the following modifications.

(2) Paragraph 3 shall have effect as if for paragraph (b) and the "and" immediately preceding it there were substituted –
"(aa)   a grant-maintained school, as defined by section 183(1) of the Education Act 1996,
(ab)   a grant-maintained special school, as defined by section 337(4) of that Act, and
(b) a special school, as defined by section 6(2) of that Act, which is neither a maintained special school, as defined by section 337(3) of that Act, nor a grant-maintained special school.".

(3) Paragraph 4(b)(i) shall have effect as if for the words from "foundation", in the first place where it occurs, to "1998)" there were substituted "or grant-maintained school".

SCHEDULE 12
ACCESSIBLE PUBLIC RECORDS

Meaning of "accessible public record"

1. For the purposes of section 68 "accessible public record" means

any record which is kept by an authority specified –
      (a) as respects England and Wales, in the Table in paragraph 2,
      (b) as respects Scotland, in the Table in paragraph 4, or
      (c) as respects Northern Ireland, in the Table in paragraph 6,
and is a record of information of a description specified in that Table in relation to that authority.

Housing and social services records: England and Wales

2. The following is the Table referred to in paragraph 1(a).

TABLE OF AUTHORITIES AND INFORMATION

The authorities	*The accessible information*
Housing Act local authority.	Information held for the purpose of any of the authority's tenancies.
Local social services authority.	Information held for any purpose of the authority's social services functions.

3. – (1) The following provisions apply for the interpretation of the Table in paragraph 2.

(2) Any authority which, by virtue of section 4(e) of the Housing Act 1985, is a local authority for the purpose of any provision of that Act is a "Housing Act local authority" for the purposes of this Schedule, and so is any housing action trust established under Part III of the Housing Act 1988.

(3) Information contained in records kept by a Housing Act local authority is "held for the purpose of any of the authority's tenancies" if it is held for any purpose of the relationship of landlord and tenant of a dwelling which subsists, has subsisted or may subsist between the authority and any individual who is, has been or, as the case may be, has applied to be, a tenant of the authority.

(4) Any authority which, by virtue of section 1 or 12 of the Local Authority Social Services Act 1970, is or is treated as a local authority for the purposes of that Act is a "local social services authority" for the purposes of this Schedule; and information contained in records kept by such an authority is "held for any purpose of the authority's social services functions" if it is held for the purpose of any past, current or proposed exercise of such a function in any case.

(5) Any expression used in paragraph 2 or this paragraph and in Part II of the Housing Act 1985 or the Local Authority Social Services Act 1970 has the same meaning as in that Act.

Housing and social services records: Scotland

4. The following is the Table referred to in paragraph 1(b).

TABLE OF AUTHORITIES AND INFORMATION

The authorities	The accessible information
Local authority. Scottish Homes.	Information held for any purpose of any of the body's tenancies.
Social work authority.	Information held for any purpose of the authority's functions under the Social Work (Scotland) Act 1968 and the enactments referred to in section 5(1B) of that Act.

5. – (1) The following provisions apply for the interpretation of the Table in paragraph 4.

(2) "Local authority" means –
(a) a council constituted under section 2 of the Local Government etc (Scotland) Act 1994,
(b) a joint board or joint committee of two or more of those councils, or
(c) any trust under the control of such a council.

(3) Information contained in records kept by a local authority or Scottish Homes is held for the purpose of any of their tenancies if it is held for any purpose of the relationship of landlord and tenant of a dwelling-house which subsists, has subsisted or may subsist between the authority or, as the case may be, Scottish Homes and any individual who is, has been or, as the case may be, has applied to be a tenant of theirs.

(4) "Social work authority" means a local authority for the purposes of the Social Work (Scotland) Act 1968; and information contained in records kept by such an authority is held for any purpose of their functions if it is held for the purpose of any past, current or proposed exercise of such a function in any case.

Housing and social services records: Northern Ireland

6. The following is the Table referred to in paragraph 1(c).

TABLE OF AUTHORITIES AND INFORMATION

The authorities	The accessible information
The Northern Ireland Housing Executive.	Information held for the purpose of any of the Executive's tenancies.
A Health and Social Services Board.	Information held for the purpose of any past, current or proposed exercise by the Board of any function exercisable, by virtue of directions under Article 17(1) of the Health and Personal Social Services (Northern Ireland) Order 1972, by the Board on behalf of the Department of Health and Social Services with respect to the administration of personal social services under – (a) the Children and Young Persons Act (Northern Ireland) 1968; (b) the Health and Personal Social Services (Northern Ireland) Order 1972; (c) Article 47 of the Matrimonial Causes (Northern Ireland) Order 1978; (d) Article 11 of the Domestic Proceedings (Northern Ireland) Order 1980; (e) the Adoption (Northern Ireland) Order 1987; or (f) the Children (Northern Ireland) Order 1995.
An HSS trust.	Information held for the purpose of any past, current or proposed exercise by the trust of any function exercisable, by virtue of an authorisation under Article 3(1) of the Health and Personal Social Services (Northern Ireland) Order 1994, by the trust on behalf of a Health and Social Services Board with respect to the administration of personal social services under any statutory provision mentioned in the last preceding entry.

7. – (1) This paragraph applies for the interpretation of the Table in paragraph 6.

(2) Information contained in records kept by the Northern Ireland Housing Executive is "held for the purpose of any of the Executive's tenancies" if it is held for any purpose of the relationship of landlord and tenant of a dwelling which subsists, has subsisted or may subsist between the Executive and any individual who is, has been or, as the case may be, has applied to be, a tenant of the Executive.

SCHEDULE 13

MODIFICATIONS OF ACT HAVING EFFECT BEFORE 24th
OCTOBER 2007

1. After section 12 there is inserted –

> "**12A** – (1) A data subject is entitled at any time by notice in writing –
>> (a) to require the data controller to rectify, block, erase or destroy exempt manual data which are inaccurate or incomplete, or
>> (b) to require the data controller to cease holding exempt manual data in a way incompatible with the legitimate purposes pursued by the data controller.
>
> (2) A notice under subsection (1)(a) or (b) must state the data subject's reasons for believing that the data are inaccurate or incomplete or, as the case may be, his reasons for believing that they are held in a way incompatible with the legitimate purposes pursued by the data controller.
>
> (3) If the court is satisfied, on the application of any person who has given a notice under subsection (1) which appears to the court to be justified (or to be justified to any extent) that the data controller in question has failed to comply with the notice, the court may order him to take such steps for complying with the notice (or for complying with it to that extent) as the court thinks fit.
>
> (4) In this section "exempt manual data" means –
>> (a) in relation to the first transitional period, as defined by paragraph 1(2) of Schedule 8, data to which paragraph 3 or 4 of that Schedule applies, and
>> (b) in relation to the second transitional period, as so defined, data to which paragraph 14 of that Schedule applies.
>
> (5) For the purposes of this section personal data are incomplete if, and only if, the data, although not inaccurate, are such that their incompleteness would constitute a contravention of the third or

443

fourth data protection principles, if those principles applied to the data.".

2. In section 32 –
    (a) in subsection (2) after "section 12" there is inserted –
    "(dd)   section 12A,", and
    (b) in subsection (4) after "12(8)" there is inserted ", 12A(3)".

3. In section 34 for "section 14(1) to (3)" there is substituted "sections 12A and 14(1) to (3)."

4. In section 53(1) after "12(8)" there is inserted ", 12A(3)".

5. In paragraph 8 of Part II of Schedule 1, the word "or" at the end of paragraph (c) is omitted and after paragraph (d) there is inserted

"or
(e) he contravenes section 12A by failing to comply with a notice given under subsection (1) of that section to the extent that the notice is justified.".

SCHEDULE 14
TRANSITIONAL PROVISIONS AND SAVINGS

Interpretation

1. In this Schedule –

"the 1984 Act" means the Data Protection Act 1984;

"the old principles" means the data protection principles within the meaning of the 1984 Act;

"the new principles" means the data protection principles within the meaning of this Act.

Effect of registration under Part II of 1984 Act

2. – (1) Subject to sub-paragraphs (4) and (5) any person who, immediately before the commencement of Part III of this Act –
    (a) is registered as a data user under Part II of the 1984 Act, or
    (b) is treated by virtue of section 7(6) of the 1984 Act as so registered,
is exempt from section 17(1) of this Act until the end of the registration period or, if earlier, 24th October 2001.

(2) In sub-paragraph (1) "the registration period", in relation to a person, means –
    (a) where there is a single entry in respect of that person as a data user, the period at the end of which, if section 8 of the 1984 Act had remained in force, that entry would have fallen to be removed unless renewed, and
    (b) where there are two or more entries in respect of that person as a data user, the period at the end of which, if that section had remained in force, the last of those entries to expire would have fallen to be removed unless renewed.

(3) Any application for registration as a data user under Part II of the 1984 Act which is received by the Commissioner before the commencement of Part III of this Act (including any appeal against a refusal of registration) shall be determined in accordance with the old principles and the provisions of the 1984 Act.

(4) If a person falling within paragraph (b) of sub-paragraph (1) receives a notification under section 7(1) of the 1984 Act of the refusal of his application, sub-paragraph (1) shall cease to apply to him –
    (a) if no appeal is brought, at the end of the period within which an appeal can be brought against the refusal, or
    (b) on the withdrawal or dismissal of the appeal.

(5) If a data controller gives a notification under section 18(1) at a time when he is exempt from section 17(1) by virtue of sub-paragraph (1), he shall cease to be so exempt.

(6) The Commissioner shall include in the register maintained under section 19 an entry in respect of each person who is exempt from section 17(1) by virtue of sub-paragraph (1); and each entry shall consist of the particulars which, immediately before the commencement of Part III of this Act, were included (or treated as included) in respect of that person in the register maintained under section 4 of the 1984 Act.

(7) Notification regulations under Part III of this Act may make provision modifying the duty referred to in section 20(1) in its application to any person in respect of whom an entry in the register maintained under section 19 has been made under sub-paragraph (6).

(8) Notification regulations under Part III of this Act may make further transitional provision in connection with the substitution of Part III of this Act for Part II of the 1984 Act (registration), including provision modifying the application of provisions of Part III in transitional cases.

Rights of data subjects

3. – (1) The repeal of section 21 of the 1984 Act (right of access to personal data) does not affect the application of that section in any case in which the request (together with the information referred to in paragraph (a) of subsection (4) of that section and, in a case where it is required, the consent referred to in paragraph (b) of that subsection) was received before the day on which the repeal comes into force.

(2) Sub-paragraph (1) does not apply where the request is made by reference to this Act.

(3) Any fee paid for the purposes of section 21 of the 1984 Act before the commencement of section 7 in a case not falling within sub-paragraph (1) shall be taken to have been paid for the purposes of section 7.

4. The repeal of section 22 of the 1984 Act (compensation for inaccuracy) and the repeal of section 23 of that Act (compensation for loss or unauthorised disclosure) do not affect the application of those sections in relation to damage or distress suffered at any time by reason of anything done or omitted to be done before the commencement of the repeals.

5. The repeal of section 24 of the 1984 Act (rectification and erasure) does not affect any case in which the application to the court was made before the day on which the repeal comes into force.

6. Subsection (3)(b) of section 14 does not apply where the rectification, blocking, erasure or destruction occurred before the commencement of that section.

Enforcement and transfer prohibition notices served under Part V of 1984 Act

7. – (1) If, immediately before the commencement of section 40 –
    (a) an enforcement notice under section 10 of the 1984 Act has effect, and
    (b) either the time for appealing against the notice has expired or any appeal has been determined,
then, after that commencement, to the extent mentioned in sub-paragraph (3), the notice shall have effect for the purposes of sections 41 and 47 as if it were an enforcement notice under section 40.

(2) Where an enforcement notice has been served under section 10 of the 1984 Act before the commencement of section 40 and immediately before that commencement either –

(a) the time for appealing against the notice has not expired, or

(b) an appeal has not been determined,

the appeal shall be determined in accordance with the provisions of the 1984 Act and the old principles and, unless the notice is quashed on appeal, to the extent mentioned in sub-paragraph (3) the notice shall have effect for the purposes of sections 41 and 47 as if it were an enforcement notice under section 40.

(3) An enforcement notice under section 10 of the 1984 Act has the effect described in sub-paragraph (1) or (2) only to the extent that the steps specified in the notice for complying with the old principle or principles in question are steps which the data controller could be required by an enforcement notice under section 40 to take for complying with the new principles or any of them.

8. − (1) If, immediately before the commencement of section 40 −

(a) a transfer prohibition notice under section 12 of the 1984 Act has effect, and

(b) either the time for appealing against the notice has expired or any appeal has been determined,

then, on and after that commencement, to the extent specified in sub-paragraph (3), the notice shall have effect for the purposes of sections 41 and 47 as if it were an enforcement notice under section 40.

(2) Where a transfer prohibition notice has been served under section 12 of the 1984 Act and immediately before the commencement of section 40 either −

(a) the time for appealing against the notice has not expired, or

(b) an appeal has not been determined,

the appeal shall be determined in accordance with the provisions of the 1984 Act and the old principles and, unless the notice is quashed on appeal, to the extent mentioned in sub-paragraph (3) the notice shall have effect for the purposes of sections 41 and 47 as if it were an enforcement notice under section 40.

(3) A transfer prohibition notice under section 12 of the 1984 Act has the effect described in sub-paragraph (1) or (2) only to the extent that the prohibition imposed by the notice is one which could be imposed by an enforcement notice under section 40 for complying with the new principles or any of them.

Notices under new law relating to matters in relation to which 1984 Act had effect

9. The Commissioner may serve an enforcement notice under section

40 on or after the day on which that section comes into force if he is satisfied that, before that day, the data controller contravened the old principles by reason of any act or omission which would also have constituted a contravention of the new principles if they had applied before that day.

10. Subsection (5)(b) of section 40 does not apply where the rectification, blocking, erasure or destruction occurred before the commencement of that section.

11. The Commissioner may serve an information notice under section 43 on or after the day on which that section comes into force if he has reasonable grounds for suspecting that, before that day, the data controller contravened the old principles by reason of any act or omission which would also have constituted a contravention of the new principles if they had applied before that day.

12. Where by virtue of paragraph 11 an information notice is served on the basis of anything done or omitted to be done before the day on which section 43 comes into force, subsection (2)(b) of that section shall have effect as if the reference to the data controller having complied, or complying, with the new principles were a reference to the data controller having contravened the old principles by reason of any such act or omission as is mentioned in paragraph 11.

Self-incrimination, etc

13. – (1) In section 43(8), section 44(9) and paragraph 11 of Schedule 7, any reference to an offence under this Act includes a reference to an offence under the 1984 Act.

(2) In section 34(9) of the 1984 Act, any reference to an offence under that Act includes a reference to an offence under this Act.

Warrants issued under 1984 Act

14. The repeal of Schedule 4 to the 1984 Act does not affect the application of that Schedule in any case where a warrant was issued under that Schedule before the commencement of the repeal.

Complaints under section 36(2) of 1984 Act and requests for assessment under section 42

15. The repeal of section 36(2) of the 1984 Act does not affect the application of that provision in any case where the complaint was received by the Commissioner before the commencement of the repeal.

16. In dealing with a complaint under section 36(2) of the 1984 Act or a request for an assessment under section 42 of this Act, the Commissioner shall have regard to the provisions from time to time applicable to the processing, and accordingly –

(a) in section 36(2) of the 1984 Act, the reference to the old principles and the provisions of that Act includes, in relation to any time when the new principles and the provisions of this Act have effect, those principles and provisions, and

(b) in section 42 of this Act, the reference to the provisions of this Act includes, in relation to any time when the old principles and the provisions of the 1984 Act had effect, those principles and provisions.

Applications under Access to Health Records Act 1990 or corresponding Northern Ireland legislation

17. – (1) The repeal of any provision of the Access to Health Records Act 1990 does not affect –

(a) the application of section 3 or 6 of that Act in any case in which the application under that section was received before the day on which the repeal comes into force, or

(b) the application of section 8 of that Act in any case in which the application to the court was made before the day on which the repeal comes into force.

(2) Sub-paragraph (1)(a) does not apply in relation to an application for access to information which was made by reference to this Act.

18. – (1) The revocation of any provision of the Access to Health Records (Northern Ireland) Order 1993 does not affect –

(a) the application of Article 5 or 8 of that Order in any case in which the application under that Article was received before the day on which the repeal comes into force, or

(b) the application of Article 10 of that Order in any case in which the application to the court was made before the day on which the repeal comes into force.

(2) Sub-paragraph (1)(a) does not apply in relation to an application for access to information which was made by reference to this Act.

Applications under regulations under Access to Personal Files Act 1987 or corresponding Northern Ireland legislation

19. – (1) The repeal of the personal files enactments does not affect

the application of regulations under those enactments in relation to —
(a) any request for information,
(b) any application for rectification or erasure, or
(c) any application for review of a decision,
which was made before the day on which the repeal comes into force.

(2) Sub-paragraph (1)(a) does not apply in relation to a request for information which was made by reference to this Act.

(3) In sub-paragraph (1) "the personal files enactments" means —
(a) in relation to Great Britain, the Access to Personal Files Act 1987, and
(b) in relation to Northern Ireland, Part II of the Access to Personal Files and Medical Reports (Northern Ireland) Order 1991.

Applications under section 158 of Consumer Credit Act 1974

20. Section 62 does not affect the application of section 158 of the Consumer Credit Act 1974 in any case where the request was received before the commencement of section 62, unless the request is made by reference to this Act.

SCHEDULE 15
MINOR AND CONSEQUENTIAL AMENDMENTS

Public Records Act 1958 (c 51)

1. – (1) In Part II of the Table in paragraph 3 of Schedule 1 to the Public Records Act 1958 (definition of public records) for "the Data Protection Registrar" there is substituted "the Data Protection Commissioner".

(2) That Schedule shall continue to have effect with the following amendment (originally made by paragraph 14 of Schedule 2 to the Data Protection Act 1984).

(3) After paragraph 4(1)(n) there is inserted –
"(nn) records of the Data Protection Tribunal".

Parliamentary Commissioner Act 1967 (c 13)

2. In Schedule 2 to the Parliamentary Commissioner Act 1967 (departments etc subject to investigation) for "Data Protection Registrar" there is substituted "Data Protection Commissioner".

3. In Schedule 4 to that Act (tribunals exercising administrative functions), in the entry relating to the Data Protection Tribunal, for "section 3 of the Data Protection Act 1984" there is substituted "section 6 of the Data Protection Act 1998".

Superannuation Act 1972 (c 11)

4. In Schedule 1 to the Superannuation Act 1972, for "Data Protection Registrar" there is substituted "Data Protection Commissioner".

House of Commons Disqualification Act 1975 (c 24)

5. – (1) Part II of Schedule 1 to the House of Commons Disqualification Act 1975 (bodies whose members are disqualified) shall continue to include the entry "The Data Protection Tribunal" (originally inserted by paragraph 12(1) of Schedule 2 to the Data Protection Act 1984).

(2) In Part III of that Schedule (disqualifying offices) for "The Data Protection Registrar" there is substituted "The Data Protection Commissioner".

Northern Ireland Assembly Disqualification Act 1975 (c 25)

6. – (1) Part II of Schedule 1 to the Northern Ireland Assembly Disqualification Act 1975 (bodies whose members are disqualified) shall continue to include the entry "The Data Protection Tribunal" (originally inserted by paragraph 12(3) of Schedule 2 to the Data Protection Act 1984).

(2) In Part III of that Schedule (disqualifying offices) for "The Data Protection Registrar" there is substituted "The Data Protection Commissioner".

Representation of the People Act 1983 (c 2)

7. In Schedule 2 of the Representation of the People Act 1983 (provisions which may be included in regulations as to registration etc), in paragraph 11A(2) –
    (a) for "data user" there is substituted "data controller", and
    (b) for "the Data Protection Act 1984" there is substituted "the Data Protection Act 1998".

Access to Medical Reports Act 1988 (c 28)

8. In section 2(1) of the Access to Medical Reports Act 1988 (interpretation), in the definition of "health professional", for "the Data Protection (Subject Access Modification) Order 1987" there is substituted "the Data Protection Act 1998".

Football Spectators Act 1989 (c 37)

9. – (1) Section 5 of the Football Spectators Act 1989 (national membership scheme: contents and penalties) is amended as follows.

(2) In subsection (5), for "paragraph 1(2) of Part II of Schedule 1 to the Data Protection Act 1984" there is substituted "paragraph 1(2) of Part II of Schedule 1 to the Data Protection Act 1998".

(3) In subsection (6), for "section 28(1) and (2) of the Data Protection Act 1984" there is substituted "section 29(1) and (2) of the Data Protection Act 1998".

Education (Student Loans) Act 1990 (c 6)

10. Schedule 2 to the Education (Student Loans) Act 1990 (loans for students) so far as that Schedule continues in force shall have effect as if the reference in paragraph 4(2) to the Data Protection Act 1984 were a reference to this Act.

Access to Health Records Act 1990 (c 23)

11. For section 2 of the Access to Health Records Act 1990 there is substituted –

    "2. In this Act "health professional" has the same meaning as in the Data Protection Act 1998."

12. In section 3(4) of that Act (cases where fee may be required) in paragraph (a), for "the maximum prescribed under section 21 of the Data Protection Act 1984" there is substituted "such maximum as may be prescribed for the purposes of this section by regulations under section 7 of the Data Protection Act 1998".

13. In section 5(3) of that Act (cases where right of access may be partially excluded) for the words from the beginning to "record" in the first place where it occurs there is substituted "Access shall not be given under section 3(2) to any part of a health record".

14. In Article 4 of the Access to Personal Files and Medical Reports (Northern Ireland) Order 1991 (obligation to give access), in paragraph (2) (exclusion of information to which individual entitled under section 21 of the Data Protection Act 1984) for "section 21 of the Data Protection Act 1984" there is substituted "section 7 of the Data Protection Act 1998".

15. In Article 6(1) of that Order (interpretation), in the definition of "health professional", for "the Data Protection (Subject Access Modification) (Health) Order 1987" there is substituted "the Data Protection Act 1998".

Tribunals and Inquiries Act 1992 (c 53)

16. In Part 1 of Schedule 1 to the Tribunals and Inquiries Act 1992 (tribunals under direct supervision of Council on Tribunals), for paragraph 14 there is substituted —

"Data Protection

14.(a) The Data Protection Commissioner appointed under section 6 of the Data Protection Act 1998;
(b) the Data Protection Tribunal constituted under that section, in respect of its jurisdiction under section 48 of that Act."

Access to Health Records (Northern Ireland) Order 1993 (1993/1250 (NI 4))

17. For paragraphs (1) and (2) of Article 4 of the Access to Health Records (Northern Ireland) Order 1993 there is substituted —

"(1)   In this Order "health professional" has the same meaning as in the Data Protection Act 1998.".

18. In Article 5(4) of that Order (cases where fee may be required) in subparagraph (a), for "the maximum prescribed under section 21 of the Data Protection Act 1984" there is substituted "such maximum as may be prescribed for the purposes of this Article by regulations under section 7 of the Data Protection Act 1998".

19. In Article 7 of that Order (cases where right of access may be partially excluded) for the words from the beginning to "record" in the first place where it occurs there is substituted "Access shall not be given under Article 5(2) to any part of a health record".

SCHEDULE 16
REPEALS AND REVOCATIONS

Part I
Repeals

Chapter	Short title	Extent of repeal
1984 c 35.	The Data Protection Act 1984.	The whole Act.
1986 c 60.	The Financial Services Act 1986.	Section 190.
1987 c 37.	The Access to Personal Files Act 1987.	The whole Act.
1988 c 40.	The Education Reform Act 1988.	Section 223.
1988 c 50.	The Housing Act 1988.	In Schedule 17, paragraph 80.
1990 c 23.	The Access to Health Records Act 1990.	In section 1(1), the words from "but does not" to the end.
		In section 3, subsection (1)(a) to (e) and, in subsection (6)(a), the words "in the case of an application made otherwise than by the patient".
		Section 4(1) and (2).
		In section 5(1)(a)(i), the words "of the patient or" and the word "other".
		In section 10, in subsection (2) the words "or orders"

		and in subsection (3) the words "or an order under section 2(3) above".
		In section 11, the definitions of "child" and "parental responsibility".
1990 c 37.	The Human Fertilisation and Embryology Act 1990.	Section 33(8).
1990 c 41.	The Courts and Legal Services Act 1990.	In Schedule 10, paragraph 58.
1992 c 13.	The Further and Higher Education Act 1992.	Section 86.
1992 c 37.	The Further and Higher Education (Scotland) Act 1992.	Section 59.
1993 c 8.	The Judicial Pensions and Retirement Act 1993.	In Schedule 6, paragraph 50.
1993 c 10.	The Charities Act 1993.	Section 12.
1993 c 21.	The Osteopaths Act 1993.	Section 38.
1994 c 17.	The Chiropractors Act 1994.	Section 38.
1994 c 19.	The Local Government (Wales) Act 1994.	In Schedule 13, paragraph 30.
1994 c 33.	The Criminal Justice and Public Order Act 1994.	Section 161.
1994 c 39.	The Local Government etc (Scotland) Act 1994.	In Schedule 13, paragraph 154.

Part II
Revocations

Number	Title	Extent of revocation
SI 1991/1142.	The Data Protection Registration Fee Order 1991.	The whole Order.
SI 1991/1707 (NI 14).	The Access to Personal Files and Medical Reports (Northern Ireland) Order 1991.	Part II. The Schedule.
SI 1992/3218.	The Banking Co-ordination (Second Council Directive) Regulations 1992.	In Schedule 10, paragraphs 15 and 40.
SI 1993/1250 (NI 4).	The Access to Health Records (Northern Ireland) Order 1993.	In Article 2(2), the definitions of "child" and "parental responsibility". In Article 3(1), the words from "but does not include" to the end. In Article 5, paragraph (1)(a) to (d) and, in paragraph (6)(a), the words "in the case of an application made otherwise than by the patient". Article 6(1) and (2). In Article 7(1)(a)(i), the words "of the patient or" and the word "other".
SI 1994/429 (NI 2).	The Health and Personal Social Services (Northern Ireland) Order 1994.	In Schedule 1, the entries relating to the Access to Personal Files

		and Medical Reports (Northern Ireland) Order 1991.
SI 1994/1696.	The Insurance Companies (Third Insurance Directives) Regulations 1994.	In Schedule 8, paragraph 8.
SI 1995/755 (NI 2).	The Children (Northern Ireland) Order 1995.	In Schedule 9, paragraphs 177 and 191.
SI 1995/3275.	The Investment Services Regulations 1995.	In Schedule 10, paragraphs 3 and 15.
SI 1996/2827.	The Open-Ended Investment Companies (Investment Companies with Variable Capital) Regulations 1996.	In Schedule 8, paragraphs 3 and 26.

Data Protection Act 1998 (Commencement) Order 2000 SI 2000 No 183

Made   *31st January 2000*

The Secretary of State, in exercise of the powers conferred on him by sections 67(2) and 75(3) of the Data Protection Act 1998, hereby makes the following Order:

1. This Order may be cited as the Data Protection Act 1998 (Commencement) Order 2000.

2. – (1) The provisions of the Data Protection Act 1998, other than those referred to in section 75(2) (provisions coming into force on the day on which that Act was passed) and section 56 (prohibition of requirement as to production of certain records), shall come into force on 1st March 2000.

(2) The coming into force of section 62 of the Data Protection Act 1998 shall not affect the application of section 159 (correction of wrong information) or section 160 (alternative procedure for business consumers) of the Consumer Credit Act 1974 in any case where a credit reference agency has, in response to a request under section 158(1) of that Act, complied with section 158(1) and (2) or dealt with the request under section 160(3) before 1st March 2000.

Mike O'Brien
Parliamentary Under-Secretary of State
Home Office
31st January 2000

EXPLANATORY NOTE
(This note is not part of the Order)

This Order brings the Data Protection Act 1998, with the exception of section 56 and those provisions already in force by virtue of section 75(2), into force on 1st March 2000. Section 75(4) of the Act provides that section 56 (prohibition of requirement as to production of certain records) must not be brought into force before sections 112, 113 and 115 of the Police Act 1997 (which provide for the issue by the Secretary of State of criminal conviction certificates, criminal record certificates and enhanced criminal record certificates) are all in force.

The Order makes transitional provision for requests made to credit reference agencies pursuant to section 158 of the Consumer Credit Act 1974.

The provisions of the Data Protection Act 1998 implement Directive 95/46/EC on the protection of individuals with regard to the processing of personal data and on the free movement of such data.

Data Protection (Corporate Finance Exemption) Order 2000
SI 2000 No 184

Made	*31st January 2000*
Laid before Parliament	*7th February 2000*
Coming into force	*1st March 2000*

The Secretary of State, in exercise of the powers conferred on him by section 67(2) of, and paragraph 6(2) of Schedule 7 to, the Data Protection Act 1998, and after consultation with the Data Protection Commissioner in accordance with section 67(3) of that Act, hereby makes the following Order:

Citation and commencement

1. – (1) This Order may be cited as the Data Protection (Corporate Finance Exemption) Order 2000 and shall come into force on 1st March 2000.

(2) In this Order, "the Act" means the Data Protection Act 1998.

Matters to be taken into account

2. – (1) The matter set out in paragraph (2) below is hereby specified for the purposes of paragraph 6(1)(b) of Schedule 7 to the Act (matters to be taken into account in determining whether exemption from the subject information provisions is required for the purpose of safeguarding an important economic or financial interest of the United Kingdom).

(2) The matter referred to in paragraph (1) above is the inevitable prejudicial effect on –
    (a) the orderly functioning of financial markets, or
    (b) the efficient allocation of capital within the economy,
which will result from the application (whether on an occasional or regular basis) of the subject information provisions to data to which paragraph (3) below applies.

(3) This paragraph applies to any personal data to which the application of the subject information provisions could, in the reasonable belief of the relevant person within the meaning of paragraph 6 of Schedule 7 to the Act, affect –

461

(a) any decision of any person whether or not to –
  (i) deal in,
  (ii) subscribe for, or
  (iii) issue,
any instrument which is already in existence or is to be, or may be, created; or
(b) any decision of any person to act or not to act in a way that is likely to have an effect on any business activity including, in particular, an effect on –
  (i) the industrial strategy of any person (whether the strategy is, or is to be, pursued independently or in association with others),
  (ii) the capital structure of an undertaking, or
  (iii) the legal or beneficial ownership of a business or asset.

Mike O'Brien
Parliamentary Under-Secretary of State
Home Office
31st January 2000

EXPLANATORY NOTE
(This note is not part of the Order)

The Data Protection Act 1998 imposes certain obligations on data controllers to give data subjects information about the processing of personal data and to give access to personal data. By virtue of section 27(2) of that Act, the provisions imposing these obligations are referred to as "the subject information provisions". Paragraph 6 of Schedule 7 to the Act creates an exemption from these provisions where, inter alia, the exemption is required for the purpose of safeguarding an important economic or financial interest of the United Kingdom.

This Order provides that the inevitable prejudicial effect on the orderly functioning of financial markets or the efficient allocation of capital within the economy resulting from the occasional or regular application of the subject information provisions to certain data is a matter to be taken into account in determining whether exemption from the subject information provisions is required for the purpose of safeguarding an important economic or financial interest of the United Kingdom. The data in question are data to which the application of the subject information provisions could, in the reasonable belief of the relevant person as defined, affect decisions whether to deal in, subscribe for or issue instruments or decisions which are likely to affect any business activity.

This Order contributes to the implementation of Directive 95/46/EC on the protection of individuals with regard to the processing of personal data and on the free movement of such data.

A Regulatory Impact Assessment was prepared for the Data Protection Bill as it was then and the statutory instruments to be made under it, and was placed in the libraries of both Houses of Parliament. The Regulatory Impact Assessment is now available on the internet at *www.homeoffice.gov.uk*. Alternatively, copies can be obtained by post from the Home Office, LGDP Unit, 50 Queen Anne's Gate, London, SW1H 9AT.

Data Protection (Conditions under Paragraph 3 of Part II of Schedule 1) Order 2000
2000 No 185

Made   *31st January 2000*
Laid before Parliament   *7th February 2000*
Coming into force   *1st March 2000*

The Secretary of State, in exercise of the powers conferred upon him by section 67(2) of, and paragraph 3(1) of Part II of Schedule 1 to, the Data Protection Act 1998, and after consultation with the Data Protection Commissioner in accordance with section 67(3) of that Act, hereby makes the following Order:

Citation and commencement

1. This Order may be cited as the Data Protection (Conditions under Paragraph 3 of Part II of Schedule 1) Order 2000 and shall come into force on 1st March 2000.

Interpretation

2. In this Order, "Part II" means Part II of Schedule 1 to the Data Protection Act 1998.

General provisions

3. – (1) In cases where the primary condition referred to in paragraph 3(2)(a) of Part II is met, the provisions of articles 4 and 5 apply.

(2) In cases where the primary condition referred to in paragraph 3(2)(b) of that Part is met by virtue of the fact that the recording of the information to be contained in the data by, or the disclosure of the data by, the data controller is not a function conferred on him by or under any enactment or an obligation imposed on him by order of a court, but is necessary for compliance with any legal obligation to which the data controller is subject, other than an obligation imposed by contract, the provisions of article 4 apply.

Notices in writing

4. – (1) One of the further conditions prescribed in paragraph (2) must be met if paragraph 2(1)(b) of Part II is to be disapplied in respect of any particular data subject.

(2) The conditions referred to in paragraph (1) are that –
(a) no notice in writing has been received at any time by the data controller from an individual, requiring that data controller to provide the information set out in paragraph 2(3) of that Part before the relevant time (as defined in paragraph 2(2) of that Part) or as soon as practicable after that time; or
(b) where such notice in writing has been received but the data controller does not have sufficient information about the individual in order readily to determine whether he is processing personal data about that individual, the data controller shall send to the individual a written notice stating that he cannot provide the information set out in paragraph 2(3) of that Part because of his inability to make that determination, and explaining the reasons for that inability.

(3) The requirement in paragraph (2) that notice should be in writing is satisfied where the text of the notice –
(a) is transmitted by electronic means,
(b) is received in legible form, and
(c) is capable of being used for subsequent reference.

Further condition in cases of disproportionate effort

5. – (1) The further condition prescribed in paragraph (2) must be met for paragraph 2(1)(b) of Part II to be disapplied in respect of any data.

(2) The condition referred to in paragraph (1) is that the data controller shall record the reasons for his view that the primary condition referred to in article 3(1) is met in respect of the data.

Mike O'Brien
Parliamentary Under-Secretary of State
Home Office
31st January 2000

EXPLANATORY NOTE
(This note is not part of the Order)

Paragraph 2 of Part II of Schedule 1 to the Data Protection Act 1998

("Part II") provides that personal data will not be treated as processed fairly unless certain requirements are met relating to the provision to the data subject of information about the processing ("the information requirements"). Different provisions apply depending on whether data have been obtained from the data subject or from some other source.

Paragraph 3 of Part II sets out conditions which, if met, allow the data controller to disregard the information requirements in cases where the data have been obtained from a source other than the data subject. Power is given to the Secretary of State to prescribe further conditions which must be met before the information requirements can be disregarded in this way.

Article 4 of this Order prescribes further conditions for cases where the disproportionate effort ground in paragraph 3(2)(a) of Part II is being relied upon, or where the disclosure or recording of the data is necessary for compliance with a legal obligation, other than one imposed by contract or by or under an enactment or by a court order. In both cases, the Order provides that any data controller claiming the benefit of the disapplication of the information requirements must still provide the relevant information to any individual who requests it. Further, if a data controller cannot readily determine whether he is processing information about the individual concerned because of a lack of identifying information, that data controller must write to the individual explaining the position. In the former case only (disproportionate effort), article 5 of this Order provides for a further condition to be met: the data controller must keep a record of the reasons why he believes the disapplication of the information requirements is necessary.

This Order contributes to the implementation of Directive 95/46/EC on the protection of individuals with regard to the processing of personal data and on the free movement of such data.

A Regulatory Impact Assessment was prepared for the Data Protection Bill as it was then and the statutory instruments to be made under it, and was placed in the libraries of both Houses of Parliament. The Regulatory Impact Assessment is now available on the internet at *www.homeoffice.gov.uk*. Alternatively, copies can be obtained by post from the Home Office, LGDP Unit, 50 Queen Anne's Gate, London SW1H 9AT.

Data Protection (Functions of Designated Authority) Order 2000
SI 2000 No 186

Made	*31st January 2000*
Laid before Parliament	*7th February 2000*
Coming into force	*1st March 2000*

The Secretary of State, in exercise of the powers conferred upon him by sections 54(2) and 67(2) of the Data Protection Act 1998 and after consultation with the Data Protection Commissioner in accordance with section 67(3) of that Act, hereby makes the following Order:

Citation and commencement

1. This Order may be cited as the Data Protection (Functions of Designated Authority) Order 2000 and shall come into force on 1st March 2000.

Interpretation

2. – (1) In this Order:

"the Act" means the Data Protection Act 1998;

"foreign designated authority" means an authority designated for the purposes of Article 13 of the Convention by a party (other than the United Kingdom) which is bound by that Convention;

"register" means the register maintained under section 19(1) of the Act;

"request", except in article 3, means a request for assistance under Article 14 of the Convention which states –
    (a) the name and address of the person making the request;
    (b) particulars which identify the personal data to which the request relates;
    (c) the rights under Article 8 of the Convention to which the request relates;
    (d) the reasons why the request has been made;
and "requesting person" means a person making such a request.

(2) In this Order, references to the Commissioner are to the Commissioner as the designated authority in the United Kingdom for the purposes of Article 13 of the Convention.

Co-operation between the Commissioner and foreign designated authorities

3. – (1) The Commissioner shall, at the request of a foreign designated authority, furnish to that foreign designated authority such information referred to in Article 13(3)(a) of the Convention, and in particular the data protection legislation in force in the United Kingdom at the time the request is made, as is the subject of the request.

(2) The Commissioner shall, at the request of a foreign designated authority, take appropriate measures in accordance with Article 13(3)(b) of the Convention, for furnishing to that foreign designated authority information relating to the processing of personal data in the United Kingdom.

(3) The Commissioner may request a foreign designated authority to furnish to him or, as the case may be, to take appropriate measures for furnishing to him, the information referred to in Article 13(3) of the Convention.

Persons resident outside the United Kingdom

4. – (1) This article applies where a person resident outside the United Kingdom makes a request to the Commissioner under Article 14 of the Convention, including a request forwarded to the Commissioner through the Secretary of State or a foreign designated authority, seeking assistance in exercising any of the rights under Article 8 of the Convention.

(2) If the request –
(a) seeks assistance in exercising the rights under section 7 of the Act; and
(b) does not indicate that the data controller has failed, contrary to section 7 of the Act, to comply with the same request on a previous occasion,
the Commissioner shall notify the requesting person of the data controller's address for the receipt of notices from data subjects exercising their rights under that section and of such other information as the Commissioner considers necessary to enable that person to exercise his rights under that section.

(3) If the request indicates that a data protection principle has been contravened by a data controller the Commissioner shall either –

(a) notify the requesting person of the rights of data subjects and the remedies available to them under Part II of the Act together with such particulars as are contained in the data controller's entry in the register as are necessary to enable the requesting person to avail himself of those remedies; or

(b) if the Commissioner considers that notification in accordance with sub-paragraph (a) would not assist the requesting person or would, for any other reason, be inappropriate, treat the request as if it were a request for an assessment which falls to be dealt with under section 42 of the Act.

(4) The Commissioner shall not be required, in response to any request referred to in paragraphs (2) and (3) above, to supply to the requesting person a duly certified copy in writing of the particulars contained in any entry made in the register other than on payment of such fee as is prescribed for the purposes of section 19(7) of the Act.

Persons resident in the United Kingdom

5. – (1) Where a request for assistance in exercising any of the rights referred to in Article 8 of the Convention in a country or territory (other than the United Kingdom) specified in the request is made by a person resident in the United Kingdom and submitted through the Commissioner under Article 14(2) of the Convention, the Commissioner shall, if he is satisfied that the request contains all necessary particulars referred to in Article 14(3) of the Convention, send it to the foreign designated authority in the specified country or territory.

(2) If the Commissioner decides that he is not required by paragraph (1) above to render assistance to the requesting person he shall, where practicable, notify that person of the reasons for his decision.

Restrictions on use of information

6. Where the Commissioner receives information from a foreign designated authority as a result of either –
    (a) a request made by him under article 3(3) above; or
    (b) a request received by him under articles 3(2) or 4 above,
the Commissioner shall use that information only for the purposes specified in the request.

Mike O'Brien
Parliamentary Under-Secretary of State
Home Office
31st January 2000

EXPLANATORY NOTE
(This note is not part of the Order)

Section 54(1) of the Data Protection Act 1998 provides that the Data Protection Commissioner ("the Commissioner") shall continue to be the designated authority in the United Kingdom for the purposes of Article 13 of the Convention for the Protection of Individuals with regard to Automatic Processing of Personal Data which was opened for signature on 28th January 1981 ("the Convention"). Section 54(2) provides that the Secretary of State may by order make provision as to the functions to be discharged by the Commissioner in that capacity.

This Order specifies those functions. In particular, article 3 requires the Commissioner to furnish particular information to the designated authorities in other Convention countries and also provides that he may request such authorities to furnish him with information. Article 4 requires the Commissioner to assist persons resident outside the United Kingdom in exercising certain of their rights under Part II of the Act. In the circumstances specified in article 4(2), he is required to notify a resident outside the United Kingdom of certain of the rights and remedies available under Part II of the Act or to treat any request made to him by such a resident as a request for an assessment to be dealt with under section 42 of the Data Protection Act 1998. Article 5 provides that if a request for assistance in exercising, *inter alia*, rights of access to personal data in a Convention country is made by a person resident in the United Kingdom and submitted to the Commissioner, the Commissioner will send the request to the designated authority in that country.

The Convention is published in the Treaty Series at no 86 of 1990, Cm 1329. It entered into force in respect of the United Kingdom on 1st December 1987.

A Regulatory Impact Assessment was prepared for the Data Protection Bill as it was then and the statutory instruments to be made under it, and was placed in the libraries of both Houses of Parliament. The Regulatory Impact Assessment is now available on the internet at *www.homeoffice.gov.uk*. Alternatively, copies can be obtained by post from the Home Office, LGDP Unit, 50 Queen Anne's Gate, London SW1 9AT.

Data Protection (Fees under section 19(7)) Regulations 2000 SI 2000 No 187

Made	*31st January 2000*
Laid before Parliament	*7th February 2000*
Coming into force	*1st March 2000*

The Secretary of State, in exercise of the powers conferred upon him by section 19(7) of the Data Protection Act 1998, having regard to the definition of "fees regulations" in section 16(2) of that Act, and after consultation with the Data Protection Commissioner in accordance with section 67(3) of the Act, hereby makes the following Regulations:

1. These Regulations may be cited as the Data Protection (Fees under section 19(7)) Regulations 2000 and shall come into force on 1st March 2000.

2. The fee payable by a member of the public for the supply by the Data Protection Commissioner under section 19(7) of the Data Protection Act 1998 of a duly certified written copy of the particulars contained in any entry made in the register maintained under section 19(1) of that Act shall be £2.

Mike O'Brien
Parliamentary Under-Secretary of State
Home Office
31st January 2000

EXPLANATORY NOTE
(This note is not part of the Regulations)

These Regulations prescribe a fee of £2 to be paid to the Data Protection Commissioner for the supply of a duly certified copy of any data controller's entry on the register.

A Regulatory Impact Assessment was prepared for the Data Protection Bill as it was then and the statutory instruments to be made under it, and was placed in the libraries of both Houses of Parliament. The Regulatory Impact Assessment is now available on the internet at *www.homeoffice.gov.uk*. Alternatively, copies can be obtained by post from the Home Office, LGDP Unit, 50 Queen Anne's Gate, London SW1H 9AT.

Crown Copyright material reproduced with the permission of the Controller of Her Majesty's Stationery Office.

Data Protection (Notification and Notification Fees) Regulations 2000
SI 2000 No 188

Made	*31st January 2000*
Laid before Parliament	*7th February 2000*
Coming into force	*1st March 2000*

Whereas the Data Protection Commissioner has submitted to the Secretary of State proposals in accordance with section 25(1) of the Data Protection Act 1998:

And whereas the Secretary of State has considered those proposals and has consulted the Data Protection Commissioner in accordance with sections 25(4) and 67(3)(b) of that Act:

And whereas it appears to the Secretary of State that processing of a description set out in the Schedule to these Regulations is unlikely to prejudice the rights and freedoms of data subjects:

Now, therefore, the Secretary of State, in exercise of the powers conferred on him by sections 17(3), 18(2), (4) and (5), 19(2), (3), (4) and (5), 20(1), 26(1) and 67(2) of, and paragraph 2(7) and (8) of Schedule 14 to, that Act, hereby makes the following Regulations:

Citation and commencement

1. These Regulations may be cited as the Data Protection (Notification and Notification Fees) Regulations 2000 and shall come into force on 1st March 2000.

Interpretation

2. In these Regulations –

"the Act" means the Data Protection Act 1998;

"the register" means the register maintained by the Commissioner under section 19 of the Act.

Exemptions from notification

3. Except where the processing is assessable processing for the purposes of section 22 of the Act, section 17(1) of the Act shall not apply in relation to processing –

(a) falling within one or more of the descriptions of processing set out in paragraphs 2 to 5 of the Schedule to these Regulations (being processing appearing to the Secretary of State to be unlikely to prejudice the rights and freedoms of data subjects); or

(b) which does not fall within one or more of those descriptions solely by virtue of the fact that disclosure of the personal data to a person other than those specified in the descriptions—

(i) is required by or under any enactment, by any rule of law or by the order of a court, or

(ii) may be made by virtue of an exemption from the non-disclosure provisions (as defined in section 27(3) of the Act).

Form of giving notification

4. – (1) Subject to regulations 5 and 6 below, the Commissioner shall determine the form in which the registrable particulars (within the meaning of section 16(1) of the Act) and the description mentioned in section 18(2)(b) of the Act are to be specified, including in particular the detail required for the purposes of that description and section 16(1)(c), (d), (e) and (f) of the Act.

(2) Subject to regulations 5 and 6 below, the Commissioner shall determine the form in which a notification under regulation 12 (including that regulation as modified by regulation 13) is to be specified.

Notification in respect of partnerships

5. – (1) In any case in which two or more persons carrying on a business in partnership are the data controllers in respect of any personal data for the purposes of that business, a notification under section 18 of the Act or under regulation 12 below may be given in respect of those persons in the name of the firm.

(2) Where a notification is given in the name of a firm under paragraph (1) above –

(a) the name to be specified for the purposes of section 16(1)(a) of the Act is the name of the firm, and

(b) the address to be specified for the purposes of section 16(1)(a) of the Act is the address of the firm's principal place of business.

Notification in respect of the governing body of, and head teacher at, any school

6. – (1) In any case in which a governing body of, and a head teacher at, any school are, in those capacities, the data controllers in respect of any personal data, a notification under section 18 of the Act or under regulation 12 below may be given in respect of that governing body and head teacher in the name of the school.

(2) Where a notification is given in the name of a school under paragraph (1) above, the name and address to be specified for the purposes of section 16(1)(a) of the Act are those of the school.

(3) In this regulation, "head teacher" includes in Northern Ireland the principal of a school.

Fees to accompany notification under section 18 of the Act

7. – (1) This regulation applies to any notification under section 18 of the Act, including a notification which, by virtue of regulation 5 or 6 above, is given in respect of more than one data controller.

(2) A notification to which this regulation applies must be accompanied by a fee of £35.

Date of entry in the register

8. – (1) The time from which an entry in respect of a data controller who has given a notification under section 18 of the Act in accordance with these Regulations is to be treated for the purposes of section 17 of the Act as having been made in the register shall be determined as follows.

(2) In the case of a data controller who has given the notification by sending it by registered post or the recorded delivery service, that time is the day after the day on which it is received for dispatch by the Post Office.

(3) In the case of a data controller who has given a notification by some other means, that time is the day on which it is received by the Commissioner.

Acknowledgment of receipt of notification in the case of assessable processing

9. – (1) In any case in which the Commissioner considers under section 22(2)(a) of the Act that any of the processing to which a notification relates is assessable processing within the meaning of that section he shall, within 10 days of receipt of the notification, give a written notice to the data controller who has given the notification, acknowledging its receipt.

(2) A notice under paragraph (1) above shall indicate —
(a) the date on which the Commissioner received the notification, and
(b) the processing which the Commissioner considers to be assessable processing.

Confirmation of register entries

10. — (1) The Commissioner shall, as soon as practicable and in any event within a period of 28 days after making an entry in the register under section 19(1)(b) of the Act or amending an entry in the register under section 20(4) of the Act, give the data controller to whom the register entry relates notice confirming the register entry.

(2) A notice under paragraph (1) above shall include a statement of —
(a) the date on which —
(i) in the case of an entry made under section 19(1)(b) of the Act, the entry is treated as having been included by virtue of regulation 8 above, or
(ii) in the case of an entry made under section 20(4) of the Act, the notification was received by the Commissioner;
(b) the particulars entered in the register, or the amendment made, in pursuance of the notification; and
(c) in the case of a notification under section 18 of the Act, the date by which the fee payable under regulation 14 below must be paid in order for the entry to be retained in the register as provided by section 19(4) of the Act.

Additional information in register entries

11. In addition to the matters mentioned in section 19(2)(a) of the Act, the Commissioner may include in a register entry —
(a) a registration number issued by the Commissioner in respect of that entry;
(b) the date on which the entry is treated, by virtue of regulation 8 above, as having been included in pursuance of a notification under section 18 of the Act;
(c) the date on which the entry falls or may fall to be removed by virtue of regulation 14 or 15 below; and
(d) information additional to the registrable particulars for the

purpose of assisting persons consulting the register to communicate with any data controller to whom the entry relates concerning matters relating to the processing of personal data.

Duty to notify changes to matters previously notified

12. – (1) Subject to regulation 13 below, every person in respect of whom an entry is for the time being included in the register is under a duty to give the Commissioner a notification specifying any respect in which –

(a) that entry becomes inaccurate or incomplete as a statement of his current registrable particulars, or

(b) the general description of measures notified under section 18(2)(b) of the Act or, as the case may be, that description as amended in pursuance of a notification under this regulation, becomes inaccurate or incomplete,

and setting out the changes which need to be made to that entry or general description in order to make it accurate and complete.

(2) Such a notification must be given as soon as practicable and in any event within a period of 28 days from the date on which the entry or, as the case may be, the general description, becomes inaccurate or incomplete.

(3) References in this regulation to an entry being included in the register include any entry being treated under regulation 8 above as being so included.

Duty to notify changes—transitional modifications

13. – (1) This regulation applies to persons in respect of whom an entry in the register has been made under paragraph 2(6) of Schedule 14 to the Act.

(2) In the case of a person to whom this regulation applies, the duty imposed by regulation 12 above shall be modified so as to have effect as follows.

(3) Every person in respect of whom an entry is for the time being included in the register is under a duty to give the Commissioner a notification specifying–

(a) his name and address, in any case in which a change to his name or address results in the entry in respect of him no longer including his current name and address;

(b) to the extent to which the entry relates to eligible data –

(i) a description of any eligible data being or to be processed by him or on his behalf, in any case in which such processing is of personal data of a description not included in that entry;

(ii) a description of the category or categories of data subject to which eligible data relate, in any case in which such category or categories are of a description not included in that entry;

(iii) a description of the purpose or purposes for which eligible data are being or are to be processed in any case in which such processing is for a purpose or purposes of a description not included in that entry;

(iv) a description of the source or sources from which he intends or may wish to obtain eligible data, in any case in which such obtaining is from a source of a description not included in that entry;

(v) a description of any recipient or recipients to whom he intends or may wish to disclose eligible data, in any case in which such disclosure is to a recipient or recipients of a description not included in that entry; and

(vi) the names, or a description of, any countries or territories outside the United Kingdom to which he directly or indirectly transfers, or intends or may wish directly or indirectly to transfer, eligible data, in any case in which such transfer would be to a country or territory not named or described in that entry; and

(c) to the extent to which sub-paragraph (b) above does not apply, any respect in which the entry is or becomes inaccurate or incomplete as –

(i) a statement of his current registrable particulars to the extent mentioned in section 16(1)(c), (d) and (e) of the Act;

(ii) a description of the source or sources from which he currently intends or may wish to obtain personal data; and

(iii) the names or a description of any countries or territories outside the United Kingdom to which he currently intends or may wish directly or indirectly to transfer personal data;

and setting out the changes which need to be made to that entry in order to make it accurate and complete in those respects.

(4) Such a notification must be given as soon as practicable and in any event within a period of 28 days from the date on which –

(a) in the case of a notification under paragraph (3)(a) above, the entry no longer includes the current name and address;

(b) in the case of a notification under paragraph (3)(b) above, the specified practice or intentions are in the particulars there mentioned of a description not included in the entry; and

(c) in the case of a notification under paragraph (3)(c) above, the entry becomes inaccurate or incomplete in the particulars there mentioned.

(5) For the purposes of this regulation, personal data are "eligible data" at any time if, and to the extent that, they are at that time subject to processing which was already under way immediately before 24th October 1998.

Retention of register entries

14. – (1) This regulation applies to any entry in respect of a person which is for the time being included, or by virtue of regulation 8 is treated as being included, in the register, other than an entry to which regulation 15 below applies.

(2) In relation to an entry to which this regulation applies, the fee referred to in section 19(4) of the Act is £35.

Retention of register entries—transitional provisions

15. – (1) This regulation applies to any entry in respect of a person which is for the time being included in the register under paragraph 2(6) of Schedule 14 to the Act or, as the case may be, such an entry as amended in pursuance of regulation 12 (including that regulation as modified by regulation 13).

(2) Section 19(4) and (5) of the Act applies to entries to which this regulation applies subject to the modifications in paragraph (3) below.

(3) Section 19(4) and (5) of the Act shall be modified so as to have effect as follows –

"(4)   No entry shall be retained in the register after—
    (a) the end of the registration period, or
    (b) 24th October 2001, or
    (c) the date on which the data controller gives a notification under section 18 of the Act,
whichever occurs first.
(5) In subsection (4) "the registration period" has the same meaning as in paragraph 2(2) of Schedule 14.".

Mike O'Brien
Parliamentary Under-Secretary of State
Home Office
31st January 2000

SCHEDULE
PROCESSING TO WHICH SECTION 17(1) DOES NOT APPLY

Interpretation

1. In this Schedule –

"exempt purposes" in paragraphs 2 to 4 shall mean the purposes specified in sub-paragraph (a) of those paragraphs and in paragraph 5 shall mean the purposes specified in sub-paragraph (b) of that paragraph;

"staff" includes employees or office holders, workers within the meaning given in section 296 of the Trade Union and Labour Relations (Consolidation) Act 1992, persons working under any contract for services, and volunteers.

Staff administration exemption

2. The processing –
(a) is for the purposes of appointments or removals, pay, discipline, superannuation, work management or other personnel matters in relation to the staff of the data controller;
(b) is of personal data in respect of which the data subject is –
(i) a past, existing or prospective member of staff of the data controller; or
(ii) any person the processing of whose personal data is necessary for the exempt purposes;
(c) is of personal data consisting of the name, address and other identifiers of the data subject or information as to –
(i) qualifications, work experience or pay; or
(ii) other matters the processing of which is necessary for the exempt purposes;
(d) does not involve disclosure of the personal data to any third party other than –
(i) with the consent of the data subject; or
(ii) where it is necessary to make such disclosure for the exempt purposes; and
(e) does not involve keeping the personal data after the relationship between the data controller and staff member ends, unless and for so long as it is necessary to do so for the exempt purposes.

Advertising, marketing and public relations exemption

3. The processing –

(a) is for the purposes of advertising or marketing the data controller's business, activity, goods or services and promoting public relations in connection with that business or activity, or those goods or services;

(b) is of personal data in respect of which the data subject is—

    (i) a past, existing or prospective customer or supplier; or

    (ii) any person the processing of whose personal data is necessary for the exempt purposes;

(c) is of personal data consisting of the name, address and other identifiers of the data subject or information as to other matters the processing of which is necessary for the exempt purposes;

(d) does not involve disclosure of the personal data to any third party other than –

    (i) with the consent of the data subject; or

    (ii) where it is necessary to make such disclosure for the exempt purposes; and

(e) does not involve keeping the personal data after the relationship between the data controller and customer or supplier ends, unless and for so long as it is necessary to do so for the exempt purposes.

Accounts and records exemption

4. – (1) The processing –

(a) is for the purposes of keeping accounts relating to any business or other activity carried on by the data controller, or deciding whether to accept any person as a customer or supplier, or keeping records of purchases, sales or other transactions for the purpose of ensuring that the requisite payments and deliveries are made or services provided by or to the data controller in respect of those transactions, or for the purpose of making financial or management forecasts to assist him in the conduct of any such business or activity;

(b) is of personal data in respect of which the data subject is –

    (i) a past, existing or prospective customer or supplier; or

    (ii) any person the processing of whose personal data is necessary for the exempt purposes;

(c) is of personal data consisting of the name, address and other identifiers of the data subject or information as to –

    (i) financial standing; or

    (ii) other matters the processing of which is necessary for the exempt purposes;

(d) does not involve disclosure of the personal data to any third party other than –

    (i) with the consent of the data subject; or

(ii) where it is necessary to make such disclosure for the exempt purposes; and

(e) does not involve keeping the personal data after the relationship between the data controller and customer or supplier ends, unless and for so long as it is necessary to do so for the exempt purposes.

(2) Sub-paragraph (1)(c) shall not be taken as including personal data processed by or obtained from a credit reference agency.

Non profit–making organisations exemptions

5.   The processing –

(a) is carried out by a data controller which is a body or association which is not established or conducted for profit;

(b) is for the purposes of establishing or maintaining membership of or support for the body or association, or providing or administering activities for individuals who are either members of the body or association or have regular contact with it;

(c) is of personal data in respect of which the data subject is—

(i) a past, existing or prospective member of the body or organisation;

(ii) any person who has regular contact with the body or organisation in connection with the exempt purposes; or

(iii) any person the processing of whose personal data is necessary for the exempt purposes;

(d) is of personal data consisting of the name, address and other identifiers of the data subject or information as to –

(i) eligibility for membership of the body or association; or

(ii) other matters the processing of which is necessary for the exempt purposes;

(e) does not involve disclosure of the personal data to any third party other than –

(i) with the consent of the data subject; or

(ii) where it is necessary to make such disclosure for the exempt purposes; and

(f) does not involve keeping the personal data after the relationship between the data controller and data subject ends, unless and for so long as it is necessary to do so for the exempt purposes.

EXPLANATORY NOTE
(This note is not part of the Regulations)

These Regulations set out a number of arrangements in respect of the giving of notifications to the Data Protection Commissioner by data controllers under Part III of the Data Protection Act 1998.

Regulation 3 makes provision exempting data controllers carrying out certain processing from the need to notify. The descriptions of the exempt processing operations are set out in the Schedule to the Regulations, and cover processing operations involving staff administration, advertising, marketing and public relations, accounts and record keeping and certain processing operations carried out by non profit-making organisations. Exemption from notification is lost if the processing falls within any description of assessable processing specified by the Secretary of State under section 22 of the Act.

Regulation 4 makes general provision for the form of all such notifications to be determined by the Commissioner. Regulations 5 and 6 make special provision in two cases where there is more than one data controller in respect of personal data; regulation 5 provides for notification by business partners to be in the name of the partnership, and regulation 6 for notification by the governing body and head teacher of a school to be in the name of the school.

Regulation 7 prescribes fees to accompany a notification under section 18 of the Act. A fee of £35 is prescribed.

Regulation 8 provides that an entry in the register of notifications maintained by the Commissioner under section 19 of the Act is to be taken to have been made, for the purposes of avoiding the prohibition in section 17 of the Act on processing without a register entry, in the case of a notification sent by registered post or recorded delivery service on the day after the day it was received by the Post Office, and in any other case on the day it was received by the Commissioner.

Regulation 9 requires the Commissioner to give written notice to a data controller acknowledging receipt of any notification which he considers relates to assessable processing within the meaning of section 22 of the Act. The notice must be given within 10 days of receipt of the notification and must indicate the date of receipt and the processing considered to be assessable processing.

Regulation 10 requires the Commissioner to give notice to a data controller confirming his register entry. The notice must be given as soon as practicable and in any event within 28 days of making a register entry under section 19 of the Act or of amending it under section 20. It must contain the date on which the entry is deemed by regulation 8 to have been made or as the case may be the date of alteration, the particulars entered or amended, and, in the case of a notification under section 18, the date on which the fee provided for by regulation 14 falls due.

Regulation 11 authorises the Commissioner to include certain matters in a register entry additional to the registrable particulars set out in section 16 of the Act. Those matters are a registration number, the deemed date of the entry provided by regulation 8, the date on which the entry may lapse under regulation 14 or 15, and additional information for the purpose of assisting communication about data protection matters between persons consulting the register and the data controller.

Regulation 12 imposes on everyone who has a register entry a duty to notify the Commissioner of any respect in which the entry becomes an inaccurate or incomplete statement of his current registrable particulars or in which the latest description of security matters given under section 18(2)(b) of the Act becomes inaccurate or incomplete. The notification must set out the changes which need to be made to ensure accuracy and completeness, and be given as soon as practicable and in any event within 28 days from the time when the inaccuracy or incompleteness arises. Regulation 12 is modified by regulation 13 in its application to persons who have a register entry by virtue of the manner in which the Act's transitional provisions operate on entries in the register maintained under section 4 of the Data Protection Act 1984. In these cases, the duty under regulation 12 varies according to the extent to which the entry relates to data which are subject to processing which was already under way immediately before 24th October 1998. In respect of such data, the notification must specify certain aspects of processing which are not from time to time included in the existing register entry; in other cases it must specify any respect in which the entry becomes inaccurate or incomplete in certain respects, and set out the changes needed to ensure accuracy and completeness.

Regulation 14 provides that, other than in the transitional circumstances addressed in regulation 15, the fee to be paid annually to secure retention of a registered entry is £35.

Regulation 15 provides for the retention of register entries included by virtue of the manner in which the Act's transitional provisions operate on entries in the register maintained under section 4 of the Data Protection Act 1984; these are to be retained until the end of the defined registration period, or 24th October 2001, or the date on which notification is given under section 18 of the Act, whichever occurs first.

This Order contributes to the implementation of Directive 95/46/EC on the protection of individuals with regard to the processing of personal data and on the free movement of such data.

A Regulatory Impact Assessment was prepared for the Data Protection Bill as it was then and the statutory instruments to be made under it, and was placed in the libraries of both Houses of Parliament. The Regulatory Impact Assessment is now available on the internet at *www.homeoffice.gov.uk*. Alternatively, copies can be obtained by post from the Home Office, LGDP Unit, 50 Queen Anne's Gate, London SW1H 9AT.

Data Protection Tribunal (Enforcement Appeals) Rules 2000 SI 2000 No 189

Made	*31st January 2000*
Laid before Parliament	*7th February 2000*
Coming into force	*1st March 2000*

The Secretary of State, in exercise of the powers conferred on him by section 67(2) of, and paragraph 7 of Schedule 6 to, the Data Protection Act 1998, and after consultation with the Council on Tribunals in accordance with section 8 of the Tribunals and Inquiries Act 1992, hereby makes the following Rules:

Citation and commencement

1. These Rules may be cited as the Data Protection Tribunal (Enforcement Appeals) Rules 2000 and shall come into force on 1st March 2000.

Application and interpretation

2. – (1) These Rules apply to appeals under section 48 of the Act, and the provisions of these Rules are to be construed accordingly.

(2) In these Rules, unless the context otherwise requires –
"the Act" means the Data Protection Act 1998;

"appeal" means an appeal under section 48 of the Act;

"appellant" means a person who brings or intends to bring an appeal under section 48 of the Act;

"chairman" means the chairman of the Tribunal, and includes a deputy chairman of the Tribunal presiding or sitting alone;

"costs" –
(a) except in Scotland, includes fees, charges, disbursements, expenses and remuneration;
(b) in Scotland means expenses, and includes fees, charges, disbursements and remuneration;

"disputed decision" means —
    (a) in relation to an appeal under section 48 of the Act other than an appeal under section 48(3)(b), the decision of the Commissioner, and
    (b) in relation to an appeal under section 48(3)(b) of the Act the effect of a decision of the Commissioner,
against which the appellant appeals or intends to appeal to the Tribunal;

"party" has the meaning given in paragraph (3) below; and

"proper officer" in relation to a rule means an officer or member of staff provided to the Tribunal under paragraph 14 of Schedule 5 to the Act and appointed by the chairman to perform the duties of a proper officer under that rule.

(3) In these Rules, "party" means the appellant or the Commissioner, and, except where the context otherwise requires, references in these Rules to a party (including references in rule 12 below) include a person appointed under rule 16 below to represent his interests.

(4) In relation to proceedings before the Tribunal in Scotland, for the words "on the trial of an action" in rules 11(4), 12(8) and 23(2) below there is substituted "in a proof".

Method of appealing

3. — (1) An appeal must be brought by a written notice of appeal served on the Tribunal.

(2) The notice of appeal shall —
    (a) identify the disputed decision and the date on which the notice relating to such decision was served on or given to the appellant; and
    (b) state —
      (i) the name and address of the appellant;
      (ii) the grounds of the appeal;
      (iii) whether the appellant considers that he is likely to wish a hearing to be held or not;
      (iv) where applicable, the special circumstances which the appellant considers justify the Tribunal's accepting jurisdiction under rule 4(2) below; and
      (v) an address for service of notices and other documents on the appellant.

(3) Where an appeal is brought under section 48(1) of the Act in

relation to an information notice, the notice of appeal shall also contain a statement of any representations the appellant wishes to make as to why it might be necessary in the interests of justice for the appeal to be heard and determined otherwise than by the chairman sitting alone as provided by rule 18(2) below.

(4) A notice of appeal may include a request for an early hearing of the appeal and the reasons for that request.

Time limit for appealing

4. – (1) Subject to paragraph (2) below, a notice of appeal must be served on the Tribunal within 28 days of the date on which the notice relating to the disputed decision was served on or given to the appellant.

(2) The Tribunal may accept a notice of appeal served after the expiry of the period permitted by paragraph (1) above if it is of the opinion that, by reason of special circumstances, it is just and right to do so.

(3) A notice of appeal shall if sent by post in accordance with rule 27(1) below be treated as having been served on the date on which it is received for dispatch by the Post Office.

Acknowledgement of notice of appeal and notification to the Commissioner

5. – (1) Upon receipt of a notice of appeal, the proper officer shall send –
   (a) an acknowledgement of the service of a notice of appeal to the appellant, and
   (b) subject to paragraph (3) below, a copy of the notice of appeal to the Commissioner.

(2) An acknowledgement of service under paragraph (1)(a) above shall be accompanied by a statement of the Tribunal's powers to award costs against the appellant under rule 25 below.

(3) Paragraph (1)(b) above does not apply to a notice of appeal relating to an appeal under section 48(3) of the Act, but in such a case –
   (a) the proper officer shall send a copy of the notice of appeal to the Commissioner if the Tribunal is of the opinion that the interests of justice require the Commissioner to assist it by giving evidence or being heard on any matter relating to the appeal, and
   (b) where a copy is sent to the Commissioner under subparagraph (a) above, the jurisdiction referred to in paragraph 6(2) of Schedule 6 to the Act shall not be exercised ex parte.

Reply by Commissioner

6. – (1) The Commissioner shall take the steps specified in paragraph (2) below –
   (a) where he receives a copy of a notice of appeal under rule 5(1)(b) above, within 21 days of the date of that receipt, and
   (b) where he receives a copy of a notice of appeal under rule 5(3)(a) above, within such time, not exceeding 21 days from the date of that receipt, as the Tribunal may allow.

(2) The steps are that the Commissioner must–
   (a) send to the Tribunal a copy of the notice relating to the disputed decision, and
   (b) send to the Tribunal and the appellant a written reply acknowledging service upon him of the notice of appeal, and stating –
      (i) whether or not he intends to oppose the appeal and, if so,
      (ii) the grounds upon which he relies in opposing the appeal.

(3) Before the expiry of the period referred to in paragraph (1) above which is applicable to the case, the Commissioner may apply to the Tribunal for an extension of that period, showing cause why, by reason of special circumstances, it would be just and right to do so, and the Tribunal may grant such extension as it considers appropriate.

(4) Where the appellant's notice of appeal has stated that he is not likely to wish a hearing to be held, the Commissioner shall in his reply inform the Tribunal and the appellant whether he considers that a hearing is likely to be desirable.

(5) Where an appeal is brought under section 48(1) of the Act in relation to an information notice, the Commissioner may include in his reply a statement of representations as to why it might be necessary in the interests of justice for the appeal to be heard and determined otherwise than by the chairman sitting alone as provided by rule 18(2) below.

(6) A reply under this rule may include a request for an early hearing of the appeal and the reasons for that request.

Application for striking out

7. – (1) Subject to paragraph (3) below, where the Commissioner is of the opinion that an appeal does not lie to, or cannot be entertained by, the Tribunal, or that the notice of appeal discloses no reasonable grounds of appeal, he may include in his reply under rule 6(2) above a notice to that effect stating the grounds for such contention and applying for the appeal to be struck out.

(2) An application under this rule may be heard as a preliminary issue or at the beginning of the hearing of the substantive appeal.

(3) This rule does not apply in the case of an appeal under section 48(3) of the Act.

Amendment and supplementary grounds

8. – (1) With the leave of the Tribunal, the appellant may amend his notice of appeal or deliver supplementary grounds of appeal.

(2) Paragraphs (1) and (3) of rule 5 above apply to an amended notice of appeal and to supplementary grounds of appeal provided under paragraph (1) above as they do to a notice of appeal.

(3) Upon receipt of a copy of an amended notice of appeal or amended grounds of appeal under rule 5(1)(b) or (3)(a) above, the Commissioner may amend his reply to the notice of appeal, and must send the amended reply to the Tribunal and the appellant –
    (a) where he receives a copy of a notice of appeal under rule 5(1)(b) above, within 21 days of the date of that receipt, and
    (b) where he receives a copy of a notice of appeal under rule 5(3)(a) above, within such time, not exceeding 21 days from the date of that receipt, as the Tribunal may allow.

(4) Rule 6(3) above applies to the periods referred to in paragraph (3) above.

(5) Without prejudice to paragraph (3) above, the Commissioner may, with the leave of the Tribunal, amend his reply to the notice of appeal, and must send the amended reply to the Tribunal and the appellant.

Withdrawal of appeal

9. – (1) The appellant may at any time withdraw his appeal by sending to the Tribunal a notice of withdrawal signed by him or on his behalf, and the proper officer shall send a copy of that notice to the Commissioner.

(2) A notice of withdrawal shall if sent by post in accordance with rule 27(1) below have effect on the date on which it is received for dispatch by the Post Office.

(3) Where an appeal is withdrawn under this rule a fresh appeal may not be brought by the appellant in relation to the same disputed decision except with the leave of the Tribunal.

Consolidation of appeals

10. – (1) Subject to paragraph (2) below, where in the case of two or more appeals to which these Rules apply it appears to the Tribunal—
(a) that some common question of law or fact arises in both or all of them, or
(b) that for some other reason it is desirable to proceed with the appeals under this rule,
the Tribunal may order that the appeals be consolidated or heard together.

(2) The Tribunal shall not make an order under this rule without giving the parties an opportunity to show cause why such an order should not be made.

Directions

11. – (1) Subject to paragraphs (4) and (5) below, the Tribunal may at any time of its own motion or on the application of any party give such directions as it thinks proper to enable the parties to prepare for the hearing of the appeal or to assist the Tribunal to determine the issues.

(2) Such directions may in particular –
(a) provide for a particular matter to be dealt with as a preliminary issue and for a pre-hearing review to be held;
(b) provide for –
(i) the exchange between the parties of lists of documents held by them which are relevant to the appeal,
(ii) the inspection by the parties of the documents so listed,
(iii) the exchange between the parties of statements of evidence, and
(iv) the provision by the parties to the Tribunal of statements or lists of agreed matters;
(c) require any party to send to the Tribunal and to the other party –
(i) statements of facts and statements of the evidence which will be adduced, including such statements provided in a modified or edited form;
(ii) a skeleton argument which summarises the submissions which will be made and cites the authorities which will be relied upon, identifying any particular passages to be relied upon;

(iii) a chronology of events;

(iv) any other particulars or supplementary statements which may reasonably be required for the determination of the appeal;

(v) any document or other material which the Tribunal may require and which it is in the power of that party to deliver;

(vi) an estimate of the time which will be needed for any hearing; and

(vii) a list of the witnesses the party intends to call to give evidence at any hearing;

(d) limit the length of oral submissions and the time allowed for the examination and cross-examination of witnesses; and

(e) limit the number of expert witnesses to be heard on either side.

(3) The Tribunal may, subject to any specific provisions of these Rules, specify time limits for steps to be taken in the proceedings and may extend any time limit.

(4) Nothing in this rule may require the production of any document or other material which the party could not be compelled to produce on the trial of an action in a court of law in that part of the United Kingdom where the appeal is to be determined.

(5) It shall be a condition of the supply of any information or material provided under this rule that any recipient of that information or material may use it only for the purposes of the appeal.

(6) The power to give directions may be exercised in the absence of the parties.

(7) Notice of any directions given under this rule shall be served on the parties, and the Tribunal may, on the application of any party, set aside or vary such directions.

Power to require entry of premises for testing of equipment or material

12. – (1) Subject to paragraph (8) below, the Tribunal may, for the purpose of determining an appeal, make an order requiring the occupier of any premises ("the occupier") to permit the Tribunal to enter those premises at a specified time and inspect, examine, operate or test any equipment on those premises used or intended to be used in connection with the processing of personal data, and to inspect, examine or test any documents or other material on those premises connected with the processing of personal data.

(2) An order under paragraph (1) above shall also require the occupier to permit the Tribunal to be accompanied by –
    (a) the parties, and
    (b) such number of the officers or members of staff provided to the Tribunal under paragraph 14 of Schedule 5 to the Act as it considers necessary.

(3) The Tribunal shall serve a copy of the order on the occupier and the parties.

(4) The time specified in the order shall not be earlier than 7 days after the date of service of the copy.

(5) The Tribunal may upon the application of the occupier set the order aside.

(6) Subject to paragraph (4) above, the Tribunal may upon the application of any person mentioned in paragraph (3) above alter the time specified in the order without being obliged to serve further copies under that paragraph, but shall notify the other persons so mentioned of the revised time.

(7) This rule also applies where the occupier is a party to the appeal.

(8) Documents or other material which the appellant could not be compelled to produce on the trial of an action in that part of the United Kingdom where the appeal is to be determined shall be immune from inspection, examination or testing under this rule.

Power to determine without a hearing

13. – (1) Where either –
    (a) the parties so agree in writing, or
    (b) it appears to the Tribunal that the issues raised on the appeal have been determined on a previous appeal brought by the appellant on the basis of facts which did not materially differ from those to which the appeal relates and the Tribunal has given the parties an opportunity of making representations to the effect that the appeal ought not to be determined without a hearing,
the Tribunal may determine an appeal, or any particular issue, without a hearing.

(2) Before determining any matter under this rule, the Tribunal may if it thinks fit direct any party to provide in writing further information

about any matter relevant to the appeal within such time as the Tribunal may allow.

Time and place of hearings

14. – (1) Except where rule 13 above applies, as soon as practicable after notice of appeal has been given, and with due regard to the convenience of the parties and any request made under rule 3(4) or 6(6) above, the Tribunal shall appoint a time and place for a hearing of the appeal.

(2) The proper officer shall send to each party a notice informing him of the time and place of any hearing.

(3) The reference to a "party" in paragraph (2) above does not include the Commissioner in the case of an appeal under section 48(3) of the Act other than a case to which rule 5(3)(a) above applies.

(4) The time notified under paragraph (1) above shall not be earlier than 14 days after the date on which the notice is sent unless –
(a) the parties agree otherwise, or
(b) the appellant agrees otherwise, and the hearing relates to an appeal under section 48(3) of the Act.

(5) A notice to a party under this rule shall inform him of the effect of rule 17 below.

(6) The Tribunal may –
(a) postpone the time appointed for any hearing;
(b) adjourn a hearing to such time as the Tribunal may determine; or
(c) alter the place appointed for any hearing;
and, if it exercises any of the above powers, it shall notify each party previously notified of that hearing under this rule, and any person summoned under rule 15 below to attend as a witness at that hearing, of the revised arrangements.

Summoning of witnesses

15. – (1) Subject to paragraph (2) below, the Tribunal may by summons require any person in the United Kingdom to attend as a witness at a hearing of an appeal at such time and place as may be specified in the summons and, subject to rule 23(2) and (3) below, at the hearing to answer any questions or produce any documents in his custody or under his control which relate to any matter in question in the appeal.

(2) No person shall be required to attend in obedience to a summons under paragraph (1) above unless he has been given at least 7 days' notice of the hearing or, if less than 7 days, he has informed the Tribunal that he accepts such notice as he has been given.

(3) The Tribunal may upon the application of a person summoned under this rule set the summons aside.

(4) A person who has attended a hearing as a witness in obedience to a summons shall be entitled to such sum as the Tribunal considers reasonable in respect of his attendance at, and his travelling to and from, the hearing; and where the summons was issued at the request of a party such sum shall be paid or tendered to him by that party.

(5) In relation to proceedings before the Tribunal in Scotland, in this rule "summons" means citation and the provisions of this rule are to be construed accordingly.

Representation at a hearing

16. – (1) At any hearing by the Tribunal a party may conduct his case himself or may appear and be represented by any person whom he may appoint for the purpose.

(2) In this rule, references to a "party" do not include the Commissioner in the case of an appeal under section 48(3) of the Act other than a case to which rule 5(3)(a) above applies.

Default of appearance at hearing

17. If, without furnishing the Tribunal with sufficient reason for his absence, a party fails to appear at a hearing, having been duly notified of the hearing, the Tribunal may, if that party is the appellant, dismiss the appeal or, in any case, hear and determine the appeal, or any particular issue, in the party's absence and may make such order as to costs as it thinks fit.

Hearings and determinations in the case of appeals against an information notice

18. – (1) This rule applies to any appeal under section 48(1) of the Act in respect of an information notice.

(2) Subject to paragraph (3) below, any hearing of or relating to an appeal to which this rule applies shall be by the chairman sitting alone,

and any appeal or issue relating to an appeal to which this rule applies shall be determined by the chairman sitting alone.

(3) Paragraph (2) above does not apply where it appears to the chairman that a hearing or determination by the Tribunal constituted in accordance with paragraph 4 of Schedule 6 to the Act is necessary in the interests of justice, taking into account any representations made under rule 3(3) or 6(5) above.

Hearings in public or in private

19. – (1) All hearings by the Tribunal (including preliminary hearings) shall be in public unless, having regard to the desirability of safeguarding –
    (a) the privacy of data subjects or
    (b) commercially sensitive information,
the Tribunal directs that the hearing or any part of the hearing shall take place in private.

(2) Without prejudice to paragraph (3) below, the following persons, in addition to the parties, may attend a hearing notwithstanding that it is in private –
    (a) the chairman or any deputy chairman or member of the Tribunal in his capacity as such, notwithstanding that they do not constitute the Tribunal for the purpose of the hearing; and
    (b) any other person with the leave of the Tribunal and the consent of the parties present.

(3) Whether or not a hearing is held in public, a member of the Council on Tribunals or the Scottish Committee of the Council on Tribunals in his capacity as such may attend the hearing, and may remain present during the deliberations of the Tribunal but must not take part in the deliberations.

Conduct of proceedings at hearing

20. – (1) Subject to rule 17 above, the Tribunal shall at the hearing of an appeal give to each party an opportunity –
    (a) to address the Tribunal and to amplify orally written statements previously furnished under these Rules, to give evidence and to call witnesses, and to put questions to any person giving evidence before the Tribunal, and
    (b) to make representations on the evidence (if any) and on the subject matter of the appeal generally but, where evidence is taken, such opportunity shall not be given before the completion of the taking of evidence.

(2) Subject to paragraph (3) below, in this rule, references to a "party" do not include the Commissioner in the case of an appeal under section 48(3) of the Act.

(3) In a case to which rule 5(3)(a) above applies, the Tribunal shall give the Commissioner the opportunity referred to in paragraph (1) above to the extent that it is of the opinion that the interests of justice require the Commissioner to assist it by giving evidence or being heard on any matter relating to the appeal.

(4) Except as provided by these Rules, the Tribunal shall conduct the proceedings in such manner as it considers appropriate in the circumstances for discharging its functions and shall so far as appears to it appropriate seek to avoid formality in its proceedings.

Preliminary and incidental matters

21. As regards matters preliminary or incidental to an appeal the chairman may act for the Tribunal under rules 4(2), 6(1) and (3), 8 to 12, 14(1) and (6)(a) and (c) and 15.

Burden of proof

22. In any proceedings before the Tribunal relating to an appeal to which these Rules apply, other than an appeal under section 48(3) of the Act, it shall be for the Commissioner to satisfy the Tribunal that the disputed decision should be upheld.

Evidence

23. – (1) The Tribunal may receive in evidence any document or information notwithstanding that such document or information would be inadmissible in a court of law.

(2) No person shall be compelled to give any evidence or produce any document which he could not be compelled to give or produce on the trial of an action in a court of law in that part of the United Kingdom where the appeal is to be determined.

(3) The Tribunal may require oral evidence of a witness (including a party) to be given on oath or affirmation and for that purpose the chairman or the proper officer shall have power to administer oaths or take affirmations.

Determination of appeal

24. – (1) As soon as practicable after the Tribunal has determined an appeal, the chairman shall certify in writing that determination and sign and date the certificate.

(2) The certificate shall include –
    (a) any material finding of fact, and
    (b) the reasons for the decision.

(3) The proper officer shall send a copy of the certificate to the parties.

(4) The Tribunal shall make arrangements for the publication of its determination but in doing so shall have regard to the desirability of safeguarding the privacy of data subjects and commercially sensitive information, and for that purpose may make any necessary amendments to the text of the certificate.

Costs

25. – (1) In any appeal before the Tribunal, including one withdrawn under rule 9 above, the Tribunal may make an order awarding costs –
    (a) against the appellant and in favour of the Commissioner where it considers that the appeal was manifestly unreasonable;
    (b) against the Commissioner and in favour of the appellant where it considers that the disputed decision was manifestly unreasonable;
    (c) where it considers that a party has been responsible for frivolous, vexatious, improper or unreasonable action, or for any failure to comply with a direction or any delay which with diligence could have been avoided, against that party and in favour of the other.

(2) The Tribunal shall not make an order under paragraph (1) above awarding costs against a party without first giving that party an opportunity of making representations against the making of the order.

(3) An order under paragraph (1) above may be to the party or parties in question to pay to the other party or parties either a specified sum in respect of the costs incurred by that other party or parties in connection with the proceedings or the whole or part of such costs as taxed (if not otherwise agreed).

(4) Any costs required by an order under this rule to be taxed may be taxed in the county court according to such of the scales prescribed by

the county court rules for proceedings in the county court as shall be directed by the order.

(5) In relation to proceedings before the Tribunal in Scotland, for the purposes of the application of paragraph (4) above, for the reference to the county court and the county court rules there shall be substituted references to the sheriff court and the sheriff court rules and for the reference to proceedings there shall be substituted a reference to civil proceedings.

Irregularities

26. – (1) Any irregularity resulting from failure to comply with any provision of these Rules or of any direction of the Tribunal before the Tribunal has reached its decision shall not of itself render the proceedings void, but the Tribunal may, and shall if it considers that any person may have been prejudiced by that irregularity, give such directions or take such steps as it thinks fit before reaching its decision to cure or waive the irregularity, whether by amendment of any document, the giving of notice or otherwise.

(2) Clerical mistakes in any document recording or certifying a direction, decision or determination of the Tribunal or chairman, or errors arising in such a document from an accidental slip or omission, may at any time be corrected by the chairman, by certificate signed by him.

Notices etc

27. – (1) Any notice or other document required or authorised by these Rules to be served on or sent to any person or authority may be sent by post in a registered letter or by the recorded delivery service –
    (a) in the case of the Tribunal, to the proper officer of the Tribunal;
    (b) in the case of the Commissioner, to him at his office;
    (c) in the case of an appellant, to him at his address for service under these Rules; and
    (d) in the case of an occupier within the provisions of rule 12 above, to him at the premises in question.

(2) An appellant may at any time by notice to the Tribunal change his address for service under these Rules.

Mike O'Brien
Parliamentary Under-Secretary of State
Home Office
31st January 2000

EXPLANATORY NOTE
(This note is not part of the Rules)

These Rules, which have been prepared after consultation with the Council on Tribunals regulate the exercise of the rights of appeal against decisions of the Data Protection Commissioner conferred by section 48 of the Data Protection Act 1998 and the practice and procedure of the Data Protection Tribunal in such cases.

Rule 3 requires an appeal to be made by notice of appeal served on the Tribunal, stating the grounds of appeal and other specified particulars, with provision for including a request with reasons for an early hearing. An appeal against an information notice may also include representations against a hearing by the chairman or deputy sitting alone. The notice must, under rule 4, be served within 28 days of the date on which the Commissioner's decision was served on the appellant, but in special circumstances appeals may be accepted out of time. Rule 5 provides for acknowledgement of the notice of appeal, and for service of a copy on the Commissioner except in the case of certain appeals to be heard ex parte. Rule 6 provides for a reply by the Commissioner.

Rule 7 allows the Commissioner to apply for an appeal to be struck out in limited circumstances. Rule 8 provides for the parties to amend their pleadings, in some cases with leave only, and rule 9 makes provision in respect of the withdrawal of an appeal. Provision is made as to the consolidation of appeals (rule 10).

Rule 11 provides for the giving of directions by the Tribunal, of its own motion or on the application of a party; this power may be exercised in the absence of the parties, and any party may apply to set aside or vary directions. Provision is made by rule 12 for the ordering of persons in occupation of premises to permit entry for the testing of equipment or material connected with the processing of personal data.

The Tribunal must as a general rule proceed by way of a hearing but in certain circumstances it may determine an appeal without a hearing (rule 13). Provision is made as to the appointment of time and place of a hearing (rule 14), summoning of witnesses to attend a hearing (rule 15), representation at a hearing (rule 16) and default of appearance at a hearing (rule 17). Rule 18 makes provision for the constitution of the Tribunal for hearing certain appeals against an information notice.

Hearings by the Tribunal must generally be in public, but special provision is made for private hearings in limited circumstances (rule 19). The Rules include provision as to the conduct of proceedings at a hearing (rule 20), powers of the chairman to act for the Tribunal (rule 21), evidence (rule 23), the determination of appeals (rule 24) and costs (rule 25). In all proceedings other than those relating to the inclusion of a statement of urgency in a Commissioner's notice, the onus is placed on the Commissioner of satisfying the Tribunal that his decision should be upheld (rule 22).

These Rules contribute to the implementation of Directive 95/46/EC on the protection of individuals with regard to the processing of personal data and on the free movement of such data.

Data Protection (International Co-operation) Order 2000
SI 2000 No 190

Made	*31st January 2000*
Laid before Parliament	*7th February 2000*
Coming into force	*1st March 2000*

The Secretary of State, in exercise of the powers conferred upon him by sections 54(3) and 67(2) of the Data Protection Act 1998, and after consultation with the Data Protection Commissioner in accordance with section 67(3) of that Act, hereby makes the following Order:

Citation and commencement

1. This Order may be cited as the Data Protection (International Co-operation) Order 2000 and shall come into force on 1st March 2000.

Interpretation

2. In this Order:

"the Act" means the Data Protection Act 1998;

"supervisory authority" means a supervisory authority in an EEA State other than the United Kingdom for the purposes of the Data Protection Directive;

"transfer" means a transfer of personal data to a country or territory outside the European Economic Area.

Information relating to adequacy

3. – (1) Subject to paragraph (2), this article applies in any case where the Commissioner is satisfied that any transfer or proposed transfer by a data controller has involved or would involve a contravention of the eighth principle.

(2) In cases where an enforcement notice has been served in respect of a contravention of the eighth principle, this article shall not apply unless –

(a) the period within which an appeal can be brought under section 48(1) of the Act has expired without an appeal being brought; or

(b) where an appeal has been brought under section 48(1), either –
(i) the decision of the Tribunal is to the effect that there has been a breach of that eighth principle, or
(ii) where any decision of the Tribunal is to the effect that there has not been a breach of that eighth principle, the Commissioner has appealed successfully against that finding.

(3) In cases to which this article applies, the Commissioner shall inform the European Commission and the supervisory authorities of the reasons why he is satisfied that any transfer or proposed transfer has involved or would involve a contravention of the eighth principle.

(4) In this article, "the eighth principle" means the eighth principle set out in paragraph 8 of Part I of Schedule 1 to the Act, having regard to paragraphs 13, 14 and 15 of Part II of that Schedule.

Objections to authorisations

4. – (1) This article applies where –
(a) a transfer has been authorised by another Member State in purported compliance with Article 26(2) of the Data Protection Directive, and
(b) the Commissioner is satisfied that such authorisation is not in compliance with that Article.

(2) The Commissioner may inform the European Commission of the particulars of the authorisation together with the reasons for his view that the authorisation is not in compliance with Article 26(2) of the Directive.

Requests from supervisory authorities in relation to certain data controllers

5. – (1) This article applies in any case where a data controller is processing data in the United Kingdom –
(a) in circumstances other than those described in section 5(1) of the Act, and
(b) within the scope of the functions of a supervisory authority in another EEA State.

(2) The Commissioner may, at the request of a supervisory authority referred to in paragraph (1)(b), exercise his functions under Part V of

the Act in relation to the processing referred to in paragraph (1) as if the data controller were processing those data in the circumstances described in section 5(1)(a) of the Act.

(3) Where the Commissioner has received a request from a supervisory authority under paragraph (2), he shall –
  (a) in any case where he decides to exercise his functions under Part V of the Act, send to the supervisory authority as soon as reasonably practicable after exercising those functions such statement of the extent of the action that he has taken as he thinks fit; and
  (b) in any case where he decides not to exercise those functions, send to the supervisory authority as soon as reasonably practicable after making the decision the reasons for that decision.

Requests by Commissioner in relation to certain data controllers

6. – (1) This article applies in any case where a data controller is processing data in another EEA State in circumstances described in section 5(1) of the Act.

(2) The Commissioner may request the supervisory authority of the EEA State referred to in paragraph (1) to exercise the functions conferred on it by that EEA State pursuant to Article 28(3) of the Data Protection Directive in relation to the processing in question.

(3) Any request made under paragraph (2) must specify –

  (a) the name and address in the EEA State, in so far as they are known by the Commissioner, of the data controller; and
  (b) such details of the circumstances of the case as the Commissioner thinks fit to enable the supervisory authority to exercise those functions.

General exchange of information

7. The Commissioner may supply to the European Commission or any supervisory authority information to the extent to which, in the opinion of the Commissioner, the supply of that information is necessary for the performance of the data protection functions of the recipient.

Mike O'Brien
Parliamentary Under-Secretary of State
Home Office
31st January 2000

EXPLANATORY NOTE
(This note is not part of the Order)

Section 54(3) of the Data Protection Act 1998 provides that the Secretary of State may by Order make provision as to co-operation between the Data Protection Commissioner, the European Commission and other supervisory authorities in EEA States.

Article 3(3) of this Order obliges the Commissioner to give to the European Commission and supervisory authorities his reasons for being satisfied that a transfer or proposed transfer has involved or would involve a transfer to a country or territory outside the EEA which has inadequate protection for the rights and freedoms of data subjects in relation to the processing of personal data. Such a transfer would be a breach of the eighth data protection principle in Part I of Schedule 1 to the 1998 Act. Where another Member State or its supervisory authority has authorised a transfer to such a third country or territory, article 4 allows the Commissioner to inform the European Commission.

Article 5 of the Order extends the enforcement powers of the Commissioner under Part V of the Act so that they can be exercised in relation to certain data controllers who are processing data in the United Kingdom but to whom the Act does not apply by virtue of section 5 of the Act (which relates to jurisdiction). The powers can only be exercised by the Commissioner following a request from the supervisory authority of the EEA State the laws of which apply to the data controller. Article 6 allows the Commissioner to make similar requests for assistance where a data controller within the scope of the Commissioner's functions is processing data in another EEA State.

Article 7 permits the Commissioner to supply other information to the European Commission or supervisory authorities where that information is necessary for the discharge of their data protection functions.

This Order contributes to the implementation of Directive 95/46/EC on the protection of individuals with regard to the processing of personal data and on the free movement of such data.

A Regulatory Impact Assessment was prepared for the Data Protection Bill as it was then and the statutory instruments to be made under it, and was placed in the libraries of both Houses of Parliament. The Regulatory Impact Assessment is now available on the internet at *www.homeoffice.gov.uk*. Alternatively, copies can be obtained by post from the Home Office, LGDP Unit, 50 Queen Anne's Gate, London SW1H 9AT.

Data Protection (Subject Access) (Fees and Miscellaneous Provisions) Regulations 2000 SI 2000 No 191

Made	*31st January 2000*
Laid before Parliament	*7th February 2000*
Coming into force	*1st March 2000*

The Secretary of State, in exercise of the powers conferred on him by sections 7(2), (7), (8) and (11) (having regard to the definitions of "prescribed", "the prescribed maximum" and "the prescribed period" in section 7(10)), 8(1) and 67(2) of the Data Protection Act 1998 and having consulted the Data Protection Commissioner in accordance with Section 67(3) of that Act, hereby makes the following Regulations:

Citation, commencement and interpretation

1. – (1) These Regulations may be cited as the Data Protection (Subject Access) (Fees and Miscellaneous Provisions) Regulations 2000 and shall come into force on 1st March 2000.

(2) In these Regulations "the Act" means the Data Protection Act 1998.

Extent of subject access requests

2. – (1) A request for information under any provision of section 7(1)(a), (b) or (c) of the Act is to be treated as extending also to information under all other provisions of section 7(1)(a), (b) and (c).

(2) A request for information under any provision of section 7(1) of the Act is to be treated as extending to information under the provisions of section 7(1)(d) only where the request shows an express intention to that effect.

(3) A request for information under the provisions of section 7(1)(d) of the Act is to be treated as extending also to information under any other provision of section 7(1) only where the request shows an express intention to that effect.

Maximum subject access fee

3. Except as otherwise provided by regulations 4, 5 and 6 below, the maximum fee which may be required by a data controller under section 7(2)(b) of the Act is £10.

Limited requests for subject access where data controller is credit reference agency

4. – (1) In any case in which a request under section 7 of the Act has been made to a data controller who is a credit reference agency, and has been limited, or by virtue of section 9(2) of the Act is taken to have been limited, to personal data relevant to an individual's financial standing –

    (a) the maximum fee which may be required by a data controller under section 7(2)(b) of the Act is £2, and

    (b) the prescribed period for the purposes of section 7(8) of the Act is seven working days.

(2) In this regulation "working day" means any day other than –

    (a) Saturday or Sunday,

    (b) Christmas Day or Good Friday,

    (c) a bank holiday, within the meaning of section 1 of the Banking and Financial Dealings Act 1971, in the part of the United Kingdom in which the data controller's address is situated.

(3) For the purposes of paragraph (2)(c) above –

    (a) the address of a registered company is that of its registered office, and

    (b) the address of a person (other than a registered company) carrying on a business is that of his principal place of business in the United Kingdom.

Subject access requests in respect of educational records

5. – (1) This regulation applies to any case in which a request made under section 7 of the Act relates wholly or partly to personal data forming part of an accessible record which is an educational record within the meaning of Schedule 11 to the Act.

(2) Except as provided by paragraph (3) below, a data controller may not require a fee under section 7(2)(b) of the Act in any case to which this regulation applies.

(3) Where, in a case to which this regulation applies, the obligation imposed by section 7(1)(c)(i) of the Act is to be complied with by

supplying the data subject with a copy of information in permanent form, the maximum fee which may be required by a data controller under section 7(2)(b) of the Act is that applicable to the case under the Schedule to these Regulations.

(4) In any case to which this regulation applies, and in which the address of the data controller to whom the request is made is situated in England and Wales, the prescribed period for the purposes of section 7(8) of the Act is fifteen school days within the meaning of section 579(1) of the Education Act 1996.

Certain subject access requests in respect of health records – transitional provisions
6. – (1) This regulation applies only to cases in which a request made under section 7 of the Act –
    (a) relates wholly or partly to personal data forming part of an accessible record which is a health record within the meaning of section 68(2) of the Act,
    (b) does not relate exclusively to data within paragraphs (a) and (b) of the definition of "data" in section 1(1) of the Act, and
    (c) is made before 24th October 2001.

(2) Where in a case to which this regulation applies, the obligation imposed by section 7(1)(c)(i) of the Act is to be complied with by supplying the data subject with a copy of information in permanent form, the maximum fee which may be required by a data controller under section 7(2)(b) of the Act is £50.

(3) Except in a case to which paragraph (2) above applies, a data controller may not require a fee under section 7(2)(b) of the Act where, in a case to which this regulation applies, the request relates solely to personal data which –
    (a) form part of an accessible record –
        (i) which is a health record within the meaning of section 68(2) of the Act, and
        (ii) at least some of which was made after the beginning of the period of 40 days immediately preceding the date of the request; and
    (b) do not fall within paragraph (a) or (b) of the definition of "data" in section 1(1) of the Act.

(4) For the purposes of paragraph (3) above, an individual making a request in any case to which this regulation applies may specify that his request is limited to personal data of the description set out in that paragraph.

Mike O'Brien
Parliamentary Under-Secretary of State
Home Office
31st January 2000

SCHEDULE

MAXIMUM SUBJECT ACCESS FEES WHERE A COPY OF INFORMATION CONTAINED IN AN EDUCATIONAL RECORD IS SUPPLIED IN PERMANENT FORM

1. In any case in which the copy referred to in regulation 5(3) includes material in any form other than a record in writing on paper, the maximum fee applicable for the purposes of regulation 5(3) is £50.

2. In any case in which the copy referred to in regulation 5(3) consists solely of a record in writing on paper, the maximum fee applicable for the purposes of regulation 5(3) is set out in the table below.

number of pages of information comprising the copy	maximum fee
fewer than 20	£1
20–29	£2
30–39	£3
40–49	£4
50–59	£5
60–69	£6
70–79	£7
80–89	£8
90–99	£9
100–149	£10
150–199	£15
200–249	£20
250–299	£25
300–349	£30
350–399	£35
400–449	£40
450–499	£45
500 or more	£50

EXPLANATORY NOTE
(This note is not part of the Regulations)

These Regulations make miscellaneous provision in respect of the exercise of the right of access to personal data conferred in section 7 of the Data Protection Act 1998.

Regulation 2 provides that a request for access to information under any provision of section 7(1)(a) to (c) of the Act is to be treated as extending to all such information. But a request is not to be taken to extend to information about the logic of automated decision-taking under section 7(1)(d) unless an express intention appears, and where there is such an express intention, the request is to be treated as limited to that information unless an express contrary intention appears.

Regulation 3 provides that, except in the special cases set out in regulations 4, 5 and 6, the maximum fee which a data controller may charge for access to data under section 7(2) of the Act is £10.

The Regulations make special provision as to fees and time limits in relation to three particular types of subject access request:–

In respect of limited requests as provided in section 9 of the Act, where the data controller is a credit reference agency and a subject access request is limited to personal data relevant to the applicant's financial standing, the maximum fee which may be charged by the data controller for access is prescribed as £2, and the period within which a data controller must comply with the request is prescribed as seven working days rather than the forty day period which, by virtue of section 7(10) of the Act, otherwise applies (regulation 4).

In respect of subject access requests relating to accessible records which are educational records (as defined in section 68(1) of and Schedule 11 to the Act), no access fee may be charged unless a permanent copy of the information is to be provided, in which case the maximum fee which may be charged for access is as set out in the Schedule, and varies according to the type and volume of copies in question. The prescribed period for compliance with these requests is set at fifteen school days in England and Wales (regulation 5); otherwise, again, the forty day period in section 7(10) of the Act applies.

In respect of subject access requests relating to accessible records which are health records (as defined in section 68 of the Act), and which are not exclusively automated or intended for automation within the meaning of the first two paragraphs of the definition of "data" in section 1(1) of the Act, the Regulations make transitional provision in respect of certain requests made before 24th October 2001. Firstly, where a permanent copy of the information is to be provided, the maximum fee which may be charged by the data controller for access in the case of such requests is prescribed as £50. Secondly, where the request is restricted solely to data which form part of a health record, and that record has been at least partially created within the forty days preceding the request, and no permanent copy of the information is to be provided, no fee may be charged; provision is made for requests to be specifically limited to conform to these circumstances (regulation 6). This Order contributes to the implementation of Directive 95/46/EC on the protection of individuals with regard to the processing of personal data and on the free movement of such data.

A Regulatory Impact Assessment was prepared for the Data Protection Bill as it was then and the statutory instruments to be made under it, and was placed in the libraries of both Houses of Parliament. The Regulatory Impact Assessment is now available on the internet at *www.homeoffice.gov.uk*. Alternatively, copies can be obtained by post from the Home Office, LGDP Unit, 50 Queen Anne's Gate, London SW1H 9AT.

Data Protection Tribunal (National Security Appeals) Rules 2000 SI 2000 No 206

Made	*2nd February 2000*
Laid before Parliament	*8th February 2000*
Coming into force	*1st March 2000*

The Secretary of State, in exercise of the powers conferred on him by section 67(2) of, and paragraph 7 of Schedule 6 to, the Data Protection Act 1998, hereby makes the following Rules:

Citation and commencement

1.   These Rules may be cited as the Data Protection Tribunal (National Security Appeals) Rules 2000 and shall come into force on 1st March 2000.

Application and interpretation

2. – (1) These Rules apply to appeals under section 28 of the Act, and the provisions of these Rules are to be construed accordingly.

(2)   In these Rules, unless the context otherwise requires –

"the Act" means the Data Protection Act 1998;

"appeal" means an appeal under section 28 of the Act;

"appellant" means a person who brings or intends to bring an appeal under section 28 of the Act;

"costs" –
(a) except in Scotland, includes fees, charges, disbursements, expenses and remuneration;
(b) in Scotland means expenses, and includes fees, charges, disbursements and remuneration;

"disputed certification" means –
(a) in relation to an appeal under section 28(4) of the Act, the certificate against which the appeal is brought or intended to be brought, and

513

(b) in relation to an appeal under section 28(6) of the Act, the claim by the data controller, against which the appeal is brought or intended to be brought, that a certificate applies to any personal data;

"party" has the meaning given in paragraph (3) below;

"president" means the person designated by the Lord Chancellor under paragraph 3 of Schedule 6 to the Act to preside when the Tribunal is constituted under that paragraph;

"proper officer" in relation to a rule means an officer or member of staff provided to the Tribunal under paragraph 14 of Schedule 5 to the Act and appointed by the chairman to perform the duties of a proper officer under that rule;

"relevant Minister" means the Minister of the Crown who is responsible for the signing of the certificate under section 28(2) of the Act to which the appeal relates, and except where the context otherwise requires, references in these Rules to the relevant Minister include a person appointed under rule 21 below to represent his interests; and

"respondent data controller" in relation to an appeal under section 28(6) of the Act means the data controller making the claim which constitutes the disputed certification.

(3)   In these Rules, except where the context otherwise requires, "party" means the appellant or −
    (a) in relation to an appeal under section 28(4) of the Act, the relevant Minister, and
    (b) in relation to an appeal under section 28(6) of the Act, the respondent data controller,
and, except where the context otherwise requires, references in these Rules to a party or to any such party include a person appointed under rule 21 below to represent his interests.

(4)   In relation to proceedings before the Tribunal in Scotland, for the words "on the trial of an action" in rules 15(6) and 26(2) below there is substituted "in a proof".

Constitution and general duty of the Tribunal

3. − (1) When exercising its functions under these Rules, the Tribunal shall secure that information is not disclosed contrary to the interests of national security.

(2)   Paragraph 6(1) of Schedule 6 to the Act applies only to the exercise of the jurisdiction of the Tribunal in accordance with rule 11 below.

(3)   For the purposes of paragraph (1) above, but without prejudice to the application of that paragraph, the disclosure of information is to be regarded as contrary to the interests of national security if it would indicate the existence or otherwise of any material.

Method of appealing

4. – (1) An appeal must be brought by a written notice of appeal served on the Tribunal.

(2)   The notice of appeal shall –
    (a) identify the disputed certification; and
    (b) state –
      (i)   the name and address of the appellant;
      (ii) the grounds of the appeal; and
      (iii) an address for service of notices and other documents on the appellant.

(3)   In the case of an appeal under section 28(6) of the Act, the notice of appeal shall also state –
    (a) the date on which the respondent data controller made the claim constituting the disputed certification;
    (b) an address for service of notices and other documents on the respondent data controller; and
    (c) where applicable, the special circumstances which the appellant considers justify the Tribunal's accepting jurisdiction under rule 5(3) below.

Time limit for appealing

5. – (1) In the case of an appeal under section 28(4) of the Act, a notice of appeal may be served on the Tribunal at any time during the currency of the disputed certification to which it relates.

(2)   In the case of an appeal under section 28(6) of the Act, subject to paragraph (3) below, a notice of appeal must be served on the Tribunal within 28 days of the date on which the claim constituting the disputed certification was made.

(3) The Tribunal may accept a notice of appeal served after the expiry of the period permitted by paragraph (2) above if it is of the opinion that, by reason of special circumstances, it is just and right to do so.

(4) A notice of appeal shall if sent by post in accordance with rule 30(1) below be treated as having been served on the date on which it is received for dispatch by the Post Office.

Acknowledgment of notice of appeal and notification by the Tribunal

6. – (1) Upon receipt of a notice of appeal, the proper officer shall send–
   (a) an acknowledgment of the service of a notice of appeal to the appellant, and
   (b) a copy of the notice of appeal to –
      (i) the relevant Minister,
      (ii) the Commissioner, and
      (iii) in the case of an appeal under section 28(6) of the Act, the respondent data controller.

(2) An acknowledgment of service under paragraph (1)(a) above shall be accompanied by a statement of the Tribunal's powers to award costs against the appellant under rule 28 below.

Relevant Minister's notice in reply

7. – (1) No later than 42 days after receipt of a copy of a notice of appeal under rule 6(1)(b) above, the relevant Minister shall send to the Tribunal –
   (a) a copy of the certificate to which the appeal relates, and
   (b) a written notice in accordance with paragraph (2) below.

(2) The notice shall state –
   (a) with regard to an appeal under section 28(4) of the Act, whether or not he intends to oppose the appeal and, if so –
      (i) a summary of the circumstances relating to the issue of the certificate, and the reasons for the issue of the certificate;
      (ii) the grounds upon which he relies in opposing the appeal; and
      (iii) a statement of the evidence upon which he relies in support of those grounds; and
   (b) with regard to an appeal under section 28(6) of the Act, whether or not he wishes to make representations in relation to the appeal and, if so –
      (i) the extent to which he intends to support or oppose the appeal;

(ii) the grounds upon which he relies in supporting or opposing the appeal; and

(iii) a statement of the evidence upon which he relies in support of those grounds.

(3) Except where the Tribunal proposes to determine the appeal in accordance with rule 11 below, and subject to rule 12 below, the proper officer shall send a copy of the notice to –

(a) the appellant,

(b) the Commissioner, and

(c) in the case of an appeal under section 28(6) of the Act, the respondent data controller.

Reply by respondent data controller

8. – (1) A respondent data controller shall, within 42 days of the date on which he receives a copy of a notice of appeal under rule 6(1)(b) above, send to the Tribunal a written reply acknowledging service upon him of the notice of appeal, and stating –

(a) whether or not he intends to oppose the appeal and, if so,

(b) the grounds upon which he relies in opposing the appeal.

(2) Before the expiry of the period of 42 days referred to in paragraph (1) above, the respondent data controller may apply to the Tribunal for an extension of that period, showing cause why, by reason of special circumstances, it would be just and right to do so, and the Tribunal may grant such extension as it considers appropriate.

(3) Except where the Tribunal proposes to determine the appeal in accordance with rule 11 below, the proper officer shall send a copy of the reply to –

(a) the relevant Minister; and

(b) subject to paragraph (4) and rule 12 below, the appellant and the Commissioner.

(4) No copy may be sent under paragraph (3)(b) above before the period of 42 days referred to in 12(2)(b) below has expired, otherwise than in accordance with rule 12, unless the relevant Minister has indicated that he does not object.

Amendment and supplementary grounds

9. – (1) With the leave of the Tribunal, the appellant may amend his notice of appeal or deliver supplementary grounds of appeal.

(2) Rule 6(1) above and rule 11(1)(a) below apply to an amended notice of appeal and to supplementary grounds of appeal provided under paragraph (1) above as they do to a notice of appeal.

(3) Upon receipt of a copy of an amended notice of appeal or amended grounds of appeal under rule 6(1) above, the relevant Minister may amend his notice in reply and, in the case of an appeal under section 28(6) of the Act, the respondent data controller may amend his reply to the notice of appeal.

(4) An amended notice or reply under paragraph (3) above must be sent to the Tribunal within 28 days of the date on which the copy referred to in that paragraph is received.

(5) Without prejudice to paragraph (3) above, and with the leave of the Tribunal —
    (a) the relevant Minister may amend a notice in reply, and
    (b) the respondent data controller may amend a reply to the notice of appeal.

(6) Rule 7(3) above and rules 11(1)(b) and 12(1)(a) below apply to an amended notice in reply by the relevant Minister provided under paragraph (3) or (5) above as they do to a notice in reply.

(7) Rule 8(3) and (4) above and rules 11(1)(c) and 12(1)(b) below apply to an amended reply by the respondent data controller provided under paragraph (3) or (5) above as they do to a reply.

Application for striking out

10. — (1) Where the relevant Minister or, in the case of an appeal under section 28(6) of the Act, the respondent data controller is of the opinion that an appeal does not lie to, or cannot be entertained by, the Tribunal, or that the notice of appeal discloses no reasonable grounds of appeal, he may include in his notice under rule 7 or, as the case may be, his reply under rule 8 above a notice to that effect stating the grounds for such contention and applying for the appeal to be struck out.

(2) An application under this rule may be heard as a preliminary issue or at the beginning of the hearing of the substantive appeal.

Summary disposal of appeals

11. — (1) Where, having considered —
    (a) the notice of appeal,

(b) the relevant Minister's notice in reply and,

(c) in the case of an appeal under section 28(6) of the Act, the respondent data controller's reply,

the Tribunal is of the opinion that the appeal is of such a nature that it can properly be determined by dismissing it forthwith, it may, subject to the provisions of this rule, so determine the appeal.

(2) Where the Tribunal proposes to determine an appeal under paragraph (1) above, it must first notify the appellant and the relevant Minister of the proposal.

(3) A notification to the appellant under paragraph (2) above must contain particulars of the appellant's entitlements set out in paragraph (4) below.

(4) An appellant notified in accordance with paragraph (2) above is entitled, within such time as the Tribunal may reasonably allow –

(a) to make written representations, and

(b) to request the Tribunal to hear oral representations

against the proposal to determine the appeal under paragraph (1) above.

(5) Where an appellant requests a hearing under paragraph (4)(b) above, the Tribunal shall, as soon as practicable and with due regard to the convenience of the appellant, appoint a time and place for a hearing accordingly.

(6) The proper officer shall send to the appellant a notice informing him of –

(a) the time and place of any hearing under paragraph (5) above, which, unless the appellant otherwise agrees, shall not be earlier than 14 days after the date on which the notice is sent, and

(b) the effect of rule 22 below.

(7) The Tribunal must as soon as practicable notify the appellant and the relevant Minister if, having given a notification under paragraph (2) above, it ceases to propose to determine the appeal under paragraph (1) above.

Relevant Minister's objection to disclosure

12. – (1) Where the relevant Minister objects, on grounds of the need to secure that information is not disclosed contrary to the interests of national security, to the disclosure of –

(a)   his notice in reply to the appellant, the Commissioner or, in the case of an appeal under section 28(6) of the Act, the respondent

data controller; or
(b)   the reply of a respondent data controller to the appellant or the Commissioner,
he may send a notice of objection to the Tribunal.

(2)   A notice of objection under paragraph (1) above must be sent –
(a)   where paragraph (1)(a) above applies, with the notice in reply; and
(b)   where paragraph (1)(b) above applies, within 42 days of the date on which he receives the copy mentioned in rule 8(3) above.

(3)   A notice of objection under paragraph (1) above shall –
(a)   state the reasons for the objection; and
(b)   where paragraph (1)(a) above applies, if and to the extent it is possible to do so without disclosing information contrary to the interests of national security, be accompanied by a version of the relevant Minister's notice in a form which can be shown to the appellant, the Commissioner or, as the case may be, the respondent data controller.

(4)   Where the relevant Minister sends a notice of objection under paragraph (1) above, the Tribunal must not disclose the material in question otherwise than in accordance with rule 17 below.

Withdrawal of appeal

13. – (1) The appellant may at any time withdraw his appeal by sending to the Tribunal a notice of withdrawal signed by him or on his behalf, and the proper officer shall send a copy of that notice to –
(a)   the relevant Minister,
(b)   the Commissioner, and
(c)   in the case of an appeal under section 28(6) of the Act, the respondent data controller.

(2)   A notice of withdrawal shall if sent by post in accordance with rule 30(1) below have effect on the date on which it is received for dispatch by the Post Office.

(3)   Where an appeal is withdrawn under this rule a fresh appeal may not be brought by the same appellant in relation to the same disputed certification except with the leave of the Tribunal.

Consolidation of appeals

14. – (1) Subject to paragraph (2) below, where in the case of two or

more appeals to which these Rules apply it appears to the Tribunal –
  (a) that some common question of law or fact arises in both or all of them, or
  (b) that for some other reason it is desirable to proceed with the appeals under this rule,
the Tribunal may order that the appeals be consolidated or heard together.

(2) The Tribunal shall not make an order under this rule without giving the parties and the relevant Minister an opportunity to show cause why such an order should not be made.

Directions

15. – (1) This rule is subject to rule 16 below.

(2) In this rule, references to a "party" include the relevant Minister notwithstanding that he may not be a party to an appeal under section 28(6) of the Act.

(3) Subject to paragraphs (6) and (7) below, the Tribunal may at any time of its own motion or on the application of any party give such directions as it thinks proper to enable the parties to prepare for the hearing of the appeal or to assist the Tribunal to determine the issues.

(4) Such directions may in particular –
  (a) provide for a particular matter to be dealt with as a preliminary issue and for a pre-hearing review to be held;
  (b) provide for –
    (i) the exchange between the parties of lists of documents held by them which are relevant to the appeal,
    (ii) the inspection by the parties of the documents so listed,
    (iii) the exchange between the parties of statements of evidence, and
    (iv) the provision by the parties to the Tribunal of statements or lists of agreed matters;
  (c) require any party to send to the Tribunal and to the other parties –
    (i) statements of facts and statements of the evidence which will be adduced, including such statements provided in a modified or edited form;
    (ii) a skeleton argument which summarises the submissions which will be made and cites the authorities which will be relied upon, identifying any particular passages to be relied upon;

(iii) a chronology of events;

(iv) any other particulars or supplementary statements which may reasonably be required for the determination of the appeal;

(v) any document or other material which the Tribunal may require and which it is in the power of that party to deliver;

(vi) an estimate of the time which will be needed for any hearing; and

(vii) a list of the witnesses he intends to call to give evidence at any hearing;

(d) limit the length of oral submissions and the time allowed for the examination and cross-examination of witnesses; and

(e) limit the number of expert witnesses to be heard on either side.

(5)   The Tribunal may, subject to any specific provisions of these Rules, specify time limits for steps to be taken in the proceedings and may extend any time limit.

(6)   Nothing in this rule may require the production of any document or other material which the party could not be compelled to produce on the trial of an action in a court of law in that part of the United Kingdom where the appeal is to be determined.

(7)   It shall be a condition of the supply of any information or material provided under this rule that any recipient of that information or material may use it only for the purposes of the appeal.

(8)   The power to give directions may be exercised in the absence of the parties.

(9)   Notice of any directions given under this rule shall be served on all the parties, and the Tribunal may, on the application of any party, set aside or vary such directions.

Applications by relevant Minister

16. – (1) This rule applies in any case where the Tribunal proposes to –

(a) give or vary any direction under rule 15 above or rule 18(2) below,

(b) issue a summons under rule 20 below, or

(c) certify or publish a determination under rule 27 below.

(2)   Before the Tribunal proceeds as proposed in any case to which this rule applies, it must first notify the relevant Minister of the proposal.

(3)   If the relevant Minister considers that proceeding as proposed by

the Tribunal would cause information to be disclosed contrary to the interests of national security, he may make an application to the Tribunal requesting it to reconsider the proposal or reconsider it to any extent.

(4) An application by the relevant Minister under paragraph (3) above must be made within 14 days of receipt of notification under paragraph (2), and the Tribunal must not proceed as proposed in any case to which this rule applies before that period has expired, otherwise than in accordance with rule 17 below, unless the relevant Minister has indicated that he does not object.

(5) Where the relevant Minister makes an application under this rule, the Tribunal must not proceed as proposed otherwise than in accordance with rule 17 below.

Determinations on relevant Minister's objections and applications

17. — (1) Except where rule 11 above applies, the Tribunal shall determine whether to uphold any objection of the relevant Minister under rule 12 above, and any application under rule 16 above, in accordance with this rule.

(2) Subject to paragraph (3) below, proceedings under this rule shall take place in the absence of the parties.

(3) The relevant Minister (or a person authorised to act on his behalf) may attend any proceedings under this rule, whether or not he is a party to the appeal in question.

(4) An objection under rule 12 above must be considered under this rule as a preliminary issue, and an application under rule 16 above may be considered as a preliminary issue or at the hearing of the substantive appeal.

(5) Where, in the case of an objection under rule 12 above, the Tribunal is minded to overrule the relevant Minister's objection, or to require him to provide a version of his notice in a form other than that in which he provided it under rule 12(3)(b) above, the Tribunal must invite the relevant Minister to make oral representations.

(6) Where the Tribunal under paragraph (5) above overrules an objection by the relevant Minister under rule 12 above, or requires him to provide a version of his notice in a form other than that in which he provided it under rule 12(3)(b) above, the Tribunal shall not

disclose, and the relevant Minister shall not be required to disclose, any material which was the subject of the unsuccessful objection if the relevant Minister chooses not to rely upon it in opposing the appeal.

(7) Where, in the case of an objection under rule 12 above, the Tribunal upholds the relevant Minister's objection and either –

(a) approves the version of his notice provided under rule 12(3)(b) or

(b) requires him to provide a version of his notice in a form other than that in which he provided it under rule 12(3)(b),

rule 7(3) above applies to that version of the notice.

Power to determine without a hearing

18. – (1) Without prejudice to rule 11 above, where either –

(a) the parties so agree in writing, or

(b) it appears to the Tribunal that the issues raised on the appeal have been determined on a previous appeal brought by the appellant on the basis of facts which did not materially differ from those to which the appeal relates and the Tribunal has given the parties an opportunity of making representations to the effect that the appeal ought not to be determined without a hearing,

the Tribunal may determine an appeal, or any particular issue, without a hearing.

(2) Before determining any matter under this rule, the Tribunal may, subject to rule 16 above, if it thinks fit direct any party to provide in writing further information about any matter relevant to the appeal within such time as the Tribunal may allow.

Time and place of hearings

19. – (1) Except where rule 11 or 18 above applies, as soon as practicable after notice of appeal has been given, and with due regard to the convenience of the parties, the Tribunal shall appoint a time and place for a hearing of the appeal.

(2) Except in relation to a hearing under rule 11(5) above, the proper officer shall send to each party, the Commissioner and the relevant Minister a notice informing him of the time and place of any hearing, which, unless the parties otherwise agree, shall not be earlier than 14 days after the date on which the notice is sent.

(3) A notice to a party under this rule shall inform him of the effect of rule 22 below.

(4) The Tribunal may –
  (a) postpone the time appointed for any hearing;
  (b) adjourn a hearing to such time as the Tribunal may determine; or
  (c) alter the place appointed for any hearing;
and, if it exercises any of the above powers, it shall notify each person previously notified of that hearing under this rule or rule 11(6) above, and any person summoned under rule 20 below to attend as a witness at that hearing, of the revised arrangements.

Summoning of witnesses

20. – (1) This rule is subject to rule 16 above.

(2) Subject to paragraph (3) below, the Tribunal may by summons require any person in the United Kingdom to attend as a witness at a hearing of an appeal at such time and place as may be specified in the summons and, subject to rule 26(2) and (3) below, at the hearing to answer any questions or produce any documents in his custody or under his control which relate to any matter in question in the appeal.

(3) No person shall be required to attend in obedience to a summons under paragraph (2) above unless he has been given at least 7 days' notice of the hearing or, if less than 7 days, he has informed the Tribunal that he accepts such notice as he has been given.

(4) The Tribunal may upon the application of a person summoned under this rule set the summons aside.

(5) A person who has attended a hearing as a witness in obedience to a summons shall be entitled to such sum as the Tribunal considers reasonable in respect of his attendance at, and his travelling to and from, the hearing; and where the summons was issued at the request of a party such sum shall be paid or tendered to him by that party.

(6) In relation to proceedings before the Tribunal in Scotland, in this rule "summons" means citation and the provisions of this rule are to be construed accordingly.

Representation at a hearing

21. – (1) At any hearing by the Tribunal, other than a hearing under rule 11 above –
  (a) a party may, subject to rules 17(2) above and 23(3) below, conduct his case himself or may appear and be represented by

any person whom he may appoint for the purpose, and

(b) the relevant Minister may appear and be represented by any person whom he may appoint for the purpose.

(2) At any hearing by the Tribunal under rule 11(5) above, the appellant may conduct his case himself or may appear and be represented by any person whom he may appoint for the purpose.

Default of appearance at hearing

22. If, without furnishing the Tribunal with sufficient reason for his absence, a party fails to appear at a hearing, having been duly notified of the hearing, the Tribunal may, if that party is the appellant, dismiss the appeal or, in any case, hear and determine the appeal, or any particular issue, in the party's absence and may make such order as to costs as it thinks fit.

Hearings to be in private

23. – (1) All hearings by the Tribunal (including preliminary hearings) shall be in private unless the Tribunal, with the consent of the parties and the relevant Minister, directs that the hearing or any part of the hearing shall take place in public.

(2) Where the Tribunal sits in private it may, with the consent of the parties and the relevant Minister, admit to a hearing such persons on such terms and conditions as it considers appropriate.

(3) Where the Tribunal considers it necessary for any party other than the relevant Minister to be excluded from proceedings or any part of them in order to secure that information is not disclosed contrary to the interests of national security, it must –

(a) direct accordingly,

(b) inform the person excluded of its reasons, to the extent that it is possible to do so without disclosing information contrary to the interests of national security, and record those reasons in writing, and

(c) inform the relevant Minister.

(4) The relevant Minister, or a person authorised to act on his behalf, may attend any hearing, other than a hearing under rule 11 above, notwithstanding that it is in private.

Conduct of proceedings at hearing

24. – (1) Subject to rules 22 and 23(3) above, the Tribunal shall at the

of an appeal give to each party and the relevant Minister an
.unity –

(a) to address the Tribunal and to amplify orally written statements
previously furnished under these Rules, to give evidence and to
call witnesses, and to put questions to any person giving evidence
before the Tribunal, and

(b) to make representations on the evidence (if any) and on the
subject matter of the appeal generally but, where evidence is taken,
such opportunity shall not be given before the completion of the
taking of evidence.

(2) Except as provided by these Rules, the Tribunal shall conduct the
proceedings in such manner as it considers appropriate in the
circumstances for discharging its functions and shall so far as appears to
it appropriate seek to avoid formality in its proceedings.

Preliminary and incidental matters

25. As regards matters preliminary or incidental to an appeal the
president may act for the Tribunal under rules 5(3), 8(2), 9, 13 to 15,
19(1) and (4)(a) and (c) and 20.

Evidence

26. – (1) The Tribunal may receive in evidence any document or
information notwithstanding that such document or information would
be inadmissible in a court of law.

(2) No person shall be compelled to give any evidence or produce
any document which he could not be compelled to give or produce
on the trial of an action in a court of law in that part of the United
Kingdom where the appeal is to be determined.

(3) The Tribunal may require oral evidence of a witness (including a
party) to be given on oath or affirmation and for that purpose the
president or the proper officer shall have power to administer oaths or
take affirmations.

Determination of appeal

27. – (1) As soon as practicable after the Tribunal has determined an
appeal, the president shall certify in writing that determination and
sign and date the certificate.

(2) If and to the extent that it is possible to do so without disclosing

information contrary to the interests of national security, and subject to rule 16 above, the certificate shall include –
  (a) any material finding of fact, and
  (b) the reasons for the decision.

(3) The proper officer shall send a copy of the certificate to –
  (a) the parties,
  (b) the relevant Minister, and
  (c) the Commissioner.

(4) Subject to rule 16 above, the Tribunal shall make arrangements for the publication of its determination but in doing so shall have regard to –
  (a) the desirability of safeguarding the privacy of data subjects and commercially sensitive information, and
  (b) the need to secure that information is not disclosed contrary to the interests of national security,
and for those purposes may make any necessary amendments to the text of the certificate.

(5) For the purposes of this rule (but without prejudice to its generality), the disclosure of information is to be regarded as contrary to the interests of national security if it would indicate the existence or otherwise of any material.

Costs

28. – (1) In any appeal before the Tribunal, including one withdrawn under rule 13 above, the Tribunal may make an order awarding costs –
  (a) in the case of an appeal under section 28(4) of the Act –
    (i) against the appellant and in favour of the relevant Minister where it considers that the appeal was manifestly unreasonable;
    (ii) against the relevant Minister and in favour of the appellant where it allows the appeal and quashes the disputed certification, or does so to any extent;
  (b) in the case of an appeal under section 28(6) of the Act –
    (i) against the appellant and in favour of any other party where it dismisses the appeal or dismisses it to any extent;
    (ii) in favour of the appellant and against any other party where it allows the appeal or allows it to any extent; and
  (c) where it considers that a party has been responsible for frivolous, vexatious, improper or unreasonable action, or for any failure to comply with a direction or any delay which with diligence could have been avoided, against that party and in favour of the other.

(2) The Tribunal shall not make an order under paragraph (1) above awarding costs against a party without first giving that party an opportunity of making representations against the making of the order.

(3) An order under paragraph (1) above may be to the party or parties in question to pay to the other party or parties either a specified sum in respect of the costs incurred by that other party or parties in connection with the proceedings or the whole or part of such costs as taxed (if not otherwise agreed).

(4) Any costs required by an order under this rule to be taxed may be taxed in the county court according to such of the scales prescribed by the county court rules for proceedings in the county court as shall be directed by the order.

(5) In relation to proceedings before the Tribunal in Scotland, for the purpose of the application of paragraph (4) above, for the reference to the county court and the county court rules there shall be substituted references to the sheriff court and the sheriff court rules and for the reference to proceedings there shall be substituted a reference to civil proceedings.

Irregularities

29. – (1) Any irregularity resulting from failure to comply with any provision of these Rules or of any direction of the Tribunal before the Tribunal has reached its decision shall not of itself render the proceedings void, but the Tribunal may, and shall if it considers that any person may have been prejudiced by that irregularity, give such directions or take such steps as it thinks fit before reaching its decision to cure or waive the irregularity, whether by amendment of any document, the giving of notice or otherwise.

(2) Clerical mistakes in any document recording or certifying a direction, decision or determination of the Tribunal or president, or errors arising in such a document from an accidental slip or omission, may at any time be corrected by the president by certificate signed by him.

Notices etc

30. – (1) Any notice or other document required or authorised by these Rules to be served on or sent to any person or authority may be sent by post in a registered letter or by the recorded delivery service –
    (a) in the case of the Tribunal, to the proper officer of the Tribunal;

(b) in the case of an appellant or a respondent data controller, to him at his address for service under these Rules;

(c) in the case of the relevant Minister or the Commissioner, to him at his office.

(2) An appellant or respondent data controller may at any time by notice to the Tribunal change his address for service under these Rules.

Mike O'Brien
Parliamentary Under-Secretary of State
Home Office
2nd February 2000

EXPLANATORY NOTE
(This note is not part of the Rules)

These Rules regulate the exercise of the rights of appeal conferred by section 28 of the Data Protection Act 1998 (relating to Ministerial certification that exemption from provisions of the Act is or was required for the purpose of safeguarding national security), and the practice and procedure of the Data Protection Tribunal in such cases.

Rule 3 places a general duty on the Tribunal in such cases to secure that information is not disclosed contrary to the interests of national security, and limits the ex parte jurisdiction of the Tribunal to matters concerning the summary disposal of appeals under rule 11.

Rule 4 requires an appeal to be made by notice of appeal served on the Tribunal, stating the grounds of appeal and other specified particulars, and rule 5 makes provision as to the time limits for appealing. Rule 6 provides for acknowledgment of the notice of appeal, and for service of copies. Rule 7 provides for a notice in reply by the Minister who signed the certificate, and rule 8 for a reply by the data controller in section 28(6) cases who is claiming the application of a certificate. Rule 9 provides for the parties to amend their pleadings, in some cases with leave only. Rule 10 allows the Minister or the data controller to apply for an appeal to be struck out in limited circumstances.

Rule 11 enables the Tribunal to dismiss an appeal on the basis of consideration of the notice of appeal, the Minister's notice, and any reply by a data controller, where it considers it proper to do so, but it must first allow the appellant to make representations, written and oral, against a proposal to deal with the appeal under this procedure.

Rule 12 permits the Minister to object, on national security grounds, to the disclosure of his notice in reply, or any data controller's reply, to a party (or the Data Protection Commissioner). Where he does so, he must give reasons and if possible supply a version of the notice which can be disclosed, and the procedure set out in rule 17 applies to the objection.

Rules 13 and 14 make provision in respect of the withdrawal of an appeal and the consolidation of appeals. Rule 15 provides for the giving of directions by the Tribunal, of its own motion or on the application of a party; this power may be exercised in the absence of the parties, and any party may apply to set aside or vary directions.

Rule 16 provides for the Minister to be able to apply, on national security grounds, for the Tribunal to reconsider proposals to exercise certain of its powers (including giving directions, issuing a witness summons or publishing a determination). The procedure in rule 17 applies to such an application.

Rule 17 provides for the Tribunal to adjudicate on objections and applications of the Minister made on national security grounds.

Other than in cases to which rule 11 applies, the Tribunal must as a general rule proceed by way of a hearing but in certain additional circumstances it may determine an appeal without a hearing (rule 18). Provision is made as to the appointment of time and place of a hearing (rule 19), summoning of witnesses to attend a hearing (rule 20), representation at a hearing (rule 21) and default of appearance at a hearing (rule 22).

Hearings by the Tribunal must generally be in private, but provision is made for public hearings, and the admission of other persons, in limited circumstances (rule 23). The Rules include provision as to the conduct of proceedings at a hearing (rule 24), powers of the president to act for the Tribunal (rule 25), evidence (rule 26), the determination of appeals (rule 27) and costs (rule 28).

These Rules contribute to the implementation of Directive 95/46/EC on the protection of individuals with regard to the processing of personal data and on the free movement of such data.

Crown Copyright material reproduced with the permission of the Controller of Her Majesty's Stationery Office.

Data Protection (Subject Access Modification) (Health) Order 2000
SI 2000 No 413

Made	*17th February 2000*
Coming into force	*1st March 2000*

Whereas a draft of this Order has been laid before and approved by a resolution of each House of Parliament:

Now, therefore, the Secretary of State, in exercise of the powers conferred on him by sections 30(1) and (4) and 67(2) of the Data Protection Act 1998 and after consultation with the Data Protection Commissioner in accordance with section 67(3) of that Act, hereby makes the following Order:

Citation and commencement

1. This Order may be cited as the Data Protection (Subject Access Modification) (Health) Order 2000 and shall come into force on 1st March 2000.

Interpretation

2. In this Order –

"the Act" means the Data Protection Act 1998;

"the appropriate health professional" means –
(a) the health professional who is currently or was most recently responsible for the clinical care of the data subject in connection with the matters to which the information which is the subject of the request relates; or
(b) where there is more than one such health professional, the health professional who is the most suitable to advise on the matters to which the information which is the subject of the request relates; or
(c) where –
(i) there is no health professional available falling within paragraph (a) or (b), or
(ii) the data controller is the Secretary of State and data to which this Order applies are processed in connection with the exercise of the functions conferred on him by or under

the Child Support Act 1991 and the Child Support Act 1995 or his functions in relation to social security or war pensions,

a health professional who has the necessary experience and qualifications to advise on the matters to which the information which is the subject of the request relates;

"care" includes examination, investigation, diagnosis and treatment;

"request" means a request made under section 7;

"section 7" means section 7 of the Act; and

"war pension" has the same meaning as in section 25 of the Social Security Act 1989 (establishment and functions of war pensions committees).

Personal data to which Order applies

3. – (1) Subject to paragraph (2), this Order applies to personal data consisting of information as to the physical or mental health or condition of the data subject.

(2) This Order does not apply to any data which are exempted from section 7 by an order made under section 38(1) of the Act.

Exemption from the subject information provisions

4. – (1) Personal data falling within paragraph (2) and to which this Order applies are exempt from the subject information provisions.

(2) This paragraph applies to personal data processed by a court and consisting of information supplied in a report or other evidence given to the court by a local authority, Health and Social Services Board, Health and Social Services Trust, probation officer or other person in the course of any proceedings to which the Family Proceedings Courts (Children Act 1989) Rules 1991, the Magistrates' Courts (Children and Young Persons) Rules 1992, the Magistrates' Courts (Criminal Justice (Children)) Rules (Northern Ireland) 1999, the Act of Sederunt (Child Care and Maintenance Rules) 1997 or the Children's Hearings (Scotland) Rules 1996 apply where, in accordance with a provision of any of those Rules, the information may be withheld by the court in whole or in part from the data subject.

Exemptions from section 7

5. – (1) Personal data to which this Order applies are exempt from section 7 in any case to the extent to which the application of that section would be likely to cause serious harm to the physical or mental health or condition of the data subject or any other person.

(2) Subject to article 7(1), a data controller who is not a health professional shall not withhold information constituting data to which this Order applies on the ground that the exemption in paragraph (1) applies with respect to the information unless the data controller has first consulted the person who appears to the data controller to be the appropriate health professional on the question whether or not the exemption in paragraph (1) applies with respect to the information.

(3) Where any person falling within paragraph (4) is enabled by or under any enactment or rule of law to make a request on behalf of a data subject and has made such a request, personal data to which this Order applies are exempt from section 7 in any case to the extent to which the application of that section would disclose information –
    (a) provided by the data subject in the expectation that it would not be disclosed to the person making the request;
    (b) obtained as a result of any examination or investigation to which the data subject consented in the expectation that the information would not be so disclosed; or
    (c) which the data subject has expressly indicated should not be so disclosed,
provided that sub-paragraphs (a) and (b) shall not prevent disclosure where the data subject has expressly indicated that he no longer has the expectation referred to therein.

(4) A person falls within this paragraph if –
    (a) except in relation to Scotland, the data subject is a child, and that person has parental responsibility for that data subject;
    (b) in relation to Scotland, the data subject is a person under the age of sixteen, and that person has parental responsibilities for that data subject; or
    (c) the data subject is incapable of managing his own affairs and that person has been appointed by a court to manage those affairs.

Modification of section 7 relating to data controllers who are not health professionals

6. – (1) Subject to paragraph (2) and article 7(3), section 7 of the Act is modified so that a data controller who is not a health professional shall not communicate information constituting data to which this Order applies in response to a request unless the data controller has first consulted the person who appears to the data controller to be the appropriate health professional on the question whether or not the exemption in article 5(1) applies with respect to the information.

(2) Paragraph (1) shall not apply to the extent that the request relates to information which the data controller is satisfied has previously been seen by the data subject or is already within the knowledge of the data subject.

Additional provision relating to data controllers who are not health professionals

7. – (1) Subject to paragraph (2), article 5(2) shall not apply in relation to any request where the data controller has consulted the appropriate health professional prior to receiving the request and obtained in writing from that appropriate health professional an opinion that the exemption in article 5(1) applies with respect to all of the information which is the subject of the request.

(2) Paragraph (1) does not apply where the opinion either –
   (a) was obtained before the period beginning six months before the relevant day (as defined by section 7(10) of the Act) and ending on that relevant day, or
   (b) was obtained within that period and it is reasonable in all the circumstances to re-consult the appropriate health professional.

(3) Article 6(1) shall not apply in relation to any request where the data controller has consulted the appropriate health professional prior to receiving the request and obtained in writing from that appropriate health professional an opinion that the exemption in article 5(1) does not apply with respect to all of the information which is the subject of the request.

Further modifications of section 7

8. In relation to data to which this Order applies –
   (a) section 7(4) of the Act shall have effect as if there were inserted after paragraph (b) of that subsection "or, (c) the information is contained in a health record and the other individual is a health professional who has compiled or contributed to the health record or has been involved in the care of the data subject in his capacity as a health professional";
   (b) section 7(9) shall have effect as if –

(i) there was substituted –

"(9)   If a court is satisfied on the application of –
(a) any person who has made a request under the foregoing provisions of this section, or
(b) any other person to whom serious harm to his physical or mental health or condition would be likely to be
caused by compliance with any such request in contravention of those provisions,
that the data controller in question is about to comply with
or has failed to comply with the request in contravention of
those provisions, the court may order him not to comply or,
as the case may be, to comply with the request."; and

(ii) the reference therein to a contravention of the foregoing
provisions of that section included a reference to a
contravention of the provisions contained in this Order.

Mike O'Brien
Parliamentary Under-Secretary of State
Home Office
17th February 2000

EXPLANATORY NOTE
(This note is not part of the Order)

This Order provides for the partial exemption from the provisions of
the Data Protection Act 1998 which confer rights on data subjects to
gain access to data held about them of data relating to the physical or
mental health or condition of the data subject (article 3(1)). The Order
does not apply to any data to which any order made under section
38(1) of the Act applies (article 3(2)).

An exemption from section 7 of the Act is conferred by article 5(1)
only to the extent to which the supply to the data subject of particulars
of the information constituting the data would be likely to cause serious
harm to his or any other person's physical or mental health or condition.
Before deciding whether this exemption applies (and, accordingly,
whether to grant or withhold subject access) a data controller who is
not a health professional is obliged by articles 5(2) and 6(1) to consult
the health professional responsible for the clinical care of the data subject
or, if there is more than one, the most suitable available health
professional or, if there is none available or the data controller is the
Secretary of State exercising his functions relating to social security,
child support or war pensions, a health professional who has the

necessary experience and qualifications to advise on the matters to which the information which is requested relates (definition in article 2). This obligation to consult does not apply where the data subject has already seen or knows about the information which is the subject of the request (article 6(1)), nor in certain limited circumstances where consultation has been carried out prior to the request being made (article 7(1) and (2)).

A further exemption from section 7 of the Act is conferred in certain circumstances where a third party is making the request for access on behalf of the data subject and the data subject does not wish that information to be disclosed to that third party (article 5(3)).

In the case of court reports in certain proceedings where information in the report may be withheld by the court, article 4 provides an exemption from section 7 of the Act and also a complete exemption from the first data protection principle to the extent to which it requires compliance with paragraph 2 of Part II of Schedule 1 to the Act (which confers obligations on data controllers to give certain information to data subjects relating to data held about them).

Article 8 modifies section 7 of the Act so that a data controller cannot refuse access on the grounds that the identity of a third party would be disclosed in cases where the information is contained in a health record and the third party is a health professional who has compiled or contributed to that health record or has been involved in the care of the data subject in his capacity as a health professional, unless serious harm to that health professional's physical or mental health or condition is likely to be caused by giving access such that the exemption in article 5(1) applies.

This Order contributes to the implementation of Directive 95/46/EC on the protection of individuals with regard to the processing of personal data and on the free movement of such data.

A Regulatory Impact Assessment was prepared for the Data Protection Bill as it was then and the statutory instruments to be made under it, and was placed in the libraries of both Houses of Parliament. The Regulatory Impact Assessment is now available on the internet at *www.homeoffice.gov.uk*. Alternatively, copies can be obtained by post from the Home Office, LGDP Unit, 50 Queen Anne's Gate, London SW1H 9AT.

Data Protection (Subject Access Modification) (Education) Order 2000
SI 2000 No 414

Made	*17th February 2000*
Coming into force	*1st March 2000*

Whereas a draft of this Order has been laid before and approved by a resolution of each House of Parliament:

Now, therefore, the Secretary of State, in exercise of powers conferred upon him by sections 30(2) and (4) and 67(2) of the Data Protection Act 1998, and after consultation with the Data Protection Commissioner in accordance with section 67(3) of the Act, hereby makes the following Order:

Citation and commencement

1. This Order may be cited as the Data Protection (Subject Access Modification) (Education) Order 2000 and shall come into force on 1st March 2000.

Interpretation

2. In this Order –
"the Act" means the Data Protection Act 1998;

"education authority" in article 6 has the same meaning as in paragraph 6 of Schedule 11 to the Act;

"Principal Reporter" means the Principal Reporter appointed under section 127 of the Local Government etc (Scotland) Act 1994 or any officer of the Scottish Children's Reporter Administration to whom there is delegated under section 131(1) of that Act any function of the Principal Reporter;

"request" means a request made under section 7; and

"section 7" means section 7 of the Act.

Personal data to which the Order applies

3. – (1) Subject to paragraph (2), this Order applies to personal data consisting of information constituting an educational record as defined in paragraph 1 of Schedule 11 to the Act.

(2)   This Order does not apply –
(a) to any data consisting of information as to the physical or mental health or condition of the data subject to which the Data Protection (Subject Access Modification) (Health) Order 2000 applies; or
(b) to any data which are exempted from section 7 by an order made under section 38(1) of the Act.

Exemption from the subject information provisions

4. – (1) Personal data falling within paragraph (2) and to which this Order applies are exempt from the subject information provisions.

(2)   This paragraph applies to personal data processed by a court and consisting of information supplied in a report or other evidence given to the court in the course of proceedings to which the Magistrates' Courts (Children and Young Persons) Rules 1992, the Magistrates' Courts (Criminal Justice (Children)) Rules (Northern Ireland) 1999, the Act of Sederunt (Child Care and Maintenance Rules) 1997 or the Children's Hearings (Scotland) Rules 1996 apply where, in accordance with a provision of any of those Rules, the information may be withheld by the court in whole or in part from the data subject.

Exemptions from section 7

5. – (1) Personal data to which this Order applies are exempt from section 7 in any case to the extent to which the application of that section would be likely to cause serious harm to the physical or mental health or condition of the data subject or any other person.

(2)   In circumstances where the exemption in paragraph (1) does not apply, where any person falling within paragraph (3) is enabled by or under any enactment or rule of law to make a request on behalf of a data subject and has made such a request, personal data consisting of information as to whether the data subject is or has been the subject of or may be at risk of child abuse are exempt from section 7 in any case to the extent to which the application of that section would not be in the best interests of that data subject.

(3) A person falls within this paragraph if –
(a) the data subject is a child, and that person has parental responsibility for that data subject; or
(b) the data subject is incapable of managing his own affairs and that person has been appointed by a court to manage those affairs.

(4) For the purposes of paragraph (2), "child abuse" includes physical injury (other than accidental injury) to, and physical and emotional neglect, ill-treatment and sexual abuse of, a child.

(5) Paragraph (2) shall not apply in Scotland.

Modification of section 7 relating to Principal Reporter

6. Where in Scotland a data controller who is an education authority receives a request relating to information constituting data to which this Order applies and which the education authority believes to have originated from or to have been supplied by or on behalf of the Principal Reporter acting in pursuance of his statutory duties, other than information which the data subject is entitled to receive from the Principal Reporter, section 7 shall be modified so that –
(a) the data controller shall, within fourteen days of the relevant day (as defined by section 7(10) of the Act), inform the Principal Reporter that a request has been made; and
(b) the data controller shall not communicate information to the data subject pursuant to that section unless the Principal Reporter has informed that data controller that, in his opinion, the exemption specified in article 5(1) does not apply with respect to the information.

Further modifications of section 7

7. – (1) In relation to data to which this Order applies –
(a) section 7(4) of the Act shall have effect as if there were inserted after paragraph (b) of that subsection "or (c) the other individual is a relevant person";
(b) section 7(9) shall have effect as if –
(i) there was substituted –

"(9)   If a court is satisfied on the application of –
(a) any person who has made a request under the foregoing provisions of this section, or
(b) any person to whom serious harm to his physical or mental health or condition would be likely to be caused by compliance with any such request in contravention of those provisions,

540

that the data controller in question is about to comply with or has failed to comply with the request in contravention of those provisions, the court may order him not to comply or, as the case may be, to comply with the request."; and

(ii) the reference to a contravention of the foregoing provisions of that section included a reference to a contravention of the provisions contained in this Order.

(2) After section 7(ii) of the Act insert –

"(12) A person is a relevant person for the purposes of subsection (4)(c) if he –
(a) is a person referred to in paragraph 4(a) or (b) or paragraph 8(a) or (b) of Schedule 11;
(b) is employed by an education authority (within the meaning of paragraph 6 of Schedule 11) in pursuance of its functions relating to education and the information relates to him, or he supplied the information in his capacity as such an employee; or
(c) is the person making the request.".

Mike O'Brien
Parliamentary Under-Secretary of State
Home Office
17th February 2000

EXPLANATORY NOTE
(This note is not part of the Order)

This Order provides for the partial exemption from the provisions of the Data Protection Act 1998, which confer rights on data subjects to gain access to data held about them, of certain data (education records) where the exercise of those rights would be likely to cause serious harm to the physical or mental health or condition of the data subject or another person, or, in some circumstances, (except in the case of Scotland) would disclose information as to whether the data subject is or has been the subject of or may be at risk of child abuse which disclosure would not be in the best interests of that data subject. The Order does not apply to any data to which the Data Protection (Subject Access Modification) (Health) Order 2000 (SI 2000/413) or any order made under section 38(1) of the Act applies (article 3(2)).

In the case of court reports in certain proceedings where information in the report may be withheld by the court, there is a complete exemption under article 4 of the Order from both section 7 of the Act and the first data protection principle to the extent to which it requires compliance with paragraph 2 of Part II of Schedule 1 to the Act (which confers obligations on data controllers to give certain information to data subjects relating to data held about them). For other personal data to which the Order applies, there is an exemption from section 7 of the Act only (article 5).

Article 7 of the Order also modifies section 7 of the Act so that a data controller cannot refuse access on the grounds that the identity of a third party would be disclosed in cases where the third party is a relevant person (as defined), unless serious harm to that relevant person's physical or mental health or condition is likely to be caused such that the exemption in article 5(1) applies.

In the case of data controllers which are education authorities in Scotland who receive certain data from the Principal Reporter, article 6 requires such data controllers to obtain the Principal Reporter's opinion on whether the disclosure of the information might cause serious harm to anyone before responding to any section 7 request.

This Order contributes to the implementation of Directive 95/46/EC on the protection of individuals with regard to the processing of personal data and on the free movement of such data.

A Regulatory Impact Assessment was prepared for the Data Protection Bill as it was then and the statutory instruments to be made under it, and was placed in the libraries of both Houses of Parliament. The Regulatory Impact Assessment is now available on the internet at *www.homeoffice.gov.uk*. Alternatively, copies can be obtained by post from the Home Office, LGDP Unit, 50 Queen Anne's Gate, London SW1H 9AT.

Data Protection (Subject Access Modification) (Social Work) Order 2000
SI 2000 No 415

Made   *17th February 2000*
Coming into force   *1st March 2000*

Whereas a draft of this Order has been laid before and approved by a resolution of each House of Parliament:

Whereas the Secretary of State considers that the application of the subject information provisions (or those provisions without modification) in the circumstances and to the extent specified in this Order would be likely to prejudice the carrying out of social work:

Now, therefore, the Secretary of State, in exercise of the powers conferred on him by sections 30(3) and (4) and 67(2) of the Data Protection Act 1998, and after consultation with the Data Protection Commissioner in accordance with section 67(3) of that Act, hereby makes the following Order:

Citation and commencement

1. This Order may be cited as the Data Protection (Subject Access Modification) (Social Work) Order 2000 and shall come into force on 1st March 2000.

Interpretation

2. – (1) In this Order –
"the Act" means the Data Protection Act 1998;

"compulsory school age" in paragraph 1(f) of the Schedule has the same meaning as in section 8 of the Education Act 1996, and in paragraph 1(g) of the Schedule has the same meaning as in Article 46 of the Education and Libraries (Northern Ireland) Order 1986;

"Health and Social Services Board" means a Health and Social

Services Board established under Article 16 of the Health and Personal Social Services (Northern Ireland) Order 1972;

"Health and Social Services Trust" means a Health and Social Services Trust established under the Health and Personal Social Services (Northern Ireland) Order 1991;

"Principal Reporter" means the Principal Reporter appointed under section 127 of the Local Government etc (Scotland) Act 1994 or any officer of the Scottish Children's Reporter Administration to whom there is delegated under section 131(1) of that Act any function of the Principal Reporter;

"request" means a request made under section 7;

"school age" in paragraph 1(h) of the Schedule has the same meaning as in section 31 of the Education (Scotland) Act 1980;

"section 7" means section 7 of the Act; and

"social work authority" in article 6 means a local authority for the purposes of the Social Work (Scotland) Act 1968.

(2) Any reference in this Order to a local authority in relation to data processed or formerly processed by it includes a reference to the Council of the Isles of Scilly in relation to data processed or formerly processed by the Council in connection with any functions mentioned in paragraph 1(a)(ii) of the Schedule which are or have been conferred upon the Council by or under any enactment.

Personal data to which Order applies

3. – (1) Subject to paragraph (2), this Order applies to personal data falling within any of the descriptions set out in paragraphs 1 and 2 of the Schedule.

(2) This Order does not apply –
(a) to any data consisting of information as to the physical or mental health or condition of the data subject to which the Data Protection (Subject Access Modification) (Health) Order 2000 or the Data Protection (Subject Access Modification) (Education) Order 2000 applies; or
(b) to any data which are exempted from section 7 by an order made under section 38(1) of the Act.

Exemption from subject information provisions

4. Personal data to which this Order applies by virtue of paragraph 2 of the Schedule are exempt from the subject information provisions.

Exemption from section 7

5. – (1) Personal data to which this Order applies by virtue of paragraph 1 of the Schedule are exempt from the obligations in section 7(1)(b) to (d) of the Act in any case to the extent to which the application of those provisions would be likely to prejudice the carrying out of social work by reason of the fact that serious harm to the physical or mental health or condition of the data subject or any other person would be likely to be caused.

(2)   In paragraph (1) the "carrying out of social work" shall be construed as including –
>   (a) the exercise of any functions mentioned in paragraph 1(a)(i), (d), (f) to (j), (m) or (o) of the Schedule;
>   (b) the provision of any service mentioned in paragraph 1(b), (c) or (k) of the Schedule; and
>   (c) the exercise of the functions of any body mentioned in paragraph 1(e) of the Schedule or any person mentioned in paragraph 1(p) or (q) of the Schedule.

(3)   Where any person falling within paragraph (4) is enabled by or under any enactment or rule of law to make a request on behalf of a data subject and has made such a request, personal data to which this Order applies are exempt from section 7 in any case to the extent to which the application of that section would disclose information –
>   (a) provided by the data subject in the expectation that it would not be disclosed to the person making the request;
>   (b) obtained as a result of any examination or investigation to which the data subject consented in the expectation that the information would not be so disclosed; or
>   (c) which the data subject has expressly indicated should not be so disclosed,

provided that sub–paragraphs (a) and (b) shall not prevent disclosure where the data subject has expressly indicated that he no longer has the expectation referred to therein.

(4)   A person falls within this paragraph if –
>   (a) except in relation to Scotland, the data subject is a child, and that person has parental responsibility for that data subject;
>   (b) in relation to Scotland, the data subject is a person under the

age of sixteen, and that person has parental responsibilities for that data subject; or

(c) the data subject is incapable of managing his own affairs and that person has been appointed by a court to manage those affairs.

Modification of section 7 relating to Principal Reporter

6. Where in Scotland a data controller who is a social work authority receives a request relating to information constituting data to which this Order applies and which originated from or was supplied by the Principal Reporter acting in pursuance of his statutory duties, other than information which the data subject is entitled to receive from the Principal Reporter, section 7 shall be modified so that –

(a) the data controller shall, within fourteen days of the relevant day (within the meaning of section 7(10) of the Act), inform the Principal Reporter that a request has been made; and

(b) the data controller shall not communicate information to the data subject pursuant to that section unless the Principal Reporter has informed that data controller that, in his opinion, the exemption specified in article 5(1) does not apply with respect to the information.

Further modifications of section 7

7. – (1) In relation to data to which this Order applies by virtue of paragraph 1 of the Schedule –

(a) section 7(4) shall have effect as if there were inserted after paragraph (b) of that subsection "or, (c) the other individual is a relevant person";

(b) section 7(9) shall have effect as if –

(i) there was substituted –

"(9)   If a court is satisfied on the application of –
(a) any person who has made a request under the foregoing provisions of this section, or
(b) any person to whom serious harm to his physical or mental health or condition would be likely to be caused by compliance with any such request in contravention of those provisions,
that the data controller in question is about to comply with or has failed to comply with the request in contravention of those provisions, the court may order him not to comply or, as the case may be, to comply with the request."; and

(ii) the reference to a contravention of the foregoing provisions of that section included a reference to a contravention of the provisions contained in this Order.

(2) After section 7(11) of the Act insert –

"(12) A person is a relevant person for the purposes of subsection (4)(c) if he –
(a) is a person referred to in paragraph 1(p) or (q) of the Schedule to the Data Protection (Subject Access Modification) (Social Work) Order 2000; or
(b) is or has been employed by any person or body referred to in paragraph 1 of that Schedule in connection with functions which are or have been exercised in relation to the data consisting of the information; or
(c) has provided for reward a service similar to a service provided in the exercise of any functions specified in paragraph 1(a)(i), (b), (c) or (d) of that Schedule,
and the information relates to him or he supplied the information in his official capacity or, as the case may be, in connection with the provision of that service.".

Mike O'Brien
Parliamentary Under-Secretary of State
Home Office
17th February 2000

SCHEDULE
Personal Data to which this Order Applies
Article 3

1.   This paragraph applies to personal data falling within any of the following descriptions –
(a) data processed by a local authority -
(i) in connection with its social services functions within the meaning of the Local Authority Social Services Act 1970 or any functions exercised by local authorities under the Social Work (Scotland) Act 1968 or referred to in section 5(1B) of that Act, or
(ii) in the exercise of other functions but obtained or consisting of information obtained in connection with any of those functions;
(b) data processed by a Health and Social Services Board in connection with the provision of personal social services within the meaning of the Health and Personal Social Services (Northern

Ireland) Order 1972 or processed by the Health and Social Services Board in the exercise of other functions but obtained or consisting of information obtained in connection with the provision of those services;

(c) data processed by a Health and Social Services Trust in connection with the provision of personal social services within the meaning of the Health and Personal Social Services (Northern Ireland) Order 1972 on behalf of a Health and Social Services Board by virtue of an authorisation made under Article 3(1) of the Health and Personal Social Services (Northern Ireland) Order 1994 or processed by the Health and Social Services Trust in the exercise of other functions but obtained or consisting of information obtained in connection with the provision of those services;

(d) data processed by a council in the exercise of its functions under Part II of Schedule 9 to the Health and Social Services and Social Security Adjudications Act 1983;

(e) data processed by a probation committee established by section 3 of the Probation Service Act 1993 or the Probation Board for Northern Ireland established by the Probation Board (Northern Ireland) Order 1982;

(f) data processed by a local education authority in the exercise of its functions under section 36 of the Children Act 1989 or Chapter II of Part VI of the Education Act 1996 so far as those functions relate to ensuring that children of compulsory school age receive suitable education whether by attendance at school or otherwise;

(g) data processed by an education and library board in the exercise of its functions under article 55 of the Children (Northern Ireland) Order 1995 or article 45 of, and Schedule 13 to, the Education and Libraries (Northern Ireland) Order 1986 so far as those functions relate to ensuring that children of compulsory school age receive efficient full-time education suitable to their age, ability and aptitude and to any special educational needs they may have, either by regular attendance at school or otherwise;

(h) data processed by an education authority in the exercise of its functions under sections 35 to 42 of the Education (Scotland) Act 1980 so far as those functions relate to ensuring that children of school age receive efficient education suitable to their age, ability and aptitude, whether by attendance at school or otherwise;

(i) data relating to persons detained in a special hospital provided under section 4 of the National Health Service Act 1977 and processed by a special health authority established under section 11 of that Act in the exercise of any functions similar to any social services functions of a local authority;

(j) data relating to persons detained in special accommodation provided under article 110 of the Mental Health (Northern Ireland) Order 1986 and processed by a Health and Social Services Trust in the exercise of any functions similar to any social services functions of a local authority;

(k) data processed by the National Society for the Prevention of Cruelty to Children or by any other voluntary organisation or other body designated under this sub-paragraph by the Secretary of State or the Department of Health, Social Services and Public Safety and appearing to the Secretary of State or the Department, as the case may be, to be processed for the purposes of the provision of any service similar to a service provided in the exercise of any functions specified in sub-paragraphs (a)(i), (b), (c) or (d) above;

(l) data processed by –

(i) a Health Authority established under section 8 of the National Health Service Act 1977;

(ii) an NHS Trust established under section 5 of the National Health Service and Community Care Act 1990; or

(iii) a Health Board established under section 2 of the National Health Service (Scotland) Act 1978,

which were obtained or consisted of information which was obtained from any authority or body mentioned above or government department and which, whilst processed by that authority or body or government department, fell within any sub-paragraph of this paragraph;

(m) data processed by an NHS Trust as referred to in sub-paragraph (l)(ii) above in the exercise of any functions similar to any social services functions of a local authority;

(n) data processed by a government department and obtained or consisting of information obtained from any authority or body mentioned above and which, whilst processed by that authority or body, fell within any of the preceding sub-paragraphs of this paragraph;

(o) data processed for the purposes of the functions of the Secretary of State pursuant to section 82(5) of the Children Act 1989;

(p) data processed by any guardian ad litem appointed under section 41 of the Children Act 1989, Article 60 of the Children (Northern Ireland) Order 1995 or Article 66 of the Adoption (Northern Ireland) Order 1987 or by a safeguarder appointed under section 41 of the Children (Scotland) Act 1995;

(q) data processed by the Principal Reporter.

2. This paragraph applies to personal data processed by a court and consisting of information supplied in a report or other evidence given to the court by a local authority, Health and Social Services Board, Health and Social Services Trust, probation officer or other person in the course of any proceedings to which the Family Proceedings Courts (Children Act 1989) Rules 1991, the Magistrates' Courts (Children and Young Persons) Rules 1992, the Magistrates' Courts (Criminal Justice (Children)) Rules (Northern Ireland) 1999, the Act of Sederunt (Child Care and Maintenance Rules) 1997 or the Children's Hearings (Scotland) Rules 1996 apply where, in accordance with a provision of any of those Rules, the information may be withheld by the court in whole or in part from the data subject.

EXPLANATORY NOTE
(This note is not part of the Order)

This Order provides for the partial exemption from the provisions of the Data Protection Act 1998, which confer rights on data subjects to gain access to data held about them, of certain data where the exercise of those rights would be likely to prejudice the carrying out of social work by causing serious harm to the physical or mental health or condition of the data subject or another person (article 3(1)). The Order does not apply to any data to which the Data Protection (Subject Access Modification) (Health) Order 2000 (SI 2000/413), the Data Protection (Subject Access Modification) (Education) Order 2000 (SI 2000/414) or any order made under section 38(1) of the Act applies (article 3(2)).

In the case of court reports in certain proceedings where information in the report may be withheld by the court, article 4 of, and paragraph 2 of the Schedule to, this Order provide a complete exemption from section 7 of the Act and also a complete exemption from the first data protection principle to the extent to which it requires compliance with paragraph 2 of Part II of Schedule 1 to the Act (which confers obligations on data controllers to give certain information to data subjects relating to data held about them). In all other cases, article 5(1) confers an exemption from section 7(1)(b) to (d) of the Act, leaving the right of the data subject to be informed by any data controller whether data about him are being processed by or on behalf of that data controller.

Article 7 modifies section 7 of the Act so that a data controller cannot refuse access on the grounds that the identity of a third party would be disclosed in cases where the third party is a relevant person (as defined), unless serious harm to that relevant person's physical or mental health or condition is likely to be caused by giving access such that the exemption in article 5(1) applies.

A further exemption from section 7 of the Act is conferred by article

5(3) in certain circumstances where a third party is making the request for access on behalf of the data subject and the data subject does not wish that information to be disclosed to that third party.

By virtue of paragraph 1 of the Schedule to this Order, it principally applies to data processed by local authorities, in relation to their social services and education welfare functions, and health authorities to whom such data are passed and by probation committees and the National Society for the Prevention of Cruelty to Children. This Order also applies to data processed for similar purposes by the corresponding bodies in Northern Ireland. Data processed by government departments for certain purposes connected with social work and by officers such as guardians ad litem and (in Scotland) the Principal Reporter of the Scottish Children's Reporter Administration are also within the scope of the Order. Provision is made enabling other voluntary organisations or other bodies to be added to the list of bodies whose data are subject to the provisions of the Order where the data are processed for purposes similar to the social services functions (or in Scotland social work functions) of local authorities.

In the case of social work authorities in Scotland who receive certain data from the Principal Reporter, article 6 requires such data controllers to obtain the Principal Reporter's approval before responding to any section 7 request.

This Order contributes to the implementation of Directive 95/46/EC on the protection of individuals with regard to the processing of personal data and on the free movement of such data.

A Regulatory Impact Assessment was prepared for the Data Protection Bill as it was then and the statutory instruments to be made under it, and was placed in the libraries of both Houses of Parliament. The Regulatory Impact Assessment is now available on the internet at *www.homeoffice.gov.uk.* Alternatively, copies can be obtained by post from the Home Office, LGDP Unit, 50 Queen Anne's Gate, London SW1H 9AT.

Data Protection (Crown Appointments) Order 2000
SI 2000 No 416

Made	*17th February 2000*
Coming into force	*1st March 2000*

Whereas a draft of this Order has been laid before and approved by a resolution of each House of Parliament:

Now, therefore, the Secretary of State, in exercise of the powers conferred upon him by paragraph 4 of Schedule 7 to the Data Protection Act 1998, and after consultation with the Data Protection Commissioner in accordance with section 67(3) of that Act, hereby makes the following Order:

1. This Order may be cited as the Data Protection (Crown Appointments) Order 2000 and shall come into force on 1st March 2000.

2. There shall be exempted from the subject information provisions of the Data Protection Act 1998 (as defined by section 27(2) of that Act) personal data processed for the purposes of assessing any person's suitability for any of the offices listed in the Schedule to this Order.

Mike O'Brien
Parliamentary Under-Secretary of State
Home Office
17th February 2000

SCHEDULE
Exemptions from Subject Information Provisions
Article 2

Offices to which appointments are made by Her Majesty: −
    (a) Archbishops, diocesan and suffragan bishops in the Church of England
    (b) Deans of cathedrals of the Church of England
    (c) Deans and Canons of the two Royal Peculiars
    (d) The First and Second Church Estates Commissioners
    (e) Lord-Lieutenants

(f) Masters of Trinity College and Churchill College, Cambridge
(g) The Provost of Eton
(h) The Poet Laureate
(i) The Astronomer Royal

EXPLANATORY NOTE
(This note is not part of the Order)

The Data Protection Act 1998 imposes certain obligations on data controllers to give data subjects information about the processing of their personal data and access to those personal data. By virtue of section 27(2) of that Act, the provisions imposing these obligations are referred to as the "subject information provisions".

This Order exempts from the subject information provisions processing of personal data for the purposes of assessing any person's suitability for certain offices to which appointments are made by Her Majesty.

This Order contributes to the implementation of Directive 95/46/BC on the protection of individuals with regard to the processing of personal data and on the free movement of such data.

A Regulatory Impact Assessment was prepared for the Data Protection Bill as it was then and the statutory instruments to be made under it, and was placed in the libraries of both Houses of Parliament. The Regulatory Impact Assessment is now available on the internet at *www.homeoffice.gov.uk*. Alternatively, copies can be obtained by post from the Home Office, LGDP Unit, 50 Queen Anne's Gate, London SW1H 9AT.

Data Protection (Processing of Sensitive Personal Data) Order 2000
SI 2000 No 417

Made	*17th February 2000*
Coming into force	*1st March 2000*

Whereas a draft of this Order has been laid before and approved by a resolution of each House of Parliament:

Now, therefore, the Secretary of State, in exercise of the powers conferred on him by section 67(2) of, and paragraph 10 of Schedule 3 to, the Data Protection Act 1998 and after consultation with the Data Protection Commissioner in accordance with section 67(3) of that Act, hereby makes the following Order:

1. – (1) This Order may be cited as the Data Protection (Processing of Sensitive Personal Data) Order 2000 and shall come into force on 1st March 2000.

(2)   In this Order, "the Act" means the Data Protection Act 1998.

2.   For the purposes of paragraph 10 of Schedule 3 to the Act, the circumstances specified in any of the paragraphs in the Schedule to this Order are circumstances in which sensitive personal data may be processed.

Mike O'Brien
Parliamentary Under-Secretary of State
Home Office
17th February 2000

SCHEDULE
Circumstances in which Sensitive Personal Data may be Processed
Article 2

1. – (1) The processing –
    (a) is in the substantial public interest;
    (b) is necessary for the purposes of the prevention or detection

of any unlawful act; and

(c) must necessarily be carried out without the explicit consent of the data subject being sought so as not to prejudice those purposes.

(2) In this paragraph, "act" includes a failure to act.

2. The processing –
(a) is in the substantial public interest;
(b) is necessary for the discharge of any function which is designed for protecting members of the public against –
    (i) dishonesty, malpractice, or other seriously improper conduct by, or the unfitness or incompetence of, any person, or
    (ii) mismanagement in the administration of, or failures in services provided by, any body or association; and
(c) must necessarily be carried out without the explicit consent of the data subject being sought so as not to prejudice the discharge of that function.

3. – (1) The disclosure of personal data –
(a) is in the substantial public interest;
(b) is in connection with –
    (i) the commission by any person of any unlawful act (whether alleged or established),
    (ii) dishonesty, malpractice, or other seriously improper conduct by, or the unfitness or incompetence of, any person (whether alleged or established), or
    (iii) mismanagement in the administration of, or failures in services provided by, any body or association (whether alleged or established);
(c) is for the special purposes as defined in section 3 of the Act; and
(d) is made with a view to the publication of those data by any person and the data controller reasonably believes that such publication would be in the public interest.

(2) In this paragraph, "act" includes a failure to act.

4. The processing –
(a) is in the substantial public interest;
(b) is necessary for the discharge of any function which is designed for the provision of confidential counselling, advice, support or any other service; and
(c) is carried out without the explicit consent of the data subject

because the processing –

(i) is necessary in a case where consent cannot be given by the data subject,

(ii) is necessary in a case where the data controller cannot reasonably be expected to obtain the explicit consent of the data subject, or

(iii) must necessarily be carried out without the explicit consent of the data subject being sought so as not to prejudice the provision of that counselling, advice, support or other service.

5. – (1) The processing –

(a) is necessary for the purpose of –

(i) carrying on insurance business, or

(ii) making determinations in connection with eligibility for, and benefits payable under, an occupational pension scheme as defined in section 1 of the Pension Schemes Act 1993;

(b) is of sensitive personal data consisting of information falling within section 2(e) of the Act relating to a data subject who is the parent, grandparent, great grandparent or sibling of –

(i) in the case of paragraph (a)(i), the insured person, or

(ii) in the case of paragraph (a)(ii), the member of the scheme;

(c) is necessary in a case where the data controller cannot reasonably be expected to obtain the explicit consent of that data subject and the data controller is not aware of the data subject withholding his consent; and

(d) does not support measures or decisions with respect to that data subject.

(2) In this paragraph –

(a) "insurance business" means insurance business, as defined in section 95 of the Insurance Companies Act 1982, falling within Classes I, III or IV of Schedule 1 (classes of long term business) or Classes 1 or 2 of Schedule 2 (classes of general business) to that Act, and

(b) "insured" and "member" includes an individual who is seeking to become an insured person or member of the scheme respectively.

6. The processing –

(a) is of sensitive personal data in relation to any particular data subject that are subject to processing which was already under way immediately before the coming into force of this Order;

(b) is necessary for the purpose of –

(i) carrying on insurance business, as defined in section 95 of the Insurance Companies Act 1982, falling within Classes I, III or IV of Schedule 1 to that Act; or

(ii) establishing or administering an occupational pension scheme as defined in section 1 of the Pension Schemes Act 1993; and

(c) either –

(i) is necessary in a case where the data controller cannot reasonably be expected to obtain the explicit consent of the data subject and that data subject has not informed the data controller that he does not so consent, or

(ii) must necessarily be carried out even without the explicit consent of the data subject so as not to prejudice those purposes.

7. – (1) Subject to the provisions of sub-paragraph (2), the processing –

(a) is of sensitive personal data consisting of information falling within section 2(c) or (e) of the Act;

(b) is necessary for the purpose of identifying or keeping under review the existence or absence of equality of opportunity or treatment between persons –

(i) holding different beliefs as described in section 2(c) of the Act, or

(ii) of different states of physical or mental health or different physical or mental conditions as described in section 2(e) of the Act,

with a view to enabling such equality to be promoted or maintained;

(c) does not support measures or decisions with respect to any particular data subject otherwise than with the explicit consent of that data subject; and

(d) does not cause, nor is likely to cause, substantial damage or substantial distress to the data subject or any other person.

(2) Where any individual has given notice in writing to any data controller who is processing personal data under the provisions of sub-paragraph (1) requiring that data controller to cease processing personal data in respect of which that individual is the data subject at the end of such period as is reasonable in the circumstances, that data controller must have ceased processing those personal data at the end of that period.

8. – (1) Subject to the provisions of sub-paragraph (2), the processing –

(a) is of sensitive personal data consisting of information falling within section 2(b) of the Act;

(b) is carried out by any person or organisation included in the register maintained pursuant to section 1 of the Registration of Political Parties Act 1998 in the course of his or its legitimate political activities; and

(c) does not cause, nor is likely to cause, substantial damage or substantial distress to the data subject or any other person.

(2) Where any individual has given notice in writing to any data controller who is processing personal data under the provisions of sub-paragraph (1) requiring that data controller to cease processing personal data in respect of which that individual is the data subject at the end of such period as is reasonable in the circumstances, that data controller must have ceased processing those personal data at the end of that period.

9. The processing –

(a) is in the substantial public interest;

(b) is necessary for research purposes (which expression shall have the same meaning as in section 33 of the Act);

(c) does not support measures or decisions with respect to any particular data subject otherwise than with the explicit consent of that data subject; and

(d) does not cause, nor is likely to cause, substantial damage or substantial distress to the data subject or any other person.

10. The processing is necessary for the exercise of any functions conferred on a constable by any rule of law.

EXPLANATORY NOTE
(This note is not part of the Order)

The first data protection principle set out in paragraph 1 of Schedule 1 to the Data Protection Act 1998 prohibits the processing of sensitive personal data unless one of the conditions in Schedule 3 to the Act is met. The condition set out in paragraph 10 of that Schedule is that the processing of sensitive personal data is carried out in circumstances specified by the Secretary of State. The Schedule to this Order specifies ten such circumstances.

Paragraph 1 of the Schedule to this Order covers certain processing for the purposes of the prevention or detection of any unlawful act, where seeking the consent of the data subject to the processing would prejudice those purposes. Paragraph 2 is a similar provision for cases where the processing is required to discharge functions which protect members of the public from certain conduct which may not constitute an unlawful act, such as incompetence or mismanagement.

Paragraph 3 of the Schedule covers certain disclosures for journalistic, artistic or literary purposes of personal data relating to a wide range of conduct (eg unlawful acts, dishonesty and incompetence etc).

Paragraph 4 of the Schedule covers processing required to discharge functions involving the provision of services such as confidential counselling and advice, in circumstances where the consent of the data subject is not obtained for one of the specified reasons set out in the paragraph.

Paragraph 5 of the Schedule covers processing in certain insurance or occupational pension scheme contexts, where details of particular relatives of the principal insured or member are required (eg health details of relatives used to calculate the life expectancy of the insured). The data controller must not process these data to make decisions or take actions with respect to the relatives, nor if he is aware of the relative withholding his consent to the processing.

Paragraph 6 of the Schedule covers the processing of sensitive data that were already being processed before the coming into force of this Order in certain insurance and pension contexts. Like the provision in paragraph 5, the data controller must not continue to process these data if he is aware of the data subject withholding his consent to the processing. Alternatively, the data controller may continue the processing in the case of group insurance or pension schemes even without the explicit consent of the data subject to avoid prejudice to that insurance policy or pension scheme.

Paragraph 9 of Schedule 3 to the Data Protection Act 1998 provides as a condition relevant for the purposes of the first data protection principle that the processing is of personal data relating to racial or ethnic origin for the purposes of ethnic monitoring. Paragraph 7 of the Schedule to this Order makes similar provision in relation to the monitoring of equality between persons with different religious beliefs or between persons of differing physical or mental states or conditions.

Paragraph 8 of the Schedule relates to the processing of information about political opinions by registered political parties, provided such processing does not cause substantial damage or distress to any person. Paragraph 9 of the Schedule covers, for example, processing in the course of maintaining archives where the sensitive personal data are not used to take decisions about any person without their consent and no substantial damage or distress is caused to any person by the keeping of those data.

Paragraph 10 of the Schedule covers processing by the police in the exercise of their common law powers.

This Order contributes to the implementation of Directive 95/46/EC on the protection of individuals with regard to the processing of personal data and on the free movement of such data.

A Regulatory Impact Assessment was prepared for the Data Protection Bill as it was then and the statutory instruments to be made under it, and was placed in the libraries of both Houses of Parliament. The Regulatory Impact Assessment is now available on the internet at *www.homeoffice.gov.uk*. Alternatively, copies can be obtained by post from the Home Office, LGDP Unit, 50 Queen Anne's Gate, London SW1H 9AT.

Data Protection (Designated Codes of Practice) Order 2000 SI 2000 No 418

Made	*17th February 2000*
Coming into force	*1st March 2000*

Whereas a draft of this Order has been laid before and approved by a resolution of each House of Parliament:

Now, therefore, the Secretary of State, in exercise of the powers conferred upon him by section 32(3) of the Data Protection Act 1998, and after consultation with the Data Protection Commissioner in accordance with section 67(3) of that Act, hereby makes the following Order:

1. This Order may be cited as the Data Protection (Designated Codes of Practice) Order 2000 and shall come into force on 1st March 2000.

2. The codes of practice listed in the Schedule to this Order shall be designated for the purposes of section 32(3) of the Data Protection Act 1998.

Mike O'Brien
Parliamentary Under-Secretary of State
Home Office
17th February 2000

SCHEDULE
Designated Codes of Practice
Article 2

1. The Code on Fairness and Privacy issued by the Broadcasting Standards Commission in June 1998 pursuant to sections 107 and 108 of the Broadcasting Act 1996.

2. The ITC Programme Code issued by the Independent Television Commission in Autumn 1998 pursuant to section 7 of the Broadcasting Act 1990.

3. The Code of Practice published by the Press Complaints Commission in December 1997.

4. The Producers' Guidelines issued by the British Broadcasting Corporation in November 1996.

5. The Programme Code issued by the Radio Authority in March 1998 pursuant to section 91 of the Broadcasting Act 1990.

EXPLANATORY NOTE
(This note is not part of the Order)

This Order designates certain codes of practice issued by various media organisations. As designated codes of practice, compliance with them may be taken into account when determining for the purposes of section 32(1)(b) of the Data Protection Act 1998 whether a data controller reasonably believes that publication of any journalistic, literary or artistic material would be in the public interest.

A Regulatory Impact Assessment was prepared for the Data Protection Bill as it was then and the statutory instruments to be made under it, and was placed in the libraries of both Houses of Parliament. The Regulatory Impact Assessment is now available on the internet at *www.homeoffice.gov.uk*. Alternatively, copies can be obtained by post from the Home Office, LGDP Unit, 50 Queen Anne's Gate, London SW1H 9AT.

Data Protection (Miscellaneous Subject Access Exemptions) Order 2000
SI 2000 No 419

Made   *17th February 2000*
Coming into force   *1st March 2000*

Whereas a draft of this Order has been laid before and approved by a resolution of each House of Parliament:

Whereas the Secretary of State considers it necessary for the safeguarding of the interests of data subjects or the rights and freedoms of other individuals that the prohibitions or restrictions on disclosure contained in the enactments and instruments listed in the Schedule to this Order ought to prevail over section 7 of the Data Protection Act 1998:

Now, therefore, the Secretary of State, in exercise of the powers conferred on him by sections 38(1) and 67(2) of the Data Protection Act 1998, and after consultation with the Data Protection Commissioner in accordance with section 67(3) of that Act, hereby makes the following Order:

1. This Order may be cited as the Data Protection (Miscellaneous Subject Access Exemptions) Order 2000 and shall come into force on 1st March 2000.

2. Personal data consisting of information the disclosure of which is prohibited or restricted by the enactments and instruments listed in the Schedule to this Order are exempt from section 7 of the Data Protection Act 1998.

Mike O 'Brien
Parliamentary Under–Secretary of State
Home Office
17th February 2000

SCHEDULE
Exemptions From Section 7
Article 2
Part I
Enactments and Instruments Extending to the United Kingdom

Human fertilisation and embryology: information about the provision of treatment services, the keeping or use of gametes or embryos and whether identifiable individuals were born in consequence of treatment services.

Sections 31 and 33 of the Human Fertilisation and Embryology Act 1990.

Part II
Enactments and Instruments Extending to England and Wales

(a) Adoption records and reports

Sections 50 and 51 of the Adoption Act 1976.

Regulations 6 and 14 of the Adoption Agencies Regulations 1983, so far as they relate to records and other information in the possession of local authorities.

Rules 5, 6, 9, 17, 18, 21, 22 and 53 of the Adoption Rules 1984.
Rules 5, 6, 9, 17, 18, 21, 22 and 32 of the Magistrates' Courts (Adoption) Rules 1984.

(b) Statement of child's special educational needs

Regulation 19 of the Education (Special Educational Needs) Regulations 1994.

(c) Parental order records and reports

Sections 50 and 51 of the Adoption Act 1976 as modified by paragraphs 4(a) and (b) of Schedule 1 to the Parental Orders (Human Fertilisation and Embryology) Regulations 1994 in relation to parental orders made under section 30 of the Human Fertilisation and Embryology Act 1990.

Rules 4A.5 and 4A.9 of the Family Proceedings Rules 1991.

Rules 21E and 21I of the Family Proceedings Courts (Children Act 1989) Rules 1991.

Part III
Enactments and Instruments Extending to Scotland

(a) Adoption records and reports

Section 45 of the Adoption (Scotland) Act 1978.

Regulation 23 of the Adoption Agencies (Scotland) Regulations 1996, so far as it relates to records and other information in the possession of local authorities.

Rule 67.3 of the Act of Sederunt (Rules of the Court of Session 1994) 1994.

Rules 2.12, 2.14, 2.30 and 2.33 of the Act of Sederunt (Child Care and Maintenance Rules) 1997.

Regulation 8 of the Adoption Allowance (Scotland) Regulations 1996.

(b) *Information provided by principal reporter for children's hearing*
Rules 5 and 21 of the Children's Hearings (Scotland) Rules 1996.

(c) *Record of child or young person's special educational needs*
Section 60(4) of the Education (Scotland) Act 1980.
Proviso (bb) to regulation 7(2) of the Education (Record of Needs) (Scotland) Regulations 1982.

(d) *Parental order records and reports*
Section 45 of the Adoption (Scotland) Act 1978 as modified by paragraph 10 of Schedule 1 to the Parental Orders (Human Fertilisation and Embryology) (Scotland) Regulations 1994 in relation to parental orders made under section 30 of the Human Fertilisation and Embryology Act 1990.

Rules 2.47 and 2.59 of the Act of Sederunt (Child Care and Maintenance Rules) 1997.

Rules 81.3 and 81.18 of the Act of Sederunt (Rules of the Court of Session 1994) 1994.

Part IV
Enactments and Instruments Extending to Northern Ireland
(a) *Adoption records and reports*
Articles 50 and 54 of the Adoption (Northern Ireland) Act 1987.

Rule 53 of Order 84 of the Rules of the Supreme Court (Northern Ireland) 1980.

Rule 22 of the County Court (Adoption) Rules (Northern Ireland) 1980.

Rule 32 of Order 50 of the County Court Rules (Northern Ireland) 1981.

(b) *Statement of child's special educational needs*
Regulation 17 of the Education (Special Educational Needs) Regulations (Northern Ireland) 1997.

(c) *Parental order records and reports*
Articles 50 and 54 of the Adoption (Northern Ireland) Order 1987 as modified by paragraph 5(a) and (e) of Schedule 2 to the Parental Orders (Human Fertilisation and Embryology) Regulations 1994 in respect of parental orders made under section 30 of the Human Fertilisation and Embryology Act 1990.

Rules 4, 5 and 16 of Order 84A of the Rules of the Supreme Court (Northern Ireland) 1980.

Rules 3, 4 and 15 of Order 50A of the County Court Rules (Northern Ireland) 1981.

EXPLANATORY NOTE
(This note is not part of the Order)

This Order exempts from section 7 of the Data Protection Act 1998, which entitles individuals to gain access to personal data held about them, personal data the disclosure of which is prohibited or restricted by certain enactments and subordinate instruments in the interests of safeguarding the interests of the data subject himself or the rights and freedoms of some other individual (article 2).

The personal data which are exempted by the Order concern: human fertilisation and embryology information in the United Kingdom; information contained in adoption and parental order records and reports, and statements and records of the special educational needs of children in England or Wales, Scotland and Northern Ireland; and, in Scotland only, information provided by reporters for the purposes of a children's hearing (the Schedule).

This Order contributes to the implementation of Directive 95/46/EC on the protection of individuals with regard to the processing of personal data and on the free movement of such data.

A Regulatory Impact Assessment was prepared for the Data Protection Bill as it was then and the statutory instruments to be made under it, and was placed in the libraries of both Houses of Parliament. The Regulatory Impact Assessment is now available on the internet at *www.homeoffice.gov.uk*. Alternatively, copies can be obtained by post from the Home Office, LGDP Unit, 50 Queen Anne's Gate, London SW1H 9AT.

Tables

Table of Cases

Table of Statutes

Table of Statutory Instruments

European Material

Index